RELIGIONS OF
THE WEST
TODAY

RELIGIONS OF THE WEST TODAY

Third Edition

JOHN L. ESPOSITO
Georgetown University

DARRELL J. FASCHING
University of South Florida

TODD T. LEWIS
College of the Holy Cross

New York   Oxford
OXFORD UNIVERSITY PRESS

Oxford University Press is a department of the University of Oxford. It furthers the University's
objective of excellence in research, scholarship, and education by publishing worldwide.

Oxford   New York
Auckland   Cape Town   Dar es Salaam   Hong Kong   Karachi
Kuala Lumpur   Madrid   Melbourne   Mexico City   Nairobi
New Delhi   Shanghai   Taipei   Toronto

With offices in
Argentina   Austria   Brazil   Chile   Czech Republic   France   Greece
Guatemala   Hungary   Italy   Japan   Poland   Portugal   Singapore
South Korea   Switzerland   Thailand   Turkey   Ukraine   Vietnam

For titles covered by Section 112 of the US Higher Education Opportunity Act,
please visit www.oup.com/us/he for the latest information about
pricing and alternate formats.

Published by Oxford University Press
198 Madison Avenue, New York, NY 10016
www.oup.com

Library of Congress Cataloging-in-Publication Data

Esposito, John L.
   Religions of the West today / John L. Esposito, Georgetown University; Darrell J. Fasching,
University of South Florida; Todd T. Lewis, College of the Holy Cross.—THIRD EDITION.
      pages cm
ISBN 978-0-19-999963-7
   1. Western countries—Religion—Textbooks.   2. Religions—Textbooks.   I. Fasching, Darrell J.,
1944–   II. Lewis, Todd, 1952–   III. Title.
BL689.E87 2014
200.9182′1—dc23

                                                                                    2014008987

Printing number: 9 8 7 6 5 4 3 2 1
Printed in the United States of America
on acid-free paper

For Jean Esposito and Melissa and Nathan Lewis,
and in memory of Harold and Lillian Gushin

BRIEF CONTENTS

CONTENTS

Chapter 4   CHRISTIAN DIVERSITY AND THE ROAD TO MODERNITY   147

PREFACE

Religion is unquestionably a dynamic spiritual and political force in the world today. Around the globe religious experiences and beliefs profoundly change individual lives even as they influence politics and play a powerful role in international affairs. This third edition of *Religions of the West Today* addresses this reality with an introductory volume for college and university students.

Although this is a multiauthored text, with each author taking primary responsibility for different chapters (John Esposito: Islam; Darrell Fasching: Judaism, Christianity, and New Age Religions and Globalization; and Todd Lewis: Indigenous Religions), it has truly been a collaborative project from start to finish. Throughout the entire process we shared and commented on each other's material.

Religions of the West Today grew out of our several decades of experience in teaching world religions. It is a product of our conviction that, for our students to understand the daily news accounts of religions in our global situation, they need more than just the ancient foundations of the world's religions. Textbooks on world religions have too often tended to emphasize historical origins and doctrinal developments, focusing on the past and giving short shrift to the "modern" world. Many stressed a textual, theological/philosophical, or legal approach, one that gave insufficient attention to the modern alterations of these traditions. Most gave little attention to their social institutions or their connections to political power. As a result, students came away with a maximum appreciation for the origins and development of the classical traditions but a minimum awareness of the continued dynamism and relevance of religious traditions today. So, despite the growing visibility and impact of a global religious resurgence and of the unprecedented globalization of all world religions, most textbooks have not quite caught up. *Religions of the West Today* extends our commitment to address this situation for Hinduism, Buddhism, East Asian religions, and Islam, with short chapters also devoted to indigenous religions and global religions.

A short comment on the selection of this volume's title, *Religions of the West Today*, and that of its companion volume, *Religions of Asia Today*: Both books grew out of our larger text, *World Religions Today*, now in its fifth edition. These titles, while illustrating our contemporary emphasis, also highlight the difficulties of choosing apt language in our postmodern, globalized world. The authors engaged in a spirited debate to find agreement on the question of what terms to use as titles of the two new volumes. Going back to the nineteenth century, a Eurocentric vantage point on the world created the dichotomy "Western" religions versus "Eastern" (or "Oriental") religions. While it is true that any geographic, directional terms are arbitrary, the fact remains that the power of imperial Europe and its creation of the new field of knowledge, religious studies, created these terms. As Kipling wrote, "East is East, and West is West, and never the twain shall meet." In this process, Islam was commonly—and erroneously—shunted away from the "West" and distanced from the "Western" monotheisms Christianity and Judaism. All of Asia was likewise lumped together, misleadingly, as "Eastern religions" despite extraordinary diversity found there.

So we, as authors, found it problematic to either assent to this now archaic dichotomy or to find a completely satisfactory alternative. How could we craft a textbook for the twenty-first century, highlighting postcolonial and postmodern perspectives, while labeling our textbooks with nineteenth-century, colonial terms? Such terms recall the stereotypes of the mysterious, mystical, and unchanging (and therefore backward and unscientific) East. And yet today, in an age of globalization, our students learn advanced mathematics, chemistry, and physics from their professors from India, China, Japan, and other Asian countries. Moreover, they are most likely to associate the term "The East" with the superiority of Japanese and Korean automobiles, cutting-edge electronic technology, and the growing international dominance of the Chinese economy. Nevertheless, there are those who remember the preglobalization era and fear the old colonial stereotypes may still linger.

Our solution is an awkward one, one that suggests we are still in transition to a new way of looking at the world. We chose to mix geographic metaphors. So we have *Religions of the West Today* to highlight the grouping of the Abrahamic faiths together; and to group Hinduism, Buddhism, and the traditions of East Asia all under the title *Religions of Asia Today*, with the plural *religions* underlining their plurality. One of the problems with this choice is that Islam today is also a major religion in Asia, with substantial communities in Pakistan, Bangladesh, India, Indonesia, Malaysia, and China. For this reason, we include a chapter on Islam in the *Religions of Asia Today* volume to reflect this reality. We feel that this addition empowers instructors to include in their courses the discussion of Islam in Asia, a possibility that recent events in the world certainly justifies. Of course, this still leaves the growing role of Christianity in China and the major social and political role of Christianity in South Korea treated only in passing (in the East Asian Religions chapter). One can see why we, as authors, had an extended and not fully resolved conversation about both content and titles. It is a conversation that mirrors the complexities and perplexities of our new global situation.

New to the Third Edition

The book's major theme and chapter structure have been retained from the earlier editions, though they have been updated and revised. We have also updated chapter content to reflect recent events at the time of writing. In response to reviewer suggestions, we have included the following new content:

- NEW marginal definitions of Key Terms help students understand each term within its immediate context.
- NEW coverage of Zoroastrianism (Chapter 4), Baha'i (Chapter 6), and Jehovah's Witnesses (Chapter 6)

Features

Each chapter is enriched by a wide variety of thematic and special-topic boxes that explore particular ideas or practices in some depth. It is our hope that these lively and interesting boxes are seen as an integral part of the text, allowing students to imagine how religion today is among the most colorful, lively, and striking of human endeavors.

- "Gender Focus" boxes present additional information, beyond that in the regular text, about different practices by believers of different sexes.
- "Rituals and Rites" boxes describe the ritual practices of believers, often with a focus on ways these rites have changed over time.
- "Contrasting Religious Visions" boxes compare the beliefs of two significant adherents of a faith who each see the demands of their religion calling believers in very different directions in the modern age. These demonstrate that, no matter what religion we are examining, that very same religious tradition can be used to promote both peacemaking and conflict.
- "Teachings of Religious Wisdom" boxes offer some of the primary texts and formal teachings of different religions.
- "Tales of Spiritual Transformation" offer descriptions of religious experiences in the believers' own words.

Supplementary Materials

The ancillary materials for *World Religions Today*, Fifth Edition, can be paired with *Religions of the West Today*, Third Edition.

For the instructor: Supplementary materials are available on the Oxford University Press **Ancillary Resource Center (ARC)**, a convenient, instructor-focused single destination for resources to accompany your text. Accessed online through individual user accounts, the ARC provides instructors with access to up-to-date ancillaries at any time while guaranteeing the security of grade-significant resources. In addition, it allows OUP to keep instructors informed when new content becomes available. Available on the ARC:

- The Instructor's Manual, which includes the following:

    Chapter summaries
    Chapter goals
    Key terms with definitions
    Lecture outlines
    Suggested web links and other resources

- A **Computerized Test Bank**, including 40 fill-in-the-blank, 40 multiple-choice, 40 true/false, and 12 essay/discussion questions per chapter
- **Lecture outlines** as PowerPoint®-based slides

A link to the ARC is available on the **Companion Website** (www.oup.com/us /esposito).

For the student: The **Companion Website** (www.oup.com/us/esposito) includes the following student resources:

- Chapter goals
- Flashcards of key term
- Suggested web links and other resources
- Self-quizzes, containing 20 fill-in-the-blank, 20 multiple-choice, 20 true/ false, and 6 essay/discussion questions per chapter, selected from the Test Bank in the ARC

The Instructor's Manual and Computerized Test Bank, as well as the student material from the Companion Website, are also available in **Learning Management System Cartridges**, in a fully downloadable format for instructors using a learning management system in their courses.

Acknowledgments

This third edition of *Religions of the West Today* has been substantially revised in light of the valuable comments we continue to receive from colleagues across the country who have used it and in light of our own subsequent experiences and reflections. We offer special thanks to the following professors and to the other, anonymous, reviewers. This edition is much stronger because of their thoughtful comments:

Todd M. Brenneman, University of Central Florida
Robert Brown, James Madison University
David Kitts, Carson-Newman University
Peter David Lee, Columbia College—California
Robin L. Owens, Mount St. Mary's College
Linda Pittman, College of William and Mary
Paul Schneider, University of South Florida
Caleb Simmons, University of Mississippi
Phillip Spivey, University of Central Arkansas
Mlen-Too Wesley, Penn State University
Mark Whitters, Eastern Michigan University
Simon A. Wood, University of Nebraska—Lincoln

Thanks also to the reviewers of the previous editions for their lasting input on the work: Constantina Rhodes Bailly, Eckerd College; Herbert Berg, University of North Carolina–Wilmington; Sheila Briggs, University of Southern California; Terry L. Burden, University of Louisville; Dexter E. Callender Jr., University of Miami;

David Capes, Houston Baptist University; James E. Deitrick, University of Central Arkansas; Sergey Dolgopolski, University of Kansas; Joan Earley, State University of New York at Albany; James Egge, Eastern Michigan University; John Farina, George Mason University; Debora Y. Fonteneau, Savannah State University; Liora Gubkin, California State University–Bakersfield; William David Hart, University of North Carolina–Greensboro; William Hutchins, Appalachian State University; Father Brad Karelius, Saddleback Community College; Sandra T. Keating, Providence College; Mohammad Hassan Khalil, University of Illinois; Louis Komjathy, University of San Diego; Ian Maclean, James Madison University; Sean McCloud, University of North Carolina at Charlotte; Tim Murphy, University of Alabama; Nancy Nahra, Champlain College; Jason Neelis, University of Florida; Patrick Nnoromele, Eastern Kentucky University; Catherine Orsborn, University of Denver; Andrew Pavelich, University of Houston–Downtown; Kris Pratt, Spartanburg Methodist College; Rick Rogers, Eastern Michigan University; Barry R. Sang, Catawba College; Brooke Schedneck, Arizona State University; D. Neil Schmid, North Carolina State University; Martha Ann Selby, University of Texas at Austin; Theresa S. Smith, Indiana University of Pennsylvania; Yushau Sodiq, Texas Christian University; Bruce Sullivan, Northern Arizona University; Aaron J. Hahn Tapper, University of San Francisco; James H. Thrall, International College–University of Bridgeport; Eglute Trinkauske, Nazareth College; Peter Umoh, University of Bridgeport; Hugh B. Urban, Ohio State University; Anne Vallely, University of Ottawa; Andrew Christian Van Gorder, Baylor University; Glenn Wallis, University of Georgia; Tammie Wanta, University of North Carolina at Charlotte; Catherine Wessinger, Loyola University New Orleans.

We have been fortunate to work with an excellent, supportive, and creative team at Oxford University Press, led by Robert Miller, Executive Editor in Oxford's Higher Education Group. Senior Production Editor Barbara Mathieu, Editorial Assistants Kaitlin Coats and Emily Krupin, and Senior Development Editor Meg Botteon have been extraordinarily supportive throughout the writing process. Our thanks also to Robin Tuthill, who prepared the student and instructor support materials for the first four editions of the book, and to Kate Kelley, who updated them for this fifth edition.

John L. Esposito
Darrell J. Fasching
Todd T. Lewis

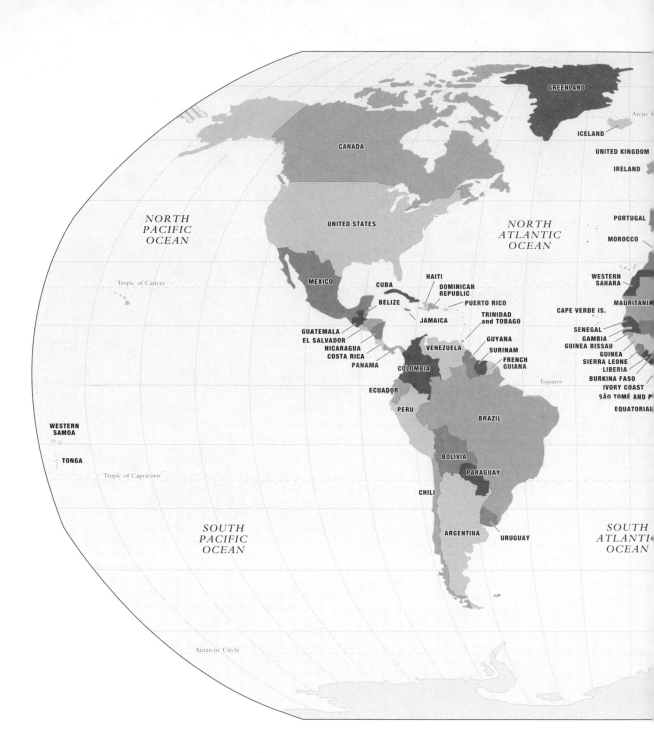

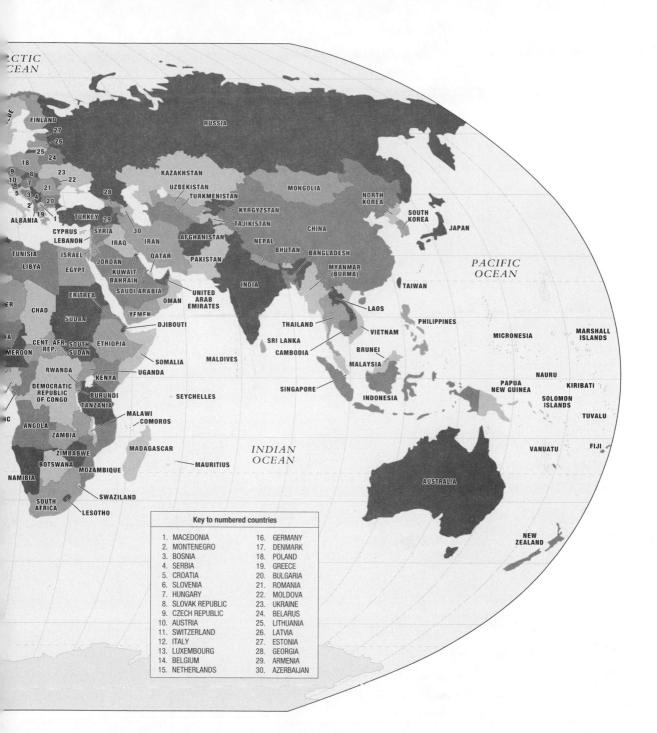

ARCTIC
OCEAN

FINLAND
27
26
25 24
18
9 8 23 22
10 7 21
16 3 4 20 28
5 2 19 1
ALBANIA
TURKEY 29
CYPRUS SYRIA 30
LEBANON
TUNISIA ISRAEL JORDAN IRAN
LIBYA EGYPT KUWAIT QATAR
BAHRAIN
ERITREA SAUDI ARABIA OMAN UNITED
ARAB
CHAD YEMEN EMIRATES
SUDAN DJIBOUTI
CENT. AFR. SOUTH ETHIOPIA
CAMEROON REP. SUDAN
SOMALIA MALDIVES
RWANDA KENYA UGANDA
DEMOCRATIC
REPUBLIC BURUNDI SEYCHELLES
OF CONGO TANZANIA
MALAWI
ANGOLA COMOROS
ZAMBIA
ZIMBABWE MADAGASCAR
BOTSWANA INDIAN
NAMIBIA MOZAMBIQUE MAURITIUS OCEAN
SWAZILAND
SOUTH
AFRICA LESOTHO

RUSSIA

KAZAKHSTAN
UZBEKISTAN MONGOLIA NORTH
TURKMENISTAN KOREA
KYRGYZSTAN SOUTH
TAJIKISTAN KOREA JAPAN
AFGHANISTAN CHINA
NEPAL
PAKISTAN BHUTAN BANGLADESH PACIFIC
MYANMAR OCEAN
INDIA (BURMA)
TAIWAN
THAILAND LAOS
SRI LANKA VIETNAM PHILIPPINES
CAMBODIA
BRUNEI MARSHALL
MALAYSIA MICRONESIA ISLANDS
SINGAPORE
INDONESIA NAURU
PAPUA KIRIBATI
NEW GUINEA SOLOMON
ISLANDS
TUVALU
VANUATU FIJI
AUSTRALIA

NEW
ZEALAND

Key to numbered countries	
1. MACEDONIA	16. GERMANY
2. MONTENEGRO	17. DENMARK
3. BOSNIA	18. POLAND
4. SERBIA	19. GREECE
5. CROATIA	20. BULGARIA
6. SLOVENIA	21. ROMANIA
7. HUNGARY	22. MOLDOVA
8. SLOVAK REPUBLIC	23. UKRAINE
9. CZECH REPUBLIC	24. BELARUS
10. AUSTRIA	25. LITHUANIA
11. SWITZERLAND	26. LATVIA
12. ITALY	27. ESTONIA
13. LUXEMBOURG	28. GEORGIA
14. BELGIUM	29. ARMENIA
15. NETHERLANDS	30. AZERBAIJAN

RELIGIONS OF THE WEST TODAY

INTRODUCTION

1

Globalization: World Religions in Everyone's Hometown

I n an age of globalization, human events reach through time and around the world to transform our personal, social, and political lives. In 2008 the citizens of the United States elected their first African American president, Barack Obama. This would not have been possible without the civil rights movement of nonviolent protest against racial injustice led by a black Baptist minister, Dr. Martin Luther King Jr. Fifty-some years earlier King's movement brought racial equality and equal voting rights to the United States. Likewise, Dr. King's commitment to bringing about racial equality through the use of nonviolent protest would not have been imaginable without the civil rights revolution brought about in the British empire a generation earlier. In South Africa and then India this revolution was led by the great Hindu religious teacher of nonviolence, Mohandas K. Gandhi. Dr. King took Gandhi as his model and learned about nonviolence by studying Gandhi's teachings. America has never been the same since.

In 1950 a black president would have been unimaginable. Then the United States was considered a white Protestant nation whose majority was just beginning to grudgingly accept Catholics and Jews as equal citizens. At that time race still deeply divided America. In many parts of the country, black citizens were forbidden to share the same water fountain or use the same bathrooms as whites. In 1960 the startling news was that John F. Kennedy had been elected the first Catholic president of the United States. Then in 1964 the landmark Civil Rights Act was passed by Congress not long after President Kennedy's assassination.

Just as important as the Civil Rights Act of 1964 was the Immigration Act of 1965, signed by President Lyndon Johnson. This act abolished the immigration system set up in 1924 and modified in 1952. The earlier system heavily favored immigration from

Europe and severely restricted immigration from other parts of the world, especially Asia. The 1965 legislation dramatically changed the face of America. According to government figures, in 1950 about 3.6 percent of immigrants were from Asia; by the year 2000, more than 30 percent were. In the fall of 2010 the news headlines reported that for the first time there were no Protestants on the Supreme Court and with the 2012 national election, the governor of one southern state is now of Hindu descent and another is of Sikh descent. All of this indicates that the process of globalization that began in earnest after World War II is profoundly transforming American culture.

In the 1950s, if you walked down the streets of almost any city in the United States, you would have expected to find churches, both Catholic and Protestant, and Jewish synagogues. When people thought about religious diversity, it was limited largely to Protestants, Catholics, and Jews. In the twenty-first century the situation is dramatically different. Almost daily the newspapers take note of new religious members of the community—announcing such events as a meditation retreat at a Korean Zen center in the suburbs of Providence, Rhode Island; the opening of an Islamic mosque in St. Louis, Missouri; or the dedication of a Hindu temple in Tampa, Florida.

Figure 1.1, compiled by Todd Lewis from PEW Foundation reports, census data, and other studies, offers a very rough approximation of the number of adherents of the various religions found in the world today, and their numbers in relation to each other. There is no reliable exact count available or even possible for many reasons: the lack of surveys utilizing the same criteria; disagreements about what is a branch of a world religion and what is a "new religion"; and the lack of any census/survey data from the world's two most populous nations, India and China. Existing surveys that summarize religious identity on a global level are extremely problematic due to these issues of definition, limited global scope, and affiliation.

Central to any survey data is the assumption that a person can be listed under one variable and be only that; but such an exclusive choice of one and only one religion does not very well capture the reality of world religions today. (For this reason, the estimated percentages assigned to each tradition in Figure 1.1 exceed 100%.) Even among those professing to be monotheists, there are now many hyphenated identities (such as Buddhist Jew, Zen Christian, or agnostic Yoga devotee). Singular identity is even more problematic to represent the religious reality for most people in Asia and across the various indigenous peoples across the world, where many follow more than one tradition. As we discuss elsewhere in this textbook, there are many native religions blended with Christianity, or Buddhism, or the ancestor veneration practices rooted in Confucian tradition; in other words, individuals can adhere to two or more traditions and feel no need or compulsion to choose just one. In East Asia, individuals typically follow the "diffuse religious tradition," a mixture founded on Confucianism, with elements of Daoism, Buddhism, and often shamanism. If we listed those in the world who believe in and resort to spirit mediums (shamans, oracles, etc.), it is possible that their total number (from Hindus, Buddhists, East Asians, and indigenous peoples) would be greater than those counted in the largest organized religion, Christianity. And those now following one of the world's "new religions" embrace a new tradition that combines elements from the major world religions with one or more others such

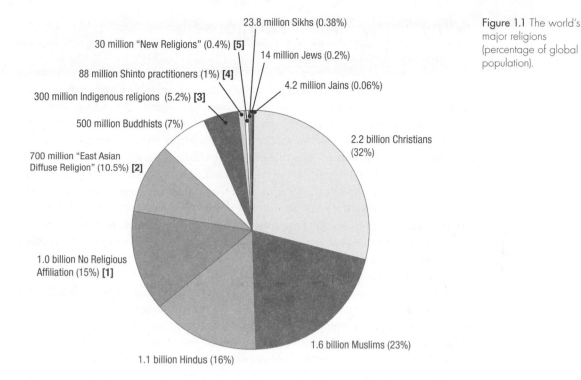

23.8 million Sikhs (0.38%)

30 million "New Religions" (0.4%) **[5]**

14 million Jews (0.2%)

88 million Shinto practitioners (1%) **[4]**

4.2 million Jains (0.06%)

300 million Indigenous religions (5.2%) **[3]**

500 million Buddhists (7%)

2.2 billion Christians (32%)

700 million "East Asian Diffuse Religion" (10.5%) **[2]**

1.0 billion No Religious Affiliation (15%) **[1]**

1.6 billion Muslims (23%)

1.1 billion Hindus (16%)

Figure 1.1 The world's major religions (percentage of global population).

Notes:

[1] Includes atheists, agnostics, and people who do not self-identify with any particular religion in surveys. Studies have also revealed that many of the "religiously unaffiliated" do have some religious beliefs. Some of the religiously unaffiliated, for example, do express belief in God or a higher power, a view shared, for example, by 7% of Chinese unaffiliated adults, 30% of French unaffiliated adults, and 68% of unaffiliated U.S. adults. Some of the unaffiliated also engage in certain kinds of religious practices. For example, 7% of unaffiliated adults in France and 27% of those in the United States say they attend religious services at least once a year.

[2] A combination of Confucian, Daoist, and local religious devotions. This figure was estimated based on a Chinese government statistic indicating that 44% of adults reported that they had worshiped at a graveside or tomb in the survey year.

[3] Practice various folk or traditional religions, including African traditional religions, Indian tribal traditions, Native American religions, and Australian aboriginal religions.

[4] This number for adherents to Shinto in Japan is based on recent surveys that have shown that 80% of Japanese register their newborn children at a Shinto shrine, and that roughly the same number visit these temples on New Year's Day and other major traditional holidays.

[5] The formation of new religions has been a key hallmark of global religious life since 1750, and it has been recorded on every continent. Some have come and gone (such as the "Shakers" in Colonial America); some have arisen and command the loyalty of few until today; most have arisen and spread in a particular region; a few have become global in membership.

as ancestral cults, martial arts, and new Western philosophies or psychologies. It is easy for demographers to give a false certainty to the pluralistic and fluid boundaries of the world's religions today.

Why Study World Religions?

In the emerging global economy, most neighborhoods, workplaces, and schools reflect this diversity as well. The beliefs and practices of world religions have become part of the mosaic of American society. *Karma* has become part of the American vocabulary, Hindu visualization practices are used in sports training, and Buddhist meditation techniques have been adopted in programs of stress management. No matter where we live today, it is more and more likely that our next-door neighbors are ethnically, politically, and, yes, even religiously diverse—coming from many parts of the globe (see Map 1.1). To understand other religions is no longer an "elective" activity that one might do just because it is interesting. Today understanding diverse religions is a necessity because it is now about understanding our neighbors. If we do not understand each other, our misunderstandings may well lead to prejudice, conflict, and even violence.

The academic study of religion is one of the newest disciplines in the modern university. Its beginnings go back to the emergence of the social sciences in the nineteenth century, with the appearance of such fields as anthropology, sociology, and comparative linguistics. One of the great founding fathers of this study was the Indologist Max Muller (1825–1900), who argued that "the person who knows only one religion understands none."[1] It is only by studying the diverse expressions of religion throughout history and across cultures that we come to understand its unity and diversity.

Prior to the 1960s, in the United States, for instance, one could not have studied religions comparatively in secular and state universities. Only religious colleges and universities offered courses on religion, and these were typically on the teachings of their own denominations. If other religions came up for discussion it was usually to point out their "erroneous teachings." Then in the 1960s departments of religious studies began to appear in nonreligious colleges and secular state universities. Responding to the new diversity brought on by globalization, these departments began to offer courses on Asian traditions such as Hinduism and Buddhism, on Islam and comparative religions. What they attempted was completely new in history: They sought to empathetically understand the diverse religious traditions of the world in an objective manner.

The academic study of religion requires a new way of looking at the religion of others. It requires the courage and compassion to sympathetically understand the diverse worldviews of others and the willingness to learn from each. Its goal is not to show one religion is right and all others wrong but rather to show what humans have found compelling in each and how each tradition has shaped history. The task in the study of world religions today is to overcome stereotypes and glimpse the wisdom found in each of these traditions. To judge another's religion without understanding it and what it means to its members is to "prejudge" them—that is the meaning of the word *prejudice*. When encountering beliefs and practices we do not understand, it is

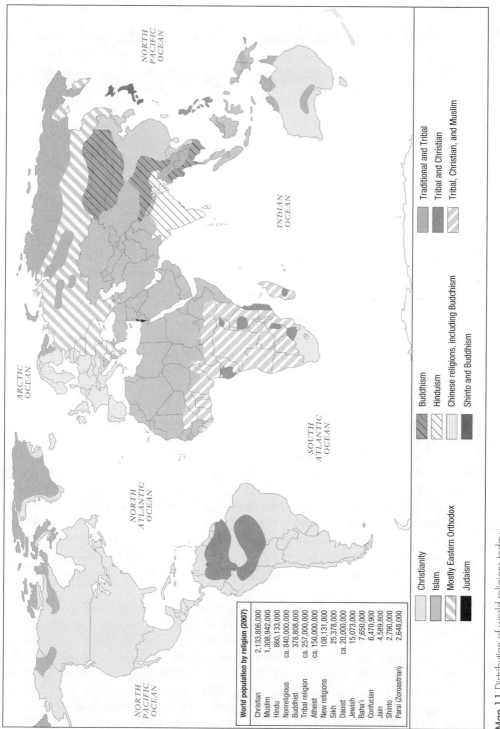

World population by religion (2007)

Christian	2,133,806,000
Muslim	1,308,942,000
Hindu	860,133,000
Nonreligious	ca. 840,000,000
Buddhist	378,808,000
Tribal religion	ca. 257,000,000
Atheist	ca. 150,000,000
New religions	108,131,000
Sikh	25,378,000
Daoist	ca. 20,000,000
Jewish	15,073,000
Baha'i	7,650,000
Confucian	6,470,900
Jain	4,589,800
Shinto	2,790,000
Parsi (Zoroastrian)	2,648,000

Christianity
Islam
Mostly Eastern Orthodox
Judaism

Buddhism
Hinduism
Chinese religions, including Buddhism
Shinto and Buddhism

Traditional and Tribal
Tribal and Christian
Tribal, Christian, and Muslim

Map 1.1 Distribution of world religions today

In surveying world religions today, we shall not be able to cover everything that could be said about them. Our selection will be governed primarily by the following question: What do we need to know about the past to understand the role of religion in the world we live in today?

easy to fall into the trap of ridiculing them, saying, "How can anyone possibly believe that?" Certainly each of us wants to be understood and respected, not stereotyped and dismissed. We need to extend that same courtesy to all others as well. So in the academic study of religion we agree to "bracket" our preconceptions and prejudices—that is, put them aside and simply try to understand and appreciate the meaning others find in their beliefs and practices.

Our Task

In this book we focus on the diverse ways in which human beings have been religious in the past and are religious today. Indeed, the last decades of the twentieth century brought a global religious resurgence, a development that defied countless predictions that the irresistible secularization of civilization would lead to the disappearance of religion. Religions, it was thought, are tied to ancient premodern worldviews, and these would inevitably be replaced by a worldview based on modern science. Indeed, the clash of traditional religions with contemporary scientific and secular society is a major concern of this textbook. Awareness of this conflict is essential if we are to understand the interactions between religions and cultures in the world today. We will begin every chapter not with a discussion of the origins and early history of each religious tradition, but with examples of a major controversy or significant tension each religion faces in the world today.

With the Space Age, awareness that all humans share life in a global village has come to the religions and cultures of the earth.

We describe our present time as one in transition between "modernity" and a new "postmodern" era of globalization that is emerging. To understand what is "new" about our situation, we will have to understand the premodern period of the different religious traditions and how the premodern worldview of each relates to and contrasts with the modern period. In particular, we will have to compare the premodern period in each tradition with the changes brought about by an era that began with the rise of modern science after 1500 and declined after World War II. In surveying world religions today, we shall not be able to cover everything that could be said about them. Our selection will be governed primarily by the following question: What do we need to know about the past to understand the role of religion in the world we live in today? In order to understand many of the conflicts that we read about in the newspaper or watch on cable news, we need to understand how religious traditions profoundly shaped the world to be the way it is today. Since religious beliefs are at the center of the individual's core values, and because religious communities are major actors in our world today, studying world religions provides crucial insights for understanding our world. And to do that we must begin by introducing some basic concepts.

Understanding Religious Experience and Its Formative Elements

Wherever we find religious practice, as we shall come to see, we will find certain key elements:

The Experience of Sacredness

Myth or Symbolic Story (typically embodied in sacred writing or *scripture* and expressed in a system of *beliefs*)

Ritual

Community

Morality

Religious Leaders/Experts

religion: the sense of being tied or bound by sacred obligations to powers believed to govern our destiny

Let us begin with a working definition of the term ***religion***. Suppose we have a time machine and can transport ourselves back to the city of Rome in the first century. Why are we interested in that time and place? The word *religion* has its roots in Latin, the language of the Romans, so understanding how the Romans defined the concept helps us understand our topic.

Imagine yourself now walking down a street in Rome in the first century CE. You approach a small group of people on a street corner and ask them: "What religion are you?" They look at you strangely. They understand the individual words you have spoken, but they don't normally put those words together as you have done. Some give you blank stares, while others just look puzzled. Frustrated, you try rephrasing your question: "Are you religious?" Suddenly their faces light up and they smile and say, "Of course, but who isn't?"

By its wording, the original question assumes that *religion* is a noun applied to distinct social bodies in the world, such that you can be a member of one only if you are not a member of another. So the question seeks to find out the distinct religious group to which you belong. This way of understanding religion naturally arises among monotheists, who by definition have chosen one god and excluded all others. However, such an exclusiveness was foreign to antiquity. In rephrasing the original question as "Are you religious?" you are no longer treating *religion* as a noun, describing something you join. Instead, you are treating it as an adjective, describing an attitude toward the human condition—a way of seeing, acting, and experiencing all things. In most times and places throughout history, religion and culture were like two sides of the same coin. Therefore people did not think of their practices as "a religion"—a separate reality they had to choose over and against another. Today in Japan, for instance, it is possible to practice Buddhism, Daoism, Confucianism, and Shintoism all at the same time. This seems odd from the monotheistic perspective of Western religions, where one can be, for instance, a Muslim or a Christian or a Jew but not two or more at the same time. And yet, paradoxically, Jews, Christians, and Muslims all claim to worship the same God.

In first-century Rome, with very few exceptions, people didn't belong to a religion in any exclusive sense. They were, however, religious. Our first-century respondents would probably continue the discussion you had started something like this: "Being religious is simply a matter of common sense. I respect all those powers that govern my destiny. Therefore I worship all the gods and goddesses. It would be stupid not to. If I must go to war I want the god of war on my side. So I would perform the correct ritual sacrifices before going into battle. And when I looked for someone to marry, I petitioned the goddess of love to help me. And needless to say, when I plant my crops every spring, I do everything possible to ensure that the goddess of fertility and the gods of wind and rain are on my side. I am not a complete idiot. To ignore or antagonize the gods would be stupid."

The Sacred

What does our discussion with the ancient Romans about "religion" tell us? It tells us that religion is about what people hold sacred, what matters more than anything else to them—namely, their destiny individually and collectively. For the ancient Romans, and nearly all other human beings in all places and all times throughout history, religion has been about power and meaning in relation to human destiny. Although its exact root is uncertain, the word *religion* is probably derived from the Latin *religare*, which literally means "to tie or bind" and has the connotation of "acting with care." It expresses our sense of being "tied and bound" by relations of obligation to whatever powers we believe govern our destiny—whether these powers be natural or supernatural, personal or impersonal, one or many.

Ancient peoples everywhere believed that the powers governing their destiny were the forces of nature. Why? Because nature was experienced as that awesome collection of powers that surround and, at times, overwhelm human beings. On the one hand, nature provides life and all its necessities (food, clothing, shelter, etc.); but on the other hand, nature may turn on people, destroying them quite capriciously through earthquakes, storms, floods, and so on. Therefore the forces of nature evoke in human beings the ambivalent feeling of both fascination and dread. Rudolf Otto (1869–1937), a pioneer in the comparative study of religions, argued that the presence of these two ambivalent emotions is a sure sign that one is in the presence of the sacred. They are a defining mark of religious experience across cultures. They are the emotions that are elicited by the uncanny experience of being in the presence of that power or powers one believes have the ability to determine whether one lives or dies and, beyond that, how well one lives.

Religion as a form of human experience and behavior, therefore, is not just about purely "spiritual" things. Nor can the study of religion in global perspective be defined only by gods or God. People's religiousness over the millennia and around the earth has proven to be as diverse as the forms of power they believe govern human destiny. These powers have ranged from gods as forces of nature to the unseen ancestral spirits or spirits associated with sacred places, to more impersonal sacred forces or energies; or finally the mysterious power(s) that govern history (including the seemingly secular powers associated with wealth and politics that get treated as if "sacred"). Hence, whatever powers we believe govern our destiny will elicit a religious response from us and inspire us to wish "to tie or bind" ourselves to these powers in relations of ritual obligation. Thus tied or bound, we will act respectfully and carefully in relation to these powers, to ensure that they will be on our side.

How do we know what our obligations to these powers are? Throughout history this knowledge has been passed down from one generation to the next through myth and ritual.

Myth, Scripture, and Beliefs

Our word **myth** comes from the Greek *mythos*, which means "story." Myth, we could say, is a symbolic story about the origins of the world and destiny of human beings; myth "ties and binds" human beings in relations of obligation to whatever powers they believe ultimately govern their destiny and explains what these powers expect of them. Unlike the contemporary English use of *myth* to indicate an untrue story or a misunderstanding based on ignorance, in every religious tradition, myths

myth: symbolic story about the origins and destiny of human beings and their world

A Shinto priest and believers purify their bodies in icy water for the New Year's ceremony at the Teppozu Shrine in Tokyo.

To live well, have many descendants, and live a long life—these are three great treasures in Chinese culture. A Chinese woman prays for prosperity, posterity, and longevity at a Buddhist temple on the island of Lantau.

convey the deepest and most profound truths about life. These truths are expressed through grand stories of creation and destiny rather than in abstract theories. After the invention of writing (about 3000 BCE), these stories came to be written down, creating what we now call the "scriptures" of the various religions. Because these scriptures tell the stories about the power or powers that govern human destiny, they have been treated as sacred scriptures and passed on from one generation to the next.

The fact that the word used to designate these great religious stories, *myth*, came to be understood in modern contemporary language as meaning a "false story" reveals one of the most challenging tasks facing anyone trying to understand religious language. That challenge is understanding the symbolic nature of much of religious language. To understand a religious story literally can often lead to mis-understanding its meaning and so make it seem false. For example, in Western biblical tradition, the Psalms say "God is my shepherd," just as Buddhist scriptures refer to their founder, the Buddha, as "a bull of a man." We know such statements are not meant literally: God is not literally a shepherd, nor is the Buddha literally a bull.

To speak like this is to speak metaphorically, that is, to use things that are more familiar to help explain what is less familiar, a reality that is mysterious or even beyond human language. Shepherds and bulls we can see and know something about, but God or a Buddha is a little more mysterious. A person who says "God is our shepherd" has expressed the thought that God is like a shepherd, in the sense that God watches over and cares for persons in the same way a shepherd tends his sheep. Similarly, "Buddha was a bull of a man" expresses the conviction that the man who achieved enlightenment was a strong and powerful enlightened man. These metaphors both assert that the Buddha and God are realities that can always be relied upon.

Not all religious experiences are theistic, reflecting belief in one or more gods. Theravada Buddhists in ancient India refused to use the Hindu words roughly equivalent to the English word *God* to describe their religious understanding. Instead they spoke of the emptiness and inadequacy of all spoken metaphors to explain their goal, the blissful state of *nirvana*. And yet they too used metaphors to try to help people understand what they had experienced as the "blowing out of the flame of desire," which leads to liberation from all suffering.

In fact, the word *God*, which is so central to the Abrahamic religious traditions (Judaism, Christianity, Islam), is just one of many diverse terms used in different religions and cultures across the world to designate the **ultimate reality**, that which is the highest in value and meaning for the group. This class of terms includes not only the personal God of Western theism but also the impersonal Brahman of Hinduism, the transpersonal nirvana of Buddhism, and the impersonal power of the *Dao* at work in all things that is central to Chinese religions. At the same time one can find some parallels to Western personalistic theism in Asia, too: D'ien (Heaven) and Shang Di (Lord of Heaven) in China; incarnations of Brahman in gods such as Shiva and Krishna in devotional schools of Hinduism; and the cosmic Buddhas and bodhisattvas to whom Mahayana Buddhists pray for help.

> **ultimate reality:** that which has the highest value and meaning to a group

All these expressions for what is truly ultimate and meaningful may in fact refer to different ultimate realities—or perhaps different people use language unique to their own cultures and times to point to what may ultimately be the same reality. Here lies the challenge, mystery, and fascination of studying the religions of the world: Do differences in religious terminology reflect experiences of different realities? Or are they different expressions of or ways of describing the same reality? Because religious metaphors come out of particular historical and cultural times and places and because they are symbolic forms of expression, to understand the religious languages and messages of different religious traditions requires that we put ourselves in the time and place of their origins and use our **sympathetic imagination** to understand the metaphors used.

> **sympathetic imagination:** empathy; necessary to understand the religious languages and messages of different times and places

If religious language is primarily symbolic, where do these metaphors and symbolic expressions come from? To answer this question requires putting yourself imaginatively in the following situation: Think of a beautiful warm summer evening. The sky is clear, and millions of stars are shining brightly. The evening is so breathtaking that you decide to go for a walk in the rolling hills just outside the city. As you walk, you are suddenly in the grip of an experience so overwhelming that it cannot be expressed in words. After a short time, which seems in retrospect like an eternity, you return to your normal consciousness and wander back to the city, where you run into some friends at the local cafe. You order a latte and then you say to them, "You'll never guess what happened to me tonight. I had the most incredible experience, so incredible it defies description." Yet paradoxically, your friends immediately ask, "What was it like?" With that question, we have entered the realm of metaphor and symbolic language.

Your friends are asking you to describe what you have just said is indescribable. To answer at all, you must draw analogies to things they already know about. So you might say that the experience was like being in the presence of a shepherd who really cares for his flock. At least you might say that if you and your friends were nomads familiar with the raising of sheep, like the people of ancient Israel. Roughly a thousand years before the start of the Common Era, however, the people stopped being nomads and settled into a fixed territory under the rule of a king. Although many continued to raise sheep, they started speaking of God as a king who protects his subjects. In this way different cultures and different generations have each contributed to the rich variety of metaphors used to illuminate the mystery and meaning of human existence.

via analogia: a way of explaining spiritual reality by using analogies from particular finite qualities and characteristics

via negativa: a way of explaining spiritual reality by negating all finite qualities and characteristics

transcendent: beyond all finite things

Religious language, as symbolic language, can take one of two forms: analogy or negation. The metaphors just quoted ("God is my shepherd" and "God is my rock") are examples of the way of analogy (***via analogia***). In these metaphors, we use familiar words to create an analogy that describes something less familiar. However, there is another form of religious language, the way of negation (***via negativa***). This way of speaking religiously proceeds not by asserting what God or ultimate reality is (or is like) but by saying what it is not. This approach is very typical of mystical traditions. The Muslim mystic declares that Allah is "nothing," stating that Allah (God) is beyond (i.e., transcends) or is different from anything in our material universe and experience. Allah is not this thing and not that thing. Allah is in fact no "thing" at all. Being beyond all finite things and thus **transcendent**, Allah must be said to be no-thing.

In general, Western monotheism has emphasized the way of analogy by saying that there is one God who is like humans, able to "know" and to "love," but in a superior fashion. Thus, God is described as all-knowing, all-loving, or all-powerful. By contrast, Buddhism, of all the religions, has emphasized most strongly the way of negation, insisting that what is most valuable or true cannot be either named or imaged. Yet both ways are found in all traditions. Some Jewish, Christian, and Muslim mystics have referred to God as a "Nothingness," even as some Hindus have referred to the ultimate reality as a cosmic person (*purusha*) rather than an impersonal power (Brahman). Moreover, we should note that these two ways are not really in conflict, for the way of analogy itself implies the way of negation. That is, every time we say God is *like* some thing, we are at the same time saying God is not literally that thing. Every analogy implies a negation.

Our discussion of religious language should help us to appreciate just how challenging and at times confusing it can be to study and compare various religious traditions. Just as religious communities and religious traditions from different parts of the world use different metaphors and symbols, they also mix the way of analogy and the way of negation in varying degrees. Therefore, two different traditions sometimes talk about the same human experience in ways that seem to be totally contradictory. For example, it may seem that a Jewish theist and a Theravada Buddhist hold diametrically opposed religious beliefs, for Jews believe in a personal God who created the universe and Theravada Buddhists do not. Yet, when we look more closely at Jewish beliefs, we discover that Jews believe that God can be neither named nor imaged, even as Theravada Buddhists believe that ultimate truth is beyond all names and images. And yet, in both traditions, experiencing the nameless is said to make one more human or compassionate, not less.

After learning about the traditions covered in this book, you might conclude that perhaps theistic and nontheistic religious experiences are really not far apart. However, it is also possible that they might be seen as truly different. To pursue this great human question, we must begin by "bracketing" or withholding judgment and simply try to understand how stories and rituals shape people's lives—their views, values, and behavior. Perhaps the real measure of comparison should be how people live their lives rather than the apparently diverse images and concepts they hold. If both Jews and Buddhists, for example, are led by their religious experiences and beliefs to express compassion for those who suffer or are in need, then clearly the two faiths are similar in that very important respect.

Ritual

Like myths, **ritual** actions "tie and bind" the individual and the community to the sacred. Such actions often involve the symbolic reenactment of the stories that are passed on from one generation to the next. Typically myth and ritual are closely tied to the major festivals or holy days of a religious tradition and illuminate the meaning of human destiny in relation to sacred powers. By celebrating a cycle of festivals spread throughout the year, people come to dwell in the stories that tell them who they are, where they came from, and where they are going.

Carefully choreographed religious rituals recall important events in the history of each faith: the "Night Journey" of the Prophet Muhammad, the enlightenment of the Buddha, the birthday of Confucius. In other rituals, the faithful donate gifts to the supernatural beings to whom they ascribe a power to profoundly affect their lives. Still other rituals require circumcision, tattoos, or burn marks to set the believers off from nonbelievers, fostering in-group solidarity. The consumption of certain foods as part of some rituals suggests that the believer can acquire the "same essence" as the **divine** through ingestion, as in the Christian communion, Hindu puja, or tribal eating of a totemic animal to affirm common identity.

We should not assume that rituals only communicate ideas or beliefs. Religions are not confined to doctrines regarding the sacred. Rather, they include many *careful acts* that, in their own right, *tie and bind* people to each other and to cosmic meaning. Being religious thus entails taking decisive action at times, abstaining from certain acts at others—offering, for instance, precious gifts to supernatural beings, making pilgrimages to sacred places, or engaging in meditation or other disciplined spiritual practices.

For many believers, acting in the prescribed manner, called **orthopraxy** (correct practice), is more important than **orthodoxy** (correct belief)—acceptance of the often intricate doctrines set forth in texts and formulated by scholars. Performing the five daily Muslim prayers, visiting a Buddhist or Hindu temple to offer flowers on the full moon day, cleaning a Chinese family's ancestral grave during the spring festival, or being baptized as a Christian—all these acts are as central to "being religious" as is adopting beliefs or doctrines defined as orthodox.

The great annual festivals in the world's religions give devotees a break from the profane time of normal working life, times for special rituals, for fasts or feasting, and periods of rest and reflection on the fundamental truths. These events also reinforce

ritual: actions that link the individual and the community to each other, through the sacred

divine: highest spiritual reality

orthopraxy: practice of "right actions" as prescribed by sacred traditions

orthodoxy: acceptance of "right beliefs" based on sacred texts as formulated by religious authorities

important ties with family and fellow devotees. The need to orchestrate such crucial ritual actions also leads followers to create the religious institutions that come to occupy central places in their societies.

Community and Morality

Myth and ritual express the communal nature of human experience and shape unique communities to foster the way of life that emerges out of their religious experiences. So Buddhists form sanghas, Jews form synagogues, Christians form churches, Muslims form ummahs, and so on.

We live in communities of shared language—we share stories and we share a way of life. Religion not only ties us to the sacred powers we believe govern our destiny; it also binds us to each other. Consequently, in most religious traditions, ritual and **morality** have been closely intertwined. "Right" is often defined by "rite"—the ritual patterns of behavior that keep life sacred. Morality is an inherent dimension of religious experience, for religion not only concerns sacred powers but also describes the way of life the powers require and make possible.

morality: right action

A Tlingit shaman performing a healing ceremony.

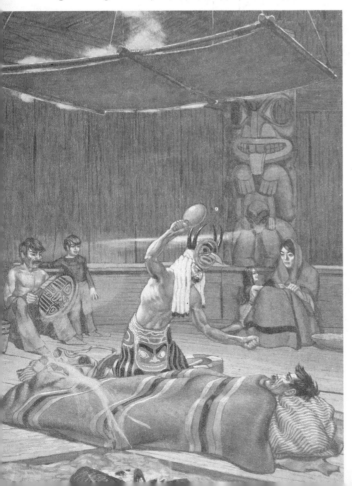

The sacred—what matters most to a given community—provides the ground for the moral experience of the virtuous life, a yardstick for measuring the rightness of any human action. The blueprint for what is just or moral is expressed in myth and ritual. Take, for example, the Jewish festival of Yom Kippur. This is the occasion at the beginning of a new year for each person to repent, to seek and offer forgiveness for the ways each has harmed others; each person also resolves to live more compassionately and justly in the new year.

This is just one example of how a religious tradition shapes morality. Even the most secular and seemingly nonreligious morality, insofar as it treats anything as sacred, can be understood as having a religious dimension. In the self-proclaimed atheist nation of the former Soviet Union, a major world power rivaling the United States in the decades after World War II, May Day was a great national festival celebrating the Russian revolution of 1917 and the founding of an atheistic state. At this celebration, the values of the way of life in the USSR were held up as sacred—worth living for and worth dying for. Although not connected in any way to the world's religions, this festival served a profound religious purpose: It told Soviet citizens that their individual lives were important and that they were tied and bound into a great historical drama that would inevitably lead to a communist society in which all would be equal.

Once we realize that religion is about what people hold sacred and the way of life that is called for by such beliefs, then it makes sense to say that all morality has a religious dimension, because every morality is grounded in religious experience, namely in the experience of what is held sacred (i.e., what matters most) in a given community. In this sense even the morality of atheists or others who may not think of themselves as religious can be said to have a religious dimension—to the degree that certain values are held sacred. Such an observation still leaves open the philosophical question of the degree to which a tradition's sacred morality is truly ethical, for ethics is the questioning of sacred moralities, asking whether what people customarily say is good or virtuous really is good or virtuous.

Religious Leaders/Experts

In every religion we will find interpretive and ritual specialists: the shamans, priests, ministers, monks, scholars, and teachers who mediate between the sacred power(s) and the community by explaining the myths and performing the rituals. The world's oldest religious specialist is the shaman, a man or woman who goes into a trance to leave his or her body to go to the spirit realm and communicate with sacred ancestors and supernatural beings (spirits, gods, demons, ghosts). Practitioners of this art (also called *mediums*

A two-year-old Muslim boy, living in predominantly Catholic East Timor, prays alongside his father at a mosque in Dili.

or *oracles*) are depicted on cave walls across Eurasia from the Neolithic period 25,000 years ago. Shamans still exist in many parts of the world, not only among the remaining indigenous peoples but also within the great world religions (see Chapter 2).

Since the invention of writing in 3000 BCE, the great world religions have relied on written materials and on scholars who have learned to write and read and thereby interpret the sacred texts. These keepers of the sacred writings translate their meanings for the great majority of rank-and-file followers, most of whom, until the modern era, were illiterate. The Confucian masters, the Muslim ulama, and the Hindu brahmin are examples of this religious specialist. And then there are those who specialize in being spiritual teachers, such as the Hindu guru, the Jewish rabbi, or the Sufi Muslim shaykh. Although we can point to interesting comparative patterns among religious rituals and between religious teachers, it is also true to say that each tradition can and must be known by its own unique set of religious practitioners and institutions.

The Great Religious Stories of the World

Since the beginning of the human race, people have told stories. We human beings are not just storytellers, we are "storydwellers." We live in our stories and make sense of the world through them. Even our understanding of what is good and evil, right and wrong, is shaped by the kind of story we see ourselves in and the role we see ourselves playing in that story. Although religious stories need not only be about gods and other spiritual beings, most of the earliest stories that have shaped human religious life have been.

While specific religious stories are indeed unique and diverse, we can group religious stories into four main types, each of which presents a symbolic story of the origins and destiny of human beings and the challenges they face in striving to realize their sacred destiny. These four main types of sacred story are:

the myths of nature
the myths of harmony
the myths of liberation
the myths of history (see Figure 1.2)

The Myths of Nature

If one goes back far enough into the history of any society, the earliest religious stories, found everywhere, are myths of nature. These are stories about the powers of nature that govern human destiny, which portray them as either personal beings (gods, spirits, and sacred ancestors) or impersonal powers. Such religions tend to see time as cyclical, always returning to the moment just before and after creation. Just as winter and death are followed by spring and new life, starting the earthly cycles all over again, time is an endless loop. Myth and ritual are the means to erase the distance between "now" and the time of origins, "in the beginning," when the gods or ancestral spirits first created the world fresh and new. In such stories one key problem of life is time. Time is the enemy. Time brings decay. It inevitably brings sickness, decline, and death. The ideal in human life is to return to the newness of life at the beginning of creation, before time began.

The means for bringing about this return is the recitation of the myths and the performance of rituals reenacting creation. Hunter-gatherer stories emphasize the fertility of the earth, the relations with animals and plants, the need for the ritual renewal of life in harmony with the seasons, and the role the tribe plays in maintaining the eternal cosmic order. In many of these societies, a shaman is the spiritual leader; as will be seen in the next chapter, the shaman's trance journeys restore harmony between the human community, spirits, and the forces of nature.

China and the Myths of Harmony

In China the great cosmic story that emerged was that of the Dao (sometimes rendered Tao). The universal Dao, which all beings share, is the source of harmony in the universe at work but hidden in all the forces of nature. One's true self is knowable only in relation to the Dao. All of creation works through combinations of complementary opposites of *yin* and *yang*, of dark and light, of earth and heaven, of female and male. Yin and yang are never polar opposites; rather, each flows into the other with no absolute division, the way day flows into night and night into day. There is a little day in every night, a little male in every female (and vice versa). The ideal for human life, then, is balance and harmony. The great problem of existence is the disharmony that occurs when the elements of society and/or the universe are out of balance.

To restore balance, two different religions emerged in China: Both Daoism and Confucianism sought to bring harmony between heaven and earth, self and society. These two traditions offered very different means to overcome the problem and realize the ideal. Daoist sages urged humans to seek harmony with the rhythms of nature through cultivating *wu-wei*, the art of "not doing," or not interfering with the natural flow of life. Out of that harmony, the harmony of society would flow spontaneously. By contrast, the Confucian sages urged humans to establish harmony in society through the practice of *li*, the ritual observance of obligations attached to one's station in society. They taught that people can be in harmony with the rhythms of the universe only when individuals know their place (as child, parent, citizen), cultivate their character, and sacrifice their self-interest for the good of the whole society.

India and the Myths of Liberation

In India, life was also seen in relationship to the cycles and rhythms of nature, and its ancient priests enacted careful, powerful rituals to control the gods behind all cosmic activity. But in India these worldly rhythms and concerns were ultimately to be

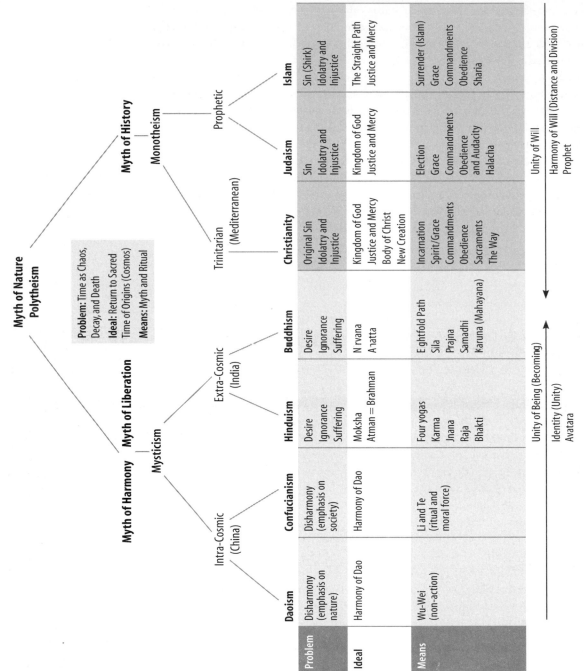

Figure 1.2 The world's religions in perspective.

20

escaped, not affirmed. Human existence was seen as distorted by delusion and suffering, not because there is nothing good about life but because no matter how good it is, it is transient and always ends in old age, sickness, and death. The problem of life is human entrapment in an endless cycle of suffering and rebirth; the highest goal was to overcome these bonds. The ultimate goal of all the great religions originating there is to destroy the illusions fostered by our selfish desires, for only when these are mastered can humans be freed from the wheel of death and rebirth (*samsara*). In that moment of liberation or enlightenment, one will come to realize the ultimate reality and find blissful union with it.

For most Hindus, the true self (*atman*) is merged with the eternal Brahman in either the personal or impersonal form. Buddhism offers the possibility of removing selfish attachments and realizing complete enlightenment within the suffering and impermanence of life, achieving the indescribable and transpersonal reality called *nirvana*.

Hinduism and Buddhism developed a variety of means, called yogas, for achieving release from samsara. These range widely, from disciplined ritual activity and the selfless performance of one's duties, to seeking spiritual knowledge through meditation, or cultivating selfless devotion toward a particular god.

Hindu women pay homage to the god of the sun during the Chat Puja festival on the banks of the Hooghly River in the eastern Indian city of Calcutta. Thousands of Hindu devotees reached the riverside at sunset and will spend the night praying.

The Middle East and the Myths of History

The myths of nature, of harmony, and of liberation use the human experience of the rhythms and cycles of nature as the basis for religious metaphors and symbolic language expressed in sacred stories. In the myths of history, by contrast, it is not nature but history that comprises the realm of human experience from which the metaphors for religious experience are primarily drawn. While all religions communicate their traditions by telling stories, only the religions of the Middle East, beginning with Judaism, make "story" itself the central metaphor of religious expression. Unlike the eternally cyclical rhythms of nature, stories have a beginning and an end. Ancient Judaism conceived of the cosmos as a great unfolding story told by a great divine storyteller (God): In the beginning God spoke, the world was created, and the story of revelation began.

Three versions of this story of revelation arose in the Middle East—first the Judaic, then the Christian, and finally the Islamic. For each of these, human beings are considered human by virtue of being children of the one God who created all things. All three traditions tell the myth of Adam and Eve as the first human beings, and venerate the patriarch Abraham, whom each considers to be the true model of faith and obedience to divine revelation. In all three, the problem of life is viewed as "sin"—failing to follow God's laws, a combination of idolatry and human selfishness that leads to injustice. The ideal goal of life is for humans to be in harmony with the will of God, whereupon peace and justice will reign and death will be overcome. The means for bringing this about are obedience to the will of God but also even debate

All that remains of the great temple in Jerusalem, destroyed by the Romans in 70 BCE, is the Western Wall. It is considered to be the holiest of sites where observant Jews come to pray.

with God (Judaism), acceptance of divine grace or aid through the incarnation of God (Christianity), and submission to the will of God (Islam). Although each of the three Abrahamic religions has its own story of the cosmos full of many trials, triumphs, and tragedies, each tells of the human-divine story having a happy ending, though only for faithful believers. In contrast to the myths of nature, harmony, and liberation, traditions founded on myths of history regard time not as the enemy but as the vehicle for encountering the ultimate reality, which is God, for eternity. The goal is not to escape time by returning to the beginning through ritual, nor rising above time in mystical ecstasy, but of meeting the one God in time and making a journey with God through time. Time for the faithful is promising, and the future is ultimately hopeful.

Religious Diversity and Historical Change: The Structure of This Book

Each of the great religious traditions addressed the problem of mortality. In India and China the ultimate answer was essentially mystical: All find their true identity through inner transformation, achieving union or harmony with the same ultimate reality (whether Brahman or the Dao) or, in the case of Buddhism, experiencing the same ultimate destiny of nirvana. In the Middle East, the answer was not primarily mystical but apocalyptic—the union with God at the end of time, which leads to the resurrection of the dead and eternal life.

Each of these traditions speaks to the problem of morality as well, by helping the individual to get beyond the self-centeredness that came with urban individualism and to grasp the essential unity and interdependence of all human beings. And each sought to provide life with meaning by depicting individuals and communities as participating in a great cosmic story that gives drama and purpose to human life. These were stories that were not made absurd by death; rather, their purpose was to show individuals a way to overcome the finality of death.

Finally, we need to qualify our statements about the unity and diversity of religions. When we stand back at a great distance we can use the four types of myth or story—those of nature, harmony, liberation, and history—to classify the various religions. As we get closer, we discover that each of these stories has variations expressing internal differences in doctrine and in practice. Those familiar with Christianity need only recall how many different kinds of Christianity there are. There is such a great difference between church rituals conducted by contemplative Quakers, enthusiastic Southern Baptists, and the more formal rituals of Anglicans that it is hard to believe they are all examples of the same religion. In fact, this range of diversity is true of every religious tradition.

In the chapters to come we will be examining how human beings struggle to continue the religiousness of their ancestors in a radically different, fast-changing, and globalizing world. We will see how Western civilization gave birth to modernity and, through its colonial expansion, spread its religious and cultural influence around the world, disrupting premodern religious cultures everywhere. By *colonialism* we mean the political, social, cultural, and economic domination of one society by another. Colonialism is as old as civilization and is part of the story of virtually all religions and civilizations, East and West. But after 1492, modern Western colonialism came closest to achieving global domination. Propelled by European colonialism, Christianity became the first faith to spread globally, forcing every religion to reckon with its beliefs, its practices, and its critiques of non-Christians.

We will also describe how colonialism, in turn, provoked postcolonial reactions that have divided those in each religious tradition into three groups:

fundamentalist: one who rejects aspects of modernity and wants to return to the perceived foundational purity of an ancestral sacred social/political order, or way of life

1. **Fundamentalists**, who reject important aspects of modernity and want to go back to what they perceive as the purity of an "authentic" social/political order manifested in the sacred way of life of their ancestors.
2. Modernists, who seek an accommodation of their religious tradition to the insights of science and the social and political realities of modern life.
3. Postmodernists, who, while rejecting the dominance of science and Western modernity, seek to go forward into a new situation that affirms the role of religion in public life in a way that embraces religious diversity and is open to change in their religious tradition in this regard.

While some fundamentalists reject everything modern, most accept modern technology while rejecting changes suggested by the sciences that would call into question the fundamentalists' religious worldview. Earlier we spoke of "orthodoxy" as "right belief," and while many fundamentalists would consider themselves orthodox, not all who call themselves orthodox would consider themselves fundamentalists. Very often orthodox movements will interpret their scriptures allegorically or symbolically, while fundamentalists tend to interpret their scriptures literally. For instance, an orthodox Christian might interpret the seven days of creation as symbolic periods of undetermined length. A fundamentalist, however, would be inclined to say, "No, we are talking about creating the world literally in seven 24-hour periods of time, so scientific accounts of the origin and development of the universe over millennia are false."

Among modernists and postmodernists, most argue that some parts of the religious tradition must change. What is distinctive about the modernist end of the spectrum is the view that the human understanding of religious truth and practice is subject to historical change and development, a notion that fundamentalists find abhorrent, even blasphemous.

As Figure 1.3 indicates, religions are not monolithic. And they should not be studied as vague, disembodied abstractions but as vibrant multifaceted phenomena embraced by real people. Humans are different, too, and born with different talents and shaped by varying experiences; they are diverse in how they engage with their surroundings. The template of the bell curve (Figure 1.3) is useful to display the universal pattern of the range of beliefs that humans adopt in adhering to a given world religion. Although impossible to graph with exactitude in each case, the effort to understand

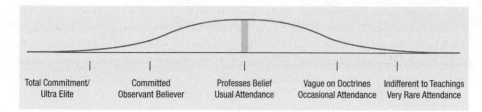

Figure 1.3 Mapping the typical spectrum of believers in religious communities.

how religion exists for the elite, the average believer, and the hardly observant is a valuable exercise. The vertical axis plots the percentage of believers; the horizontal axis is a measure of belief vitality and ritual attendance. On the left side are the elite who have complete commitment and lifestyle to the highest religious ideals. They are "all in." Examples include the Tibetan Buddhist nun doing a three-year cave meditation retreat, and the Hindu holy man or Daoist monk who has turned the remainder of life into a religious pilgrimage. On the far right are those who are indifferent to doctrine or who disbelieve. (Yes, their presence is also universal; the records of skeptics and disbelievers are as ancient as those of believers.) In learning about world religions, being attentive to this variance guides our efforts to explain how world religions captured the imagination and elicited the loyalty of believers in every society. Here are also clues about how religion has brought out the best and worst of humanity in history.

Our treatment of the history of each tradition in each chapter will be organized as follows:

- Overview
- Encounter with Modernity
- Premodern
- Modern
- Postmodern
- Conclusion

The overview at the start of each chapter introduces the basic worldview of the religious tradition. The section that follows, "Encounter with Modernity," describes a particular moment in which premodern religious traditions clashed with the modern worldview and explains the diverse responses that emerged from that encounter. Next, each chapter will shift back to the *premodern* period and begin to trace the origins and development of the tradition, to better explain why modernity represents a challenge to it. This period is accounted for in two phases—a *formative period*, which traces the origins of the traditions, and a *classical period*, which explains its fully developed premodern beliefs, rituals, and institutions.

The section on *modernity* traces the diverse fundamentalist and modernist responses that developed in each tradition as it was challenged and threatened by Western colonialism and its modern scientific/technological worldview. This is followed by a *postmodern* section, in which we survey the most recent reactions to the adaptations each tradition has made to the modern world. These reactions tend to be postcolonial attempts (in most regions, after 1945) to reclaim religious and cultural identities that existed before the advent of modern Western colonialism. In this way we show why the world, with all its possibilities for coexistence and conflict, is the way it is today. The *conclusion* to each chapter addresses the implications of this history for the future of each tradition.

Historical Overview: From Premodern to Postmodern

The structure of this book revolves around two great transitions in human history that we are positing:

Premodern to Modern
Modern to Postmodern

The first began with urbanization, and the second begins with globalization.

From about 8000 BCE the domestication of plants and animals made village life possible. Acquisition of agricultural skill then allowed the development of the first great cities, from approximately 3000 BCE, bringing about a great transformation in human experience. Urban life drew people together out of different social groups, each with a different culture. In the earliest indigenous human groups, everyone lived close to the rhythms of nature, in extended families or clans that shared a common way of life and lived by the same myths and rituals. In the cities people came together from different groups, bringing with them different stories, different rituals, and different family identities.

The complexities and new possibilities of urban life led to the specialization of labor. Whereas in small-scale indigenous societies everyone shared the hunting and gathering or simple agriculture, in the cities the agricultural surplus created by peasant farmers made it possible for some to engage in diverse occupations such as carpentry, blacksmithing, and record keeping. Society became more complex and differentiated into classes (peasants, craftsmen, noblemen, priests, etc.). In a parallel fashion, elaborate and detailed new mythologies emerged in the cities, assigning special powers and tasks to each of the many gods and spirits of the different tribes now embraced as the gods of the city.

These changes fundamentally transformed the economies and cultures of the new urban centers. The human situation evolved. In the indigenous group, identity was collective because everybody shared the same stories and hunting and gathering activities. The cities, by contrast, were communities of strangers. People did not automatically share a collective sense of identity. Urban life enhanced awareness of how one person differed from another.

The loss of collective sense of identity and the emergence of large, impersonal, and often-brutal urban city-states in Egypt, India, China, and Mesopotamia led to growing populations for whom the experience of the world was marked by suffering and cruelty. Populated by strangers and ruled by emperors, kings, or Pharaohs considered divine or representatives of the gods, these new city-states eventually faced a threefold crisis.

First, tribal collective identity was experienced as eternal—the tribe never dies. However, under the impact of urban individuation humans began to think of themselves as individuals, and death suddenly loomed as a personal problem even as life seemed more cruel and uncertain. With the greater development of individual self-awareness, death presented people with a new and unsettling problem: What happens to my (individual) "self" when I die?

Second, urban life created the new problems of law and morality. In the isolated indigenous group the right thing to do was prescribed by ritual, and the same rites were known and respected by all. In cities, people from a variety of religious traditions lived together; yet as individuals, each looked out for his or her own good, if necessary at the expense of others. Thus in the cities law emerged to set the minimum order necessary to sustain human life, and it became necessary to develop a system of ethics to persuade people to live up to even higher ideals.

Third, the situation evoked a crisis of meaning. Can life really have any meaning if it is filled with injustice and ends in meaningless death? The first written expression of this great question appeared in the ancient Near East at the beginning of the urban period (ca. 3000–1500 BCE) and is known as the *Epic of Gilgamesh*.

The great world religions emerged in the three great centers of civilization in the ancient world—China, India, and the Middle East—as their founders and prophets responded to critical questions about the meaning of life, mortality, and morality. Between 800 BCE and 600 CE all developed their classical expressions, dividing much of the world among them (see Map 1.2) in the context of the formation of great empires that united peoples of various tribes and city-states into larger political entities. These new political orders created a need for a more inclusive understanding of human identity. Sages and prophets arose who redefined the meaning of being human in terms beyond the boundaries of the tribe and the city-state, seeing a higher unity to reality beyond the many local gods and spirits. In China, for example, all humans were said to share in common the *Dao* (the hidden power of harmony that governs the universe), and the effect of a truly humane ruler was believed to radiate outward to ensure social harmony. In India, for Hindus it was the reality of *Brahman* (the universal, impersonal, eternal spirit that is the source of all things), and for Buddhists, the universal causality of interdependent becoming. In the Middle East, Judaism, Christianity, and later Islam each developed as religious traditions that emphasized that they were children of the one God who created all things. Biblical figures such as Abraham, Moses, Jesus, and Muhammad emphasized that their community had a special covenant with God. These ideas about the meaning of the divine-human relationship remain central to the world's great religions.

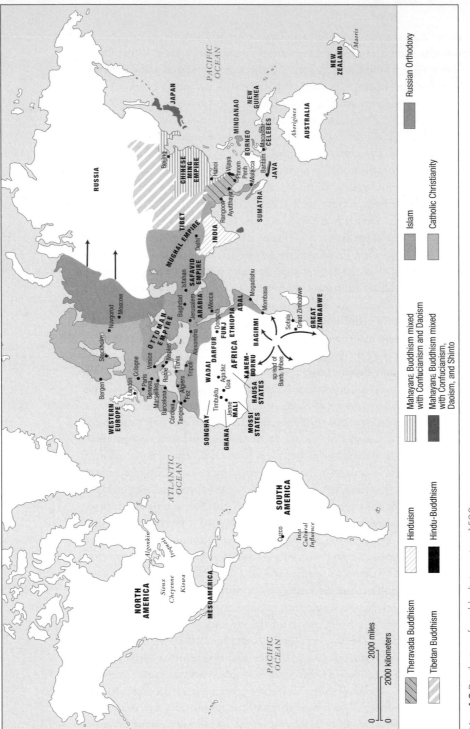

Map 1.2 Distribution of world religions circa 1500 CE.

Today the secularizing influences of modernization and the unprecedented international migration are transforming the ancient geographic division of the world's religions. Before we can move on to explore the struggle of peoples everywhere to continue the religiousness of their ancestors in today's very different world, we need to be clear about the terms **premodern**, **modern**, and **postmodern**.

In general, premodern history around the globe describes a wide range of cultures in which religion played the decisive role in explaining and ordering life. In premodern societies, religion provided the most certain knowledge one could have of the world, and consequently religious authority played a central role in each culture's social, political, and economic ordering of public life. In this respect, all premodern cultures have more in common with each other than with modern **secular** (i.e., nonreligious) culture. With the advances in science that gathered steam in the eighteenth century, the scientific worldview spread globally and, for many, came to replace religion as the most certain form of knowledge. The modern period is marked by a tendency for individuals to view religion as a matter of personal faith or opinion. Gradually most areas of public life were secularized. That is, religious doctrines and officials no longer played central roles in politics, economics, or public education. The most dramatic institutional expression of this change in the West was the emergence of the separation of church and state. The secular state was the expression of "modern" reality—politics governed a society's public life, and religion was a private matter for individuals and their families. From the end of the nineteenth century up until the early 1970s, many scholars even predicted the end of religion and a coming nonreligious, or *secular*, stage in world history.

Every premodern society saw the universe through explicitly religious eyes and pronounced its vision of life sacred. Since all premodern societies were dominated by the influence of religious authority, they all understood and ordered their worlds through religious myths and rituals that had been passed down for many generations. Modern culture, by contrast, tends to emphasize the centrality of rational and empirical science. And, as we shall see in Chapter 4, the scientific worldview brought with it certain distinctive features, especially the tendency to reject the premodern past and to regard its beliefs and traditions as irrational and superstitious. In addition, history was understood as representing inevitable progress toward an ideal future, and the knowledge that would bring about this glorious future could be had only through science, with its "objective view" of the world, finally ending the centuries of human hatred and bloodshed caused by religions.

While much more can and will be said in the remaining chapters about this premodern/modern contrast, we have at least suggested that the contrast between premodern and modern is dramatic and clear. But a word needs to be said about our use of the third term in this sequence, the *postmodern* situation. According to the postmodernist thinker Jean-François Lyotard, this era is characterized by the collapse of all the grand, all-encompassing sacred stories through which human beings interpreted life in their respective cultures.[2] In ancient societies, these **metanarratives** (to use Lyotard's term) were the religious myths of the four types

premodern: civilization in which there is no separation between a dominant religion and society

modern: civilization that separates its citizens' lives into public and private spheres, restricting religion to private life

postmodern: society typified by accepting public diversity in both religious beliefs and social practices

secular: sociologically used to mean "nonreligious"

metanarrative: grand cosmic and/or historical story accepted by majority of a society as expressing its beliefs about its origins, destiny, and sacred identity

we have described; the notion that they were true for all times and places went virtually unquestioned. In modern culture the primary metanarrative has been the story of history as progress driven by science and technology. However, the globalization of religious and cultural interaction that began in the twentieth century has tended to relativize them all, to see each as a historical construction, and regard none as ultimately, universally true. Significantly, this includes the modern myth of inevitable scientific progress.

In the premodern world a single grand narrative or religious worldview was typically experienced as true, valuable, and meaningful by the overwhelming majority of people. It is this kind of metanarrative that has collapsed for many in our day. For Lyotard, "postmodern" is more a style of thinking than a stage of history. It is a decentered style of thinking that invites pluralism and rejects imposing a single truth on all. In our postmodern world a new type of metanarrative is arising globally, an anti-metanarrative accepting the reality of religious and cultural pluralism. In this anti-metanarrative, no single story is all-encompassing for all people in a given culture—especially as a global culture emerges and practitioners of the world's religions are found in everyone's hometown. The grand stories of the world religions have thereby become miniaturized and globalized. Everyone has his or her own stories, knowing full well that other people in one's neighborhood and around the world live by other stories.

The very creation of textbooks on world religions encourages just such a postmodern awareness. In this situation the adherents of each religious tradition have to deal with diversity within their own traditions as well as diversity among religious traditions. All, but especially those who follow the great missionary faiths—Christianity, Islam, Buddhism—are challenged to explain how it is that the world continues in this ever-multiplying religious pluralism and why their own understanding of ultimate reality (God, Allah, Brahman, Buddha nature, Dao, etc.) has not led all the world into their own path.

We also suggest that there is a strong correlation between the postmodern challenge to modernity and the postcolonial challenge to colonialism. A postcolonial era typically begins with a rejection of the modern Western historical metanarrative of scientific-technological progress and in this way opens the door to postmodern awareness and critiques. However, that door swings two ways: some seek a return to premodern fundamental notions of religious truth and practice, insisting that there is only one true religious story and way of life; others embrace the postmodern situation and seek to accommodate the reality of diversity. What these fundamentalisms and postmodern pluralisms have in common is a rejection of the modern strategy of privatizing religion. Both insist that religion ought to play a role in influencing not only private but also public life. But fundamentalists

An adult pilgrim is baptized in the Jordan River, Israel.

advocate accomplishing this by returning to an absolute religious metanarrative and work to impose a political order that should shape public life for everyone; postmodernists (as we use the term) accept a plurality of narratives, recognizing the public benefits of embracing religious pluralism in an age of globalization.

We use the contrast between *modern* and *postmodern* to describe not a philosophy or an existing historical period but, rather, a newly emerging historical trend. A postmodern trend deserves to be called "new" because it challenges the assumptions of modernity without simply reverting to premodern views of reality. In particular, postmodern pluralism challenges modern "science" as the single form of objective knowledge about the world and also the modern practice of privatizing religion. Today, all the world's religions are caught up in the struggle between their premodern, modern, and possible postmodern interpretations.

Because Christianity is the dominant religion of Western civilization, the civilization that produced modernization, it went through the trauma of accommodation to modernity first. Being the first, it had the luxury of embracing modernization in slower stages than those religions that did not encounter modernization until it had attained a more developed form. Therefore Chapter 4, on Christianity, will have to tell two stories. One is an outline of the intellectual and social history of the West that resulted in modernization, and the other is the story of the role that Christianity played in that history, both in promoting modernization and in resisting it.

Some have charged that modernization is a form of Western cultural and perhaps even religious imperialism that has been forced on other cultures. However, modernization and secularization challenge all sacred traditions and identities, including those of Western religions. As we shall see in the remaining chapters of this book, the patterns of modernization's impact on diverse religions and cultures are quite variable, as are the responses elicited. Modernization did not have an impact on all religions simultaneously, nor did all react in exactly the same way, although there are striking similarities. Therefore, we should not expect all religions and societies to exhibit exactly the same patterns and responses.

The Modern/Postmodern Transition: Colonialism, the Socialist Challenge, and the End of Modernity

In the nineteenth century the synergy of Western science, economics (capitalism), and technology fostered among the dominant European nations, especially England and France, a thirst for building colonial empires. These colonial ambitions were paralleled in the modern period by those of only one Asian nation—Japan. By 1914 most of the world was under the domination of Western European culture.

Geographically the Russians and the British controlled about a third of the globe. In terms of population, the British Empire controlled about a fifth of the human race—nearly 400 million people—while France controlled over 50 million colonial subjects (see Map 1.3).

Colonial dominance and paternalism (the British spoke of "the white man's burden" and the French of their "mission to civilize") was accompanied by the spread of science, technology, and capitalism, which proved traumatic to indigenous cultures and their religious traditions. The impressive achievements of Western civilization often prompted an initial phase of emulation of Western ways by elites, leading them to embrace modernization and secularization. Almost inevitably, however, there was a religious and political backlash, seen in struggles for national liberation as indigenous peoples sought to reclaim their independence and autonomy and to reaffirm the value of their original ways of life. This backlash often included a resurgence of religious influence as a force in anticolonial struggles. Most independence movements readily adopted a key element of Western civilization—nationalism—in their attempts to resist foreign occupation and to protect their religious and cultural identities by resisting exploitation.

Many of these movements paradoxically struck an alliance with socialism, the philosophical and political movement that arose in the nineteenth century in Europe among the new urban working class as a protest against the poverty and social dislocation created by early capitalism and the Industrial Revolution. Socialism was itself a modernist movement, sustained by a vision of scientific progress, yet it also championed premodern values of community against the rampant individualism of modern capitalism. In Karl Marx's formulation of "scientific socialism," it became an international movement that had an impact on world history as profound as that of any world religion. Indeed, as religious societies around the globe revolted against European imperialism, most experimented with some form of socialism as a modern way of protesting and of dialing back modernity itself. The twentieth century produced examples around the world of Jewish, Christian, Islamic, Hindu, Buddhist, and neo-Confucian forms of socialism. In its secular form socialism or communism became the dominant element in Russian culture, spreading throughout Eastern Europe and across Asia like a new missionary religion, most prominently "converting" China, the largest country of Asia, by 1949.

Consistent with the myth of modernity, the German socialist Karl Marx (1818–83) saw history as progressively unfolding in three stages. He defined these stages in terms of a class theory of society that went from primitive communism (tribal societies), in which all were equal; through the rise of complex urban civilizations, which gave birth to societies ruled by bureaucracies, pitting privileged classes against the masses; to a final stage of history in which society would once more be communistic. In this last age all were again to be equal—for all complex, class-defined institutions would wither away, and people would live together in spontaneous harmony. As many who have studied Marx and his followers have suggested, this vision takes the biblical myth of history, culminating in the appearance of the messianic age, and recasts it in secular form as the coming to earth of a classless society in an earthly paradise.

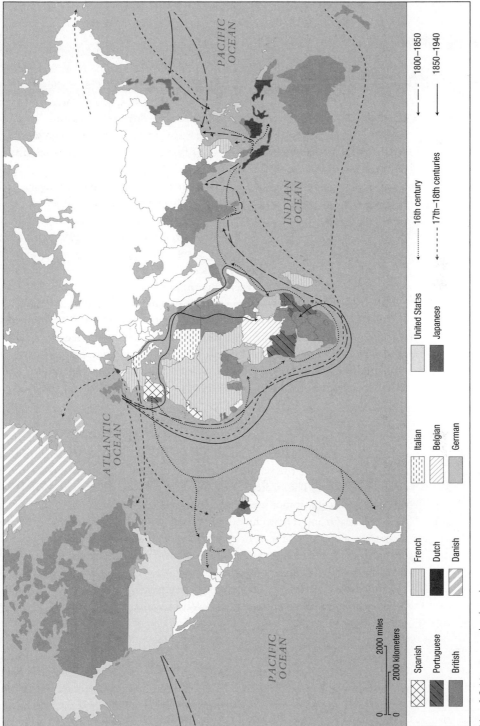

Map 1.3 Missions and colonialism.

Legend:

Spanish
Portuguese
British

French
Dutch
Danish

Italian
Belgian
German

United States
Japanese

16th century
17th–18th centuries

1800–1850
1850–1940

PACIFIC OCEAN

INDIAN OCEAN

ATLANTIC OCEAN

PACIFIC OCEAN

0   2000 miles
0   2000 kilometers

Marx secularized the biblical myth of history by replacing the will of God as the directing force of history with what he maintained were "scientific" laws of social development that guide the progressive unfolding of history. Marx believed that capitalism depended on a large class of urban workers, who, once they were gathered together in the industrial cities of the modern world, would organize, creating an international workers union that would lead a worldwide revolution. This revolution would result in the replacement of capitalist societies, based on hereditary wealth and privileges, with a new, classless society of freedom, equality, and social justice for all.

Socialism represents an ambivalent rejection of a modern scientific world dominated by an economic system, capitalism, that seemed to make the rich richer and the poor poorer. It claimed to be "modern," "secular," and "scientific." Yet Marxism, unlike capitalism, retained much of the religious and ethical power of biblical tradition, with its emphasis on justice for the poor, the widow, the orphan, and the stranger as the final outcome of history.

While socialism provided a vehicle to protest the impact of modernity on society, two world wars decisively undermined belief in inevitable progress toward greater scientific understanding, prosperity, and benevolent coexistence. World War I (1914–18) and World War II (1939–45) were the great wars of modern technology that shattered this myth. Science and technology, which had been viewed as the engines of progress, had become, as well, the means of unprecedented destruction. The utopian dream of technological progress ended as a nightmare in August 1945, when newly invented atomic bombs were dropped on the Japanese cities of Hiroshima and Nagasaki.

The use of nuclear weapons brought World War II to an end, only to usher in a "cold war" between the Soviet Union and the United States. Throughout the second half of the twentieth century, an armed standoff between these two superpowers threatened to plunge the whole human race into a third and final war of thermonuclear annihilation. The makers of the modern myth of progress had failed to foresee that a technology that increases efficiency can be applied not only to the improvement of public health and the production of less expensive consumer goods, but also to the invention of weapons of mass destruction. Indeed, since World War II progress in the means of destroying large numbers of humans has been staggering. It took the Nazis six years to kill 6 million Jews and others in their death camps. Today, nuclear war could destroy virtually the whole human race in a few days.

Finally, it is important to note that World War I and especially World War II not only called into question the "scientific age of progress" but also brought an end to the modern age of empires. The twentieth century saw the withdrawal of European powers from the Middle East, South Asia, Southeast Asia, East Asia, and Africa. European colonial powers left behind independent nation-states whose rulers were unelected. Many of these new political entities had arbitrarily drawn boundaries. Often, moreover, people were divided without regard to ethnic identity or religious communities, and the legacy of exploitative colonial practices was economic poverty.

Postmodern Trends in a Postcolonial World

In the modern period the social authority of religion was undermined by the new scientific rationalists, whose descriptions of reality, they believed, explained how the world "really is," in contrast to the fanciful myths of religions. The postmodern world begins with the further loss of innocence, as many have argued that not only religious knowledge but also scientific knowledge is relative in important ways. That is, science too is an imaginative interpretation of the world based on faith (faith in the intelligibility of the world) and cannot offer the final truth about reality. Of course, many today dispute this understanding of science. Nevertheless, these arguments are similar to the arguments between premodern religious philosophers (defending religion) and the new secular scientists (challenging religion) at the beginning of the modern period. No matter who is ultimately correct, the very existence of such disputes suggests that the postmodern situation is one in which unquestioning faith in science, which characterized the modern era, no longer exists.

From the perspective of postmodernists, all knowledge is relative, including religious and scientific knowledge. Postmodern trends seem to promote cultural and ethical relativism. Some rejoice in this, arguing that it means the end of all the absolutes that have been used to justify violence by some against others. Still others are afraid that total relativism will lead to the end of civilization and the beginning of a new barbarism—that once we have relativized the absolute distinction between good and evil, we will plunge into an ethical void in which any atrocity can be justified.

Thus for individuals living in the postmodern period, scientific knowledge now competes on equal intellectual footing with religious knowledge. They are equally relative and equally subject to criticism by those who reject their main precepts. Therefore the position that scientific secularism is a source of public and certain knowledge, while religious knowledge is mere private opinion, no longer seems as valid as it once did. Consequently, the appearance of postmodern trends has been accompanied by a resurgence of religion in the public realm—a resurgence whose diverse forms are responses to both the threat and promise of postmodernity.

In the new, postmodern civilization, another stage in the history of religions has emerged, one in which the world religions encounter each other as they spread via **globalization**. Until the modern period the great world religions had largely divided the globe among them, with some modest overlap. But in the postmodern world, more and more, all the world's religions have members in every country or society. Just as Christians had migrated to every city in the world by 1850, today Hindus, Buddhists, and Muslims are now found in significant numbers in all large American and European cities and increasingly in smaller ones. Today, anyone using the Internet can take in a live web-cam view in major temples, shrines, churches, mosques, and monasteries from around the world; devotees can offer prayers, order rituals, or make monetary offerings through their websites. This is globalization.

globalization: in terms of world religions, the idea that all the world's religions have members in almost every country or society; technology affords access to all key religious sites and practices

Conclusion: We Are All Heretics in Our Postmodern Situation

In the premodern period, people, for the most part, acquired their religious identities because of where they were born. In the postmodern world, however, every individual is faced with what sociologist Peter Berger calls "the heretical imperative."[3] *Heretic* comes from an ancient Greek word that means "to choose." In our postmodern world every religious person becomes a **heretic**, that is, one who is no longer simply born into a given religion or identity but must choose it, even if it is only to retain the identity offered by the circumstances of his or her birth.

In this world of "heretics," all the world's religions, each of which originated to provide a universal answer to the questions of human identity, have been forced to take account of the others. Today global media allow distant viewers to experience the positives and negatives, both exemplary and scandalous actions, of individuals acting in the name of their religions as never before. Around the globe, religious adherents and skeptics come face to face with their own particularism amid the undeniable reality of the world's enduring diverse faiths.

Until postmodern trends set in, other people's religions could be readily dismissed in a series of negative stereotypes. When people of diverse religions are neighbors, this option is both more difficult and more dangerous. To the degree that stereotyping and discrimination persist, they promote prejudice, conflict, and violence. The alternative is to develop new understandings of the relation between world religions and the societies around the world—one that allows the peoples of the earth to follow their respective faith traditions, including nonbelief, yet also share their wisdom with each other in an atmosphere of mutual respect and understanding. This alternative—to appreciate what we have in common as well as to acknowledge our distinctive differences—has been explored brilliantly by two of the great religious figures of the twentieth century, Mohandas K. Gandhi and Martin Luther King Jr. Each spiritual leader "passed over" from his native religion and culture to the religious world of the other and came back enriched by that second tradition without having abandoned his own. You are invited to embark on a similar journey through the study of the world's religions today.

heretic: from the ancient Greek term for "one who chooses," used to communicate the postmodern idea that there is no longer a single center of "taken-for-granted commonly shared truth" in society and so everyone has no choice but to choose his or her beliefs

"Modernity multiplies choices. . . . The modern individual is faced not just with the opportunity but with the necessity to make choices as to his beliefs. This fact constitutes the heretical imperative."

—Peter Berger

Discussion Questions

1. Define religion in terms of its six characteristics—sacred, myth, ritual, community, morality, and religious leaders—and explain the possible relations among them.

2. What do the authors mean when they argue that all morality is religious, even that of atheists?

3. In what way does religious language complicate the question of whether there is agreement or disagreement among religions on various issues? Describe in terms of the *via analogia* and the *via negativa*, giving examples of each.

4. Explain the four types of religious story and give a historical example of each.

5. Why did urbanization lead to the emergence of the great world religions? That is, what new urban problems did these religions address?

6. What is colonialism, and what is its significance for religions and cultures in the modern period?

7. How are the terms *premodern*, *modern*, and *postmodern* being used in this text, and how are they related to modern colonialism?

8. According to the authors, modernization privatizes religion, whereas in premodern and postmodern religious movements religion plays a public role in society but in different ways. Explain.

9. Explain Marxist socialism, and tell why it was an attractive option to religious movements protesting modernity.

10. How might you justify the statement that both postmodernist and fundamentalist religious movements are examples of Peter Berger's "heretical imperative"?

Key Terms

divine	myth	secular
fundamentalist	orthodoxy	sympathetic
globalization	orthopraxy	imagination
heretic	postmodern	transcendent
metanarrative	premodern	ultimate reality
modern	religion	*via analogia*
moral	ritual	*via negativa*

Notes

1. F. Max Muller, *Lectures on the Origin and Growth of Religion as Illustrated by the Religions of India* (London: Longmans Green, 1880), p. 218.
2. Jean-François Lyotard, *The Postmodern Condition: A Report on Knowledge* (Minneapolis: University of Minnesota Press, 1984).
3. Peter Berger, *The Heretical Imperative* (New York: Doubleday, 1979), p. 60.

INDIGENOUS RELIGIONS

2

Overview

Across all the earth's inhabited continents today are thousands of different *indigenous peoples*, ethnic groups whose ties to their lands go back a millennium or much longer. Some have migrated to new homelands and changed their ways of life in recent centuries; others have been relocated in recent generations to "reservations" within modern states; still others (in growing numbers) live in two worlds, moving between life in their modern countries and their native group. Indigenous peoples today defy easy characterization: In remote Highland New Guinea, the village headman wears only a penis sheath as he performs a ritual to protect his home. More typical is a Kayapo chief in the Amazon rain forest who one day dresses in little more than body paint and on another wears western clothes. A visitor to a Lakota ceremonial leader in the North American Plains would find him in blue jeans, western-style shirt, and a Stetson hat.

All surviving indigenous peoples (or *first peoples*) have been affected by the modern world and its trade, technologies, or communications. The cultural traditions and religious lives of all these peoples have been altered, often dramatically, by outsiders encroaching on their lands, exposing them to new diseases, and imposing laws to take their lands and assimilate them into the majority citizenry. Around the world and over recent centuries, hundreds of indigenous groups have succumbed or been assimilated, their religions like their languages forever gone.

The religious traditions discussed in this chapter are different from those of the great world religions covered in the other chapters of this book. Yet these indigenous peoples and their religions remain a noteworthy part of the world's religious landscape today, despite their small populations. Few possess literary texts or great temples. Yet these independent, ethnic, and land-bounded religions are themselves worthy of study; they also help us understand the general phenomenon of humanity as a religious species. The treatment of indigenous peoples by the great world religions gives us important insights about the latter's role in the historical expansion of early states and modern nations; and we can see beliefs and practices of the world's indigenous religions being assimilated into the new religions forming across the globe today.

This chapter will begin by looking back to prehistory to understand the long history of some of the common worldviews, religious roles, and ritual practices evident among early *Homo sapiens*. We will then examine case studies of the world's last living hunter-gatherers and simple agriculturalists to sample indigenous religions across the globe today. The world's surviving indigenous religions would best be represented, due to their richness and diversity, by a series of chapters devoted to each one. The scope of this textbook precludes this; however, the short, introductory treatment here inevitably requires making generalizations and relies on somewhat arbitrary but representative case studies. Beyond conveying an awareness of the spiritual vitality and the neglected histories of these extraordinary indigenous traditions, we want to show that understanding religions today is enriched by seeing how all humanity, even in isolated nonliterate groups, has always been "religious."

Origins of *Homo religiosus*: Prehistory

At some point around a hundred thousand years ago, *Homo sapiens* emerged from a 4-million-year process of hominid evolution to become the animal who speaks, makes tools, buries its dead, and thinks symbolically. Long before agriculture and urbanization, the first *Homo sapiens* lived in hunter-gatherer societies. By studying their artifacts as well as the small-scale societies that still subsist in this mode of life, we can imagine what their existence was like. We know our ancestors lived and ate well, yet without the material possessions and conveniences we now consider to be essential. We know they made efforts to communicate with the spirits of their ancestors and with animals. Most likely, they regularly sought assistance from these spirits through trance and altered states of consciousness, which may have been the origins of religion.

Just as the core meanings of modern English words can be discovered by looking up their origins in Latin or Greek history, our appreciation of world religions can be enriched by understanding the origins of religion itself, by comparing the archaeological record with the customs of well-studied modern indigenous peoples.

Although the earliest humans used language, writing had not yet been invented. Consequently, these societies had oral cultures in which everything that was known

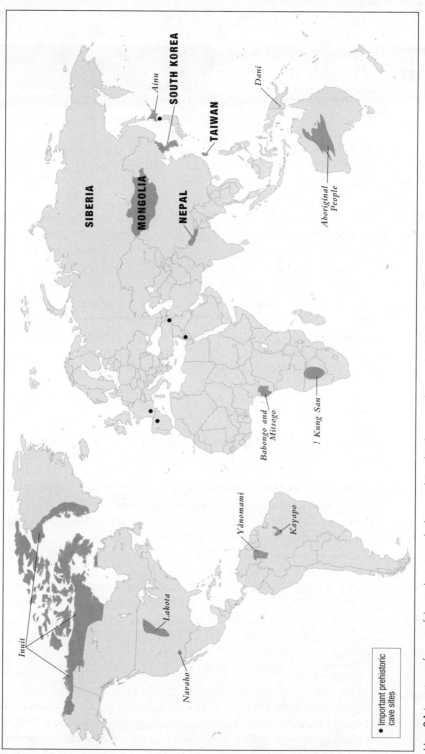

Map 2.1 Locations of some of the prehistoric and ethnographic cultural groups discussed in this book.

41

Timeline

2 million	Early hominids use the first stone tools
½ mill	Fire domesticated
100,000	*Homo sapiens:* Neanderthals and another line present evidence of ritual burial
40,000 BCE	Modern man biologically; hunting-gathering societies found across Africa and Eurasia
	Humans just "another animal" on earth
30,000	Human language and symbolic thought reach new level of advancement
15,000	Human burials across Africa and Eurasia with offerings, reflecting afterlife belief
10,000	*Homo sapiens* from Siberia disperse across North and South America via Bering Strait
9,000	Domestication of sheep/goats
7,000	Beginnings of settled agriculture, first cities
5,000	Earliest archaeological evidence of Australian aboriginal belief connected with the Rainbow Serpent, perhaps the oldest continuing belief in the world
2,000	Major states arise on the Yellow River, China; Indus River, India; Babylon on Tigris-Euphrates; Nile in Egypt
800 BCE–**200** CE	Axial Age, era of lasting formulations of social-spiritual teachings defining ethical modes of human existence in cities
100 BCE	States expanding into wilderness frontiers; Axial Age traditions legitimate expansion, assimilation of indigenous peoples
1400	Growing populations in Americas live in hierarchically organized chiefdoms or small kingdoms
1492 CE	Columbus reaches America. He writes that the native peoples encountered "are the best people in the world and above all the gentlest." His record is nonetheless filled with accounts of enslavement, murder, and rape.
1492–1600	Europeans make first contact with native peoples of Western Hemisphere continents
	Introduction of the horse alters human ecology across the "New World"
	Peoples having no natural immunological defenses to Eurasian microbes succumb to diseases in great numbers; 90 percent mortality in many settlements
	Christian missionaries travel on the networks of exploration and empire, making Christianity the world's first global religion
1546	The "New Laws" barring enslavement of indigenous peoples were repealed; "New World" colonists form societies and economies dependent on slave labor
1606	Earliest recorded contact between Europeans and Australian Aborigines
1616	Smallpox epidemic decimates native tribes in New England region
1709	A slave market erected on Wall Street in New York; African Americans and Native American men, women, and children are daily declared the property of the highest cash bidder
1716	Alamo Mission in San Antonio is authorized by the viceroy of Mexico. The mission becomes an educational center for Native Americans who converted to Christianity.
1808–1811	Tecumseh, chief of the Shawnees, organizes a defensive confederacy of Northwest frontier tribes, attempting to make the Ohio River a permanent boundary between the United States and indigenous peoples' land
1811	William Henry Harrison, governor of Ohio, leads the ferocious Battle of Tippecanoe, which destroys Tecumseh's town as well as the remnants of Tecumseh's indigenous confederacy

1830	Indian Removal Act passed; over next ten years U.S. government forcibly removes thousands of indigenous peoples west of the Mississippi
1838	"Trail of Tears": Native Americans force-marched by U.S. military to settle in Oklahoma
1850–1875	Hunting by American colonists leads to near extermination of buffalo herds, undermining Plains Indians' survival
1871	1871 Indian Appropriation Act specifies that no tribe thereafter would be recognized as an independent nation
1876	Colonel George Custer leads army attack on assembled native tribes and all 250 soldiers are killed. Afterward, U.S. Army orders troops "to attack and kill every male Indian over twelve years of age."
1888	The White Australia Policy articulated
1889–1890	Wovoka, the Paiute spiritual leader, has vision and spreads message of the Ghost Dance
1890	Massacre of Sioux at Wounded Knee, South Dakota
1910	Bwiti, a West Central African religion, is founded among the forest-dwelling Babongo and Mitsogo people of Gabon and the Fang people of Gabon and Cameroon
1918	Native American Church founded in Oklahoma, combining use of peyote with Christian beliefs of morality and self-respect. Church prohibits alcohol, requires monogamy and family responsibility, and promotes hard work.
1920	Santo Daime, a syncretistic religion based on ceremonial ayahuasca (called daime) ingestion, is begun in western Brazil by Raimundo Irineu Serra
1930	Stalin begins Soviet repression of shamans in Siberia and in their satellite, Outer Mongolia, that lasts until 1989
1950	People's Republic of China labels shamanism a "superstition" and represses spirit mediums across China
1951	Australian government formally adopts assimilation policy toward aboriginal peoples
1961	União do Vegetal, a syncretistic religion based on the use of ayahuasca and elements of folk Christianity, shamanism, and ancient Incan soul traditions, is founded by Jose Porto Velho
1975	The Australian Senate acknowledges prior ownership of country by aboriginal people and seeks compensation for their dispossession. The World Council of Indigenous People is founded.
1978	Religious Freedom Act promises to "protect and preserve" for Native Americans "freedom to believe, express, and exercise" traditional religions, "including but not limited to access to sites, use and possession of sacred objects, and the freedom to worship through ceremonial and traditional rites"
1989	Kayapo people joined by international indigenous group rights advocates to protest dam project at Altamira
1992	Australian High Court rules that native title to land has not been extinguished, rejecting 200-year-old settler claims that aboriginal lands were *terra nullius*, "no one's land"
2004	Smithsonian Institution's National Museum of the American Indian opens in Washington, DC
2008	Australian and Canadian governments issue formal apologies to aboriginal peoples for policies detrimental to integrity of lives, including forcibly sending children to Christian boarding schools
2013	Kayapo clans oppose new Amazon basin dam project on the Xingu River that will flood tribal lands

was known only because someone remembered it. And memories were made readily accessible because they were expressed in stories—stories of sacred ancestors, spirit beings, and heroes. Not recorded in written texts, these stories were kept alive in song and dance.

Moreover, time and space were not cold abstractions but were reckoned according to ancestral myths and sacred experiences. Religion likely began at sites where people believed the powers that govern the universe first manifested themselves. Whether in sacred groves, on riverbanks, or on mountaintops, human beings experienced such places of revelation as "centers of the world" (*axes mundi*). Indeed, in the indigenous religions, most everything is spiritually alive, a collective of living entities to which people must relate. The trees, the mountains, the rivers, special stones, animals, and, of course, humans are said to have souls or spirits that give them life, or *animate* them. Anthropologists once used the term **animism** to describe a worldview in which a measure of conscious life is attributed to these entities.

animism: belief in an inner soul that gives life and identity to living things and emphasizes rituals in which humans interact with other souls

cosmogony: mythological account of the world's creation

Each of the thousands of indigenous peoples have (or had) a unique **cosmogony**, or account of the world's origins and its essential powers. Because in most cosmogonies the group telling the story was a part of the everlasting cycle of nature's rhythms, the group is assumed to be an integral part of the cosmos. Everything in premodern indigenous group life reinforced a collective sense of common identity: All shared the same occupations (hunting and gathering, simple agriculture), the same myths, and the same rituals; and all were integral to the group. As a result, a person's identity was deeply embedded in the collective identity and fate of the group. The group lives on and the individual can stay connected to it, even after his or her own death.

This collective worldview is radically different from the extreme individualism and social fragmentation that is common today. In the following chapters on the world's great religions, we will show how each in its own way pushed humanity, at least in part, out of the collective community mind-set and toward greater individualism. Comprehending the features of indigenous religions will make it clear how the world religions have some of the basic features of the earliest religious traditions, yet also how they have simultaneously reinterpreted and transposed them as the details of human existence have changed.

Our human nature endows us with certain qualities that underlie the most basic expressions of religion. These include a propensity for repetitive behaviors (ritual), a virtually unique cognitive ability to create meaning (symbols, ritual acts), the enhancement of survival by identification with land or territory (sacred space), and a strong mother-offspring bond (devotion).

Archaeologists have ascertained that about 30,000 years ago humans—who are distinct from hominids because they possessed the same physiology and cognitive capacity as we do—established themselves across Eurasia. They wove cloth for clothes, used finely wrought fishhooks, constructed boats that crossed large bodies of water, and were experts in subsistence wherever they lived, from the tropics up to the edge of the Ice Age glaciers. The record of human life indicates that in every society over the last 100,000 years, a progressive complexity in the mastery of tools

The Limitations of the Term *Animism*

The term *animism*, though still in widespread use, is rooted in a problematic distinction in earlier scholarship. An *animist* was said to see the world as inhabited by a host of souls (*anima*) that are embodied in a variety of life-forms. By applying the term only to indigenous peoples, who usually worship a polytheistic pantheon, early scholars tried to create the basis for a distinction between them and peoples adhering to the major monotheistic religions. (Tylor and others saw monotheism as a superior form of religion that emerged among animist peoples, in conformity to the accounts of the Jews in the Hebrew Bible.) But does belief in souls truly separate humanity's religious belief systems and its thousands of believers? All three Abrahamic faiths hold that human beings possess souls (*anima*), as do traditional Indian and Chinese religions. In that sense, most world religions are animist. Furthermore, even the monotheistic religions hold that a multitude of nonhuman "souls" inhabit the world alongside human beings: angels, ghosts, *jinn*, demons, and so on. A second limitation with the term *animism* as a blanket term is that it also masks the large array of very different conceptions of "soul" recorded in human religious history, including peoples (e.g., the early Chinese) who believed that human bodies are inhabited by two or more souls.

was accompanied by the development of language ability and the unmistakable presence of religion.

The universality of religion in human societies even led Mircea Eliade, a pioneering scholar of comparative religions, to call our species ***Homo religiosus***, or "religious humanity." In fact, now as well as from the earliest days of the modern species, religion has been at the center of human culture, reshaping social life. Thus, we can say that religion has always been an integral, at times even essential part of humanity's evolutionary path. It supported the success of small hunter-gatherer groups, the domestication of plants and animals, and then reinforced humanity's prodigious efforts to create cities, empires, and superpowers. We now turn to the very beginning of this extraordinary story.

Homo religiosus: religious humanity

Religion's Origins Among Hunter-Gatherers

For 99 percent of our species's history, all human ancestors lived as nomadic hunter-gatherers. However, our world has been transformed in so thoroughgoing a manner that few if any people anywhere on the planet still live in this mode of life.

The earliest *Homo sapiens* existed much like the people we refer to today as belonging to indigenous or *simple subsistence* societies. Small groups of related individuals (usually fewer than fifty) "lived off the land and ocean," moving with the seasons to find wild fruits and nuts and to be close to the animals or fish they hunted for food. Close-knit bonds within these living groups were essential to everyone's survival, with individuals sharing the food and relying on each other for protection. Also typical was a division of labor, with men predominantly the hunters and women the gatherers. Compared to the permanently settled societies that began in recorded human history, most of these societies were (and are) highly egalitarian, with food and wealth shared equally. Scholars have used data from anthropological studies of modern hunter-gatherer groups to reconstruct the usually good lives of early *Homo sapiens* as follows:

> Life lived by our prehistoric ancestors was not characterized by constant depri-vation . . . with both men and women contributing substantially to the family, the economy, and the social world. . . . Life was rich in human warmth and aesthetic experience and offered an enviable balance of work and love, ritual and play.[1]

The Kung San of southern Africa, one of the most studied, late-surviving hunter-gatherer groups, are typical. A nomadic people, the Kung utilize simple tools and build temporary houses. An intricate knowledge of their environment is expressed in a language that recognizes 500 species of plants and animals, yielding a diet that consists of 105 different foods. Utter mastery of an environment shared with large predators is typical of such groups. Once scholars gained firsthand knowledge of hunter-gatherers like the Kung, they began to appreciate the highly skilled nature of this mode of life, the clear rationality of the people, and the very sophisticated lan-guages and cultures that had evolved among them. This new and empirical under-standing disproved the theories of nineteenth-century social scientists, who had speculated that religion had its origins in the fear and ignorance of humans facing a threatening and incomprehensible world.

The human capacity for language to create and build culture was almost certainly present by 100,000 BCE among the Neanderthals and those who succeeded them, the *Homo sapiens*. By 30,000 BCE, humans were performing ceremonial burials, painting and carving art, keeping rudimentary records on bone and stone plaques, and crafting elaborate personal adornments. They also made music with flutes and drums.

From this time onward, the human record shows our species constantly adapting and refining their material world, and it was by this time that humans acquired the capacity to think symbolically, almost certainly as a result of their development of more complex languages. We who cannot conceive of complex thought without the medium of language can easily imagine the advantages (in hunting, warfare, etc.) that a leap ahead in linguistic capacity must have given to those early humans.

As we saw in the first chapter, religion is centered on humans establishing and expressing life's ultimate truths. Scientists, therefore, have posited a breakthrough in cognitive ability that changed the destiny of our species forever: "categorizing and naming objects and sensations in the outer and inner worlds, and making associations between resulting mental symbols . . . for only once we create such symbols can we recombine them and ask such questions as 'What if . . . ?' "[2] The simultaneous emer-gence of modern humans and religion indicates that many "what if" questions were

Prehistoric cave art: the first shaman. Over fifty examples of animal-human figures like this one suggest that shaman-ism had its origins in the prehistoric era.

Issues of Terminology and Imagination: Primitive, Indigenous

Writers who wish to refer to the peoples living in simple subsistence societies, both modern and prehistoric, face a problem of nomenclature. The term *primitive* was once popular, but it falsely suggests a lack of cultural development or factual understanding, since in fact many native peoples have complex languages and mythologies. In choosing the term *indigenous religions*, we are implying that the social and religious lives of a given people are rooted deeply in a given place. This first mode of religious life known in the record of human history is inextricably bound to the life of small groups. The reader should note that we are not equating modern hunter-gatherers with humans living in this mode of life 30,000 years ago or suggesting that these contemporary groups are "living fossils," since none today live isolated from the developed world and all have distinct histories. The term *indigenous* until recent times referred to peoples living in premodern modes of subsistence, either as hunter-gatherers or utilizing nonmechanical agricultural methods. In growing numbers, indigenous peoples today are quickly learning about the legal systems of modern states and selectively adopting modern technologies in an attempt to preserve their lands, ease the burdens of subsistence, and ensure their culture's adaptation and survival.

aimed at explaining the unseen powers of life, the inner world of personhood, and the ultimate mystery, that of death. Many artifacts of prehistoric religion have been found that reflect human engagement with each of these realms.

Fertility, Childbirth, and Survival

One striking kind of object found across Eurasia in late prehistory is what scientists have called **"Venus" figurines**, small stone sculptures of females with large breasts and hips, often with their genitalia emphasized. To understand these objects, we must enter into the reality of prehistoric human life. Small tribes were doubtless greatly concerned with ensuring the regular birth of healthy children to keep their own group numerous enough for success in subsistence, hunting, and warfare. Further, since at that time all pregnancies and all childbirths were high-risk events and since it was realized that mothers' bountiful lactation helped ensure the survival of newborn children, it is likely that the figurines are related to concerns about birth and the survival of children in small groups. Some scholars therefore interpret the Venus figurines as icons representing a protecting, nurturing "mother goddess." They have speculated that the makers of these objects recognized and revered a special female power that lay behind the mystery of conception and birth; they focused on the miracle of females producing beings from their own bodies and celebrated the ability of women to perpetuate human life.

Added to this evidence of veneration of a mother goddess is another important archaeological find: After 15,000 BCE the dead were uniformly buried in mounds or

"Venus" figurines: prehistoric Eurasian small stone figures with exaggerated female characteristics

graves in the fetal position, suggesting that people perceived the earth as a womb from which some sort of new birth was expected. Some have gone further, to conclude that the so-called Venus icons indicate the predominance of hunter-gatherer groups that were dominated by women, who led their groups in harmony with nature. This presumed matriarchal period, in which women had superior status, is said to have ended with the expansion of groups dominated by aggressive warrior males (such as the Indo-Europeans), who adopted settled agriculture and came to rule the new, patriarchal, societies. With little more than figurines and burial practices as evidence, it is difficult to prove or confirm these speculations or to declare their universality.

Religion in Prehistory: The Secret of Early Cave Rituals

In the famous cave paintings of Eurasia, hunted animals such as bison, bear, and deer are rendered with grace and subtlety in a variety of styles. Humans are also shown, some in poses that are still puzzling, challenging us to understand who created the images and the meaning of their context.

Again, we must use our imagination to understand the context and to surmise the place of religion. Caves could be dangerous places, and groups of individuals taking the trouble to go several hundred yards under the earth, traversing narrow, damp, and dark passageways, seem to engage in no ordinary task. Archaeologists surmise

Scholars believe that prehistoric hunting group initiation ceremonies were held in underground sanctuaries decorated with carefully rendered images of animals like this early masterpiece of painting from the Chauvet cave in southern France.

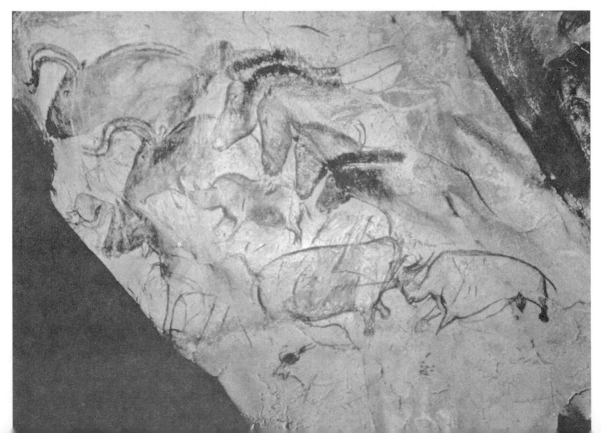

that these sites were related to the hunts undertaken by bands of able-bodied men. Hunter-gatherers needed animals for their survival. They hunted to secure the meat essential for their diet, the skins for clothing, and the bones and sinew used for tools and adornment. Some painted cave scenes also indicate that the prehistoric hunt was often dangerous: Wild bison, cave bears, and large cats are shown inflicting lethal injuries on humans.

The hunt required group coordination for success, since tracking, stalking, encircling, and using spears or stones to make kills at close range could not be achieved without coordinated action, individual bravery, and strong group loyalty. A hunting expedition could fail if a single member broke ranks and failed at his station, endangering not only himself and others in the group, but the entire tribe, which was depending on the hunters. Having documented similar rites among modern hunting tribes, scholars view some of the prehistoric caves as ritual theaters for initiating adolescent boys into the ranks of hunters, sites of instruction in hunting lore, killing practices, and ritual. Perhaps it was to these remote sites that elders brought frightened initiates and dramatically staged rituals that revealed the prey the men pursued and established the youths' new identity as adult hunters. Through this initiation ritual, young men bonded with the other adult males with whom they would risk their lives.

Such practices in the service of human survival formed the basis of the first religions according to the definitions we discussed in Chapter 1: They helped *bind* a group critical to the society's success, and they reinforced the human need to *be careful* with regard to the unseen powers surrounding them. The second point is especially

TEACHINGS OF RELIGIOUS WISDOM: The Dreamtime

In this creative era, a host of supernatural beings from an unspecified somewhere arrived and set out to populate and transform the previously flat and featureless Australian landmass. By their activities . . . they created diverse, religiously-charged landforms, richly imprinted with meaning and replete with fauna and flora. During their wanderings and numerous adventures, they established rituals and human institutions. These set in place for all time the various groups, their languages, cultural characteristics, and bound the first humans to a kind of contract. Through obedience to the laws of Dreaming, and the proper and regular performance of rituals, living Aborigines are charged with keeping the whole cosmic system of order going. This occurs under the watchful and caring gaze of the creative beings . . . who monitor human affairs without direct interference, but stay in touch via spirit-being messengers through whom they channel new knowledge and ritual elements into human society. [Humans] remain keenly aware of the proximity and relevance of the spiritual powers to their well-being and future existence. Failure by humans to uphold the human blueprint will cause the inhabitants of the spiritual realm to cut off the flow of power into human society and bring all life to an end. . . . Each succeeding generation is charged with enormous responsibility for society's continuing reproduction.

Source: Robert Tonkinson, "The Mardu Aborigines: On the Road to Somewhere," in George Spindler and Janice E. Stockard, eds. *Globalization and Change in Fifteen Cultures* (Belmont, CA: Thomson, 2007), p. 233.

important if we assume that the elders taught that each animal, like every human being, has an inner spirit or soul, one that must be respected in death and returned to the world or sent on its way back to the animal spirit world or afterlife. We now turn to this topic and trace its frequent presence in a variety of modern indigenous groups.

Indigenous Religious Traditions: Soul Belief and Afterlife

Today thousands of separate native peoples still exist, testimony to the resilience of the human spirit and the power of strong social and cultural bonds. Their religions have been an integral part of their survival, in each case somehow reflecting the group's connection with its lands, identity, modes of subsistence, and historical memory. There are indigenous peoples today who subsist primarily as hunter-gatherers, shifting slash-and-burn agriculturalists, or settled agricultural cultivators, as well as those who have assimilated in various ways into the world's modern states and economies. The traditions of these indigenous groups relating to the sacred, though uniquely grounded in each people's separate historical existence, remain an important part of the story of the world's religions today.

Studies of indigenous peoples reveal extraordinary human diversity, imagination, and religious wisdom. Their myths recount what is sacred to the group: the origins of life, its relations with animals, its connections to landforms, and the origination of the norms governing the members of the group. Indigenous religions convey the breadth of human spiritual experience across earth's diverse natural settings and reveal humanity's seemingly universal inclination for reverence. The religious experiences cultivated among these groups also show the great extent of humanity's experimentation with altered states of consciousness and extremes of bodily endurance. The rituals performed to heal, revere, and express group solidarity reveal the ways our species has conceptualized and faced the dual mysteries of birth and death.

The presence of a human belief in some sort of afterlife emerges from the earliest archaeological records of ceremonial burials. In hundreds of excavations, burial clearly was done to preserve the body and provide it with decoration (colors, jewelry, flowers, animal skulls, or antlers), foods (meat, grain), and tools (spears, sticks). These arrangements suggest that early humans felt that there was a nonmaterial component of the self, an essence that "lived on" after the physical body had perished and decayed. Thus the disposal of human corpses is clearly more than merely functional: Death seems to be likened to sleep, not mere dissolution, and the function of burial seems to be to open a gateway to an afterlife.

We noted at the start of this chapter the common belief that living beings and some inanimate objects possess a special life force which was first labeled by scholars as *animism*. An early and still widely popular articulation of soul belief was made in

"The first thing when we wake up in the morning is to be thankful to the Great Spirit for the Mother Earth: how we live, what it produces, what keeps everything alive."

—Joshua Wetsit, an Assiniboine from Montana

SOURCE: *The Sacred Ways of Knowledge, Sources of Life.*

Awakening the Spirits: A Bullroarer

Bullroarers are powerful ritual tools that convey the bond between living and dead members of scattered aboriginal groups, from those in prehistory up to those still used among native peoples in Australia. A bullroarer is a sphere that has a hole at one end, and when the device is swung around on a string, air passes through, resulting in a booming-whirring sound. The sound waves vibrate at a frequency that affects the human viscera, evoking a strange feeling, one that conveys the presence of sacred time and space.

A bullroarer painted with a serpent motif. Swinging the roarer produces a deep, piercing sound that elicits a feeling of numinosity in ritual participants.

1871 by E. B. Tylor (1831–1917), who argued that religion originated in the universal human perception that there is an invisible soul or intangible spirit inside our visible, tangible bodies. He argued that in all "primitive societies," recognition of a soul shaped similar belief systems across the world.

More recent studies of surviving indigenous religions focus less on belief in vaguely defined souls or spirits and more on the phenomenon of how indigenous peoples actually perceive and establish relations with a range of others, human and nonhuman, through their sensory experience. For them, being religious is not about creeds or texts that need interpreting; instead, people experience an embodied engagement with the environment around them, one in which certain stones, animals, trees, and the dead may "speak" to the living. Here emotions, memory, direct experiences, and altered states of consciousness play a part. Most indigenous people sustain a very close relationship with the natural world, one in which the ecosystem is deeply sensed as alive, as fertile, and in the flow of a larger, ordered cosmos.

In hunter–gatherer societies today, human life is more bound up with the recurring rhythms of nature and group interconnections than is the case today in urban industrial societies. The people live by the rising and the setting of the sun, the phases of the moon, and the seasons of the year. Time is circular. This **circular time** follows the pattern of the celestial and natural world. Human lives, too, revolve like the seasons: from life to death, as from spring to summer, fall to winter and then spring and the returning of new life, ever and again in a circle. In myth and ritual and in contact with their sacred centers of revelation, indigenous peoples feel themselves to be part of the largest rhythms of life. There is flow and a quest for equilibrium with

circular time: awareness, especially in hunter-gatherer societies, that time and life follow the same recurring cycle of time determined by the sun, moon, and the seasons

the environment; finding the good life has always meant learning to live with the plants, animals, and spirits that share the indigenous peoples' own world, discerning their motivations and intentions, their love and anger.

This practical and integral relatedness with the natural home world—of hunted animals, essential plants, and surrounding landforms—is realized through the engagement of all their five senses and is guided by myth, mind, and emotions. Resident spirit beings that have souls also have personalities and the faculty of hearing, and many command the ability to speak; indigenous traditions vary, in fact, by the ways these spirit beings speak, their personalities, and the landscapes they occupy through the seasons. The human community's attuning of its senses to these entities through ritual ensures their finding food, avoiding illness, sustaining group harmony, creating healthy children.

All known indigenous peoples have imagined their universe populated by a multitude of supernatural beings that interact with them in life. Many groups believe these ties extend into an afterlife; some assume that souls of the dead reincarnate as humans or other life forms. Relating with spirit beings (or souls) entails making ongoing, reliable connections with them; accordingly, indigenous communities tend to be very careful in performing their communal rituals.

Among most indigenous peoples today, ancestors are in some way still connected with the living; their dreams or visions support the idea that the dead can "return" in nonmaterial form. As we will see, this belief is supported by spirit mediums who serve as dramatic communicators with the dead, who enable a departed soul to speak to the living "from the other side." Although many in the contemporary Euro-American world do not take the content of dreams as seriously as facts derived from "normal waking reality," indigenous peoples today, like most humans before the modern era, regard dreams and visions as very significant sources for understanding the ultimate meanings and purposes of life.

Death is not an ultimate, irrevocable end; in most indigenous societies, it does not imply a final disconnection between the living and the dead. On the contrary, death is an elevation of one's status to that of sacred ancestor. Ancestors, in turn, are venerated as spirits who can help the living by guiding them to the hunting grounds and bringing prey animals their way or by invigorating the wild foods or cultivated crops. By the same token, misfortune in a community may be the fault of the living, who have incited the ancestors' anger and punishment by breaking a moral law or neglecting a ritual. In such situations, harmony between the living, the dead, and all of nature needs to be restored.

Ancestral spirits are seen as custodians of the traditions. They may harm those who flout custom and bless those who are faithful to it. Some scholars, following Tylor, believe that later religions evolved from early animist views of the world and efforts to manage the activities of supernatural spirit-beings. Recent archaeological evidence suggests that the most elaborate burials in late prehistory were conducted to protect the living from the power of malevolent souls. Perhaps powerful ancestral spirits (both the kind and the dangerous) became the world's first gods.

Among the Dani, a simple agricultural group in highland New Guinea, belief that the soul survives into an afterlife profoundly shapes the ways of the living. In their death rituals, the Dani try to direct the soul of a person who has just died to a distant ghost land. Yet many ghosts are thought to return to cause problems, especially if their last rites were not done properly or their death is not avenged in timely fashion. Thus Dani elders take great care when performing funerals, and they maintain small guest houses to accommodate, and pacify, the occasional ghost visitors.

Further, rival Dani villages engage continually in lethal warfare, whose main purpose is for the men to satisfy a newly departed kinsman's spirit by killing someone on the enemy's side. The Dani moral code includes the precept of "a life for a life." Moreover, since losing a kinsman inevitably weakens the collective community and each individual's soul, avenging the loss of the deceased by killing an enemy tribesman is the only means to restore the vitality of the survivors' souls. In fact, Dani kinship and food production is organized around the central need for supplying the feasts that must be held to mark deaths and celebrate revenge killings. Appeasing ancestral ghosts is always in mind.

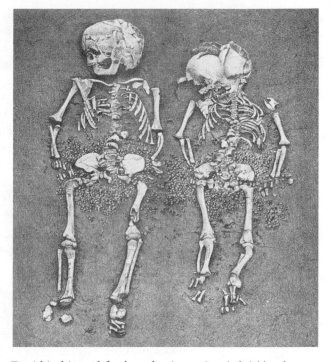

Burial of children from 20,000 BCE: With the remains are perforated shells and remnants of decorated clothing found in Grottes des Enfantes, France.

The Dani, like the Blackfoot tribe of the Northern Plains of North America, are representative of the many indigenous groups in which shamans are absent or marginal. Lacking a class of priests, every adult learns to perform the most common rituals. But there are in both societies wise religious leaders who are looked to for leading major communal festivals based on their ready knowledge of the intricate rites. Dani religious leaders are thoughtful in hosting the regular visits of ancestral ghosts; the Blackfoot wise men and women religious leaders show care in treating spirits as honored guests, feeding them, making lovely home altars, and assembling the finest medicine bundles for offerings.

Religious tradition pervades the lives of indigenous peoples. If they live in the prescribed ways, which always requires them to show respect for the beings around them (human and nonhuman), members of the group will lead successful lives.

Totemism: Australian Aboriginal Religion

Across the world, anthropologists have noted that many indigenous groups use a symbol, or totem, to establish their fundamental identity, identify proper marriage partners, promote collective solidarity, and regulate relations with outsiders. A **totem** is an

totem: symbol taken from natural world to represent common origin and essence of a social group

animal, reptile, insect, or plant that is emblematic of the community and is treated as sacred. The relationship between totems and groups reveals a special circle of kinship and a primal connection between humans and the rest of nature.

Totemism is still found among some Native Americans and is common among the various aboriginal peoples of Australia. To understand this belief system, we can take an example from the latter: Members of the aboriginal kangaroo clan believe that their origins occurred in the **Dreamtime**, when the world as we know it was being created. Their myths inform them that their clan consists of the descendants of their totemic progenitor, the first kangaroo, who created them from her own body

Dreamtime: for Australian Aborigines, the time when the world was created, and which exists in another realm

RITUALS AND RITES: Shamans Across the World

The shaman remains the key religious specialist in many societies today. The term *shaman* (alternatively pronounced "SHAY-man" or "shah-MAN") comes from the Evenk, a group of hunters and reindeer herders in Siberia. The term was adopted for all similar practitioners, however, because early scholars thought that the Siberian shaman tradition had spread across Eurasia and into the Americas, a theory that is doubted today. Four religious figures are central to an understanding of the world's religions: the shaman, the prophet, the sage, and the priest. The first is our concern in this chapter, for the shaman is still found among peoples on every inhabited continent and in the earliest records of our direct forebears.

Though differing in details of clothing and techniques, shamans are found across the world today: left, a Yanomami shaman in the Amazon; right, a Korean shaman in Seoul.

and essence, established their existence as humans, and then led them to their current home territory, making landforms, including rivers and mountains, and other creatures. Accordingly, the group members ritually decorate their bodies with kangaroo drawings; and before children are considered to be adults, they must learn the distinctive dances and songs recounting the group's totemic kangaroo story. Elder men pass down these secrets to the young men through initiation; they are most protective of the sacred symbols, the polished wood or stone *churinga* that symbolize the totem and are inscribed with the most sacred maps or tales of the founder and other heroes. The group is also protective of its own "songlines," the myths that are sung to trace in detail the progenitor's trail of creation over the land, an oral record giving the group claims to a shared identity and territory.

Harming or eating a kangaroo is almost always forbidden, or **taboo**, to members of the kangaroo clan. The totemic kangaroo spirit that dwells in the home territory is thought to be alive and protective of the group. Elders pray to and invoke it for healing and guidance. Women of the kangaroo clan who want to become pregnant visit the places where the totemic spirits reside, for they believe that conception—via spirit/soul acquisition—cannot occur without exposure to the totem's life force.

There is also a unique and regularly performed ritual that unifies the totemic group. In addition to singing and acting out their myth of origins, all the "kangaroos" in the group, on this one annual occasion, gather to renew their primordial identity and "become one flesh" again. How? By hunting down a kangaroo and ingesting its flesh. These rites are performed to increase the totemic species and give spiritual strength to individuals in the group. Here, again, in the totemic belief system, humans and nature form a spiritual totality: Although the design of the world was fixed once and for all in the Dreamtime, it is the task of humans, through their totemic rites, to maintain and renew this creation.

The French sociologist Émile Durkheim (1858–1917) argued that totemism points to a key feature in all religious life. It is the sacred totem (in our

taboo: action or object that is normally forbidden

Aboriginal men from Arnhemland, Australia, painting their bodies to show their identification with a totemic ancestor.

The art of contemporary Australian Aborigines depicts totemic beings and their role in creation during the "Dreamtime."

example, the kangaroo) that gives the group a singular focus and in so doing really stands for the group itself. For Durkheim, religion is at root about making a group's own identity, survival, and worth sacred by focusing on and identifying with a common symbol. What human groups felt as an unseen but deeply felt sacred force was really, he argued, the cohesive power of group unity. For Durkheim the central purpose of religious myth is to frame society's customs with a long and noble history such that they can be respected as sacred and bring social stability to human life.

Durkheim's influential theory is that whatever else has come to define religious beliefs across the world's human groups, religion's power to bind us together is what established it and keeps it central to human life.

Shamans: "Technicians of the Sacred"

What happens if the group's band of skilled hunters comes home empty-handed after a month? How to respond when debilitating illness marked by fever, chills, and physical weakness afflicts a growing number of villagers? Who can halt or reverse the series of misfortunes befalling a family that has let its ancestral shrine fall into ruins? Only a

spirit medium, or **shaman**, referred to variously also as *medicine man*, *folk healer*, *witch doctor*, and so on, can intervene with the unseen powers. These terms taken together designate some of the usual traits attributed to shamans.

Among the many fascinating scenes shown in prehistoric cave art are over fifty images of humans that suggest the depiction of no ordinary person. Two are famous: a bison hovering over a man, with a pole surmounted by a bird, and a human seeming to morph into a composite animal who walks hidden among a large herd of deer. These two ancient paintings may be the first recorded depictions of the shaman, an individual with special powers, whose roles, even 30,000 years ago, may have included healing the souls and bodies of others, dealing with death, and venturing into the realm of the dead. The Kung healers in recent centuries have embellished rock walls with shamanic paintings, and records of similar practices have been found in ancient caves in Europe and Asia. Scholars have posited that the prehistoric shamans are shown discerning the movements of animal herds, guiding the hunters to success, and perhaps recalling the errant souls of the living.

The term *shaman* identifies a religious specialist who mediates between the human community and the usually unseen supernatural beings also populating our world. The role varies across the world: In some indigenous societies they dominate in the group's religious life; in others, the medium remains a marginal, often-distrusted figure resorted to only in dire circumstances, where chiefs, priests, or healers perform the group's ritual and healing functions. And some indigenous societies have no tradition of spirit mediums at all.

The most common shaman's role worldwide is the ability to heal (both literally and metaphorically) through **spirit flight** achieved in trance or an altered state of consciousness; in some indigenous groups, shamans utilize psychotropic drugs found in nature to achieve or aid their otherworldly journey. Shaman healers usually cooperate with spiritual beings and in some places are distinct from **sorcerers**, mediums who manipulate the spirit world and coerce the supernaturals without their consent, often for their own benefit and against community values.

Where found, shamans are ritual specialists, intermediaries who attempt to connect this world to another realm of being that impinges on humanity. By these acts, they knit together the community in the face of the chaos of disease, death, and discord. Many shamans through their spirit flights return to teach their communities, and through trance rituals they demonstrate that the daily, ordinary world is not all there is. A deeper spiritual order enfolds the known, everyday experience of life. In most indigenous societies, the living and the dead, the community and its sacred ancestors, form one great community. Binding it all together, the shaman uses his or her body as a bridge to connect these two worlds. If harmony in an indigenous group has been shattered by troubling ancestral ghosts, only the shaman, who is able to visit both worlds and communicate the needs of one to the other, can restore balance.

Shamans have been found in over a thousand indigenous societies, though details of their practices vary. A commonly held conception in the indigenous religions is that sickness can be due to the loss of an individual's soul, by accident or by theft. In some indigenous societies, people believe that illness can be induced by an enemy's

spirit medium/ shaman: person who communicates with deities and spirits through ritually induced trance

spirit flight: shaman's attempt to locate another person's soul in another realm

sorcerers: mediums who manipulate the spirit world, often for their own benefit rather than on behalf of the community

inserting a foreign object such as a piece of bone or an insect into a victim's body. The common characteristic of their intervention is to discover this, locate the object, and remove it to cure the afflicted party.

The trance state can be reached by drumming and singing alone, but in global perspective shamans have also discovered a long list of psychotropic agents for altering consciousness to their purposes. Fasting is common, but practices may also involve the inhaling of incense, snuffs, smoke from tobacco or other psychoactive herbs, or the ingesting of mushrooms or potent plant concoctions. The shaman's trance may be marked by bodily fever, loud breathing, protruding eyes, insensitivity to temperature or pain, convulsions, or trembling. In many traditions, the shaman's soul is thought to leave the physical body, free to fly to the heavens, beneath the earth, or under the sea. On these *spirit flights*, or *soul journeys*, shamans attempt to locate another person's lost soul, perhaps because it has wandered off in this world or passed on to the afterlife. Another common belief is that the dead person's soul needs a shaman's assistance to reach the afterlife dwelling place of the clan's ancestors.

tutelary spirit:
supernatural agent,
often an ancestral spirit,
who helps a shaman

Shamans through initiation find connection with a protective spirit, or **tutelary spirit**. This is a supernatural agent, often an ancestral spirit, whose help is required to perform the difficult soul journeys, negotiate with evil spirits, compel a soul to return, or increase the shaman's healing powers. In many tribes, shamans have human helpers who watch over their unconscious bodies during trance states, for they, too, can remain stuck as spirits if their souls cannot return to their bodies.

numinous: human
perception of the
sacred

The shamanic world is one in which spirits coexist with humans in a layered cosmos, with humans occupying the earth between an upper and a lower world. The spirits are particularly accessible to humans around sacred physical objects or unusual places. As we saw in Chapter 1, each culture regards these locations as being connected to the "center of the world" (*axis mundi*). Most commonly, such sites are actual or symbolic sacred mountains or sacred trees, revered as places of original revelations, intensely alive with spiritual power, or **numinous** presence. Several examples show how shamanic traditions from around the world today share common traits.

Case Study in Healing Trance: Kung San Healers

n/um kausi: shamans
of the Kung people

The Kung San of southern Africa believe that the dead go to an afterlife, a "next world" populated by ancestors, one that is similar to this world and is linked closely to the living. Souls that miss the living return to earth as ghosts and try to sicken friends and family members in an effort to hasten their arrival in the next world. The most accomplished Kung shamans (**n/um kausi**) have the ability to enter into a trance during night-long dances, in which everyone joins in ceremonies of rhythmic drumming and singing around a fire. With this group support and social purpose, anthropologists suggest, the Kung shamans activate a natural force within their bodies, the *n/um*, a power that "boils" in and moves up the spine. The body shakes and sweats, and inhalations grow forced and deeper as the shaman slips into a trance state. Thus empowered, the shaman begins to touch the bodies of others to transfer the healing force of the boiling

A Kung healing ceremony. The trancing and healing performed by Kung shamans depends on the community's participating in drumming, singing, and dancing.

n/um into them. Expert healers can also identify and suck out poisons from the bodies of the sick; some may massage the patient with a mixture of the shaman's own sweat and blood. Healers who perceive the ghosts of troublesome ancestors watching the dance outside the community circle may shriek or hurl stones at deities in the shadows who are identified as causing difficulties. The most effective Kung shamans are honored, but they are otherwise typical members of the tribe; most are men.

The most skilled Kung shamans enter into a deep trance state (*kia*) so that their souls can leave the body and journey to the "next world." There they confirm the fate of the dead, investigate causes of sickness, or convey messages between the dead and the living. The spirit flight is a practice attributed to shamans in nearly all indigenous societies, past and present.

The shaman's role is universally regarded as mortally dangerous. The Kung call entering trance "being half-dead" and with great care guard a shaman's physical body while the healer's soul journeys to "the other world." Like many indigenous peoples, the Kung are also careful not to startle sleeping individuals, for fear that souls wandering during sleep will not have time to return to a person who has been awakened suddenly.

Men and women who become shamans in the Kung or other cultures must train through long apprenticeships. But in most groups it is common for shamans to feel that they were chosen for the role by a tutelary spirit, often in spite of their own resistance. Novice shamans must prove their ability by surviving an initiation ordeal that may require fasting and acts of extraordinary physical endurance. Each must demonstrate the capacity for trance, the grace of a tutelary spirit, and evidence of supernormal powers. Many shamans feel that they wear out their bodies by repeatedly undergoing near-death experiences in the course of soul journeys or the ingestion of spirit-infused herbs.

"You dance, dance, dance, dance. Then *n/um* lifts you up in your belly and lifts up in your back, and you start to shiver. In trance, you see everything, because you see what's troubling everybody. . . . Then *n/um* enters every part of your body, right to your feet and even your hair. . . . Then *n/um* makes your thoughts nothing in your head."

—Kinachau, a Kung San healer

SOURCE: Richard Katz, *Boiling Energy: Community Healing Among the Kalahari Kung* (Cambridge, MA: Harvard University Press, 1982).

Modern Native American art of the Ojibway depicting spirit guides in the flight of the shaman.

Case Study: Sioux Vision Quest for a Spirit Ally

Among the Lakota Sioux of North America, young men go to a sacred wilderness region on a *vision quest* in search of a personal protector spirit. After preparatory training, the apprentices fast and purify themselves in a sweat lodge. Then each one ventures out alone into the wilderness. The Lakota believe, as do the Kung, that every human being has the potential for supernatural connection and that all should be encouraged to develop this ability.

Those contacted by strong spirit allies in dreams and those who have vivid visions of the ancestors may go on to become shamans after further training with an elder practitioner. As the Lakota shaman Lame Deer recalled his experience, "All of a sudden I heard the cry of an eagle, loud and above the voices of many other birds. It seemed to say, 'We have been waiting for you. We knew you would come.' "[3] Apprentices learn the techniques of trance, the myths of the tribe, the location of "power places" in the landscape, and other healing arts that involve the use of medicines. Shamans are never the same after initiation; many receive a new name, a new identity, and in the myths they even obtain a new body. Shamans encounter evil spirits that must be tricked, seduced, or killed to complete the healing task. Given these arduous demands, becoming a shaman is often described as a death-and-rebirth experience.

Bear Sacrifice: A Widespread Arctic and Pacific Rim Tradition

We have noted how shamans can serve as mediums who bring the spirits down to earth for "ritual negotiations." An example of this practice is the bear sacrifice, once one of the most widespread rituals in the world and common across the upper Pacific

Ainu elders celebrating a Bear Feast. Offerings of food and sake are placed before the dead bear; swords and sacred quivers hang on the altar behind the men. This photograph was taken by the anthropologist Bronislaw Pilsudski (1866–1918), who lived with an Ainu community for several years in the early twentieth century.

Rim and the vast circumpolar region from northern Japan to North America. As observed in modern times, shamans carefully manage the sacrificial rituals, offering gifts from humans in exchange for an animal's life. A common belief in hunter-gatherer societies is that animals are actually spirits in disguise who assume animal bodies to interact with humans. This may have been the earliest example of humanity conceptualizing divine incarnation, the embodiment in earthly form of a supernatural being.

Among the Ainu people on Hokkaido Island in northern Japan, spirits that incarnate themselves as animals are called *kamui*. They mostly dwell in an "other world" but can have contact with humans by coming to earth and assuming life in a bear's body. The Ainu conception is that humans and *kamui* are of equal status. Although the latter (when unencumbered by a body) can fly and have magical powers, only humans can give them what they really need and want: precious sake (a wine made from rice) and *inau*, the earth's fragrant willow sticks. In the Ainu understanding, the spirits don animal bodies to acquire their fur as "clothes" to trade, for they can get *inau* and sake from humans. This transaction requires that they be ritually hunted and have their bodies killed to complete the exchange that benefits both parties.

The Ainu shaman performs special rituals to attract a spirit in its bear incarnation. Knowing that an exchange has been requested and consenting to it if humans have kept up their part in earlier exchanges, a bear cub leaves trail signs that allow hunters to track and capture it. Villages then raise the specially chosen animal until it becomes fully grown. Afterward, the shaman addresses the bear respectfully, makes the proper offerings, performs a ritual execution, and releases the *kamui* spirit to return to the other world, presumed to be happy with its gifts. The Ainu believe that if the sacred conventions of the exchange are duly observed, the *kamui* just released and other spirits will continue to assume animal form. Thus the shaman ensures that the people will have a continuous supply of meat and shelter.

Shamans Who "Repair the World"

A shaman's expertise can also be effective when a human group acts improperly. The practices of the Inuit (who dwell around the Arctic region) illustrate the shaman's role in "repairing the world." The Inuit believe that the great goddess Takanakapsaluk, Mistress of Sea Animals, lives on the ocean floor and releases whales, seals, fish, and other marine creatures so that they may be killed for human use. But the Inuit believe that when their community performs the ritual improperly or someone breaks a moral taboo, the goddess's hair "becomes soiled" and she burns in anger, holding back all creatures in her domain. The Inuit shaman must then be called for a séance. To follow one account:

> He sits behind a curtain and says again and again, "The way is made ready for me!" after which the audience responds, "Let it be so." Finally from behind the curtain, the shaman cries, "Halala-he-he-he halala-he-he!" Then he drops down a tube, which is believed to lead straight to the bottom of the sea. The shaman's voice can be heard receding further in the depths, and finally it disappears. During the shaman's absence, the audience sits in the darkened house, listening to faint sighing and groaning, while singing songs of past journeys: the shaman's dodging three deadly guard stones, averting the father of the goddess, and getting past a fierce guard dog. Approaching the goddess, the shaman finds her angry, with hair uncombed, filthy, and hanging over her eyes. The creatures of the ocean sit in a pool beside her. The shaman gently turns the goddess toward the animals and a nearby lamp, combing and washing her hair. He then asks why the animals are not coming, and she replies that they are being withheld because the people have eaten forbidden boiled meat and because the women have kept their miscarriages secret, failing to purify their homes afterward. Mollified by praises and promises to make amends, goddess Takanakapsaluk releases the animals and they are swept back into the ocean. The shaman's return is marked by a distant, then louder call of "Plu-a-he-he!" as he finally shakes in his place, gasping for breath. After a silence, he demands,

"The greatest peril in life lies in the fact that human food consists entirely of souls. All these creatures that we have to kill and eat, all we have to strike down to make clothes for ourselves, have souls, souls that do not perish and which must be pacified lest they revenge themselves on us for taking away their bodies."

—Ivaluardjuk, an Inuit healer

SOURCE: *The Sacred Ways of Knowledge, Sources of Life.*

"Your words must rise up," and then the audience members begin to confess their misdeeds. By the end of the séance, there is a mood of optimism.[4]

The Yanomami shamans of the Amazon rain forest also illustrate how mediums repair community life by bringing spirits down to earth. Village leader, curer, and defender against evil spirits, the village shaman (always male) locates and returns the disoriented souls of sick or dying villagers. If others have acted to weaken or steal someone's soul, it is the shaman who must identify both the misdeed and the perpetrators. To be initiated as shaman and to achieve such abilities, an individual must memorize chants, drumming, and struts to attract the support of his special ancestral spirits. The Yanomami shaman must also master the use of the hallucinogenic snuff called *ebene*, made from psychoactive plants that the shaman's own teacher repeatedly blew into the student's nostrils as part of his training. This powerful substance is thought to be a spirit ally that is essential for opening the Yanomami shaman's body to perceive, feel, and contact his tribe's spirit allies.

The Yanomami shaman has the power to conduct the spirits into the human world. The spirits can then be induced to enter the shaman's body and respond to questions about matters of concern, small or great. At times and without invitation, the shaman's mouth may speak the spirit's messages about group origins, life's meaning, or any hidden facts relevant to recent events.

The reliance on psychoactive substances to assist the shaman to achieve altered states of consciousness, as found among the Yanomami, is not universal. Drug-induced trances are limited mostly to groups in the Americas, where the use of the cactus peyote, the vine extract ayahuasca, and plants such as jimson and datura have long been in the shaman's medicine bag. What is universal for shamans across the world, even among

TALES OF SPIRITUAL TRANSFORMATION: The Peyote Ceremony

Divine Communion

From that time, whenever they held peyote meetings, we all attended and . . . one time something happened to me. . . . I was sitting with bowed head, . . . we prayed, . . . then I saw Jesus standing there. . . . I will pray to him, I thought. I stood up and raised my arm. I prayed. I asked for a good life—thanking God who gave me my life. And as the drum was beating, my body shook to the beat. I was unaware of it. I was just very contented. I never knew such pleasure as this. There was a sensation of great

joyousness. Now I was an angel. That is how I saw myself. Because I had wings I was supposed to fly but I could not quite get my feet off the ground. . . . I knew when I ate peyote that they were using something holy. That way is directed toward God. Nothing else on earth is holy, . . . and if someone sees something holy at a peyote meeting, that is really true. I understood that this religion is holy.

—Shirley Etsitty, Native American Church

Source: *The Sacred: Ways of Knowledge, Sources of Life* (Tsaile, AZ: Navajo Community College Press, 1996).

shamans utilizing psychoactive drugs, is reliance on the impact of rapid rhythmic drumming, dancing, chanting, and fasting to induce trance experiences. Thus, the drum or the rattle is a universal symbol of the shaman's extraordinary religious practice.

Indigenous Religions Today

The Cataclysms of Colonialism

A theme that runs throughout this book is the disruptions to life and religious traditions caused by modern European colonialism. For indigenous societies across the planet, this global expansion of invading outsiders and the political dominance they imposed has been disastrous.

This cataclysm has had many facets. Native peoples of the New World and other remote regions were decimated by the diseases of Eurasia, to which they had no natural resistance. Often simultaneously, the disease-bearing outsiders plundered the native people's riches, utilizing horses and superior weapons technology to achieve their aims. In the early colonial era, millions of people in small-scale subsistence societies were killed or enslaved. In countless instances, the outsiders appropriated and transformed the native lands when natural resources were discovered there. Whole peoples were ruthlessly swept aside, and ways of life that had evolved over centuries were cut off. Since religion is closely related to a community's way of life, the epidemics and genocide suffered by the world's indigenous peoples inevitably included the destruction and deformation of ancient religious traditions.

Over time, as the worst cruelties of colonial rule eased, the survivors and their descendants faced stark choices. Would they risk the chaos of migration by retreating into the receding natural frontiers of forests and mountains? Would they acquiesce to a nineteenth-century government's program of forced resettlement on reservations? Or would the best choice be for individuals to go their separate ways, to assimilate with the dominant society and submit to the national laws of others? Whatever the choice, the solidarity and cultural integrity of most of these displaced groups worldwide has weakened over every generation. It has inevitably been the young who have seen the limits of their minority status, rejected the old dialects and religious customs, and responded to the allure of the dominant culture by embracing assimilation.

Exposure to missionary religions and their alien exponents often contributed to the downfall of the indigenous religions. Beliefs and practices of many native peoples elicited much hostility and criticism. Governments in the Americas and Australia forced indigenous children to attend missionary schools, where Christianity was aggressively taught and in which traditional practices were ruthlessly banned. Students who spoke their native languages were subject to punishment. Missionaries viewed shamans as obstacles to the advance of the colonizing powers. Outsiders often accused

"Our church is the world."

—John Emhoolah, Kiowa leader of North America

SOURCE: *The Sacred Ways of Knowledge, Sources of Life.*

the native healers of combining evil with fakery: acting as "servants of the devil" while also being imposters or religious charlatans who exploited their own people. For the Euro-American Christian immigrants, for example, shamanism represented the chaotic wilderness, the shaman a shady character and source of disruptive chaos that threatened the colonial order. Under these circumstances, native peoples in many cases had to hide their drums, medicines, and sacred images. They believed that the only way to preserve their culture was to take it underground.

Other native peoples, however, organized in attempts to restore their place in the world and give new life to their traditions. In North America, shamans rallied to attempt to revitalize native peoples in the nineteenth century through a movement called the **Ghost Dance**. After the decimation of the buffalo by white hunters, which greatly contributed to the destruction of the indigenous way of life on the Great Plains, several elders had the same visionary revelation: Their tutelary spirits announced a way to restore the lost world by bringing back the ancestors and causing the whites to disappear. Native American religious leaders then preached that this could be accomplished if all the people performed a new dance ritual as prescribed by the spirits. Soon this Ghost Dance was practiced with fervor across the Great Plains by those whose kin had died, with the dancers falling unconscious in hopes of experiencing reunion with their deceased relatives. One leader in this movement had this vision of the Ghost Dance recorded:

> All Indians must dance, everywhere, and keep on dancing. Pretty soon in the next spring, the Great Spirit come. . . . The game be thick everywhere. All dead Indians come back and live again. . . . White can't hurt Indian then. Then big flood come like water and all white people die, get drowned. After that, water go away and then nobody but Indians everywhere and game animals of all kinds thick.[5]

The pain of engagement with outsiders is unmistakable in this new religious movement, one that sought to bind a vision of ecological renewal with the restoration of traditional religious consciousness. In 1890 the U.S. Cavalry was ordered to end this nationwide movement by massacring the men, women, and children gathered for a Ghost Dance at Wounded Knee, South Dakota.

By 2014, no indigenous societies remain that have not been exposed to the world of outsiders, with their missionaries, armies, nation-states, corporations, and technologies. Some have even been the targets of genocidal persecution. Most of the Kung people have been relocated onto reservations, forced to give up hunting, and directed to adopt agriculture or simple craft production. The Ainu of northern Japan have suffered land seizures and discrimination and are so stigmatized today that few are willing to profess knowledge of the old traditions and shamanic practices. Native peoples of the Amazon rain forest have been displaced by land-clearing settlers and threatened by multinational mining and oil drilling projects. The history of Native Americans since 1500 is a story of genocide and land taking, made worse by legal discrimination against Native American religious practices. In the twenty-first century, hundreds of

Ghost Dance: nineteenth-century Native American religious revitalization movement led by spirit mediums

"The Catholic church is a beautiful theory for Sunday, the iboga on the contrary is the practice of everyday living. In church, they speak of God, with iboga, you live God."

—Nengue Me Ndjoung Isidore, Bwiti religious leader in Africa

SOURCE: S. Swiderski, *La religion Bouiti*, vol. 1 (1990–1991).

indigenous languages and religious traditions will decline in use and disappear forever. It is hard for those centered in the dominant world civilization to absorb vicariously the shattering impact of the past centuries on the earth's "first peoples." Many groups today are involved with land ownership disputes with their federal governments, and they call for the return of human remains and the sacred items of their ancestors that were collected by museum curators in the past.

Some indigenous groups that have survived with their cultures most intact are those living far from resources the modernizing world has sought: in the trans-Arctic zone, deep in the rain forests, high in the remotest mountains, or on isolated islands far from the continental landmasses. Others have found successful means of assimilating, with members gaining education and employment outside the group and integrating modern economic life with indigenous tradition. Those groups that have retained autonomy, resisted assimilation, and worked to revitalize their identity show both the near-boundless adaptability of human culture and the deep resilience of the human spirit. An example of this indigenous vitality is in groups like the Kayapo in Brazil, who now use the Internet to share their anti-expropriation strategies and principles of cultural revitalization with other groups across the globe; their experience emphasizes

The Native American Church

In the United States today, over 550 Indian nations are recognized by the U.S. federal government, each with its own history and tribal land and each practicing its own distinct traditional religion. In the last century, there have been successful efforts to draw scattered Native Americans into new religious groups in what scholars have identified as the "pan-Americanization" of indigenous peoples.

The Native American Church is a major example of this phenomenon, one that has had one faction drawn into the orbit of Christianity and another that remains independent. But the two are united in their ceremonial use of the cactus peyote as a communal sacrament. This "melting pot" movement remains controversial among some Native Americans, who criticize how the Native American Church draws tribal members away from their own group's traditions. An additional problem this group encounters is the drug enforcement laws of the U.S. government. Similar indigenous peoples' new religions have started in South America. Two examples are Santo Daime and União do Vegetal; both are syncretistic, influenced by Christian morality and folk religion, and centered on a traditional psychotropic herb, in this case, ayahuasca. Both also have now spread across the globe, attracting nonindigenous devotees from Japan to Europe.

Source: http://www.nativeamericanchurch.net/Native_American_Church/ NATIVE_AMERICAN_CHURCH.html

the role of the young as bicultural actors who negotiate with the world outside the indigenous group. They have also harnessed the power of modern video to document infringements on their lands by outsiders and as an effective medium to communicate about group issues and share cultural teachings between Kayapo in separate regions.

Shamans in some indigenous groups were pivotal figures who led groups in facing the crises of modernity. Because traditionally they were entrusted with mediating between spirits and humans, shamans have been the natural choices to act on behalf of the group when the outside world intruded. In the face of repression, many shamans saw confrontation as the only hope for their group, led rebellions, and died in vain defense. Siberian and Mongolian shamans under Soviet rule, for example, retreated to the deep wilderness and continued to practice there.

Religious leaders found other creative responses. Some advocated **syncretism**, in which indigenous religious beliefs and practices were woven together with those of outsiders. In present-day Mexico, for example, shamans have integrated Catholic saints and sacramental theology into healing rites that utilize peyote. Another example of combining elements from different traditions to create a new religion is **Bwiti**, a West Central African religion. Organized in the early twentieth century among the forest-dwelling Babongo and Mitsogo people of Gabon and the Fang people of Gabon and Cameroon, Bwiti incorporates animism, ancestor worship, and Christianity into its belief system. As with the **Native American Church**, a mild hallucinogen plays a role, in this case the root bark of the *Tabernanthe iboga* plant, which is now specially cultivated for its religious purpose. Individuals joining the Bwiti community are taught that iboga induces a rich spiritual experience, one that allows the disciple to be healed and solve problems.

syncretism: combination of elements from different belief systems

Bwiti: west central African syncretic religion

Native American Church: modern religious group uniting native peoples of North America

Religious leaders in the Bwiti movement creatively combine regional and Christian traditions.

The Kayapo of Brazil: Selective Modernity and the Survival of Tradition

Kayapo chiefs act as religious and political leaders, trying to retain control of the land that is essential to the continuation of tradition.

The Kayapo until recent decades killed all intruders on their lands, whether lumberjacks, gold miners, or rubber-tree tappers, and were regarded as the most dangerous natives of the Amazon rain forest. Outsiders made every effort to exterminate the Kayapo, going so far as to fly over them to drop blankets infected with smallpox onto their villages. But in the middle of the twentieth century, Kayapo chiefs changed their relationship with outsiders, and in 1982 they regained ownership and control of most of their indigenous lands, the largest tract held by native peoples in South America. On a limited scale, their leaders have sold rights to cut timber and to allow outsiders to mine for gold, using the substantial rents and taxes collected to sustain and protect their culture.

The Kayapo consider themselves an integral part of the universe, bound to the cycles of the natural year and nature's ongoing rebirth. Returning from their hunts, men sing to the spirits of the game they killed in order for the animal or reptile spirits to remain in the forest. Each species is connected to a distinctive song that begins with the cry of the dead animal. A "center of the world" is located in each village's central plaza, where rituals and public life take place. To go back to the time of mythical origins and stimulate the energy required for life's prosperity and continuance, the Kayapo dance the myths recounting their origins and subsequent incidents, recalling their past to reaffirm their identity and innate vitality.

Kayapo shamans specialize in ritual healing. Their supernatural visions and capacity to contact tribal spirits enable them to perform rites that recall and restore the integrity of the *mekaron*, the soul double; at death they ensure that this soul makes a successful journey to their "village of the dead," located on tribal land, near a mountain range, where it lives an afterlife similar to that in the village of the living.

Now that some of their young men have gained an education and attracted the support of international organizations upholding the rights of native peoples, the Kayapo have secured a firm legal existence in modern Brazil. Their chiefs have acted decisively and creatively to selectively modernize yet preserve their religious traditions. From their taxes on tenant miners, they brought the group into the national cash economy, even going so far as buying airplanes and hiring Brazilian pilots to police their territory. They invested in radios and video equipment for recording group rituals and communicating with other Kayapo across their large territory, all to cultivate their common identity, ritual celebrations, and cultural survival. Traditional lip plugs and body painting remain common in village life, and group hunts keep male and female jungle survival skills honed; yet these have been integrated alongside the adoption of Western medicine, canned foods, and business connections in the global economy (such as supplying Brazilian nut oil to the corporation The Body Shoppe). As material wealth has increased, Kayapo chiefs, by adapting to the possibilities of modern life, have been outspoken in having their group maintain their jungle traditions and resist compromising their sociocultural integrity.

Many indigenous peoples, especially those decimated by disease, forced immigration, or land loss, have been attracted to missionaries of the major world religions seeking to convert them. Governments often cooperated with this goal. In many colonized lands, rituals of the indigenous religions were banned outright. It was also common that marriage was only recognized under national laws if conducted by a Christian priest. Possessing neither wealth, institutional power, nor prestige among the colonial rulers, indigenous peoples in the early contact periods who persisted in their practices were subjected to discrimination, and some states,

Protest against modern states is a regular fact of life among indigenous peoples in the world today. Struggles to retain control of the land, secure their legal rights, and ensure the education of the young are central to the survival of indigenous religious traditions today. Here, Australian Aborigines demonstrate in Sydney for the restoration of lands annexed from them by the national government.

such as the Soviet Union, imprisoned shamans in psychiatric hospitals. Many studies have found that even after an indigenous people's successful accommodation to a dominant colonial culture, what often survives as its "shamanic tradition" is only fragmentary, reduced to practical applications such as healing services.

In a world turned upside down, one in which the ancestral spirits clearly failed to protect the group or safeguard its territory, radical change was inevitable. Over generations, many shamanic traditions themselves have been diminished or reformulated to match the new life circumstances. Under colonial conditions and until today, cultures that were thriving only a few centuries ago exist only in dimming memory. What has proven the most enduring of these indigenous traditions, even in regions that came to be dominated by one or more world religion, is shamanism.

Shamanism in Modern Asia: Division of Labor Within the World Religions

Shamanism continues to exist as an integral part of the pluralistic religious cultures of Asia. In most settlements across the region, there is a shaman who can enter into the trance state, if called on to heal or to solve practical problems. Such shamanic practice today has been harmonized with the doctrines of the dominant religions and is tolerated by the Hindu, Buddhist, or Islamic religious establishments that are also by now deeply rooted in these areas.

This pattern of coexistence also includes East Asia, where shamans augment popular Confucian beliefs and ancestral rituals, a tradition of pluralistic accommodation there

"Look around. . . . So much of nature has been ruined. Spirits of trees and rocks are displaced and haunt humans because they have nowhere else to go. No wonder the country is a mess."

—Kim Myung, a Korean shaman

SOURCE: *New York Times,* July 7, 2007.

going back to the beginnings of recorded history. Here we can say that given the widespread belief in deities inhabiting this earth and in the soul's afterlife destiny, it is not surprising that East Asians still recognize the utility of spirit mediums who attempt to communicate with the dead. Divination has provided answers to such problems as where grandmother's soul might be residing, whether the ghost of a dead child is causing family troubles, or what might be done to gain the favor of a god who could help end a drought. Unhappy spirits (*kuei*) are also thought to cause distress to the living, so here, too, shamans have had an important role in healing the sick.

Typically, a client approaches a spirit medium today because of the suspicion that an illness is due to ghost possession. The medium goes into trance in the sick one's presence and speaks or acts (sometimes writing on a slate or sand-covered board) after having made contact with one or more spirits. The medium's communications are usually interpreted by an assistant, who acts as the intermediary for the family and community members present. For example, contemporary mediums in Taiwan, called *dangki*, become possessed and rapidly write divinely inspired characters in red ink on yellow papers. Sometimes the objects become amulets for their patients; alternatively, they may be burned, whereupon their ashes are mixed with water that is then drunk as medicine. The role of these spirit mediums has, if anything, *increased* with the modernization and rising prosperity of Taiwan. The same phenomenon has been reported in modern Korea as well.

Global Neo-Shamanism: Expropriation by "White Shamans"

Traditional shamanistic practices now appeal to those in the dominant societies who are drawn to the mysteries of life and want to discover them outside the practices and normative worldviews of the major world religions. With their esoteric and primordial qualities, shamanic practices are seen by some in the West as "uncontaminated," the last remaining spiritual frontier on earth. Now growing numbers of adventurers, romantics, and spiritual explorers from urban civilizations across the world seek out shamanic experience as the representative of nearly lost worlds, hoping to recover something of value. Thousands of Euro-Americans each year sign up for tours to Siberia, the Amazon, or the Himalayas to observe and even be initiated by local shamans. A number of Westerners (hence **"white shamans"**) have created global organizations propagating a purported "universal" shamanic tradition, charging high fees for tours, courses, initiations, and healing services, pledging to use some of the proceeds to assist local shamans.

white shamans: westerners who claim to be practitioners in a "universal" shamanic tradition

In indigenous societies, the shaman has a social rather than a personal reason for entering into trance and contacting the spirits, with a primary concern for the community and its well-being. This is an orientation that contrasts sharply with that of the neo-shamans, whose primary interest is in personal development and a self-healing disconnected from any wider community.

Some native peoples regard this development as an attempt by the conquerors to take the last of their possessions, their culture. Well aware of how much their peoples

GENDER FOCUS: Women Healers and Shamans Today

In most hunter-gatherer societies, where there was minimal social hierarchy and only the gendered division of subsistence labor existed, both women and men worked as healers. As indigenous societies became more complex and settled, and adopted forms of pastoralism and simple agriculture, women were subject to greater restrictions, but in some societies they still serve as healers and noted spirit mediums. In most urban communities of China and Japan, shamans are typically regarded as marginal figures of low status, but in South Korea their practices are uniquely honored and sought by people of all faiths. Korean shamans called *mudang* tend to be predominantly women, drawn into the role from one of two backgrounds: troubling personal experiences that led them to initiation; or inheritance of the role through kinship lines. An estimated 100,000 Korean shamans practice their healing arts today, dealing with life's pragmatic problems. Their séances, called *kut*, are usually held to contact a deity to request economic blessings, healing, restoration of good marital relations, or help in becoming pregnant. The *mudang* enters a trance and then begins to speak with voices attributed to deities. Typically the first statements are complaints of deficiencies in the offerings laid out or about impurity, which Korean supernaturals particularly dislike. When sponsors apologize and promise to do better next time, the divinities usually entertain the sponsor's request(s). A second type of ritual has the most proficient *mudangs* go to the next world with the soul of someone who has recently died or to check the status of a newly departed soul.

have lost and ever zealous to guard their traditional secrets, many shamans today distrust the outsiders and doubt their sincerity. Responding to these postmodern possibilities, the indigenous shaman is again mediating between worlds in creative ways. As David Chidester has noted:

> Acting on behalf of a community, even when that community was displaced and dispossessed, shamans developed new religious strategies, not only for preserving archaic techniques of ecstasy, but also for exercising new capacities for memory, concealment, performance, translation, and transformation in negotiating indigenous religious survival under difficult . . . conditions.[6]

Assimilating indigenous animistic and shamanistic traditions into urban-based civilizations goes back to the very beginnings of recorded human history, as we saw in Chapter 1. We will see in subsequent chapters how world religions from antiquity onward performed a central role in the absorption of tribal peoples into states by "converting them" away from their indigenous religions. It will also be seen in the final chapter that the "civil religions" of modern nations have been focused on legitimating the often violent work of assimilating indigenous peoples.

In the next chapters, we can find repeatedly the imprint of indigenous religions, especially soul belief and trance. Soul beliefs remain nearly universal in the great religions, with East Asia's widespread ancestor veneration an important example of archaic practices that still remain compelling and satisfying. Death rites continue to be powerful expressions of religious tradition, and states of altered consciousness are still central to spiritual growth. The metaphor of human life existing on a plane between heaven above and a netherworld below is found in all major world religions. Finally, sacred places that are believed to be at the center of the world (the *axis mundi*) in the early indigenous traditions continue to be revered in the great world religions: Divine revelations occur on mountains (as to Abraham, Moses, Muhammad, and the Daoist sages), and trees connect humans to life's sacred cosmic mysteries (Buddha was enlightened under a tree; Jesus was crucified on a wooden cross). As for the connection with shamans, when examining the lives of the founders of the world religions, prophets as well as sages, we can notice the performance of miracles such as healing the sick and ascending to the heavens on magical flights, in both cases demonstrating the mastery of what began as the chief shamanic arts.

In the last chapter of this book, we will trace further this now-global arc of interaction between indigenous religions, their leaders, shamanism, and "white shamans." We will also see how the shamanic experience of trance, communication with other worlds, and spirit flight have again found their way into the syncretistic practices of many of the "new religions" that have arisen across the world.

Conclusion

For at least the last 30,000 years, humans have evolved primarily through their cultures, not anatomy. Art, religious practices, and complex symbols were all present among modern *Homo sapiens* from the beginning. And all three emerged simultaneously. What should we understand from this circumstance? Religion is an essential element in our species's evolution: It has helped humanity bond more tightly, face the unknown, hunt more effectively, and reconcile with death. Cultural historians see all these factors helping human groups maximize the quality of their diet, which in turn enabled them to better organize, understand, and adapt to their environment as well as to each other. With more free time, there were greater possibilities for individuals to specialize, experiment, and so introduce cultural innovations.

Evidence of religion in prehistory reflects the major concerns of our species as hunter-gatherers. Fertility was important for group survival, the need to hunt for prey was a constant and central fact, and there was ongoing concern to maintain group and gender boundaries. Indigenous religions among early and later hunter-gatherers and early settled cultivators clearly aided group survival.

To the extent a group adopted religious beliefs and practices, that group obtained advantages vis-à-vis other groups. As a force binding communities, as a means of "being careful" about the unseen, and as a decisive factor in helping human groups adapt to their environment, the world's indigenous religions point out the central issues we face in understanding the continuing and universal role of religion in later human life.

Finally, we can also discern the emergence of the first religious specialist, the shaman, who cultivates the universal human capacity for entering altered states of consciousness. Both serving and leading the people, the shaman has given peoples confidence and direction in dealing with the world's unseen forces. Shamanism is still widespread in the world today. Even where one or more of the great world religions has been adopted by a population, shamanic traditions continue to find patrons. In some cases, shamans express concepts associated with one of the now-dominant world religions (e.g., the soul, hell, the force of karma). In other instances, a shamanic cosmos exists side by side with that of a world religion. Today, shamanism is practiced "underground" if there is reason to fear persecution. In most places, however, it is integrated with the dominant world religions.

Discussion Questions

1. What are the problems in knowing and understanding the religions that existed before the development of written language?

2. How might the history of religions be written by a member of an indigenous people?

3. In many hunter-gatherer groups, the people often refer to themselves as "the true people." How might sudden awareness of the existence of other people in itself undermine the cosmos posited in such indigenous religious traditions?

4. Do you think it is valid to generalize from modern hunter-gatherers back into the past to reconstruct the origins of religion? Why or why not?

5. How might a modern shaman explain the endurance of her tradition and the attraction of shamanic practices by those living in modern industrial societies?

6. Some scholars have noted that the practices of modern sports fans in the West often resemble the totemic practices of indigenous peoples. Describe these commonalities in the case of your college or for a professional team such as the Chicago Bears. How do mascots and symbolic practices function to achieve group unity and individual identity?

7. Scholars who have studied tribal peoples now counsel sympathetically imagining indigenous religions as "lived through the body" and involving the entire spectrum of human perception. Explain why this approach has value, given the practices of Kung shamanism.

8. The scholar of comparative religions Joseph Campbell once suggested that the dominant world religions all differed from the indigenous religions by their requiring followers to distance themselves from the powerful personal religious experiences that were routine in many indigenous societies. While you are invited to test this assertion in the following chapters, can you see any problems with traditions that invite everyone to have regular immersions into the sacred as described in this chapter?

9. In 1985, the anthropologist Michael Harner founded the nonprofit Foundation for Shamanic Studies, which seeks to foster "greater respect for the knowledge of indigenous peoples and ultimately help to preserve and dignify this wisdom for future generations." What questions would you have for this organization, given that they also offer workshops to train Western peoples in shamanic practices?

Key Terms

animism	*n/um kausi*	syncretism
Bwiti	Native American	taboo
circular time	Church	totem
cosmogony	numinous	tutelary spirit
Dreamtime	sorcerers	"Venus" figurines
Ghost Dance	spirit flight	"white shamans"
Homo religiosus	spirit medium/shaman	

Suggested Readings

Beck, Peggy, Anna Lee Walters, and Nia Francisco. *The Sacred: Ways of Knowledge, Sources of Life* (Tsaile, AZ: Navajo Community College Press, 1996).

Buyandelger, Manduha, *Tragic Spirits: Shamanism, Memory, and Gender in Contemporary Mongolia*. (Chicago: University of Chicago Press, 2013).

Gardner, Robert. *Gardens of War: Life and Death in the New Guinea Stone Age* (New York: Random House, 1969).

Grim, John. *The Shaman: Patterns of Religious Healing Among the Ojibway Indians* (Norman: University of Oklahoma Press, 1983).

———. *Indigenous Traditions and Ecology: The Interbeing of Cosmology and Community* (Cambridge, MA: Center for the Study of World Religions, 2001).

Harris, Marvin. *Our Kind* (New York: Harper & Row, 1989).

Hayden, Brian. *Shamans, Sorcerers and Saints: A Prehistory of Religion* (Washington, DC: Smithsonian Institution Press, 2004).

Katz, Richard. *Boiling Energy: Community Healing Among the Kalahari Kung* (Cambridge, MA: Harvard University Press, 1982).

Kendall, Laurel. *The Life and Times of a Korean Shaman* (Honolulu: University of Hawaii Press, 1988).

———. *Shamans, Housewives, and Other Restless Spirits* (Honolulu: University of Hawaii Press, 1988).

Lame Deer, and R. Erdoes. *Lame Deer: Seeker of Visions* (New York: Simon & Schuster, 1972).

Lawson, E. Thomas. *Religions of Africa: Traditions in Transformation* (San Francisco: Harper & Row, 1984).

Olupona, Jacob K. *Beyond Primitivism: Indigenous Religious Traditions and Modernity* (New York: Routledge, 2003).

Pfeiffer, J. E. *The Creative Explosion* (New York: Harper & Row, 1982).

Ritchie, Mark. *Spirit of the Rainforest: A Yanomamo Shaman's Story* (New York: Island Lake Press, 1996).

Spindler, George, and Stockard, Janice E., eds. *Globalization and Change in Fifteen Cultures* (Belmont, CA: Thomson, 2007).

Sullivan, Lawrence A., ed. *Native Religions and Cultures of North America: Anthropology of the Sacred* (New York: Continuum, 2003).

Taylor, Timothy. *The Buried Soul: How Humans Invented Death* (Boston: Beacon, 2002).

Vitebsky, Piers. *The Shaman* (New York: Macmillan, 1995).

Notes

1. Marjorie Shostack, *Nisa: Autobiography of a Kung Woman* (New York: Random House, 1982), p. 16.
2. Ian Tattersall, "Once We Were Not Alone," *Scientific American*, January 2000, p. 62.
3. Lame Deer and R. Erdoes, *Lame Deer: Seeker of Visions* (New York: Simon & Schuster, 1972), pp. 136–137.
4. Summarized from Piers Vitebsky, *The Shaman* (New York: Macmillan, 1995), p. 125.
5. Quoted in Sherman Alexie, *The Lone Ranger and Tonto Fistfight in Heaven* (New York: Atlantic Monthly Press, 1993), p. 104.
6. David Chidester, "Colonialism and Shamanism," in Mariko Walter and Eva Fridman, eds., *Shamanism: An Encyclopedia of World Beliefs, Practices, and Culture* (Santa Barbara, CA: ABC Clio, 2004), p. 48.

Additional Resources

Aboriginal Culture (http://www.aboriginalculture.com.au/index.shtml). A detailed site that contains information about traditional Australian Aboriginal Cultures, including material culture, social organization, art, and Aboriginal religion.

African Traditional Religion (http://www.afrikaworld.net/afrel/). A site with essays and links discussing the practices of African tradition religions on the continent and in diaspora.

Foundation for Shamanic Studies (http://www.shamanism.org/). Website by the nonprofit organization dedicated to the preservation of shamanic cultures and spreading their beliefs and practices across the world.

Native Languages of the Americas (http://www.native-languages.org/religion.htm). A website written by Native American scholars and practitioners, with links to other sites on a variety of themes in religion and spiritual culture.

Virtual Religion Index: American Studies (http://virtualreligion.net/vri/america.html). A rich and exhaustive listing of Web resources on every aspect of Native American religious traditions.

THE MANY STORIES OF JUDAISM
3

Sacred and Secular

Overview

Diversity, as we shall see, is an essential characteristic of all religious traditions. In this chapter we seek to understand the diversity of the Jews of yesterday and today. Jews, like all other religious people, are divided on whether diversity is a good thing or a problem. In fact, that issue is a constant theme throughout the various chapters of this book. To appreciate its manifestation in Judaism, we can start by painting a clearer picture of the diversity we are talking about: In a neighborhood in Jerusalem, on a Friday evening as dusk approaches, ultra-Orthodox Jewish men, dressed in black suits and hats, close off their streets and neighborhoods to traffic in strict observance of the rules of the Sabbath as a holy day. The majority of Jerusalem's inhabitants are secular Israelis in modern Western dress who do not consider themselves to be religious Jews. They see themselves as only ethnically Jewish and choose to ignore the Sabbath and most other religious rules. Meanwhile, in a New York City neighborhood, a male rabbi leads the traditional worship at an Orthodox **synagogue**, a role not permitted to women among the Orthodox. Nevertheless, three blocks away a woman rabbi leads her more liberal, Reform congregation in a Friday night prayer service. There is, indeed, great diversity in Judaism today. And while, since the Holocaust, the majority of Jews worldwide

synagogue: community centered on prayer and study of Torah; the building in which the community meets for these activities

Israel: Jews as a religious people; also the land and state of Israel

reside either in **Israel** or in the United States, one can still find communities of Jews throughout Europe and scattered throughout the Middle East, Africa, Latin America, and Asia, including India and China.

Behind this modern diversity and the conflicting understandings of how to live a Jewish life that they express lies premodern **Rabbinic** Judaism, which provided the model for Jewish life from about the sixth century CE until the emergence of modern forms of Judaism in the nineteenth century. Indeed, ultra-Orthodox Jews see themselves as preserving premodern Judaism against the onslaught of modern Jewish diversity. Judaism is the smallest of the great world religions; its 14 million adherents comprise .2 percent of the world's population. Yet Jews have had, and continue to have, a major impact on history. Over the millennia, Judaism has been many things to many people in different times and places. Moreover, as we have said, some people today who consider themselves to be Jewish do not identify themselves as religious. Yet secular or ethnic ways of being Jewish, as we shall see, have had profound effects on the Jewish religion and so must be included in our survey to help us understand

Rabbinic: Judaism of the postbiblical premodern period

Judaism Timeline

2000 BCE	The approximate time for the events attributed to Abraham
1280	The time of the events attributed to Moses—Exodus, and Covenant
1240	Conquest of land of Canaan under Joshua
1004–965	King David
721	Fall of northern kingdom of Israel to Assyrians
586	Fall of southern kingdom of Judah to Babylonians
538	Return from Exile
198–167	Maccabean revolt against enforced Hellenization
63	Beginning of rule by Rome
ca. 30 CE	Hillel and Shammai—first of the Tannaim
70	Destruction of the second temple
73	Fall of Zealot fortress at Masada
90	Emergence of the Academy at Yavneh
90–200	Formation of the Mishnah
200–500	Formation of the Gemara
1070	Founding of Talmudic academy by Rashi in Troyes, France
1095	First Crusade—beginnings of pogroms—mass slaughter of Europe's Jews
1306	Jews expelled from France, beginning of pattern repeated throughout Europe
1700–1760	Hasidic leader Israel ben Eliezer, the Ba'al Shem Tov
1729–1786	Moses Mendelssohn, leading figure in Jewish *Haskalah* (Enlightenment) movement/Reform Judaism

the religion of Judaism. We will find great diversity among the Jewish people, but we shall also discover a common thread. That is the task of this chapter.

Jews take as the highest reality the God of creation and history, who revealed himself at Sinai, and they believe that to act in harmony with the will of this God is the highest goal of life. Indeed, the monotheism of both Christianity and Islam is rooted in this most ancient of the three traditions. Christianity and Islam also follow Judaism in seeing the gravest problem in human life as sin—the failure to live in harmony with the will of a God who demands justice and compassion. The ideal of life is living in harmony with the will of God. Sin disrupts that life-giving harmony. In Judaism, one overcomes the problem and realizes the ideal by means of the study and practice of God's teachings or revelation: **Talmud** Torah.

Talmud: the oral Torah and its commentaries written down

In Judaism, each and every human being is free to choose good or evil because each person stands before God in the same relationship that Adam and Eve did. The idea that the sin of the first two human beings, Adam and Eve, was inherited by all descendants, the Christian concept of original sin, does not exist in Judaism (nor in

1808–1888	Samson Raphael Hirsch, leading figure in emergence of Orthodox Judaism
1860–1904	Theodor Herzl, founder of modern Zionism
1917	Balfour Declaration—proposal for Jewish homeland in Palestine endorsed by British government
1933–1945	Rise and fall of Nazi Party; the Holocaust, 6 million Jews murdered
1939–1945	World War II
May 14, 1948	Birth of state of Israel
May 11, 1949	Israel admitted to United Nations
1967	Six-Day War, followed by emergence of Judaism of Holocaust and Redemption
1973	Yom Kippur War, followed by growth of ultra-Orthodox movements
1979	Camp David peace treaty between Egypt and Israel
1980s	*Intifada*: Palestinian uprising and escalation of conflict between Palestinians and Israelis
1993	*Oslo Accord*, developing increased autonomy for Palestinians and the framework for negotiating peace with Israel, followed by continued violence on the part of radicals on both sides who view compromise as betrayal; also, continued tension between secular Israeli Jews and ultra-Orthodox haredim and between Israeli haredim and Conservative and Reform Jews of the Diaspora
1995	Oslo II agreement establishing an independent Palestinian Authority
2002	Israeli construction of a wall of separation between Israel and the territories of the Palestinian Authority; conflict between Israelis and Palestinians continues in the following years

covenant: agreement between God and Israel promising God's protection in exchange for Israel's obedience to God's commandments

halakhah: religious commandments or laws of Talmudic Judaism; God's 613 commandments

mitzvot: God's commandments requiring deeds of loving kindness

Islam). In creating the people Israel, God gave them a gift to tip the balance between good and evil in favor of good. This was the dual Torah, the sacred oral and written teachings concerning God's revelation to his people. In giving Israel the Torah, God established a **covenant** (i.e., a binding agreement) with Israel, making them a holy people and reminding them: "I will be your God and you shall be my people, I will guide and protect you and you will obey my commandments." According to the story of Torah, God set before Israel the choice between life and death and made it possible for the people to choose life. This could be accomplished by following the 613 commandments that are God's law and called *halakhah*, which means "to walk in the way of God." These commandments require deeds of loving kindness, or *mitzvot*, by which the people would embody in their lives the justice and mercy of God as a model for all the world.

It would be misleading, however, to think that this summary sketch of the religious worldview of Judaism would be agreed to by all Jews. In the remainder of this chapter we shall try to understand both the unity and the diversity of Judaism as a religious tradition and the profound impact of the emergence of modernity on its development. We begin by discussing the twentiety-century encounter of Judaism with modernity that gave rise to ultra-Orthodoxy. We then go back to the historical beginnings of Judaism and trace its history, to understand the sources of the diverse threads of contemporary Judaism and the ongoing struggle to define its future. Because our goal is to understand Judaism's encounter with modernity, we shall focus primarily on those aspects that reveal the diversity of Judaism today and show how that diversity developed.   ○ ● ○

The interior of the Touro Synagogue in Newport, Rhode Island, the oldest synagogue in the United States, consecrated in 1763.

Encounter with Modernity: Modern Judaisms and the Challenge of Ultra-Orthodoxy

Premodern Rabbinic Judaism was a world unto itself. It embraced every aspect of life and offered safe haven from the non-Jewish world that largely rejected it while greatly restricting the role of Jews in the larger society. The modern world, by contrast, seems to offer Jews a new option—the possibility of sharing in its citizenship. Thus all modern forms of Judaism draw a line between the secular (i.e., nonreligious) and the religious and allow Jews to participate in both worlds.

Each modern form of Judaism tries to preserve an essential core of Judaism in a private sphere while allowing Jews to play active "nonreligious" roles in the secular, or public, world around them. For Reform Jews the essential unchanging core of Judaism is its ethics, while all beliefs in supernatural phenomena and all traditional ritualistic requirements can be changed as needed. For Conservative Jews the rituals must remain unchanged, but beliefs about the supernatural can be changed. The Orthodox say that neither beliefs nor rituals are negotiable but still allow that some parts of a Jew's life (secular education, job, etc.) can be carried out in the secular world. The new, late-twentieth-century, ultra-Orthodox movements reject even this compromise with the world. They seek to create a Jewish way of life, totally separate from both the modernizing forms of Judaism and the surrounding **gentile** (i.e., non-Jewish) world. They accomplish this for themselves by means of segregation: creating Jewish communities where all of life (the way one dresses, how and where one works, how one spends one's leisure time) is governed by supernatural beliefs and traditional ritual.

The ultra-Orthodox seek to recapture, as far as possible, the way of premodern Jews. And they hope to see the day (at least in Israel) when all modern forms of Judaism will disappear and their own communities will be the model for the whole of society. The goal of "deprivatizing" Judaism, so that its religious vision can shape all of public life, sets ultra-Orthodox Judaism apart from other modern forms of Judaism. At the same time, ultra-Orthodoxy rejects pluralism, a key characteristic of what some call "postmodernity." Because they fear that pluralism leads to religious and ethical relativism, they rebel against modern religious pluralism, insisting that there is one truth, one way of life to which all Jews must return if they are not to drown in a sea of relativism that will undermine any sense of higher purpose for life. For the ultra-Orthodox there cannot be many ways to keep the covenant—only one way. And that one way is all-encompassing. It does not permit a Jew to parcel out his or her life into separate secular and religious portions. Nor does it permit men and women to redefine their gender roles in new and "liberating" ways. Such redefinitions, they argue, will inevitably lead to moral chaos and the collapse of the family. Although only a minority of the world's Jewish population have opted for ultra-Orthodoxy, this way of being Jewish offers a challenge to Jews the world over to examine the implications of their modern spiritual and political beliefs: Can one be both modern and Jewish without sacrificing the essence of one's religious identity?

gentile: anyone not Jewish

The Conflict over Public Life: Religion and Politics in the State of Israel

Zionism: nineteenth-century Jewish secular political movement that promoted giving Jews their own national homeland

The conflict created by ultra-Orthodoxy is most obvious in the state of Israel, where public life was shaped initially by secular Jews with a nonreligious socialist-Zionist worldview. **Zionism** is a nineteenth-century Jewish secular political movement that promoted giving Jews their own national homeland. Since the 1990s, at least 80 percent of Israelis have remained secular. However, especially since the mid-1970s, the ultra-Orthodox have formed increasingly influential religious parties that seek to undo this secularity and place the public order under the rule of *halakhah*, the religious commandments or laws of premodern Talmudic Judaism.

Although a minority with considerable diversity and disagreement among themselves, the ultra-Orthodox share in the desire to make the public life of the secular state of Israel more religiously observant. They insist, for example, that all businesses be closed on the Sabbath, and they succeeded in having the Israeli legislature, the Knesset, pass a law requiring that all marriages be performed by Orthodox rabbis. In the eyes of the ultra-Orthodox, their secular, Reform, and Conservative brethren are not really Jews, and Orthodox Jews are not orthodox enough. All non-ultra-Orthodox Jews are urged to repent and return (*teshuvah*) to the true Judaism. Consequently, both Orthodox and ultra-Orthodox Jews have campaigned to amend an Israeli law enacted in 1950, two years after Israel achieved statehood. The act, called "the law of return," assures all post-Holocaust Jews that Israel is their homeland and grants automatic Israeli citizenship to all Jews, born of a Jewish mother, who apply. Orthodox and ultra-Orthodox partisans have repeatedly tried to have the law modified to prevent anyone who has not undergone an Orthodox conversion from being accepted for citizenship.

Religious political movements and religious parties in Israel are too diverse and complex to fully account for here, but we can understand something of the dynamics of their role in Israeli society by looking at representative groups. Beyond favoring segregation and opposing pluralism, the ultra-Orthodox are themselves quite diverse. The spectrum extends from tradition-bound anti-Zionists, such as the Neturei Karta (Guardians of the City), to something quite new, the transformation of modern secular Zionism into religious Zionism with movements like the Gush Emunim (Bloc of the Faithful). In between these extremes stand various compromise movements.

haredim: ultra-Orthodox Jewish movement that rejects all modernist forms of Judaism

The Neturei Karta emulate a centuries-old way of life that comes out of the traditions of the eastern European **haredim**, or "those of true piety." They and most other ultra-Orthodox movements have their roots in a strand of vigorously anti-Zionist eastern European Orthodoxy, which, unlike most of western European Orthodoxy, made no compromise with modernity. It is because they seek to preserve the way of life of premodern eastern European Judaism that the haredim refuse to permit secular education and modern dress.

Unlike the more modern Reform, Conservative, and Orthodox Jews, the ultra-Orthodox haredim do not live in communities having gentile residents, nor are they willing to mix with modern Jews who do not share their views. Rather, they live in ghetto-like communities typically led by a rabbi revered for his piety and Talmudic skill—communities where the faith is a way of life, untarnished by the compromises with modernity regarded as unavoidable by "modern" Jews. Certain that only the coming of the messiah in God's own time can bring about a true Jewish polity, the haredim reject the state of Israel as secular and profane.

The Gush Emunim, while remaining rigorously ultra-Orthodox in their observance of Jewish law, or *halakhah*, have developed a manner of dress (e.g., jeans, short-sleeved shirts, and skullcaps for the men) that distinguishes them from the haredim, in their wide-brimmed hats and long, black coats. Rather, the Gush identify with the secular Zionists who founded the state of Israel, whom they see as their secular counterparts.

Although the Gush Emunim do not accept the Jewish state in its secular form, they, unlike the Neturei Karta, have firmly endorsed the emergence of the secular state as in accordance with the divine will, seeing it as a step on the way to a genuine (*halakhah*-based) religiously observant Jewish state. Coming into existence early in 1974, the Gush Emunim represent a distinct branch of ultra-Orthodoxy. Unlike the Neturei Karta, they sought to transform secular Zionism—to put this form of nationalism on the correct path by making public life in Israel conform to religious law, or *halakhah*.

While religious Jews make up only about 20 percent of the population in Israel (and despite the anti-Zionist stance of most of them), the various political parties that represent them have managed to play a significant role in Israeli public life, because typically neither of the major secular parties—Labor and Likud—is able to secure enough votes to form a majority government without entering into a coalition with at least some of the religious parties. This state of affairs has given such religious parties bargaining power out of all proportion to their numbers.

Ultra-Orthodoxy as a Form of Fundamentalism

The rise of Ultra-Orthodoxy in Judaism is a part of a larger religious resurgence that has been going on in all religions and cultures around the globe since the mid-1970s. The late 1960s and early 1970s were a time of radical cultural disruption in Western urban secular societies—a time when the youth of the Western world, the children of those who experienced World War II, were rejecting what they described as the emptiness of modern secular culture. In their rejection, large numbers turned to various Eastern and Western religious movements as a way of recovering a sense of meaning and purpose in life. Indeed, the less modern and secular the movement, the more attractive it appeared.

One form that this religious resurgence took was distinctively fundamentalist. What all religious fundamentalist movements have in common is a desire to return to the foundations of belief and action that existed in their respective traditions prior to the coming of modernity. These movements see in contemporary culture, where many view all truth and all values as relative, the decadence of the modern period. So they think that this is a period in which most human beings have lost their way and have ended up in a world without standards and norms.

Much of the new strength of ultra-Orthodoxy is due to significant numbers of new adherents. These are mostly former secular Jews and modern religious Jews whose dissatisfaction with life made them receptive to the ultra-Orthodox movements. These Jews have made a leap of faith out of a world that either did not ask them to give their heart to anything (pure secularism) or asked them to give only a part of their heart (modern religious forms of Judaism). They have chosen a form of Judaism that promises to bring order and meaning to the whole of life, not just to a part of it; that requires a full-time commitment, not just a part-time commitment. They have sought to return to the fundamentals of the Judaism of the **dual Torah**—that is, premodern Rabbinic Judaism.

dual Torah: the scriptures of Rabbinic Judaism, composed of the written Torah (Tanak) and the written formulation of the oral Torah (Talmud)

The fundamentalist movements challenge modern forms of Judaism by refusing to reduce being Jewish to historical heritage, morality, and ethnicity. Ultra-Orthodox Jews attempt to recover what they believe has been lost to modern Judaism, namely, the centrality of God (as a living reality), Torah (as divine revelation), and Israel (as an eternal people). Ultra-Orthodoxy rejects all forms of secular Judaism and the diversity found in Judaism today. The ultra-Orthodox wish to revert to a time when, in their view, there was one truth and one way.

The total immersion in a deliberately premodern way of life represents to the ultra-Orthodox a definitive break with what it views as the decadence of Western civilization. And while the completeness of their immersion experience emulates that of the premodern tradition of Rabbinic Judaism, its self-consciousness does not. These "new" Jews have chosen to engage in an experiment, and in this sense their religion, too, belongs to the range of forms of Judaism of the modern/postmodern period. They, like all other religious persons of the modern era, have no choice but to choose. Their choice is between withdrawal from and involvement with the modern world, either back to what they somewhat romantically view as the "one way" of premodern Judaism or forward into pluralism. To understand the implications of this choice, we must return to the beginnings of premodern Judaism in the biblical period and work our way forward.

Premodern Judaism: The Formative Era (2000 BCE–500 CE)

The Biblical Roots of Judaism

Judaism, along with Christianity and Islam, is shaped by the myth of history, a concept we learned in Chapter 1. Indeed, the myth of history begins with Judaism. Judaism finds its roots in the story of the God who made promises to Abraham and his descendants that were fulfilled centuries later. This happened when the God of Abraham sent Moses to deliver his people from slavery to the Egyptians and lead them into the "land of promise"—the land of Canaan. From these beginnings the story blossomed into the full myth of history, which tells of the God who acts in time (i.e., in history) and leads his people on a journey through time toward a day of final resurrection in which all injustice, suffering, and death will be overcome.

While all religious traditions pass on their vision of reality through stories, story plays a unique role in Jewish religion. All the great religions of the world have told stories that draw on the metaphors of nature to explain religious experience. For instance, the cycles of nature are used to explain the wheel of death and rebirth in the myths of liberation from India and the rhythms of yin and yang in the myths of harmony from the religions of China. Analogies from nature are not absent from Judaism, but there is a clear shift of emphasis from nature to history. That is, if you want to understand who the God of Israel is, you do not look primarily to nature but to history as the story of the people Israel's journey with God through time. (In this chapter, *Israel* refers to the country and "the people Israel" to the biblical people of the Mosaic covenant from which Judaism developed.)

Indeed, for Judaism God is the divine storyteller, and the unfolding of creation in history is God's story. In the beginning God said, "Let there be light," and the story began. And the unfolding story will continue to play out in history until God brings it—after many trials and tribulations—to a happy conclusion at the end of time, when the dead are raised to enjoy a new heaven and a new earth.

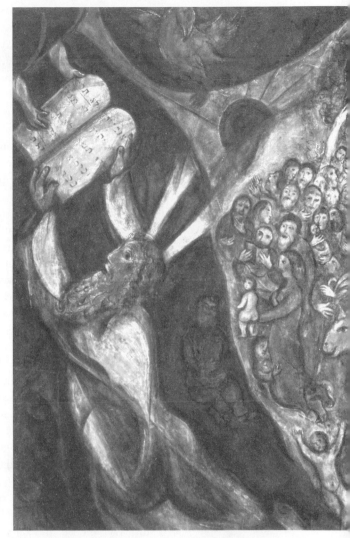

In this 1953 painting, *Moses Receiving the Tablets of the Law*, the Russian painter Marc Chagall portrays Moses receiving the Ten Commandments at Sinai. Jews trace the beginnings of Judaism to the covenant made between God and Israel at Sinai.

The Story Begins: One God Above All Others

The religiousness of ancient Israel that gave birth to Judaism developed against the background and influences of two great ancient polytheistic civilizations—Egyptian and Babylonian. Indeed, the names of the two greatest figures of the Torah, "Abraham" and "Moses," are, respectively, Babylonian and Egyptian names. And the biblical stories of both reflect this. Abraham is said to have migrated from Ur in Babylonia down into the land of Canaan, while Moses is born in Egypt, where the descendants of Abraham had migrated, seeking refuge from famine in their own land.

The great sociologist Max Weber (and many scholars since) argued that the beginning of the secularization of Western society began with the ancient Israelite religion that gave birth to Judaism. Although influenced by the religions of the Egyptians and Babylonians, ancient Israelite religion was strikingly different. For the Egyptians and the Babylonians, the world was the sacred embodiment of the gods (i.e., the waters, the land, the sun, etc., were all gods); then biblical religion came along and by the time of the Prophets had declared there is but one God and he is not the world but creator of the world. Therefore the world is secular, and God alone is holy—although the world can be sanctified, or made holy, by serving this God.

The story of the past, as it was imagined by the people Israel, proceeds from the creation of the first man and woman, Adam and Eve, to the near annihilation of humanity, as related in the story of Noah and the flood. Then came the division of humans into many language groups at the tower of Babel, God's call to Abraham to be a father of many nations, and God's promise to give the land of Canaan to the descendants of Abraham (Genesis 15). The story moves on to the migration of the family of Abraham's great-grandson Joseph into Egypt at a time of famine. It relates how the tribes of Israel, Abraham's descendants, became enslaved in Egypt and how God sent Moses to deliver them from slavery.

In the story of the Exodus, God assists Moses by sending down ten plagues on the Egyptians and then parting the waters of the Red Sea to enable the Israelites to escape to the land God gives them, in keeping with a promise made to Abraham (Genesis 15:18–21). According to this story, on the way to this land of promise God brought the people to Mount Sinai, gave the Torah to Moses, and formed a covenant with the people. As the book of Exodus (19:3–6) describes it:

> Moses went up to God, and the Lord called to him from the mountain [Mount Sinai], saying, "Thus shall you say to the house of Jacob, and tell the people of Israel; You have seen what I did to the Egyptians, and how I carried you on eagles' wings, and brought you to myself. Now therefore, if you will obey my voice indeed, and keep my covenant, then you shall be my own treasure among all peoples; for all the earth is mine; And you shall be to me a kingdom of priests, and a holy nation. These are the words which you shall speak to the people of Israel."

This description of the delivery of the covenant at Mount Sinai is a climactic moment in a powerful and dramatic story about a journey that created a holy people—the people Israel. In fact, the Hebrew word for holy (*qadosh*) suggests that to be holy is to be "set apart." So Israel was chosen out of all the nations and set apart to be God's people.

The story goes on to tell how the tribes of Israel wandered in the desert for forty years, entering the land of promise, under the leadership of Joshua only after the death of Moses (see Map 3.1). For the next 200 years they lived on the land

"I am the Lord your God who brought you out of the land of Egypt, the house of bondage: You shall have no other gods beside Me."

—NRSV, Exodus 20:1

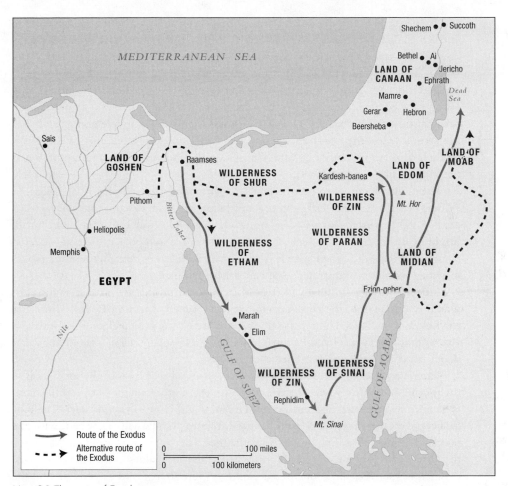

Map 3.1 The route of Exodus.

as a loose confederation under military leaders called *judges*. However, as threats of conquest from their neighbors became more frequent, many among the tribes began to demand to have a king like other nations, with a standing army to protect Israel. Some, however, argued that there could be only one king over Israel—the God of Abraham, Isaac, and Jacob. According to the story, God agreed to allow the people to have a king. And so Saul, chosen by God, was anointed with oil by a prophet, as a sign that the first king over Israel had been selected by God, not the people. Indeed, the concept of messiah (*mashiah*) has its beginnings here, for *messiah* means "anointed one," and it was understood that the one so anointed had been chosen to rule over the kingdom of God, the kingdom of Israel (1 Samuel 9:11–11:15).

Saul, however, proved to be a weak king, for he lacked independent authority and had to depend on the cooperation of the tribes, which could be uncertain. It was David, the second king over Israel, who established Israel as a nation. Under David and later his son Solomon, Israel claimed, for a brief time, to be the greatest nation in the Middle East. Stories were told of David's rise to power—how even as a young boy he had saved the tribes by slaying the Philistine giant, Goliath. Indeed, Saul, who had virtually adopted David as a member of the royal family, soon became jealous and turned on him. Forced to flee and fearing for his life, David became a Robin Hood type of figure, leading a private army of loyal followers. When Saul died in battle against the Philistines, David was proclaimed by the people and anointed as their king. Later, the northern tribes, called Israel, visited David and asked him to be their king, too. Soon he would consolidate the monarchy, becoming known as the king of all Israel and Judah.

David used his army to capture Jebus, a Canaanite city, renaming it Jerusalem, or "God's peace." Because Jerusalem had not belonged to any of the tribes of Israel, it gave David a neutral vantage point from which to rule over both Israel and Judah. David made his capital a holy city by bringing to it a sacred object, the gold-covered chest called the Ark of the Covenant, which was believed to contain the stone tablets inscribed with the commandments given at Mount Sinai.

Indeed, during David's reign it is said that God promised David that his heirs would rule Israel into the far distant future (2 Samuel 7:16). After David's death, his son Solomon succeeded him to the throne, and Israel was at the height of its power. It was Solomon who built the first **temple** so that God could dwell in a splendor greater than that of any of the gods of the other nations.

temple: the place in Jerusalem where the Jews worshiped

However, after the time of Solomon there was quarreling about the succession to the throne, and for over two centuries Israel (in the north) had one king and Judah (in the south) had another. Soon prophets like Amos and Hosea arose in Israel. The biblical prophets were revered persons believed to know God's will. They reminded the people that since abandoning their nomadic life to become farmers and city dwellers, they had been drifting further and further from the tribal values of the covenant made at Sinai. In the cities the people acted as if they were strangers to each other, and the rich mistreated the poor. The prophets warned that God would punish those who offered sacrifices in the temple while acting unjustly as citizens and neighbors. What God wants most of all, the pious believed, is the sacrifice of a pure heart committed to deeds of justice and compassion.

"Your house and your Kingdom shall be made sure forever before me; your throne shall be established forever."

—NRSV, 2 Samuel 7:16

The Story Continues with the Prophets—The One God of All

It is with the prophets that Jewish monotheism becomes fully formed, for in the tribal days of the time of Moses, Israel's commitment had been *henotheistic*—that is, to one God above all others. Thus the commandment "I am the Lord your God . . . you shall have no others beside me" did not mean that there were no other gods, only that Israel was forbidden to follow them. God was their tribal God. But after Israel was established as a great nation in the time of David, the prophets forced Israel to see that they did not own God, nor could they renege on the covenant once in the land of promise. The covenant conferred not so much privileges as responsibilities. According

to the prophets, Israel's God was the God of all the nations and he would use the other nations, if necessary, to punish Israel for any failure to keep the covenant.

King David conquered the Canaanite city of Jebus and sanctified it by placing the Ark of the Covenant there. Renamed Jerusalem by David, the city has ever since been holy for Jews.

Instructed by the prophets, the people Israel began to think of God in the manner expressed in the book of Genesis—as the creator of all things and all peoples. From the eighth century BCE forward, Israel would become progressively convinced that having "no other gods" required more than loyalty to a tribal deity. It required affirming that there were no other gods. Out of the prophetic experience came the pure and simple creed of Judaism, the **Shema**: "Hear O Israel, the Lord our God, the Lord is one" (Deuteronomy 6:4). This confession is completed by reminding the people to love this God with all their heart, soul, and strength; to pray the *Shema* on arising and retiring; and to bind its words on their hands, foreheads, and doorposts to ensure that the awareness of the one true God might permeate their every thought and action.

Shema: in Judaism, the essential confession of monotheistic faith

The prophets warned the people that if they did not return to the covenant, the God of Israel, Lord of all creation and history, would punish them. And that is exactly how the misfortunes of Israel and Judah came to be interpreted. For in 721 BCE the Assyrians conquered the kingdom of Israel and carried its inhabitants off into slavery. In 621 Judah's King, Josiah, is said to have discovered in the temple what he believed to be the long-lost book of the law (the biblical book of Deuteronomy). These writings echoed the teachings of the prophets about the need to practice justice to please

"Thus says the Lord to his anointed (messiah), to Cyrus, . . . For the sake of my servant Jacob, and Israel my chosen, I call you by your name, I surname you, though you do not know me."

—NRSV, Isaiah 45:1 & 4

God. On this basis Josiah initiated a reform that included a renewal of the covenant and designated the temple in Jerusalem as the only proper site for sacrifices. However, according to the biblical story, the reforms were not observed conscientiously, and God again allowed the people to be punished. In 586 the Babylonians conquered the Assyrians and their territories, destroyed the temple Solomon had built, and carried off the inhabitants of the southern kingdom of Judah into exile and slavery.

As the time of the Babylonian exile approached, another generation of prophets arose—Jeremiah, Ezekiel, and Isaiah—spanning the time of exile and eventual return. These prophets asserted that God was indeed punishing Israel for its failure to keep the covenant, but they added that the punishment would be temporary (to teach them a lesson). As it happened, the Persians soon conquered the Babylonians, and after only fifty years, in 538, the Israelites were permitted to return to the land. This turn of events was due to the benevolent policy of the Persian king, Cyrus. That a pagan king should so favor the Israelites was seen as miraculous, and Cyrus was declared a messiah, that is, one anointed by God to carry out God's will to return his people to their land (Isaiah 45:1–13). Cyrus himself, of course, was not aware of this role attributed to him in the destiny of Israel. Thus we see that even in the biblical period, Judaism was capable of finding religious significance in secular political events.

A model of the city of Jerusalem centered around the temple as it might have looked in 50 BCE.

The Story Becomes One of Exile and Return

When the first wave of exiles returned to the land (520–515 BCE), the leadership was weak and the people lacked a clear direction. It was not until Ezra, a priest, and Nehemiah, a gifted layman, led a second wave of exiles (458 BCE) in a return to the land of Israel that a clear pattern for a postexilic Judaism emerged. These leaders demanded that the people repent: They had married citizens of other nations and sacrificed to other gods, and now they must rededicate themselves to the covenant and repurify themselves as a holy people by separating themselves from their neighbors. It is with this priestly reform that Judaism adopted the experience of exile and return, in which they saw the liberation from slavery in Babylon as a repeat of the liberation from slavery in Egypt. So exile and return became the normative pattern through which to interpret all past and future Jewish experiences. Whenever Jews felt persecuted and exiled they would hope for the day of return—"Next year in Jerusalem" became their cry. In this sense, the experience of exile and return gave birth to Judaism.

In the fourth century BCE, Alexander the Great conquered the ancient world, and after his death in 323 his empire was divided among his generals. For over a century the Ptolemies ruled over Israel (301–198). They were replaced by the Seleucids (198–167), who began a policy of enforced Hellenization, requiring all their conquered peoples to adopt Greek customs and beliefs, including veneration of many gods. The Jews, who refused to abandon their worship of the God of Abraham, Isaac, and Jacob, were severely persecuted for their noncompliance. Thus in the middle of the second century, Judas Maccabaeus and his brothers led a revolt against the cruel Seleucid ruler Antiochus Epiphanes IV. This effort, the Maccabean revolt, was successful in bringing about a status of semi-independence, which lasted into the first century CE. However, in a bid to resist new efforts at control by the Seleucids, the Jews in 63 BCE invited in the Romans to protect them. After the Exile, the temple was rebuilt on a modest scale and then later, between 20 BCE and 60 CE under the domination of Rome, the second temple was rebuilt on a grander scale. It is from the time of Alexander through the time of the Roman Empire that the religion of ancient Israel splintered and developed into a variety of forms of Judaism, each claiming they represented the true practice of faith.

The Historical Roots of Diversity

By the first century the most important of these new Jewish movements were the Sadducees, the Pharisees, the Hellenists, the Samaritans, the Zealots, the Essenes, and the Nazarenes—all of which were engaged in ongoing debate. Today we would be tempted to say the debate was about the right way to be Jewish, but the idea of Judaism as a religion did not yet exist. Rather, the partisans of the first century saw the debate as about an attempt to define how one must live to be the "true Israel," or the true people of God. To understand this debate it is important to remember that at the beginning of the first century there was no official Bible and no set of practices and commitments accepted as normative by all Jews (see Timeline on pp. 78–79). It was only at the end of the first century that the **Tanak**, or Bible of Judaism as we have it today, came into existence, along with Rabbinic Judaism as the normative pattern of Judaism for the next 1,800 years.

Tanak: the written Torah, or Hebrew Bible

Now, let's consider each of these movements in a little more detail. The Sadducees came from the wealthy upper class, were associated with the temple tradition that was exclusive to Jerusalem, and saw their task as keeping peace with Rome. They accepted only the five books of Moses as sacred scripture and insisted on literal adherence to the written Torah.

The Pharisees were teachers associated with the synagogues (houses of study and prayer) found in every city and village; they accepted not only the books of Moses but also the historical and wisdom writings and those of the prophets. Both the Jewish Bible (Tanak) and the Christian Old Testament are largely derived from the Pharisees' selection of scriptural materials. The Pharisees taught that God revealed himself in the written Torah and through oral traditions that accompanied the giving of the Torah to Moses. Moreover, they insisted that the written word could not be properly interpreted without the oral traditions. In these teachings the Pharisees offered a precursor to the later Rabbinic doctrine of God's revelation through the dual Torah, the oral and the written. Politically, the Pharisees were neither cozy with the Romans nor openly hostile to them.

Diaspora: the dispersion of a religious people outside their geographic homeland

Jews who were dispersed in the Roman Empire (i.e., outside the protectorate of Palestine) were known as the Jews of the **Diaspora**. The leaders of their synagogues were Hellenistic Jews who used a Greek translation of scriptures that closely corresponded to the Hebrew scriptures of the Pharisees, with some important exceptions. The Hellenists were the great missionaries of Judaism, who used Greek philosophy to explain the meaning of the biblical stories. They were anxious to promote Judaism as a religion that had a place for gentiles, and they adapted Judaism to Greek customs whenever feasible. They successfully encouraged large numbers of gentiles to come and worship the one true God of Israel.

Finally, there were sectarian movements like the *Zealots*, the *Samaritans*, the *Essenes*, and the *Nazarenes* (the followers of Jesus of Nazareth). Some, like the Zealots and Essenes, were openly hostile to the gentile world, whereas the Nazarenes, like the Hellenists, were very positive toward gentiles and sought their conversion. Adherents of these movements tended to be apocalyptic, believing that God would bring the world to an end soon and so would send a messiah to judge all human beings and reward the faithful. In the first century there was no single clear definition of *messiah*. A wide variety of speculations emerged, and each sectarian group had its own ideas. Most were expecting a spiritual leader, but some, primarily the Zealots, looked for a military leader able to overthrow the Romans, whose rule in Palestine had become oppressive.

What was typical of these sectarian movements was a strong distrust of the Sadducees, who were viewed as having sold out to the Romans. The Zealots, the most hostile of all, had nothing but contempt for the Sadducees and chose to oppose them directly. If the Sadducees urged, "Don't rock the boat," the Zealots were committed to rocking the boat as often as possible. To this end, they staged random guerrilla attacks against the Roman legions. In the second century a Zealot, Simon bar Kokhba, claimed the title of messiah and was executed by the Romans.

circumcision: the cutting of the foreskin as a sign of the covenant of Abraham

Finally, at least some of the sectarian groups practiced baptismal rites, that is, ritual immersion and purification. Ritual immersion was already a requirement for any gentile convert to Judaism (along with **circumcision** for males). From the first century on, however, some groups insisted that not only gentile converts were to be immersed and purified, but also Jews, if they had strayed from the true path of Judaism as understood by the particular sectarian movement.

Exodus and Exile: Story, History, and Modernity

The difference between premodern and modern is the difference between sacred story (scripture) and secular story (history). Fundamentalists fear the incursion of time and history into their sacred story, whereas modernists welcome it. The biblical writings as we have them are organized to tell a story of God's saving journey with his people. It is, as we have noted, the story of the God who acts in time and leads his people through time toward a final fulfillment. This is a grand story that answers questions of origin and destiny for the Jews as a religious people: Where do we come from? Where are we going? When modern historians read this story, they ask different questions. Primarily they want to know if things really happened as described in the sacred texts. They try to find out by comparing the stories with what else is known about the past through ancient writings, through literary analysis of stylistic changes in the writings, and through archaeological artifacts.

When historians began to read the biblical stories critically, they believed they could identify different layers of historical development in the scriptural writings. It is on this basis that they identified four major layers of historical materials: J and E (Jahwist and Elohist, from two different Hebrew names for God), from the period of the monarchy of David and Solomon (ca. 1000 BCE); D (Deuteronomic, ca. 621 BCE), associated with the prophetically rooted reforms of King Josiah; and P (priestly, ca. 458 BCE), associated with the priestly reforms of Ezra and his administrative successor, Nehemiah. Today biblical scholars do not think that the historical materials can be sorted out quite that neatly, but the recognition of historical layers remains essential to the historical study of biblical writings.

The earliest stories (J and E) seem to have been written down in the courts of David and Solomon to tell the story of how God chose Israel, from humble beginnings, to become a great kingdom. Bringing together diverse ancient tribal narratives, the royal storytellers constructed a larger and more complex story that begins with the creation of the world and ends with the kingdom of Israel under David and Solomon as the greatest nation of the ancient Middle East. It is an unambiguous story of promise and fulfillment. However, the story had to be revised in light of the Babylonian exile. The Priestly revision describes Israel as a people shaped by seemingly broken promises that are unexpectedly fulfilled, at least in part, leading to new hope and new life—a story of exile and return.

If the Exodus was the founding event of the story of Judaism, the Exile was its formative event. As one distinguished scholar of Judaism, Jacob Neusner, has noted, it was the great crisis of exile and the astonishment of return that set the mythic pattern of Judaic thought and experience ever since.[1] The exile and return provided a story pattern through which all past and future events, whether of triumph or of tragedy, could be meaningfully integrated into Jewish identity. "Exile and return" shaped the imagination of all future generations. No longer did Israel think of itself as David did (in 1 Chronicles 22:1–19), as having an unconditionally guaranteed existence. On the contrary, its existence was dependent on its commitment to the covenant.

Therefore, the fall of the second temple at the hands of the Romans in 70 CE was a trauma and a deep blow to those who wholeheartedly believed the story of the God who leads his people through time, but the crisis was not without precedent or without meaning. For although the power of leadership shifted once more, this time from the priests to the teachers (i.e., rabbis), the rabbis immediately reverted to the priestly pattern of explanation, arguing once more that the cause of the present misfortune was that Israel had not kept the covenant faithfully enough. Consequently, although the disasters that befell the first and second temples were two of the most traumatic events in the long history of Judaism, neither destroyed the faith of Jews. On the contrary, in each case Jews came to the conclusion that the loss of the temple was not a sign of God's abandonment but a call to the people Israel to be more fully observant of the covenant. Thus today Jews willingly recall these two disastrous events on the holy day of **Tisha B'Av**, for remembering brings about not despair and hopelessness but repentance and renewal.

Tisha B'Av: day of mourning to commemorate tragedies affecting the people Israel

From Torah to Talmud

The Pharisaic Roots of Rabbinic Judaism

To follow the emergence of Rabbinic, or Talmudic, Judaism, we need to resume our discussion of the various Jewish sects and movements that existed in the first century. Such diversity was brought to an end by the destruction of the temple in 70 CE. Of the movements that had been vying to provide a model for Jewish life, only a few survived, and of these it was the Pharisees who provided new leadership. There were at least three reasons for this.

First, the political neutrality of the Pharisees in the period before the fall of the temple made them appealing to the Romans. Unlike the Zealots, the Pharisees seemed benign in their views of the Roman Empire. So the Roman authorities gave them permission to establish an academy at Yavneh on the coast of present-day Israel. There they began the task of reconstructing Judaism for a new period of exile apart from the land and the temple. Second, the Pharisees were already the leaders of the synagogue tradition and the teachers (rabbis) of the importance of the oral tradition. And finally, the oral tradition the Pharisees had espoused gave them the flexibility to interpret the requirements of Jewish life in changing circumstances. Thus when the temple priesthood disappeared, no new institutions needed to be invented. The Pharisees became the natural leaders by default everywhere in ancient Palestine.

The task of the new leadership was to transpose the priestly model focused on the temple in Jerusalem into a new key—one that would allow the people Israel, like their ancestors in Babylon, to survive as Jews apart from the land and the temple. The solution the Pharisees arrived at was a model in which the people Israel (not just the temple) were holy, and every male head of a Jewish household was in fact a priest, even as the table in every Jewish house was an altar. In this new model, the center of Jewish life shifted from written Torah to the oral tradition, from priest to rabbi, from temple to synagogue, and also from temple altar to family table.

The priestly tradition had insisted that Israel was a holy people, set apart for service to the one true God, and had established elaborate rules of ritual separation to keep the people from blending in with the general population. The Pharisees, drawing on the prophets, insisted that what God wanted more than cultic worship, with its sacrifices, was deeds of loving kindness (*mitzvot*)—that is, acts of justice and mercy. To this end, then, the Pharisees transferred the rituals of separation from the temple cult to a system of ethics. The prophets had issued sweeping demands, in the name of God, for justice and mercy. The Pharisees took these demands and made them the content for the priestly rituals of holiness, working out their application in all the details of everyday life according to the best insights of the oral tradition. Between the second and fifth centuries, Rabbinic Judaism, or the Judaism of the dual Torah, emerged as the insights of the oral tradition were written down and incorporated into what became known as the Talmud. And it was this Talmudic tradition that shaped Jewish life from the sixth century until the advent of Jewish modernizing movements in the nineteenth century.

The heart of the teachings of the Pharisees was that God was a loving personal father who chose Israel and entered into the covenant with them. This is the covenant revealed in the oral and written Torah which teaches that each and every individual who keeps this covenant can live in hope of resurrection from the dead. Although the Pharisees are depicted as legalists in some of the Christian scriptures, historians have shown quite the contrary. What the Pharisees actually taught was that the sacrifices that God wants are deeds of loving kindness rooted in a pure heart, not merely external observance of divine laws.

The Pharisees asked Jews to love God above all and their neighbor as themselves. They insisted that what is hateful to oneself must not be done to one's neighbor. They insisted that humans do not live by bread alone, and therefore one should trust in God rather than worry about tomorrow. They insisted that those who would seek the will of God would find it and that those who humbled themselves would be exalted. All these teachings were adopted by Christianity as well, as we shall see in Chapter 4.

The Rabbis and the Formation of the Talmud

Hillel and Shammai were the two leading rabbis, or teachers of oral tradition, in the first century of the common era (CE). Their influence led to the development of two major schools: the house of Hillel (*Bet Hillel*) and the house of Shammai (*Bet Shammai*). The disputes between Hillel and Shammai, and their schools, eventually became the foundation of the Talmud and set the tone of disputation and dialog that is characteristic of Talmudic Judaism. Both Hillel and Shammai sought to apply the oral Torah tradition to the details of everyday life. In general it is said that Shammai interpreted the demands of Torah more strictly and severely. Hillel tended to be more lenient and compassionate in his decisions. In general, although not always, it is the teachings of Hillel that shaped the emerging Talmudic tradition. And it was the students of Hillel who were the primary shapers of the **Mishnah**—the writings that form the core of the Talmud.

It was the disciples of Hillel and Shammai and their descendants who led the Jews into the Talmudic era. A disciple of Hillel, Johanan ben Zakkai, started the academy at Yavneh. There the first task was to settle one of the key arguments that had been going on in Judaism at the beginning of the century—namely, which writings of the

"If water, which is soft, could hollow out the hard stone, the words of the Torah, which are hard, will certainly make an impression on my soft heart."
—Rabbi Akiva

"Do not unto your neighbor what you would not have him do unto you. This is the whole of the Jewish law. All else are but commentaries."
—Rabbi Hillel

Mishnah: the writings that form the core of the Talmud

The Talmud records the ongoing discussion of Torah by the great rabbinic minds across the ages and is meant to be studied and debated in a communal setting.

tradition to regard as holy and, therefore, as revelations from God. The argument, of course, was settled by default. Since the Pharisees survived to reestablish Judaism, it was the writings they revered that were selected to comprise the canon, the official set of scriptures. Unsurprisingly, the Pharisees did not limit their choices to the Torah, that is, the books attributed to Moses. In addition to the five books called the Pentateuch (Genesis, Exodus, Leviticus, Numbers, Deuteronomy), the Pharisees included the books of the prophets (e.g., Jeremiah and Ezekiel, Amos and Hosea), some historical writings (e.g., First and Second Kings), and also the writings of the wisdom literature (e.g., Proverbs, Ecclesiastes, Job). Thus it was the academy at Yavneh that settled on the books that make up the Bible of Judaism, known as the *Tanak*—an acronym standing for

- Torah (teachings),
- Neviim (prophets), and
- Ketuvim (writings).

In Western culture it has often been thought that to compare the teachings of Judaism and Christianity, all one need do is compare the Tanak, or Hebrew Bible (which Christians call the Old Testament), with the New Testament. Such a view, however, is totally misleading. The Talmud and the New Testament are like two different sets of glasses for reading the Hebrew Bible. Through the Talmud glasses, certain passages seem very clear and easy to read, while other parts are fuzzy and unreadable. And with New Testament glasses, the fuzzy passages become clear, and vice versa. Both Jews and Christians read the Hebrew Bible through the eyes of a further revelation (Talmud and New Testament) that tells them how to read the Hebrew scriptures, including what is valid and what can be dismissed. Thus Jews and Christians who seem to be reading an important body of holy writings in common might just as well be reading two different books—which, in a sense, they are. Consequently, to understand Judaism one must understand the Talmud and the central role it plays in Judaism.

The Talmud and the Torah

With the Jewish people's sacred teachings committed to writing in the written Torah, or Tanak, the **Tannaim** ("those who study") began the paradoxical process of writing down the vast and diffuse teachings of the oral tradition and transforming this material into the oral Torah. The process occurred in two phases.

> **Tannaim:** the generation of sages who created the Mishnah

First, the Tannaim, led by Hillel and Shammai, organized the wisdom of the Jewish oral tradition into categories, or *seders*, covering six areas of everyday life: agriculture, sabbaths and festivals, women and property, civil and criminal law, laws of conduct for cultic ritual and temple, and rules for maintaining cultic purity. Then the discussions of the rabbis recalling the wisdom of the oral Torah on each of these areas were written down. This collection of materials, known as the *Mishnah*, codifies the wisdom of the oral Torah. The Mishnah was intended to show Jews how they could sanctify life (i.e., make it holy) despite their loss of the temple and absence from the land of Israel.

In the second phase of Talmudic formation, the successors to the Tannaim, the *Amoraim* ("those who interpret"), set about developing a commentary on the Mishnah that would link the oral to the written Torah. The result of their work was called the **Gemara**, and these writings in combination with the Mishnah form the Talmud (meaning "learning" or "study" as related to Torah).

> **Gemara:** commentary on the Mishnah, and part of the Talmud

Even though the Talmud (Mishnah and Gemara) is said to have been completed by the sixth century, there is a sense in which the Talmud is never complete. For example, sages in the tradition, the Geonim (eminent scholars), followed up the work of the Amoraim by providing the *Responsa*—further commentaries on the Talmud. These writings constitute answers to requests from Jews throughout the Diaspora for insight and guidance in applying the teachings of the Talmud to the problems of everyday life. The tradition of commentary, which continues from generation to generation, is integral to Judaism, leaving the Talmudic traditions, as an expression of oral Torah, open to continuous development.

Producing the Talmud by writing down the oral Torah surely seems like a self-contradictory task. And yet the genius of the Talmud is in preserving the oral character of the material in written form. To appreciate the uniqueness of the Talmud

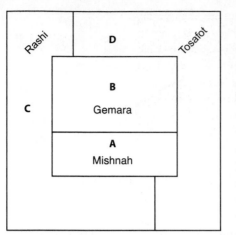

A page of the Talmud.

one really has to look at it and see how its pages are constructed. A typical page is made up of diverse and distinct parts, coexisting on the same piece of paper. These parts express the voices of the rabbis throughout the ages, and teachings about the same subject are juxtaposed on the same page. The Talmud is an ongoing dialog among Jews not only of the same time period but from age to age. At the core of a page you may find statement (A) from the Mishnah of the second century outlining the opposing points of view of Hillel and Shammai on a question of appropriate behavior. Above this text, on the same page, might be a section of the Gemara (B) from a period 200 or 300 years later, relating the Mishnah to relevant passages from the Tanak and to the diverse opinions of the Amoraim, who comment on the meaning of the Mishnah in light of the scriptures and of the opinions of the Tannaim. Typically, as well, there will be a section (C) devoted to the commentary of the greatest of the Rabbinic Talmudic scholars, Rashi. In yet another section (D) will be the commentaries of the students of Rashi from a collection known as the *Tosafot*. Each of these expresses views on the meaning of the passages of the Mishnah in light of the comments of the others and in light of additional commentaries and writings that supplement the tradition. The sections on a given page of the Talmud might span a thousand years or more.

Although Talmudic decisions are made to guide the life of the Jewish community, it would be a mistake to think that the whole point of Talmud study is to reach a conclusion. For Talmudic study is a form of religious ritual whose purpose is nothing less than to bring the student of Torah to experience God through the thrust and parry of argument about the one thing that matters most in life—God's word. That is why it is not unheard of for a debating partner to help an opponent who is stumped for a response by suggesting a line of argument that might be able to refute the point the stronger partner has just made. In this way the Talmud sanctifies doubt and questioning as a medium of religious experience that brings one in touch with God. God is in the questions even more than in the answers. For this reason too, then, the Talmud is never finished as long as there is one more Jew ready to join the debate. It is a tradition of commentary upon commentary that guarantees that the Talmud is always both ancient and ever fresh and new. The Talmud is always about how one is to make the new day holy.

This understanding of Talmudic debate echoes the Torah story that explains how Israel got its name: According to Genesis (32:23–32), one night Jacob wrestled with a stranger who refused to tell his own name but, rather, blessed Jacob and gave him a new name, Israel, meaning "one who has wrestled with God and men and prevailed." As the sun arose, Jacob limped away, convinced that he had "seen God face to face."

So the Torah teaches that Israel is the one God has chosen to wrestle with, and the way of Torah is a wrestling with the God who cannot be named (or, for that matter, imaged). The Torah teaches that the one who wrestles not only with God (and God's Torah) but with other humans (about the meaning of Torah) can prevail. Indeed, to

A page of the Torah in Hebrew, illustrating the use of a pointer called a "yad" (the Hebrew word for "hand") to follow the text.

wrestle with the Torah is to see God face to face, to be transformed and given a new name: Israel, or "wrestler with God." Hence in Rabbinic Judaism there is no higher calling than to wrestle with others over the meaning of God's Torah. This activity is one that includes rather than excludes those who disagree. According to Talmudic tradition, when the rabbis disagree on the observance of *halakhah*, the majority opinion is to prevail for the good of order. Yet it is understood that those in the minority are not necessarily wrong. The Torah is large enough to embrace everyone.

Indeed, the story of the covenant at Sinai, through which God chose Israel, suggests just such a give-and-take relationship. According to the story, the covenant established that day was a *mutual* agreement between two parties, much like a marriage contract that is both a legal arrangement and an expression of mutual love and care. In this covenant the people promise to obey the commandments of God and walk in the way of the Torah, which gives life. And God promises to guide and protect them on their journey through time. Throughout this journey, God and Israel have wrestled with each other—at one moment God is reminding Israel that by their sins the people have strayed from their promise to obey the commandments, and at another moment Israel is reminding God that he appears to have strayed from his promises to guide and protect. Within the bounds of the covenant, each party can be held accountable by the other. It is this covenant that makes Israel *Israel*—that is, the chosen people. For the rabbis, the identity of the Jews lay not in their national or ethnic history, although within the myth or symbolic story of Torah they surely embraced that history. Nor is the people's Jewishness a function of their being, by choice, members of a religion called *Judaism*; in fact, there is no word for *Judaism* in biblical Hebrew!

"The world is suspended in space and has nothing to rest on except the breath of Torah study from the mouths of students—just as a man may keep something up in the air by the blowing of his breath."
—Talmud

kosher: what
is suitable or fit,
particularly in reference
to Jewish dietary laws

Instead, the Jewish identity lies in having been chosen, before all creation, to be God's beloved eternally. The rabbis reminded the people how God had brought them to himself on eagles' wings, to be a holy people (Exodus 19:3–6), set apart to be a witness to the holiness of life. In this "setting apart" lies the ultimate meaning of the rules for **kosher** dining that forbid Jews to eat pork, to mix meat and milk, and so on. Even what one eats and the way one eats should remind the world that life is not meant to be profane and meaningless. Rather, a holy life, one that is set apart, is not one's own but belongs to God. Indeed, every act of one's life, whether in work, in eating, in the bedroom, or in prayer, should be a witness to the One who alone is truly holy and in turn sanctifies all creation.

Torah, in the Talmudic tradition, is a multidimensional word. In its narrowest sense, Torah refers to the Pentateuch, the first five books of the Bible. In a broader sense it refers to the entire Bible, or Tanak. Broader still is its meaning as the dual Torah—that is, Torah plus Talmud. And ultimately Torah is the source and pattern for all creation, for, according to the Talmud, when God created heaven and earth he did it by consulting the Torah, which was already with God in the beginning. Hence the Torah provided the pattern for the right order of the universe, a pattern revealed in the *halakhah*, given through oral and written Torah. It was this understanding of the dual Torah (Torah plus Talmud) that shaped classical Judaism.

Premodern Judaism: The Classical Era (500 CE–1729 CE)

The Premodern Rabbinic World: God, Torah, and Israel

If human beings are not only storytellers but also storydwellers, then the Torah story of the rabbis was a magnificent dwelling indeed. If religion (*religio*) is about being "tied and bound" into the cosmic drama of life by one's story symbolically told (myth) and enacted (ritual), then Torah was, and is, just such a story. The Torah story of the rabbis created the cosmic vision of classical Judaism. It is a story that embraces not only every minute, hour, and day of Rabbinic Jewish life, providing a template to make it holy, but also the whole of time, from the creation of the world to its ultimate messianic redemption.

bar mitzvah: rite of
passage for Jewish
boys to become full
members of the religion
of Judaism; the **bat
mitzvah** is a parallel
rite for girls

In the premodern world, the right to live within this story accompanied being born of a Jewish mother (and also those who were converts). While women thus determined Jewish identity, the primary guardians of Rabbinic religious life were men. Males alone had to be confirmed in their religious status through two key rituals: circumcision shortly after birth, and **bar mitzvah**, a ceremony in which they demonstrated their knowledge of the faith as they entered adulthood at age thirteen.

Observant Jews, like this young man putting on *tefillin*, declare God's oneness by binding the Torah scrolls to their bodies before daily prayer.

The Jews of the Rabbinic age of classical Judaism ate, drank, and slept Torah. The men began the day by dressing in garments with fringes (*tzitzit*) to remind them of the commandments of the covenant (Numbers 15:37–40). Before morning prayer, they wrapped the words of Torah (Deuteronomy 6:4–9) on their arms and foreheads, encased in small leather boxes known as *tefillin*, or phylacteries. Indeed, every act of the day would be couched in prayer. And every Sabbath (the seventh day of the week), all work ceased and eternity pervaded all things as the people both recalled the beginning of creation and contemplated its fulfillment to come in the messianic era at the end of time. No matter what suffering history brought to Israel, on the Sabbath an eternal people dwelled with their eternal God, savoring a foretaste of that messianic day for which all creation was made—when God will be all in all.

The meaning of the Sabbath unfolded in the portion of Torah assigned for every week of the year, organized around a great cycle of festivals. From New Year's, which begins with the story of creation on Rosh Hashanah (literally, "head of the year") and concludes ten days later with stories of divine judgment on Yom Kippur (day of atonement), through Passover (liberation/redemption of the Exodus) to the Feast of Weeks (the giving of the dual Torah and the covenant) to the Feast of Booths (the wandering in the desert, awaiting the fulfillment of the promises) as well as the commemoration of disasters averted (Purim) and not averted (Tisha B'Av), the great story unfolded. The story of Torah stretched out over the lives of Jews from the beginning of the day until the end of the day, from the beginning of the year until the end of the year, from the beginning of their lives until the end of their lives, and from the beginning of time until the end of time. In the Torah story, God and Israel

RITUALS AND RITES: Rituals of the Life Cycle

Rituals marking the important transitions in the life of the individual can be found in all religious traditions. In Judaism these are the *Bris* or *Brit milah*, the bar and bat mitzvah, and the rituals for marriage, and death.

Bris or Brit Milah

In accordance with the teachings of the Torah (Genesis 17:10–14), every male child must be circumcised when he is eight days old, as a sign of the covenant between God and his people. This ceremony is known as the *Bris* or *Brit milah* (derived from the Hebrew for "covenant" and for "circumcision"). During this ritual the child is named and the foreskin of his penis is cut off as an external sign of the covenant. This ritual ties and binds every male child's life to the eternal covenant between God and his people, renewing that covenant with each generation, child by child.

Bar and Bat Mitzvah

When a boy reaches the age of adulthood, thirteen, he is eligible to become a bar mitzvah (son of the commandments, or covenant); to this end, he is expected to demonstrate the ability to carry out his responsibilities in maintaining the religious life of the community. After intense training by his rabbi in the study of Hebrew and of Torah and Talmud, the young man is called forth at a synagogue service to recite the blessing that precedes the reading of the Torah. Then he reads the Torah portion for the week and then a portion of scripture from the Prophets. He may also be asked to comment on the meaning of the passages. By doing this the boy shows that he is able to function as a full member of the religious community. Once he has completed this ceremony he is considered to be an adult, qualified to form part of the *minyan* (ten adult males) required for any Jewish worship service. With the appearance of the Conservative and Reform Jewish communities the ritual has been extended to include young women as well. For them the ritual is called the bat mitzvah (daughter of the commandments, or covenant).

Marriage

A Jewish wedding takes place under a *huppah*, a sort of grand prayer shawl stretched over four poles that can be said to symbolize the heavens and God's creation, even as the bride and groom stand in the place of Adam and Eve, the first man and woman created by God. In the marriage ceremony, prayers and blessings sanctify the union of a man and a woman by binding them to each other and to the story of Israel's relation to God, from creation through exiles and tribulations to joyous redemption in the new Zion. Before entering under the canopy, the man places the veil over the bride's face. Under the canopy the marriage contract (*ketubah*) is witnessed, the couple are betrothed and married with an exchange of rings, and the words "Behold, you are sanctified to me by this ring in accord with the tradition of Moses and Israel" are followed by seven blessings said over a cup of wine. It is customary, at the end of the ceremony, for the groom to step on and break a glass, symbolizing the fall of the second temple. Great festivity and celebration follow.

Death

Jewish death rites are very simple. A person facing death is encouraged to say a prayer of confession, asking for forgiveness of sins and healing if possible. The prayer continues by asking that the person's death, if it is to come now, serve as atonement for all his or her sins. The prayer ends with requests ("Grant me a share in the world to come" and "Protect my beloved family") and commits the person's soul into the hands of God. Burial takes place on the day of death or the day after, without embalming. The community places the body in the ground with prayers binding the soul of the deceased to the Eternal One. The immediate family of mourners remains at home for seven days and will continue to recite memorial prayers (kaddish) for eleven months and thereafter on the anniversary of the death.

dwelled—sometimes in harmony and sometimes wrestling with each other—but always within a drama that gave life meaning in spite of the brutal incursions of the profane world that surrounded and rejected the Jews.

The genius of this Talmudic Judaism was that instead of totally rejecting the messianic apocalypticism of the biblical period, it transformed it, replacing political Zionism with an apolitical spiritual Zionism. The rabbis argued that Israel had been seduced by the Zealots into trying to force the coming of the messianic era by their own political activity. The truth is, the rabbis argued, that only God can initiate the messianic era, and God will bring the age of exile to an end and restore to Israel the land of promise only when all Israel is fully observant of *halakhah*. This view prevailed throughout the Middle Ages and was not seriously challenged until the coming of modern secular Zionism in the nineteenth and twentieth centuries.

The Medieval Journey of Judaism

Medieval Judaism reveals the precarious situation of the Jews in a world dominated by the new religion of Christianity. With the emergence of the Holy Roman Empire in 800 CE, at first Jews were more or less tolerated. By the late Middle Ages, however, this toleration gave way to persecution, except in Spain. There, for a brief period in the twelfth and thirteenth centuries CE known as the "Golden Age," Jews were welcome and Judaism flourished.

Discrimination Against Jews in the Early Middle Ages

Dwelling in the great cosmic story of Torah, the people Israel survived their journey through the medieval world of persecutions and expulsions. Their unity was then splintered by the Jewish Enlightenment in the nineteenth century and nearly shattered by the Holocaust in the twentieth century. That journey is a tale of tragic precedents for the Holocaust; and yet it is also a story of amazing spiritual endurance and creativity that enriched and expanded the house of Torah in which Israel dwelled—especially through the contributions of Kabbalistic mysticism and Hasidic piety.

The situation of the Jews deteriorated with the decline of the Roman Empire and the rise of Christianity. While Jews in Palestine, the land of Israel, were under the colonial rule of the Romans in the first four centuries, they enjoyed a unique protected status as a legal religion, despite their refusal to worship the gods of the official state cult. However, when the emperors and the empire became Christian in 380, the colonial domination of the Jews became more severe, and Jews eventually lost most of the legal protection they had enjoyed under the Romans. That domination did not really end until the establishment of the state of Israel in the twentieth century. The view that Christians had superseded or replaced the Jews as God's "chosen people" led to what in later centuries would be called "the Jewish problem"—namely, the continuing existence of Jews. Jews came to be seen as an "obstinate" and "stiff-necked" people who refused to acknowledge the truth of Christianity and convert (or, in later modern secular culture, refused to give up their Jewishness and assimilate).

RITUALS AND RITES

Major Festivals: The Days of Awe and Passover

All religions also have annual rituals that mark important events from the religious stories that shape their identity. After the Sabbath, which sets the rhythm of Jewish religious life, the Jewish New Year (Rosh Hashanah and Yom Kippur) and Passover are the most prominent of the Jewish holy days or festivals. Unlike Passover, which is focused on the home and family, Rosh Hashanah and Yom Kippur are days of communal prayer spent in the synagogue.

Rosh Hashanah and Yom Kippur

The new year begins for Jews with the Rosh Hashanah synagogue service, during which the story of creation is retold and people are reminded that God is deciding who will and who will not be written in the book of life for another year, even as he will decide the fate of nations and of the whole world. So the new year raises questions of life and death and calls for self-examination. The process ends ten days later, on Yom Kippur, a day of total fasting and repentance. When Yom Kippur ends at sunset and the fast is broken, penitents consider themselves to be both cleansed and prepared to face the new year. The solemnity of Yom Kippur is intended to fill worshippers with the appropriate awe and respect for the Lord God of the universe who governs the destiny of all.

Passover

Passover, or *Pesach*, recalls God's deliverance of the tribes of Israel from slavery in Egypt (Exodus 1–15). Passover is celebrated in the home, usually with the extended family and friends. The Passover *aggadah* is an order of service that retells the story of the liberation from Egypt with extensive commentary from the sages of the Talmud. The male head of the household presides at this retelling, which is done around the dining table, but members of the family are invited to participate, individually and collectively, in the recitation. Prominence is given to the youngest child, who must ask four key questions, the first of which is: "Why is this night different from all other nights?" In this way the story is passed on from generation to generation. As the story is retold, certain symbolic foods are eaten to remind everyone of the events that led and still lead to liberation from slavery for every Jew.

This festival is also called the feast of unleavened bread (*matzah*), for the story indicated that only bread without yeast was used at the time of the original event, since the tribes left in a hurry and did not have time to make leavened bread. To prepare for Passover all leavened bread must be removed from the premises and all utensils cleaned. Special foods used in the Seder service include wine to celebrate the joy of deliverance; bitter herbs (e.g., horseradish) to recall the bitterness of oppression

To be rescued from peril is an experience that can transform the identity of a person or of a people. The Passover meal is a ritual meal, celebrated annually, to recall God's liberation of the tribes of Israel from slavery in Egypt. A Jewish family celebrates this great story of deliverance.

by the Egyptians; saltwater to recall the tears of the tribes in slavery; celery or parsley as a sign of spring, life, and hope; one roasted or boiled egg and a roasted shank bone to recall both the destruction of the temple and Israel's redemption at the Red Sea by the "outstretched arm" of God; and a mixture of apples, walnuts, and spices, called Haroset, to recall the mortar used by Israelite slaves in building the Egyptian cities. After the symbolic foods are consumed during the telling of the story, a full family meal of celebration is eaten, and the meal concludes with further prayers and recitations from the Passover *aggadah*. During the Passover meal it is said that ordinary time is suspended and every Jew becomes part of the liberating event and so can say, "This day I too have been liberated from slavery."

Minor Festivals

In addition to the major festivals, a variety of other festivals are celebrated through the year, including the following.

Sukkot and Simchat Torah

Five days after Yom Kippur, the Festival of Booths is celebrated. Temporary dwellings (a wooden frame covered with branches) are constructed outdoors where Jews will eat their meals and may even sleep. The dwellings are to remind Jews of their journey through the wilderness to the land of promise, during which they had no permanent shelter. Sukkot is followed by Simchat Torah or the festival of "Rejoicing in the Torah." The last words of Torah (the end of the Book of Deuteronomy) are read, followed by the reading of the opening words of the first book of Torah, Genesis. This symbolizes the bringing of the year of "reading through the Torah" to an end and starting the cycle over for a new year. This is a festival of joyous celebration that includes a ritual "dancing with the Torah."

Purim

Jewish history is filled with many incidents of persecution. This joyous festival commemorates an occasion in Jewish history where an attempted Persian persecution is thwarted. The festival celebrates the tale of the book of Esther. Esther is a pretty young Jewish woman who is raised by her cousin Mordecai. She becomes one of the wives of the king of Persia, who does not know that she is Jewish. Moreover, she becomes the favorite of the king. The sinister Haman, an adviser to the king, turns the king against the Jews and seeks to exterminate them. However, Esther goes to the king and exposes Haman and his lies. As a result she wins the king's support, the Jews are saved, and Haman and his sons are executed.

Hanukkah

This is an eight-day festival of light, celebrated in the dead of winter and symbolizing the light of hope. It commemorates the reopening of the Temple in Jerusalem reclaimed from the Syrian persecutors in a Jewish revolt led by the Maccabean brothers. The temple was cleansed, and the temple menorah or candle stand needed to be relighted. However, there was only enough olive oil to burn for one day. Miraculously, the oil lasted eight days, until further oil could be supplied, keeping the fire and hope in God's love and protection alive. Today the festival is observed by lighting a special menorah that has nine branches—one to use to light each of the other eight over the successive eight days of the festival, during which family members often give each other gifts.

The First Crusade ended with the violent retaking of Jerusalem from the Muslims in 1099.

The Carolingian Era of Tolerance

For a while in Europe, under the Frankish Carolingian kings, who founded the Holy Roman Empire (800 CE), the life of Jews improved. Jews enjoyed high positions in the courts and in the professions and experienced new opportunities for wealth. And while Jews were not considered full citizens, they prospered under so-called diplomas of protection from the king's court. They became "the king's Jews." This practice was a benefit as long as Jews were favored by the king. However, in later periods the arrangement resulted in sudden reversals of fortune whenever a king (or Holy Roman Emperor) found it convenient to rescind his protection.

Centuries of Persecution and Pogrom

In the late Middle Ages, Jewish life became truly precarious in Europe. The tide turned against Jews with the launching of the First Crusade by Pope Urban II in 1095. The announced reason for the Crusades was to free Jerusalem and all of the Holy Land from the Muslims, who had taken Jerusalem in 638. In Islam as in Christianity and Judaism, Jerusalem is a holy city.

A plenary indulgence, or guarantee of forgiveness of sins and entry into heaven, was promised by the Pope to anyone who participated in the Crusades. However, as the armies raised for this purpose passed through the cities and towns of Europe on their way to rid the Holy Land of infidels (i.e., the Muslims), they decided to use the opportunity to purge the Christian world of its other "enemy" as well.

The Christian armies passing through the Rhine Valley offered Jews the choice of conversion or death. Many responded by committing suicide; many others were massacred. Few converted. The pattern of persecution and violence against Jews continued in the centuries that followed. In 1251 the Fourth Lateran Council of the Catholic Church adopted a practice first used by Muslims in eleventh-century Egypt, that of forcing Jews to wear distinctive dress. Also at this time, the Jews were forced to live in segregated quarters called *ghettos*. To the pattern of discrimination and violence was added the periodic practice of expulsion. In 1306, in a single day, all the Jews of France were arrested and ordered to be out of the country within a month. Other countries followed suit, driving the majority of Europe's Jews into eastern Europe. In 1348, as the Black Death swept across the Continent, Jews were blamed and made the scapegoats, and the Jews of many communities were executed. In Strasbourg, in the year 1349, for instance, 200 Jews were burned alive in a cemetery on the Sabbath.

The Protestant Reformation, initiated in 1517, seemed to be characterized by a more positive attitude toward Judaism. At first, Martin Luther wrote favorably of the Jews. But toward the end of his life, the German religious leader realized that Jews were no more receptive to his interpretation of the Gospel than to the Catholic interpretation. Thereafter, Luther turned viciously anti-Judaic, advocating the abuse of Jews and the burning of synagogues. Nevertheless, the aftermath of the Reformation in the sixteenth and seventeenth centuries left Christians too busy fighting each other to make the Jews a central concern. This distraction, as well as a modification of ghettos that put Jews under lock and key at night, served to reduce the violence Jews experienced at the hands of Christians.

However, at the same time, as the Jewish population of eastern Europe grew by leaps and bounds as a consequence of the expulsions from western Europe, new waves of violence broke out against Jews in eastern Europe. Between 1648 and 1658, in organized massacres called *pogroms*, over 700 Jewish communities were destroyed. Jewish deaths numbered in the hundreds of thousands. Fueling this violence in Europe was an ethos of Jew hatred that expressed itself in the rationalization that "the Jews are our misfortune" and helped prepare the way for the Holocaust.

The Jews of Italy offer a striking exception to this history of persecution: On the whole, they fared much better than the rest of European Jewry. Rome is the only major city of Europe from which Jews were never expelled. And unlike those in the rest of Europe, the Jews of Rome experienced no punitive taxes, were free to select their occupations, and were not forbidden by law to marry Christians. Nor were Jews persecuted in Italy during the Crusades and the years of the Black Death.

There were a number of reasons for this paradoxical thread in the religious history of Europe. For example, since usury was an allowable occupation for Christian financiers in Italy, Jews were not singled out for resentment as "money lenders." But perhaps the most influential factor was the relation between the popes and the Jews.

It was widely believed by medieval Christians that the gentile followers of Jesus had replaced the Jews as God's chosen people. To explain away "the Jewish problem"—why God nevertheless permitted Jews to continue to exist—the popes, from the sixth century on, turned to a theory developed by St. Augustine, the so-called "negative witness theory." According to this theory, it was God's will for Jews to wander the earth without a home, their unhappy existence functioning as a "negative witness" that proved the superiority and truth of Christianity. Consequently, the popes preached that God had rejected the Jews while, at the same time, paradoxically, acting as the legal protectors and guardians of the original chosen people, insisting that they not be physically harmed.

Although the negative witness theory shaped papal strategy for dealing with "the Jewish problem" in medieval Christendom, during the Renaissance some popes took a less biased view. Pope Sixtus IV (1471–84), for example, commissioned a Latin translation of the Kabbalah. Later Pope Clement VII sought to develop a common translation of the Old Testament by Jewish and Christian scholars, and he suspended the persecution by the Spanish Inquisition of Jews who had been forcibly baptized in Spain.

From the Golden Age in Spain to the Spanish Inquisition

In the midst of this violent history stands the Golden Age of Spain as an extraordinary interlude, when Jews were welcomed as allies against the Muslims in the portions of Spain that had been reconquered by Christians. For a time in the twelfth and early thirteenth centuries, Jews were encouraged to settle in the reconquered territories and were given unusual freedom both socially and politically, achieving important roles in the royal court and in the professions. It was a period of unprecedented intellectual exchange between the great scholars of Judaism, Islam, and Christianity.

The period came to an end in the mid-thirteenth century as a Christian backlash developed. Christians suddenly became alarmed at the growing number of Jews in high places. This fear of a "Jewish takeover" led to a new period of persecution, violence, and forced conversions, culminating in the Spanish Inquisition. Between 1480 and 1492 some 13,000 Jews, most of whom had been forcibly baptized as Christians, were condemned as **Marranos**—Jews masquerading as Christians while practicing their Judaism in secret. Many were tortured and burned at the stake. The Jews were expelled from Spain in 1492 (see Map 3.2).

Two Great Medieval Scholars: Rashi and Maimonides

The period of the late Middle Ages produced two of the greatest scholars in the history of Judaism: Rabbi Solomon ben Isaac (1040–1105), otherwise known as Rashi, and Moses ben Maimon (1135–1204), otherwise known as Maimonides. Rashi's commentaries on the Gemara of the Babylonian Talmud, which appeared in the first

---

Marranos: Jews of Spain who, although forced by the Inquisition to convert to Christianity, continued to practice Judaism in secret

---

"If there is no peace, then there is really nothing, because peace is the equivalent of all other blessings put together."

—Rashi

printed edition of the Talmud and have been in all editions since, are considered to form an essential component of the work. Rashi is hailed as the most unsurpassable teacher of Torah in the history of Talmudic Judaism. He founded an influential Talmudic academy in Troyes, France.

Maimonides, known as Rambam (for Rabbi Moses Ben Maimon), is famous for his philosophical writings, in which he uses Aristotelian concepts to explain Jewish teaching. His *Guide of the Perplexed* is well known today, and for over three centuries his compendium of Talmudic law, the *Mishnah Torah*, was the most influential guide to *halakhah* in Judaism. Although Judaism is not a religion that emphasizes *dogma* (right belief) as the test of true faith, Maimonides is credited with giving Judaism a creedal statement known as the *Thirteen Articles of Faith* (which are found on the website for this book; www.oup.com/us/esposito).

Kabbalah—Jewish Mysticism

Judaism, like all religions, has a mystical dimension. Not only in Judaism, but in the other two monotheistic traditions of Christianity and Islam, mystics have generally been viewed with an element of mistrust because mystical experience is direct and immediate and so tends to undermine traditional lines of religious authority. The mystic finds God without the guidance of either a priest or a teacher (rabbi). Moreover, the mystic often speaks of God in ways that are unconventional and sometimes seem contradictory to the nature of prophetic monotheism.

In the monotheistic traditions mysticism expresses itself in two dramatically different forms—the mysticism of love and union (the divine-human marriage) and the mysticism of identity. The place of the mystic in monotheism has always been especially ambivalent for the mystics of identity. The mystics of identity sometimes seem to say they are not just in union with God but *are* God. Whenever mystics speak in this way they are in danger of being accused of confusing themselves with God and claiming to be God. Any such representation would be heretical and blasphemous in all three biblical religions, hence would be unacceptable by any of them. And yet, despite this seemingly ever-present danger, each of the monotheistic religions has chosen to maintain an uneasy peace with its mystics, neither denying the importance and validity of mysticism nor suppressing its practice.

Although Jewish mysticism goes back to the ancient world and also reflects the influences of Neoplatonism and Gnosticism, it did not become a decisive influence in Judaism until the explicit emergence of **Kabbalah** in the late medieval period. Kabbalism sought to explain the mystery of good and evil in the universe precisely at a time of intensifying persecution and pogroms. Jews could not help but seek an understanding of God that could sustain them through a new period of suffering.

The most important Kabbalistic work is the ***Zohar*** (Book of Splendor). According to Kabbalistic teaching, there was a time when God manifested himself in the world, allowing his *Shekinah* ("divine presence") to be perceived in all things. However,

> "I believe with perfect faith that the Creator, blessed be Your name, is not a body, and that You are free from all the accidents of matter, and that You have not any form whatsoever."
>
> —Maimonides' Third Principle of Faith

Kabbalah: Jewish mystical tradition

Zohar: "Book of Splendor," the most important Kabbalistic work

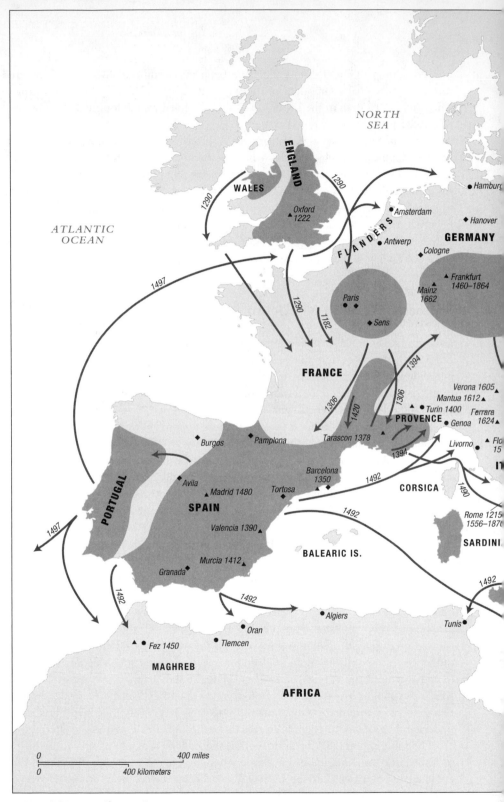

Map 3.2 Jews in Christian Europe.

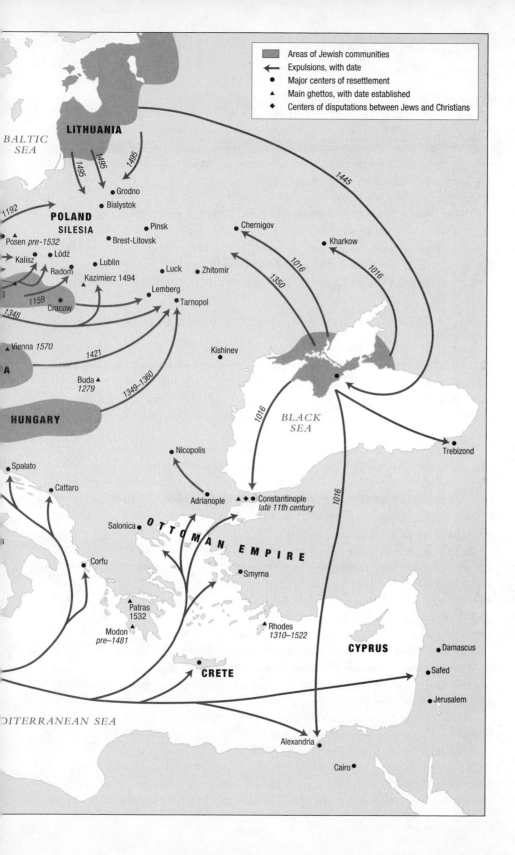

BALTIC
SEA

LITHUANIA

• Grodno
• Bialystok

1495 1495 1495

1192

POLAND
SILESIA
▲ Posen *pre-1532*

• Pinsk
• Brest-Litovsk

• Chernigov

1445

• Kharkow

Kalisz
• Lódź
Radom
Kazimierz 1494 ▲
Cracow
1159
1348

• Lublin
• Luck   • Zhitomir
Lemberg
• Tarnopol

1016   1016

1350

1016

▲ Vienna *1570*

1421

A

Buda ▲
1279

1349–1360

• Kishinev

BLACK
SEA

1016

Trebizond

HUNGARY

• Spalato
• Cattaro

• Nicopolis

• Corfu

Salonica •

• Adrianople

OTTOMAN

▲ ◆ ◆ Constantinople
late 11th century

EMPIRE

• Smyrna

1016

Patras
1532 ▲

Modon
pre–1481 ▲

▲ Rhodes
1310–1522

CYPRUS

• Damascus

CRETE

• Safed

• Jerusalem

MEDITERRANEAN SEA

Alexandria

Cairo •

because of the fall of Adam, evil entered the world and the divine presence has been exiled from its unity with God as the infinite (*En Sof*). Humans were created for *devekut* ("communion") with God, but this relationship was destroyed by Adam's sin and must be reestablished through mystical contemplation (*kavanah*) of the divine through prayer and the devout performance of the requirements of *halakhah*. The reunion of all with the infinite will bring about nothing less than the ingathering of all Jews from exile in the messianic kingdom to come.

The Kabbalistic tradition comprises a profound mystical variation on the theme of exile and return. It can be seen as a powerful religious response to the overwhelming tragedy of persecution and expulsion that marked Jewish life in Europe in the late Middle Ages and beyond. It explained the age of darkness in which Jews lived in exile and offered them a hope of transcending that darkness with a future ingathering of all Jews.

Hasidism

Hasidism: form of Judaism strongly rooted in mysticism

The mystical impulse of Kabbalism was given further embodiment in the Hasidic movement. **Hasidism** really came into its own in eastern Europe at the beginning of the eighteenth century largely in response to the pogroms endemic to the region. A *hasid* is a pious one, whose life is marked by great devotion. With Hasidism, piety took on a new intensity of meaning.

The Hasidic movement emerged in Poland with the activities of Israel ben Eliezer, who was called *the Besht* by his followers. This title was a shortened form of Ba'al Shem Tov, or "Master of the Good Name," where the "good name" was understood to be the name of God. The Besht was an ecstatic healer who worked miracles using magic, amulets, and spells. He taught that joy is the appropriate response to the world no matter how much suffering Jews experience.

In fact, although Hasidism emerged in an era of pogrom and immense suffering in eastern Europe, the Hasidim say there is no greater sin than melancholy, or sadness (*atzut*). Indeed they argue that sadness, which stems from ignorance of the pervasive presence of God in all things, is the root of all sin. According to the Besht, God hides himself in his creation. Therefore, there is no distance between God and humanity for those who have the eyes to see. And once you do see, there can be no sadness but only *simhah*—deep, pervasive, passionate joy and celebration.

The Besht was a charismatic figure whose followers hung on his every word and gesture. Their prayer circles were characterized by ecstatic singing and dancing, and they looked forward to deeply moving spiritual talks by the Besht around the Sabbath dinner table. The Besht taught that the essence of the way of Torah is to be found in devotion (*kavanah*), burning enthusiasm (*hitlahavut*), and attachment or clinging to God (*devekut*) rather than in study of the Talmud.

Tzaddik: in the Hasidic tradition, a "righteous man"—a religious leader who is as influential as a rabbi is in a traditional Talmudic community

The Besht became a model for the Hasidic notion of the **Tzaddik**, or "righteous man." The Tzaddik's authority in each Hasidic community was every bit as powerful as that of the rabbi in a traditional Talmudic community. For the Hasidim, the

For the Hasidim there is no greater sin than sadness. The proper response to God's presence, hidden everywhere in creation, is joy. One expression of that joy is to dance with the Torah, as this Hasidic man in Jerusalem is doing, accompanied by other male dancers of all ages.

Tzaddik was no ordinary person but one especially chosen by God as a direct link between heaven and earth. He was revered as a savior figure whose holiness was considered so powerful that, like Moses (Exodus 32:11–14), he could intervene on behalf of the faithful and literally change the mind of God. Like the rabbis, the Tzaddik was a religious virtuoso; however, his virtuosity was of mystical piety and devotion, not of Talmudic scholarship. His holiness was said to be spontaneously contagious: Just being near him, the Hasidim could catch his piety as a spark to light their own.

Hasidism garnered an enthusiastic popular following, for it offered even the poor and unlearned a way to move from the periphery into the heart of Judaism as they understood it. One reason for this was that in the early days, Hasidic Judaism rejected the elitism of Rabbinic Judaism, for the rabbis and their students were an intellectual elite, trained as Talmudic experts—something the average Jew could not hope to be. Hasidic Judaism offered ways to reach God other than Talmudic study: namely, devotion and prayer, which were within the reach of every sincere Jew. This path brought into popular practice the deep mystical piety of the Kabbalistic tradition.

What was most extraordinary about Hasidic mysticism was, and is, its communal nature. One cannot achieve this state of joy and selflessness by going off alone to a mountaintop but only by total immersion in the community life of the Hasidim organized around the festive worship made possible by the presence of the Tzaddik. It is this linking of deep mystical spirituality with community life that made Hasidism such a powerful force for renewal. In the nineteenth century, Hasidism moved toward reconciliation with Rabbinic Judaism by incorporating more emphasis on the study of Talmud and was eventually accepted by the rabbis who had originally rejected it.

The Kabbalistic-Hasidic tradition was deeply influenced by ancient Greek philosophy (Neoplatonism and Gnosticism). The success of its integration into the Talmudic tradition through the Hasidic movement demonstrates the extraordinary ability of Judaism to absorb and sanctify the "secular" and non-Jewish while reaffirming the practices of the tradition. This is a pattern we see repeated in the twentieth century, when many of the movements of modern and post-Holocaust Judaism have grown closer together. Judaism, despite inner tensions and conflicts, shows an amazing ability to absorb conflicting movements, which often catalyze transformation and renewal. This should not surprise anyone, for this has been true of Judaism from its very beginnings in the biblical period.

Having surveyed premodern Judaism, we are now in a position to look at the emergence of modern forms and to understand better how they are both like premodern forms of Judaism and different from them.

Judaism and Modernity (1729–1967 CE)

The Emergence of Modern Religious Forms of Judaism

Reform Judaism

From the early days of Rabbinic Judaism, between the second and fifth centuries, until the French Revolution in 1789, Jews in Europe lived as a rejected minority in a world dominated by Christians. With Enlightenment secularization, the categories of human self-understanding underwent radical revision. Enlightened Europeans were secular universalists who defined their humanity not in terms of religious myths, which they believed created divisiveness, but in terms of reason, which they held to be a capacity found universally in human beings. The ideal of this new orientation was to replace the categories of "Jew" and "Christian" with a single category: "rational human being."

For the first time in almost 2,000 years, the dominant culture looked at Jews as rational beings, equal to all other human beings, and Jews were invited to participate as citizens alongside all other individuals in the modern capitalist nation-states (see Map 3.3). This message of inclusion was widely accepted by the Jews of western Europe. It seemed that a new day was dawning. One of the leading Enlightenment scholars of the eighteenth century, Gotthold Lessing (1729–81), a gentile, wrote impassioned works proclaiming the humanity of Jews and of Muslims and arguing for their acceptance in society. Lessing befriended Moses Mendelssohn (1729–86), who became the leading figure in the Jewish Haskalah, or Enlightenment, movement, the eventual source of Reform Judaism, the first "modern" form of Judaism.

Like Hellenistic Judaism in the first century, the Haskalah movement favored partial assimilation into the gentile world, trying to show that in the 1800s, one could be an enlightened citizen of the secular world and a Jew at the same time. This required

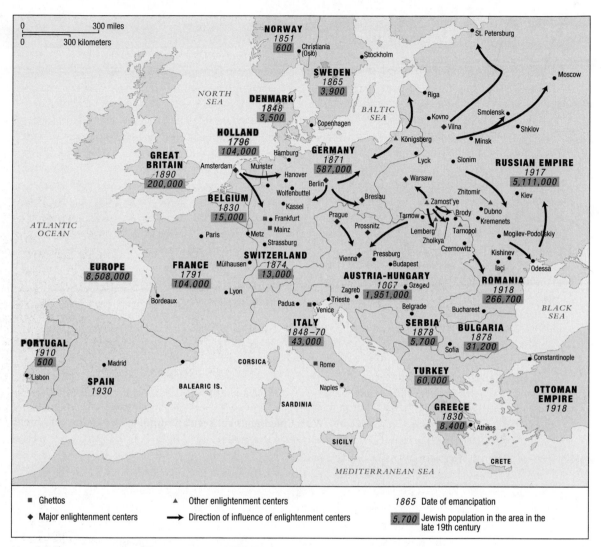

Map 3.3 The emancipation of European Jewry, 1789–1918.

the leaders of the Reform movement to answer a question that all modern forms of Judaism (including Orthodoxy) have confronted: How can I be both a Jew and a citizen of a secular state? It had been pointless to ask this question earlier, when secular states did not exist and Christian states offered Jews no possibility of citizenship.

Reform Judaism and all other forms of modern Judaism, however, have had to make a decision about how to relate to the larger secular society. Embracing the Enlightenment ideal of religion within the "limits of reason," the leaders of the Reform movement defined the essence of Judaism as a rational-ethical system rooted

GENDER FOCUS: Women in Judaism

Premodern

Talmudic Judaism shares with the emerging Judaism of the ancient biblical period a common assumption of premodern urban societies, transposed into a monotheistic frame of reference. Specifically, it was long assumed that there is a sacred natural order of the world, revealed by God, in which maleness is the normative pattern for full humanity. Traditionally, this assumption was validated by the second creation story presented in the Bible: Genesis 2:5–3:24 (as opposed to the first version, Genesis 1:1–2:4). Since in the second story God created Adam first and then Eve from the rib of Adam, men were accorded primary responsibility for the order of things, women having been created to help men. Indeed, women (like animals and slaves) are the property of men. A father could sell his daughter as payment for a debt (Exodus 21:7), for instance. Basically, a woman belonged to her father until she was given to the man who married her, to whom she then belonged. Women had no role in the public worship in the temple, but at the same time women were honored as mothers and the mainstay of the family.

The biblical attitude toward women was continued in premodern Rabbinic Judaism. However, during the biblical period certain exceptional women were revered for their wisdom and their gifts of prophecy: Miriam (the sister of Moses), Deborah (one of the judges of Israel), and Huldah (a prophetess during the reign of Josiah). Both Rabbinic and later Hasidic traditions also present models of women who were exceptions, noted for their learning and piety. Beruriah, the wife of Rabbi Meir, was noted for her skill as a Talmudic scholar, and Oudil, the daughter of the Ba'al Shem Tov, was praised for her wisdom and joyous piety. Nevertheless, such women were not the norm. They remained the exception that proved the rule.

Modern

The Enlightenment brought with it a gradual change in the status of women in Western culture, and women have progressively claimed autonomy, that is, control of their own lives. Modern forms of Judaism tend to demythologize traditional Jewish gender roles as inessential historical accretions that may even contradict fundamental insights of Judaism concerning justice and human dignity. Thus, it is probably fair to say that the greatest equality for women has been among the secular forms of Judaism, especially Jewish socialism

in the prophetic-ethical ideal of justice—an ethic that was Judaism's gift to humanity. Like their Hellenistic counterparts, they did not think that this ethic was for Jews alone but rather that Judaism was its source and purest form. This universal rational ethic was the essence of Judaism; all other aspects of Judaism were open to negotiation.

As Reform Judaism developed, it showed a remarkable openness to secular society. For instance, Jews could use the vernacular instead of Hebrew in worship; thus synagogue prayers and sermons could be spoken in the local language (German, French, English, etc.). As the movement developed in the late nineteenth century, it was also prepared to abandon the observance of kosher laws, restricting the foods Jews can eat, and other "historical accretions" as inessential to being Jewish. Indeed, it rejected the Talmud as revelation, seeing it instead as simply a human historical tradition. And it rejected belief in a literal coming of the messiah, replacing it with a belief in a messianic age

and Zionism, and among the most secular forms of religious Judaism—Reform first, then Conservative, and least among the Orthodox.

The Declaration of Independence of the State of Israel, drawing on the nation's secular socialist and Zionist roots, asserts complete equality of men and women in social and political rights. The Equal Rights for Women law of 1951 guarantees women the same rights enjoyed by men to own property and to make decisions on behalf of their children. Among the explicitly religious forms of Judaism, the Reform movement has led the way. As early as 1846 a movement to declare women equal appeared in Germany. Nevertheless, the desire of women to become rabbis was not discussed seriously until the 1920s, and it was not until the 1970s that women began to be ordained (although one private ordination is said to have occurred in 1935 in a German Reform congregation).

Today it is not uncommon, in both Reform and Conservative synagogues in America, for a young woman to celebrate her bat mitzvah as a parallel rite to a brother's bar mitzvah. Nor is it unusual for women

Today in both Reform Judaism and Conservative Judaism women are ordained to the rabbinate. Here Barbara Aiello, the first female rabbi in Italy, lights Hanukkah candles.

to read the Torah scrolls at a Sabbath service. And it is even becoming more common for women cantors to chant such services and for women rabbis to conduct them. All of this was unthinkable in premodern Judaism. And it remains unthinkable among the ultra-Orthodox.

that could easily be identified with the goal of the modern age of scientific and rational progress. Finally, it renounced any desire to return to the land of Israel, insisting that Jews were not a people tied to a specific land but a "religious community."

What especially marks the Reform movement as modern is its openness to secular learning and historical consciousness. In premodern Rabbinic Judaism (with such notable exceptions as Maimonides), the only learning worthy of consideration was the study of Torah and Talmud. But among enlightened Jews, secular learning not only was permitted but took precedence. For instance, in deciding what is and what is not essential to Judaism, Reform Judaism argued not from the "revealed will of God," as had premodern Judaism, but from the history of the development of Judaism as a religion. Thus "history" and "Judaism," not "God" and "Torah," became the defining categories. Religious disputes were to be settled primarily by appeal to the developmental history of Judaism. After all, what history reveals, Reform Jews argued, is that Judaism is a religion not of eternal, unchanging truths but of constant change. From their perspective, Reform Judaism is the true Judaism for the modern world and the logical successor, in the authentic unfolding of the historical tradition, to premodern Rabbinic Judaism.

Reform Judaism explained how one could be a Jew and still be part of a larger secular society. Reform Judaism, which initiated the journey of Judaism into the modern world, was the pioneer of all modern Judaisms. For some, Reform Judaism was a model to be emulated with modifications, especially the more secular forms of Judaism—ethnic Judaism, Jewish socialism, and Zionism (to be discussed shortly). Indeed, it would be hard to imagine the secular state of Israel without the path opened up by Reform Judaism. Yet other Jews believed that this was the wrong direction. Indeed, it was only after the bold statements of Reform Judaism that a second form of modern Judaism appeared: Orthodox Judaism, which vigorously rejected the claims of the Reform movement.

Orthodox Judaism

To call Orthodox Judaism a modern form of Judaism may seem contradictory, for orthodoxy claims that it continues the ancient tradition of premodern Rabbinic Judaism. Reform Judaism, of course, also claims to continue the same tradition. Orthodoxy, however, defined continuity in terms of resisting all change, whereas Reform Judaism thought it meant being true to the historical law of constant change. The issue between Reform and Orthodox Jews was whether, as Reform Jews held, God was acting through an ever-changing history, progressing toward an age of messianic freedom, or whether the Orthodox were correct in their view that God revealed himself only in the eternal, unchanging covenant given at Sinai. This reflects the choice modernization puts to all religions—whether to embrace historical change or reject it out of faithfulness to a view of premodern unchanging fundamental truths and practices.

Reform Jews argued for changes that would accommodate the modern world, while the Orthodox want to refuse all accommodation, although they seldom fully achieve this. Orthodox Jews wanted to present their choice of orthodoxy as if it were no choice. But clearly, the very appearance of Reform Judaism meant that one could no longer just be a Jew; one had to choose to be a Jew of a certain kind. In agreeing that it was necessary to choose, Orthodoxy gave evidence that it too was a Judaism of the modern period. From now on, like Reform Judaism, it would have to think of itself as one religious community alongside others. Premodern Rabbinic Jews had no such dilemma, for there was no "Judaism" to choose, only God, Torah, and Israel, the givens of one's birth into the chosen people.

Orthodoxy became, in many ways, the mirror image of Reform Judaism, for mirror images reverse the original that they reflect. Thus if Reform Jews prayed in the vernacular, the Orthodox insisted that all prayers be in Hebrew. If Reform Jews insisted on historical change, the Orthodox insisted on eternal unchanging truth. If Reform Jews decided issues of religious practice on the basis of history, the Orthodox decided them on the basis of the eternal word of God given in the Torah and the

Talmud. If Reform Jews abandoned literal messianic beliefs, the Orthodox reaffirmed them. If Reform Jews dismissed the Talmudic requirements (*halakhah*) as historical accretions, the Orthodox insisted on continued observance of the requirements of the dual Torah (the written Torah and the oral Torah). And if Reform Jews abandoned any ambition to return to the land of Israel, the Orthodox prayed "next year in Jerusalem" while awaiting the deliverance of the messiah.

In western Europe even the Orthodox saw the futility of separating themselves completely from the secular world and allowed that in "inessentials," such as clothing, secular education, and choice of job or career, Jews may be like everyone else. Indeed, Orthodoxy's first great intellectual defender, Samson Raphael Hirsch (1808–88), sought to show that one can live as a Jew in a secular nation-state and remain fully Orthodox. Therefore, above all, what makes Orthodoxy a modern Judaism is that, like Reform Judaism, it divides the world into the religious and the secular, separating religion and politics in a way that allows Orthodox Jews to be both Jews and citizens of a secular nation-state. However, the ultra-Orthodox set out on a path of segregation, challenging the integrationism of Reform Jews and even the minimal accommodation to the "outside world" of the Orthodox. Eastern European haredim tried to shut out modernity altogether, but this meant doing what no premodern Rabbinic Jew had ever had to do—become a sectarian.

Conservative Judaism

Once the lines had been drawn between the first two modern ways of being Jewish, it was perhaps inevitable that a third option would emerge, seeking a compromise. That option was Conservative Judaism. The Orthodox saw Jewish life as the life of an eternal people; Reform Jews saw Jewish life as the life of a historical religious community. Conservative Jews saw Jewish life as the life of a historically ethnic people that included but was not limited to the religious dimension. Conservative Judaism arose among Jews who were deeply committed to the Orthodox way of life yet sympathetic to the "modern" intellectual worldview of Reform Judaism.

The message of the leaders of Conservative Judaism was "Think whatever you like, but do what the law requires." Thus on the question of the relationship to the secular, Conservative Judaism focused on practice rather than belief. This compromise gave Conservative Jews considerable intellectual freedom of interpretation—one could believe or disbelieve any or all elements of the supernatural worldview of premodern Rabbinic Judaism and still be a Jew, as long as one observed Talmudic law in everyday life (although modest compromises in this area were permitted). This position puts the emphasis on orthopraxy (right practice) as opposed to orthodoxy (right belief).

Conservative Judaism fits very well with the pragmatic attitude of modern (especially American) culture. Like Reform Jews, Conservative Jews see Judaism as a historically unfolding religion; but unlike the Reform Jews and more like the Orthodox, the Conservative Jews emphasize an organic continuity. Historical change does not produce abrupt reorientations but gradual development—a development of the unfolding essence of Judaism. And that essence is found not so much in belief as in practice. In this way, Conservative Judaism, like Reform and Orthodox Judaism, sees itself as the logical continuation of the tradition. Conservative Judaism, as the third option, is largely an American phenomenon and is the most widely embraced form of Judaism practiced in America.

Reconstructionism

In addition to the three main strands of modern Judaism there is another movement, known as Reconstructionism, founded in America in the 1930s by Mordecai Kaplan. Kaplan cast his understanding of Judaism in almost completely secular terms drawn from the modern social and historical sciences. Kaplan defined Judaism as the religion of Jewish civilization, where "religion" was understood not in supernatural terms but as the embodiment of the ideals and group identity of a culture. But for that very reason, the practice of the religious rituals of the tradition was an important means of preserving the identity and continuing vitality of Jewish civilization. For Kaplan, Judaism must not be about life beyond death but about improving the individual's life here and now by working for the progress of society. Membership in the Reconstructionist movement is modest, but many of its themes are found in the three main types of secular Judaism that, as we shall see, found the need for religious ritual less compelling.

The Emergence of Secular Forms of Judaism

The dawning of the age of Enlightenment created an optimistic mood among Jews. But that mood did not last, for the promise of inclusion for Jews turned out to be false. The hidden premise of the new offer became apparent in the aftermath of the French Revolution, which had offered full citizenship to Jews. The offer, however, gave *everything to Jews as individuals and nothing to the Jews as a people*. To be a citizen in the new secular society, one had to trade one's religious identity for a secular or nonreligious one.

But even the considerable number of Jews who paid the high price never were accorded the equality that had been promised. The ideals of the Enlightenment were genuine enough, but they quickly crashed on the rocks of the intractability of human prejudice. As more and more Jews were "secularized" in Europe, either abandoning or minimizing their Judaism, they entered into the political and economic life of their respective countries. As they achieved success, a backlash occurred. Throughout Europe, non-Jews began to fear that the Jews were taking over "their" society.

By the end of the nineteenth century a secular, supposedly scientific, definition had come to replace the old religious definition of the Jews. The Jews became defined as a race—an inferior race that had a biologically corrupting influence on society. With the introduction of the language of race, all the old Christian stereotypes of Jews as a rejected people were resurrected in a new guise. Theoretically, at least, the Jews as a religious people could be converted—hence, "the Jewish problem" could be solved.

But race is perceived as a biologically unchangeable fact; people cannot convert from one race to another. Moreover, the advocates of the "scientific" theory of race viewed any attempt at assimilation through intermarriage as racial pollution. In the 1930s the Nazi Party in Germany could begin to exploit this new kind of prejudice against "the Jewish race" to devastating effect.

In the United States, Jews fared better than in Europe. America was forged as a nation of many peoples fleeing religious intolerance in England and on the continent. Anti-Semitism and other forms of religious bigotry were not absent from America's formative history, but Jews in America never experienced pogroms and mass expulsions. American individualism allowed more space for diverse ethnic and religious communal identities.

Jewish immigrants to the United States came in two waves. The first and more modest wave, dating from 1654, consisted of seekers of religious freedom, Jews of Spanish or Portuguese extraction, known as **Sephardic** Jews. The second and much larger wave began in the nineteenth century among the **Ashkenazi**, Jews of eastern Europe who were fleeing persecution and pogrom. By the beginning of World War II, approximately a third of the world's Jews lived in the United States. After World War II, twice as many Jews lived in the United States as in all of Europe.

Sephardic: Jews whose traditions originated in Spain or Portugal

Ashkenazi: Jews whose traditions originated in central and eastern Europe

While Jews in America were being integrated into society, in the late 1800s and early 1900s the Jews of western Europe were once more being persecuted. Most of the Jews of eastern Europe never did sense that they had been invited to join a new Enlightenment order of equality and inclusion. On the contrary, they experienced an increase in persecutions and pogroms. The challenge was to devise a strategy for surviving in societies that were replacing religious anti-Judaism with secular anti-Semitism. And it was among the more fully assimilated and secularized Jews that the new responses emerged, responses that would form a bridge from the modern forms of Judaism (Reform, Orthodox, and Conservative) to the postmodern and postcolonial Judaism of Holocaust and Redemption. These new secular forms of Judaism were Jewish socialism, ethnic (Yiddish) Judaism, and Zionism, each one offering a distinct way of being Jewish. Yet they were capable of combining in interesting and powerful ways that set the stage for the emergence of the Judaism of Holocaust and Redemption.

Jewish Socialism

Some of the strongest currents of Jewish socialism came out of eastern Europe, where secularized Jews saw in socialism another way of resolving the tension between being Jewish and being modern. As noted in Chapter 1, socialism, especially the later "scientific" socialism of Karl Marx, offered an essentially secularized version of the Jewish and Christian myths of history. It was a view of history as a story of exile and return, in which human beings begin in paradise (primitive communism), only to be expelled from the garden into a world of selfishness and sin (class conflict). Socialism, however, promises an eventual transformation into a future global, classless, society in which suffering and injustice will be overcome (including anti-Semitism) and all will live in perfect harmony—a vision very much like that of the messianic kingdom of God. Perhaps this is no coincidence, given that Karl Marx, whose father was a convert to Christianity, was the grandson of a rabbi.

For the many "secularized" Jews of Europe, the socialist story of history offered a new, yet very familiar, framework in which to understand their place in the drama of history. This new secular story gave the Enlightenment-oriented secular Jews a secular way of being Jewish. In this, Jewish socialism adapted the spirit of Reform Judaism, opting for historical development as the key to continuity in Jewish history and for a secular vision of Judaism that favored the prophetic witness of the written Torah (redefined as socialist ethics) over that of the oral Torah traditions of the Talmud. And, like Reform Jews, the Jewish socialists did not need to regard their message as exclusive to Judaism. For them it was enough to see Judaism as the unique contributor of the ideal of social justice to an international ethic for the whole human race. However, unlike their Reform counterparts, Jewish socialists no longer represented themselves as "religious"—for religion belonged to the prescientific age that was passing away.

Who was attracted to this way of being Jewish? In the wake of the Russian Revolution of 1917, socialism was especially attractive to the Jews of Russia and eastern Europe and to the poor Jewish immigrants from these areas who came to the United States. These were Jews who were victims not only of anti-Semitism but also of economic depression and unemployment. The pivotal date for Jewish socialism is usually said to be 1897, the year of the formation of the Bund, or Jewish Worker's Union, in Poland. Many secular Jews joined the socialist movement but rejected all connections with Judaism. They thought of themselves as purely secular, nonreligious persons. Some even vigorously disavowed their Jewish roots, going so far as to contribute to existing currents of anti-Semitism.

Yiddish Ethnic Judaism

Other Jewish socialists, however, wished to retain and affirm their ties to the history of the Jewish people. And so they turned to ethnicity as the key to Jewish identity—an ethnicity that was primarily identified with speaking the Yiddish language.

Even secular Jews who no longer used or knew Hebrew knew Yiddish, the common language of European Jews that developed from about the eleventh century—an amalgam of Hebrew and German. The focus on Yiddish language, and especially Yiddish literature, which often echoes Talmudic and biblical stories, gave secular Jews a way to identify with Judaism without being "religious" and to draw on the wisdom of the tradition.

Yiddish was more than a language. It stood for a way of experiencing and interpreting the world that was still deeply rooted in Judaism. Indeed, ever since the first nation-states emerged in Europe in the seventeenth century, language had been the key to national identity. Through Yiddish, Jews, otherwise dispersed—without a land of their own—sought to sustain their identity as a people in a secular age. As the language of working-class Jews, Yiddish gave Jews a deep sense of "ethnicity," of

being bound together in a common historical tradition that offered, as well, a unique identity. That
ethnicity could easily be tapped by Jewish socialists
to mobilize Jews, that is, to organize them for the
workers' revolution that was part of the Marxian
scheme of history.

From the end of the nineteenth century until
the end of World War II, Jewish socialism was the
predominant secular response to modernity among
Jews in both Europe and America. But it was not the
only response, for there emerged in the nineteenth
century another Jewish movement that, in the long
run, would be even more influential—Zionism.

The Origins of Zionism

Zionism was born out of disenchantment with
modernity and its Enlightenment promises. Unlike
Jewish socialism, Zionism did not hold out much
hope for a future in which Jews would be accepted
as equals in society. In the Zionist view, the only
viable solution for Jews in light of the long history of rejection, first by Christendom and then by
modern secular society, was to have a state of their
own where they could protect themselves.

Theodor Herzl, founder
of the Zionist movement
to create a Jewish state.

Zion is a biblical term used to refer to the city of David—Jerusalem. The word
Zionism, coined in 1893, represents a longing virtually as old as Judaism itself: to
return from exile, home to Zion. In premodern Rabbinic Judaism, this longing was
expressed in a messianic belief that someday God would send a messiah and reestablish
a homeland for his people in the land of Israel. For premodern Rabbinic Judaism as
well as for much of modern Orthodoxy and ultra-Orthodoxy, the return of Jews to
their own land can only be the work of God. Any attempt by Jews to create a Jewish
state on their own is presumptuous to the point of blasphemy. Thus when Zionism
appeared at the end of the nineteenth century, this secular movement to organize Jews
for the creation of a homeland in Palestine was vehemently rejected by the Orthodox
and ultra-Orthodox. Reform Jews, having defined themselves as a religious community rather than as a "people," showed little interest in returning to the Middle
East. In truth, Zionism did not come into its own until after the Holocaust, when it
seemed clear to Jews everywhere that Jews could never count on being accepted as
equals in Europe and that the only protection available to them would be in their own
homeland—their own state.

A pivotal event in the development of secular (political) Zionism was the Dreyfus
affair in France. This trial of a Jewish army officer on charges of treason had a profound

"Distress binds us together and, thus united, we suddenly discover our strength. . . . Let sovereignty be granted us over a portion of the globe large enough to satisfy the rightful requirements of a nation; the rest we shall manage for ourselves."

—Theodor Herzl on Zionism

influence on a young Jewish journalist, Theodor Herzl (1860–1904). The outcome of the trial—conviction of Dreyfus, who was innocent—convinced Herzl that assimilation would never be a feasible option for Jews. In 1896 he wrote *The Jewish State*, in which he rejected assimilation and proposed the creation of a Jewish state. Thus was born a movement that was destined to change the future of Judaism: secular political Zionism. Herzl convened the First Zionist Congress in Basel, Switzerland, in 1897, the same year as the formation of the Jewish socialist Bund in Poland. At this conference the World Zionist Organization was founded. In addition to Palestine, Herzl considered sites for a Jewish homeland in Cyprus. Later, the Sixth Zionist Congress rejected a British offer for a colony in Uganda, then a British protectorate. From that time forward Palestine became the sole option for Zionists. Herzl even wrote a utopian novel, *Altneuland*, imagining a Jewish state in Palestine.

Herzl's Dream and Its Ramifications

Theodor Herzl died in 1904, but not his dream. He left behind a thriving and committed body of political Zionists, the World Zionist Organization. In 1911 this organization began a modest but persistent program of colonizing areas in Palestine, which was then under British colonial control. In 1917, as a result of Zionist efforts, the British foreign secretary, Lord James Balfour, wrote the letter now known as the Balfour Declaration, pledging Britain's support for a Jewish national home in Palestine. France, Italy, and the United States endorsed the idea. One cannot overestimate the tremendous importance of the organizational infrastructure developed in both Jewish socialism (embodied in the Bund) and in Zionism (embodied in the World Zionist Organization). The skills developed in these organizations and transferred to the early settlements in Palestine, with ongoing support from Jews all over the world, made possible the "sudden" emergence of the state of Israel in 1948 with sponsorship by the United Nations.

This 1948 poster illustrates a vision of the strength and power of the Israeli Jew, a vision fostered by a Zionist movement prepared to defend the new nation of Israel.

Like Reform Judaism, Zionism relied on history and historical change as its link to the premodern traditions of the Jewish people. But unlike Reform Judaism, political Zionism did not think of itself as a religious movement. Therefore, unlike Reform Judaism, Zionism sought continuity in the idea of the Jews as a historical people. Zionists reappropriated the biblical stories of the origins of Israel as part of their story, but the biblical narratives were to serve not as religious stories of God's actions in history but as "secular" stories of the Jewish people's struggles to achieve and preserve their national identity.

Therefore, Zionists retold the stories of origins from a perspective other than that of the premodern Rabbinic tradition of the dual Torah. That tradition had its beginnings in the failure of ancient militant Jewish political messianism (with the defeat of the Zealots) and the success of a political policy of neutrality practiced by the Pharisees. The Zionists reacted to what they perceived as the failure (after almost

2,000 years) of the Rabbinic strategy of accommodation to the surrounding non-Jewish world and to the more recent Reform strategy of partial assimilation. They were not content to wait to be emancipated by others (whether God or modern gentiles). They were looking for Jewish heroes who were prepared to emancipate themselves. Thus they retold the stories of Moses and David as stories of nation builders and militant revolutionary political leaders.

For the Zionists, the interesting stories were the marginal ones of the Maccabean revolts of the second century BCE and those of the Maccabees' successors, the Zealots, who would rather kill themselves (as they did at Masada in 73 CE) than let the fight for their land end in surrender. The Zionists were looking for militant heroes who could serve as prototypes for a new kind of Jew, one prepared to fight to the last against all odds. This hero, they imagined, was the kind of Jew who would reestablish a homeland in Israel.

And yet, while calling for a new kind of Jew, Zionism was repeating the formative pattern of Judaism, telling a story of exile and return—a people who originated in the land of Israel, were forcibly dispersed for almost 2,000 years, and now sought to return. Moreover, like Jewish socialism, Zionism offered secular Jews a powerful secular version of the goal of history. In the Zionist vision, however, the Jewish people were not incidental but essential. This vision recalls the biblical prophecies (Isaiah 65:17–18) that God will create not only a new heaven and a new earth but also a new Jerusalem, namely, a reestablished Jewish homeland. All in all, they made much more comprehensive and creative use of the stories of the biblical past than did the Yiddish-speaking Jewish socialists.

Like Jewish socialism, Zionism created a new way for secular Jews to be Jewish, reappropriating the tradition through story, language (which for Zionists was the recovery and reconstruction of Hebrew as a modern language), and social organization. While before World War II Jewish socialism had more adherents than Zionism, it was later eclipsed by a Zionism that absorbed and transformed its vision. After the Holocaust and the destruction of nearly a third of the world's Jews, the validity and the urgency of the Zionist message seemed self-evident to the overwhelming majority of Jews, both religious and secular. If they were to survive, Jews must have their own national homeland.

An aerial view of Masada, where first-century Jews who had resisted Rome chose suicide rather than surrender. The defenders of Masada were an important symbol of courage and resistance to Zionists.

CONTRASTING RELIGIOUS VISIONS

As the following contrasting visions indicate, every religious tradition is capable of generating both visions that encourage peace and understanding and visions that encourage conflict and violence.

Abraham Joshua Heschel, 1907–72

On June 16, 1963, Rabbi Abraham Joshua Heschel sent a telegram to the President of the United States, John F. Kennedy. Heschel and other religious leaders were scheduled to meet with the president the next day to discuss race relations and civil rights in America. The rabbi proposed that the president declare a state of "moral emergency" to aid black Americans. "We forfeit the right to worship God as long as we continue to humiliate negroes. . . . Let religious leaders donate one month's salary toward a fund for negro housing and education. . . . The hour calls for high moral grandeur and spiritual audacity."

Abraham Joshua Heschel, 1907–72, a great Hasidic Jewish scholar and rabbi who marched with Martin Luther King Jr. at Selma and championed the way of nonviolence.

Abraham Joshua Heschel was born in Warsaw, Poland, on January 11, 1907. He was the son of a Hasidic rebbe and a long line of distinguished Hasidic teachers who were deeply steeped in Jewish mysticism. Heschel was a child prodigy. By age fourteen, he had mastered the Talmud and was himself writing Talmudic commentaries. As a young university student he was expelled from Germany by the Nazis and fled back to Poland and then to America, by way of England, shortly before the invasion of Poland. He taught first at Hebrew Union College in Cincinnati and then, for most of his career, at the Jewish Theological Seminary in New York. He is the author of numerous books that have deeply influenced modern Judaism, including *Man Is Not Alone*, *The Sabbath*, *God in Search of Man*, and *Man's Quest for God*.

Heschel's life demonstrates the capacity of Orthodox Judaism to embrace the pluralism of the modern world. As a great Jewish scholar and Hasidic rabbi, Heschel was the leading Jewish voice responding to social injustices in America during the civil rights/Vietnam War era of the 1950s and 1960s. An advocate of nonviolent civil disobedience, Heschel marched with Martin Luther King Jr. from Selma to Montgomery, Alabama, in the spring of 1965 in defense of civil rights for black Americans. "Any god who is mine but not yours, any god concerned with me but not with you," Heschel asserted, is an "idol," or false god. To segregate the races, he insisted, is nothing short of "segregating God."

As a leader of Clergy and Laymen Concerned about Vietnam, the Center for Nonviolent Social Change, and also the Jewish Peace Fellowship, Heschel convinced Dr. King to join the protest against the Vietnam War. To this end, the rabbi introduced the Baptist pastor to the leader of the Vietnamese Buddhist Peace Movement, the monk Thich Nhat Hanh. In this act Heschel showed himself to be a revolutionary not only in his advocacy for social justice for all peoples but in his openness to other religions, working closely with Christians and Buddhists to bring about social justice. Holiness, he insisted, is not to be limited to those of any one religion, not even Judaism. Holiness is defined by the intention of the heart and the righteousness of the deed. To equate God and any one religion is, for Heschel, the essence of idolatry, for God is the all-inclusive reality. The will of God is to be found, he argues, not in uniformity but in diversity. Thus whenever we meet and welcome each other as human beings, sharing a common humanity despite our differences, we encounter the presence of God.

Meir Kahane, 1932–90

Meir Kahane was born in Brooklyn, New York, on August 1, 1932. The son of a rabbi deeply involved in the Zionist movement, he too became a rabbi. In 1968 he founded the JDL, or Jewish Defense League. Kahane was no advocate for nonviolence. On the contrary, he argued that Jews cannot depend on others to defend them and need to learn to protect themselves, using violence if necessary.

Kahane's life illustrates the insistence of ultra-Orthodoxy that there can only be "one way" for all Jews, a way that protects them from pollution by the secular world and all religious diversity. In 1971 he moved to Israel and founded the anti-Arab Kach Party, which called for the forcible removal of all Arabs. This party attracted a strong following among the Gush Emunim and other religious Zionists. In 1984 Kahane was elected to the Knesset, but his party was banned before the next election, in 1988, on the grounds that Kach incited racism. Kahane was assassinated by an Egyptian Muslim radical in New York City on November 5, 1990, after a speech urging all American Jews to return to Israel to protect the land from the Arabs. In the speech he had warned of a coming apocalypse in which the American stock market would collapse, leading to a new holocaust against all Jews who were still in the United States.

Meir Kahane, 1932–90, did not share Rabbi Abraham Joshua Heschel's commitment to nonviolence. His party was banned from the Knesset (the Israeli governing body) in 1984 for inciting racism.

Kahane was an advocate of a messianic Zionism that was violently apocalyptic, expecting the messiah to come soon and lead the Jews in driving all Arabs out of Israel. He rejected the view of some religious Zionists that a secular state might be a stepping-stone to the final appearance of a genuinely religiously Jewish state. Kahane had little patience with the secular state of Israel and saw its secular leaders as the enemies of all religious Jews and hinderers of the creation of a genuine Jewish state. For Kahane, any act that elevated Jews and humiliated Arabs and all other enemies of the Jews was viewed as sanctifying God's name and hastening the coming of the messiah.

In 1994 the Kach Party and its offshoot, Kahane Chai, were designated terrorist organizations by both the Israeli government and the U.S. government. This labeling was largely in response to the 1994 attack on a mosque in Hebron during which a Kach member, Baruch Goldstein, killed thirty-four Muslims. Then, in 1995, another Kahane admirer, Yigal Amir, assassinated the prime minister of Israel, Yitzhak Rabin, to put a stop to his attempts to make peace with the Palestinians. Rabin's willingness to consider compromising with the Palestinians on land issues was viewed as treason by these radical Zionists, and in their eyes this justified his murder. While most Jews remember Kahane as a terrorist, some hold him up as a hero, martyr, and true revolutionary for a militant Zionism that preaches that, by divine command, Israel is for Jews only.

Quotations from: Abraham Joshua Heschel, *Moral Grandeur and Spiritual Audacity* (essays edited by Susannah Heschel) (New York: Farrar, Straus and Giroux, 1996).

Some Sabras, secular Jews who led the Zionist movement to create an Israeli state, stand guard over their fields on a kibbutz in Israel in the early days of the new nation.

Zionism shaped a nation and turned a utopian dream into a reality—the state of Israel. Jewish ethnic socialism and Zionism together represented a powerful, if ambivalent, rejection of the modern era and its ideal of assimilation as defined by the Enlightenment. It was the amalgamation of these ways of thinking that made a natural bridge to the Judaism of Holocaust and Redemption, for without the socialist-Zionist revolution, there would be no state of Israel. And without the state of Israel, there would be only Holocaust and no sense of redemption—no sense of rescue from the forces of slavery and death similar to their ancient deliverance from slavery in Egypt into the "promised land."

The new state of Israel became a haven for Jews from around the world, including these Ethiopian schoolchildren.

Judaism and Postmodern Trends in a Postcolonial World (1967–)

Challenges to Jewish Faith After the Holocaust

In 1933 Adolf Hitler and the Nazi Party came to power in Germany. By 1939 they had drawn Europe into World War II, a six-year war of expansion that was meant to give additional *Lebensraum* ("living space") to what the Nazis considered to be the superior Aryan race of Germany. Near the end, however, when Germany was losing badly and soldiers and supplies were desperately needed at the front, trains were diverted to the task of transporting Jews to the death camps. Hitler was more desperate to rid the world of Jews than he was to win the war.

The **Holocaust** was a singular event in human history that brought the modern era of progress to an end in mass death. *Holocaust* (which means "burnt sacrifice") is the name given to the attempt by Nazi Germany to eliminate an entire people, the Jews. Unlike the millions of others who died on the battlefronts of World War II, the Jews were not military combatants (see Map 3.4). The Jews of Germany were not enemies of Germany, but citizens. There was no military or territorial advantage to be had by systematically killing them. They were marked for death simply because they existed. Germans, defeated and humiliated in World War I (1914–18) and suffering from extreme economic depression as a result of war reparations, chose not to blame these troubles on the aggressive military actions of their government during the war. Instead, they said, "The Jews are our misfortune"—they are to blame. The Nazis rose to power partly by portraying the Jews as a racial pollutant or a diseased growth on the healthy body of the German people that had to be surgically cut out if the nation was to be restored to health and greatness.

When the Nazi Party came to power, the Jews were stripped of their citizenship and all their legal rights; their homes and businesses were appropriated; and they were herded into boxcars that delivered them to an elaborate system of death camps, where they were either worked to death as slaves or murdered in specially designed gas chambers made to order for mass killings. At the most infamous of the camps, Auschwitz, in Poland, it is estimated that 2 million Jews were executed.

One has to ask: Why the Jews? Blaming a scapegoat for misfortune is not unusual in history, but what induced the Nazis to pick the Jews for this role? The answer takes us back in large part to the story of the beginnings of Christianity (which we will discuss further in Chapter 4). As a Jewish sect that came to be dominated by non-Jews, gentiles saw themselves as having superseded and replaced the Jews as God's chosen people. The establishment of Christianity as the dominant religion of the Roman Empire led to both legal discrimination and popular discrimination that often was expressed in violence against Jews as "the children of the devil"—a people most Christians believed had been rejected by God for their role in the "killing of Jesus, the Son of God."

Holocaust: the attempt by Nazi Germany to exterminate the Jewish people

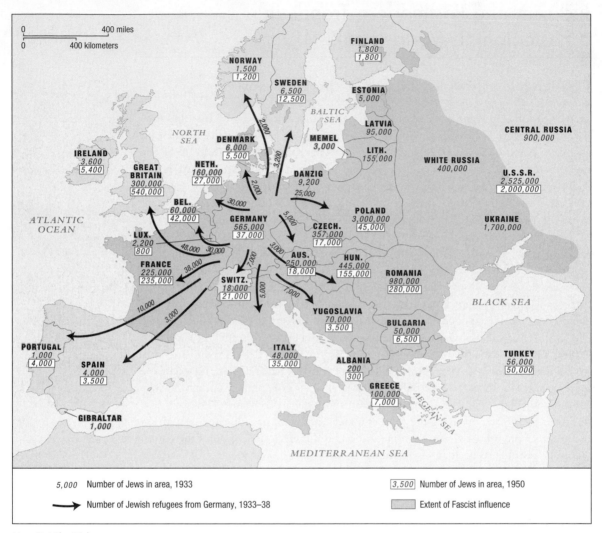

Map 3.4 The Holocaust.

Moreover the "negative witness" theory suggested by the influential Christian theologian Augustine of Hippo portrayed the Jews as condemned to wander the earth without a home, their misery supposedly offering negative proof of the truth of Christianity. From the time of this early theologian (354–430) forward, through the Middle Ages and into the modern period, Jews were the scapegoats, blamed for whatever misfortunes occurred in Western civilization. Indeed, Hitler played on popular Christian anti-Jewish sentiments to rise to the position of chancellor of Germany. Later, neither the Catholic nor the Protestant churches of Germany officially protested the Nazi treatment of the Jews—only the treatment of Jewish converts to Christianity.

The Nazis rounded up European Jews and sent them to the death camps in boxcars. These Jewish prisoners, some of them children, were photographed at the infamous Auschwitz death camp.

It took more than Christian anti-Judaism to make the Holocaust possible: For instance, the rise of secularism and scientific-bureaucratic forms of social control played an important part. Nevertheless, it is hard to imagine the Holocaust's occurring without the significant contribution of Christian anti-Semitism.

The Holocaust deeply challenges the Jewish faith orientation promoted in the stories of the exodus and exile traditions. If these stories promised a God who would always be with the people of the covenant, guiding and protecting them, then the Holocaust seemed to prove this promise a lie. Many Jews felt that God had failed to keep his promises.

After the Holocaust, some of the most Orthodox of Jews wanted to treat the Holocaust as a tragedy of the same type as the fall of the first and second temples, where these tragedies had been explained as due to a failure to keep the covenant. In fact, they proposed that the best way to remember the Holocaust was to include it in the period of fasting and mourning of Tisha B'Av. But to many other Jews, both secular and religious, this seemed wholly inappropriate. For the main victims of the Holocaust were not the most liberal and secularized Jews but rather the most orthodox and observant population in Jewry, the Jews of eastern Europe. Moreover, for many

Jews the scope of the tragedy was so great that the argument of "failure to keep the covenant" faithfully enough seemed inadequate to explain it.

How does one commemorate such an event? And how, after the Holocaust, could Jews go on believing the promises of God to guide and protect them on their journey through time? Indeed, a major debate is being carried out in contemporary Judaism in which a number of important authors offer suggestions on how Jews should respond to the Holocaust.

One author, Richard Rubenstein, says that God died at Auschwitz, and Jews will have to go on with their stories and their rituals without God. Emil Fackenheim argues that, on the contrary, God is still present in history. He justifies this view by suggesting that it is as if Jews had heard a silent yet commanding voice from Auschwitz, giving them a new commandment, a 614th commandment to be added to the 613 in the Torah. This commandment demands that Jews remain Jewish lest they allow Judaism to die, thus giving Hitler a posthumous victory.

Elie Wiesel, the Nobel Prize–winning author who is himself a survivor of Auschwitz, sees it somewhat differently.[2] Only the Jew knows, says Wiesel, that one can have the *chutzpah* (audacity) to argue with God as long as it is in defense of God's creation—as Abraham argued with God over the fate of the innocent at Sodom (Genesis 18:22–33). Indeed, a Jew has the right to put God on trial and find him guilty of abandoning the Jews during the Holocaust.

Another major Holocaust scholar, Irving Greenberg, argues that after Auschwitz, Jews can only live a "momentary faith"—tossed back and forth between the stories of the Exodus and the stories of the Holocaust. In one moment a Jew might believe in the promises of Sinai, only in the next moment to have them clouded over by memories of the smokestacks of Auschwitz. Like Wiesel, Greenberg argues that Jews

TEACHINGS OF RELIGIOUS WISDOM:
The 614th Commandment

The post-Holocaust Jewish scholar Emil Fackenheim, himself a survivor of the Holocaust, argues that Jews must not give in to despair and abandon their faith after the atrocities of the Holocaust. God, he says, speaks even from Auschwitz and gives Jews a new commandment to be added to the 613 he gave at Sinai.

Jews are forbidden to hand Hitler posthumous victories. They are commanded to survive as Jews, lest the Jewish people perish. They are commanded to remember the victims of Auschwitz lest their memory perish. They are forbidden to despair of man and his world, and to escape into either cynicism or otherworldliness, lest they cooperate in delivering the world over to the forces of Auschwitz. Finally, they are forbidden to despair of the God of Israel, lest Judaism perish. . . . A Jew may not respond to Hitler's attempt to destroy Judaism by himself cooperating in its destruction. In ancient times, the unthinkable Jewish sin was idolatry. Today, it is to respond to Hitler by doing his work.

Source: Emil L. Fackenheim, *God's Presence in History* (Northvale, NJ, and Jerusalem: Jason Aronson Inc., 1997), p. 84.

cannot be required to embrace the covenant, and yet they do so freely. Greenberg observes that this embrace takes on a wide variety of forms, from the extremely orthodox to the extremely secular. And after Auschwitz, he insists, all Jews, from the extremely orthodox to the extremely secular, are obligated to accept each other as Jews, accepting contemporary Jewish pluralism as an authentic covenantal pluralism. For Jews to turn their backs on other Jews, as some of the ultra-Orthodox in the state of Israel do when they refuse to acknowledge the Jewishness of non-Orthodox Jews, is another way of granting Hitler a posthumous victory. In a post-Holocaust and postcolonial world, Jews find themselves once more facing the question that arose in the first century of the common era: Which of all the ways of being Jewish is the right way? What has changed after Auschwitz, says Greenberg, is that Jews are free to observe or not to observe the covenant; they are not, however, free to reject Jews who exercise this freedom.

Post-Holocaust Judaism offers an alternative to the "one way" of ultra-Orthodoxy. This is a postmodern form of Judaism, in which there is not one single way to truth and to faithfulness but many. Covenantal pluralism is affirmed insofar as great diversity in thought *and* practice, both secular and religious, is allowed. Only one practice is not negotiable: the obligation of post-Holocaust Jews to accept one another in their diversity. Both ultra-Orthodoxy and the Judaism of Holocaust and Redemption seek a way out of what they see as the spiritual poverty of a modernism that made the Holocaust possible. The choice they offer to all Jews is either withdrawal from or involvement in the modern world, either back to what they view as premodern uniformity or forward to a new age of postmodern Jewish pluralism.

Finally, the post-Holocaust Jewish scholar Marc Ellis insists that Israeli Jews must never use the suffering of Jews in the Holocaust as an excuse for the oppression of their Palestinian neighbors. They must remember that the covenant relation of the Jews to the land includes the demands to ensure justice for all and to show compassion to the stranger. Not only must Jews accept other Jews in their diversity, they must accept their Christian and Muslim Palestinian neighbors in Israel in an environment of justice and peace for all. Such a task is not easy when extremists on all sides seek to undermine genuine efforts at compromise and cooperation, and yet many in the state of Israel continue the struggle to find that middle ground.

Challenges to Jewish Existence After the Holocaust

This new Judaism of Holocaust and Redemption, which has proven very attractive to American Judaism, Israeli Judaism, and Israeli nationalism, has a postmodern and postcolonial orientation. That is, instead of seeking to return to some premodern orthodoxy emphasizing one truth and one way, it attempts to find unity in the diversity of religious and secular Jews. Even its new "holy days" (or "holidays") display characteristics of both the holy and the secular. Indeed, two days that seem to be entering the Jewish calendar are recollections of seemingly secular events—*Yom Hashoah* (Day

TALES OF SPIRITUAL TRANSFORMATION

The Nobel Prize–winning author Elie Wiesel, a survivor of Auschwitz, remembers an event that took place while he was a prisoner there. His tale shows that not even consignment to the death camps of the Holocaust could destroy Jewish faith.

The Jewish festival of the giving of the Torah by God to Moses, *Simhath Torah*, arrived. However, there was no Torah in the camp that Jews could use to ritually carry in celebration. Indeed, during this celebration Hasidic Jews pick up the Torah and literally dance with it to express their joy. So an old man looks around for a substitute to use for the Torah celebration. He sees a young boy and asks him,

"Do you remember what you learned in heder (Torah school)?" "Yes I do," replied the boy. "Really," said the man, "you really remember Sh'ma Yisrael" (the confession of faith in the oneness of God). "I remember much more," said the boy. "Sh'ma Yisrael is enough," said the man. And he lifted the boy, clasped him in his arms and began dancing with him—as though *he* were the Torah. And all joined in. They all sang and danced and cried. They wept, but they sang with fervor—never before had Jews celebrated *Simhath Torah* with such fervor.

Source: Elie Wiesel, *A Jew Today* (New York: Random House, 1978), p. 146.

---

of Desolation), recalling the Holocaust, and *Yom Ha'atzmaut* (Independence Day), celebrating the founding of the modern state of Israel.

The impact of the Holocaust on Jewish consciousness cannot be overstated. During the Holocaust the Nazis nearly succeeded in their goal of eliminating Jews from the face of the earth. Nearly a third of all Jews died in the Holocaust; nearly two-thirds of the Jews of Europe died. The eastern European Jewish communities were hit the hardest. Ninety percent of these Jews and more than 80 percent of all the rabbis, Talmudic scholars, and Talmudic students then alive were murdered.

Jews might have despaired after the devastation of the Holocaust, but the founding of the state of Israel by the United Nations in 1948 gave them hope. The counterbalancing of the Holocaust and the founding of the state of Israel fits the great formative story of Jewish existence—exile and return. After 2,000 years without a homeland, many Jews experienced the ability to return to Israel as a Jewish state as a miraculous act of divine redemption akin to the return to the land of promise after slavery in Egypt or after exile in Babylon. That redemption makes it possible for Jews to remember the Holocaust without despairing.

It is in this context that we review the history of the establishment and development of the state of Israel, which marks an important turning point in the demise of colonialism and the emergence of a postcolonial, post-Holocaust Judaism. In 1922 the League of Nations gave Britain a mandate over Palestine, which had been under Muslim control. Meanwhile, the Balfour Declaration of 1917 had already set the stage for the establishment of a homeland for Jews in the area, alongside the existing Palestinian population. In supporting this policy, Britain legitimated the goal of the international Zionist movement while doing little to hasten its implementation. Thus at the conclusion of World War II, Palestine was still under the British mandate.

In 1947, as a member of the newly formed United Nations, Britain asked the General Assembly to establish a special committee on Palestine. The report of this committee, UNSCOP, led to a resolution to divide Palestine into two states—one Jewish and the other Arab (see Map 3.5). The state of Israel was established on May 14, 1948, the date on which Great Britain gave up official control of the area. Within a year Israel would be admitted to the United Nations.

The creation of a Jewish state was supported by two key UN member nations, the United States and the Soviet Union, and it represented the triumph of the Zionist movement. The Arab states, however, refused to accept the UN partition plan, and on May 15, 1948, the armies of seven Arab states invaded the newly formed nation and the war for independence was under way. The war was fought in

Leon Greenman, a Jewish survivor of Auschwitz, displays his Auschwitz serial number tattoo after addressing an Anti-Nazi League meeting in Brighton, England.

two phases, with an intervening cease-fire, and ended in the defeat of the Arab forces and an armistice with the Egyptians in February 1949. Later agreements were signed with Jordan, Lebanon, and Syria; however, none was signed with Iraq. Relations with neighboring Arab states remained tense throughout the decades that followed, flaring again into the wars of 1967 and 1973.

It is hard to overstate the impact of the 1967 war on Judaism. In June of that year, the state of Israel was seriously threatened by four predominantly Muslim nations: Egypt, Jordan, Syria, and Iraq. Israeli forces were overwhelmingly outnumbered, and the country was surrounded by 250,000 troops, having at their disposal some 2,000 tanks as well as 700 fighter planes and bombers. A UN Emergency Force had withdrawn in May, and Israeli diplomatic initiatives seeking intervention from European

Map 3.5 The creation of the state of Israel.

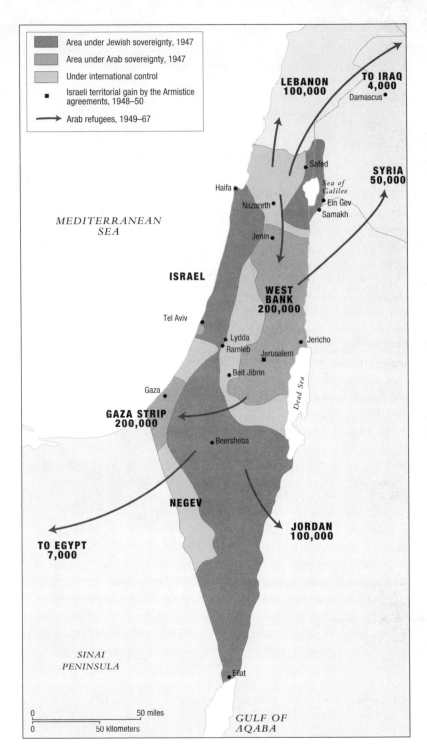

▓	Area under Jewish sovereignty, 1947
▓	Area under Arab sovereignty, 1947
░	Under international control
■	Israeli territorial gain by the Armistice agreements, 1948–50
→	Arab refugees, 1949–67

LEBANON 100,000

TO IRAQ 4,000

Damascus

Safed

SYRIA 50,000

Haifa

Sea of Galilee

Nazareth

Ein Gev

Samakh

MEDITERRANEAN SEA

Jenin

ISRAEL

WEST BANK 200,000

Tel Aviv

Lydda

Jericho

Ramleh

Jerusalem

Beit Jibrin

Dead Sea

Gaza

GAZA STRIP 200,000

Beersheba

NEGEV

JORDAN 100,000

TO EGYPT 7,000

SINAI PENINSULA

Eilat

0   50 miles

0   50 kilometers

GULF OF AQABA

This Israeli Rosh Hashanah card celebrates Moshe Dayan and Yitzhak Rabin as heroes of the victory of Israel in the 1967 Six-Day War.

countries and America met with feeble responses. Israel perceived itself to be alone, without allies and doomed to what many feared would be a second holocaust. Israeli armed forces, under the leadership of General Yitzhak Rabin, staged a surprise air attack on the morning of June 5. In a brilliant series of military moves, Israel routed the combined Arab forces in a war that was over in six days.

At the end of the war, Israel occupied territory formerly under the control of the Egyptians and the Syrians—from the Suez Canal to the Golan Heights. In the process Israel had taken control of the entire area west of the Jordan River, including the Old City of Jerusalem (on June 7), recovering one of the holiest places for all Jews, the Western Wall of the Second Temple (destroyed by the Romans in 70 CE), which had been under Jordanian control (see Map 3.6). As the dust of the Six-Day War settled, Jews both in the land of Israel and in Diaspora were overwhelmed with a sense of awe at their seemingly miraculous deliverance. Even among the most secular or nonreligious Jews, many could not help but see the redemptive hand of God in these events.

In response to this unexpected defeat, at a conference held in Khartoum in August 1967, Arab nations adopted a policy of no recognition of or negotiations with Israel. Under new leadership, the three-year-old Palestinian Liberation Organization began a long and systematic policy of guerrilla warfare against Israel.

But the essential fact for Jews has been that Israel exists and has withstood all onslaughts against it. For many Jews the 1967 war was the turning point. From that time forward the meaningful connection between the

Youths celebrate the founding of the modern state of Israel at the Western Wall, waving an Israeli flag. The new state has deep religious significance for many Jews, who see it as a sign of God's saving activity after the near annihilation of European Jews in the Holocaust.

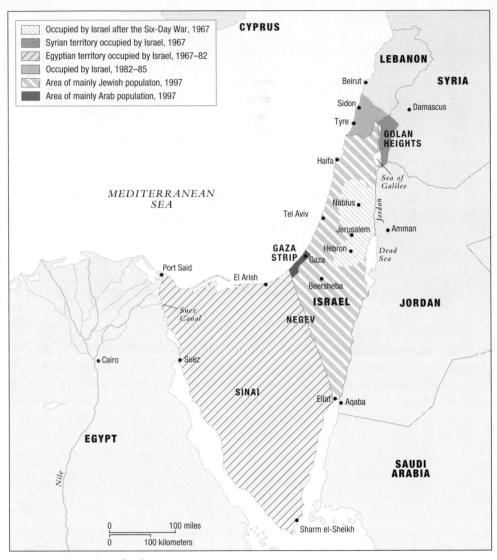

Map 3.6 Arab-Israeli conflict from 1967.

Holocaust and the founding of the state of Israel could not be ignored. The two events became indissolubly linked in Jewish minds, and the days of remembrance of these two events became ever more prominent in the Jewish calendar.

The Yom Kippur War of 1973 was less decisive than the 1967 war in military terms, but it sparked a resurgence of religious Zionism. On October 6, 1973, the Egyptian army penetrated the Israeli-occupied territory of the Sinai peninsula, while the Syrians invaded the Golan Heights. The surprise attack occurred on Yom Kippur, one of the holiest days in the Jewish calendar. Although caught off guard, Israel

The signing of the Camp David Peace Accord on March 26, 1979. U.S. President Jimmy Carter (center) is flanked by President Anwar Sadat of Egypt on his right and Israeli premier Menachem Begin on his left.

rallied and successfully rebuffed its attackers, but the event undermined confidence in the leadership of the Labor Party. Thus the ground was prepared for the rise of the conservative Likud Party, with the election of Menachem Begin as prime minister in 1977. Another result was increased political influence from religious Zionists like the Gush Emunim.

The Gush Emunim were committed to the notion that none of the occupied territories from the 1967 War was to be given back in any peace agreement after the 1973 war. Believing strongly that the Jews were chosen by God to inherit this land, they were no more inclined to share it with their Palestinian neighbors than many Christian and Muslim Palestinians were to share it with the Jews. Consequently, the Gush Emunim began an intensive program of establishing settlements in the occupied territory, an activity that was not authorized by the Israeli government. When Menachem Begin came to power, however, he supported the settlements. In this fashion, religious Zionism began to play an important role in Israeli public policy.

While the settlements were in their infancy, however, Begin signed a peace treaty with the president of Egypt, Anwar Sadat. This agreement, signed at Camp David in 1979 with the encouragement of U.S. President Jimmy Carter, called for Israel to return occupied territory in the Sinai. The Gush Emunim saw the territorial rollback as a betrayal of God's will. The movement splintered in 1982 with the death of its spiritual leader, Rabbi Zvi Yehuda Kook, and some adherents began to wage guerrilla warfare against Palestinian militants. Some even planned to blow up the mosque on the Temple Mount in Jerusalem, but they were discovered before the plan could be carried out. The leaders were arrested in 1984, and the movement lost a large measure of the public support it had enjoyed.

The Struggle over Jerusalem

The present struggle for sovereignty over Jerusalem is symbolic of the convergence of the spiritual and the physical, the religious and the political in the Middle East. This "holy" city is historically as well as scripturally claimed by Jews, Muslims, and Christians. For the Jews, Jerusalem is the "mountain of the Lord." The Mishnah (second-century compendium of Jewish laws) asserts that the Shekinah, or divine presence, has never left the Western Wall. Jerusalem is a predominant symbol and source of Jewish religious as well as nationalist identity.

In 70 CE the Romans destroyed the second temple in Jerusalem and expelled its Jewish population. Jews scattered throughout the world. Although many assimilated into the countries of their Diaspora, they retained their faith and Jewish identity. Each year, Jews across the world conclude the Passover ceremonies with the determined wish "Next Year in Jerusalem." The prophetic idea of an eventual gathering of all Jewish exiles into the land of their origin has influenced the attitudes of Westerners, Jewish as well as Christian, toward Jerusalem. The repeated assertion by Israeli leaders that a united Jerusalem is the eternal capital of Israel is an articulation of this biblical belief translated into a political vision. For 2,000 years, Jews have nursed the idea of returning to reclaim Jerusalem.

For Christians, Jerusalem is the site of their faith's origins and early history, where Jesus preached his message, was crucified, died, and was buried. It was there that in Christian belief Jesus was miraculously resurrected from the grave and ascended into heaven. The religious significance of Jerusalem was translated into the political when Pope Urban II summoned the First Crusade to recover Jerusalem and establish a Christian kingdom there.

Christian political interest in Jerusalem was manifest more recently in the British mandate over Palestine and in continuing U.S. support for Israel. Christian groups and institutions such as the World Council of Churches and the Vatican have also maintained keen interest in the status of Jerusalem.

At the same time, Jerusalem and Palestine continue to be the home of Arab Christians, who have lived there for centuries. It is also significant to the many Christians who make pilgrimages to the historical Christian churches and sites in Jerusalem.

Jerusalem is one of the three most sacred places of Islam. It was the first city to which Muslims turned in prayer (subsequently changed to Mecca), and in Muslim belief it is the place from which the Prophet Muhammad ascended to the heavens (*miraj haqq*) on a winged horse. According to Muslim eschatology (an aspect of theology that addresses the final events of human history), Jerusalem is the place where the end of time commences. Today, the loss of control of Jerusalem indicates to Muslims their ultimate defeat in what many regard as the unending Crusades launched by Christians against Islam. Failure to regain sovereignty over Jerusalem, they believe, is indicative of the decline of Islamic civilization and the failure of Palestinian aspirations to decolonize their land.

Jerusalem has also become a symbol of Western imperialism for many Muslims, who see the continued expansion of Israel as a Western plot to dominate their lands and destroy Islam. They fear that under Israeli rule, Islam's third most important mosque (al-Aqsa/Bait-ul-Maqdis) will eventually be destroyed. Indeed, some Jewish religious leaders and groups have expressed plans to rebuild the temple of King Solomon on that very site. The continued settlement of Jews in Arab East Jerusalem and the forced evacuation of Palestinians, both Christian and Muslim, have only reinforced Muslim fears.

Finally, the myth of supersession shared by Christians and Muslims further complicates things. Much as Christians have seen themselves as inheritors of Judaism who supersede or replace Judaism with a new and more complete revelation (Christianity), so Muslims see themselves as the inheritors of Judaism and Christianity. They believe that Islam is a continuation and completion of Abraham's faith and that the Quran is the final revelation sent by the same God who sent his revelations through Moses and Jesus. In that same vein, many believe that they are the true inheritors of the Holy Land, symbolized by the conquest of Jerusalem by Umar ibn al-Khattab, the second of the "Rightly Guided Caliphs," in 637 CE.

The situation became more complicated in contemporary times. In 1948, the status of Jerusalem became a global issue when, in the aftermath of the Holocaust, the United Nations partitioned Palestine to create the state of Israel as a homeland for the Jews.

The struggle for Jerusalem is indeed representative of the intersection of religion and politics in the Middle East, now with global ramifications. It is in Jerusalem that the temporal, spiritual, political, cultural, and territorial converge. Jerusalem is both modern and traditional. It is modern in its status as the aspiration of Jewish and Palestinian nationalism, and it is traditional in its sacred significance to three religions. For many there can be no political solution for Jerusalem without a religious solution. In Israel, where some forms of Zionism fuse religion and nationalism, the modern and the traditional are not distinguishable; neither are the religious and the political.

A particular reading of postcolonial history created the false expectation that the Middle East was well on the way toward secularization. History is not progressing according to the script that modernity had envisaged for the region. Religion has once again become a major theme in the study of world politics, particularly in the context of the Middle East. Rather than receding, religion has returned to the center stage. The region is developing both in political as well as economic terms, but not along the lines that Western social sciences had predicted. The long history of the nexus between power and religion and current conditions in the Middle East suggests that Western-style secularism will continue to be challenged by the contemporary religious resurgence.

In recent years, new Islamic republics have been declared in Iran, Sudan, and Afghanistan.

In Morocco, as in Saudi Arabia, the monarchy is strongly legitimized by its close association with Islam. In Jordan, King Hussein never forgot to mention his lineage, which he traced back to the Prophet Muhammad. Muslim rulers remain acutely sensitive to the power of religion, and opposition movements also appeal to Islam for legitimacy and popular support.

Similarly, Israel's very existence and identity remain tied to Judaism. Many believers base their political agenda on issues and sites that their faith holds sacred. Whether to defend the status quo or to condemn it, politicians in the Middle East, Jews as well as Muslims, invoke religious categories. The difference between the role of religion in contemporary politics, in politics in the precolonial past, and in politics in the postcolonial secular era has been one of degree, not of kind.

In the twenty-first century, religion will continue to be a major driving force in global politics. It performs many political functions, just as politics serves many religious functions in the traditional land of God, the Middle East. Religion is a source of identity as well as signification, providing symbols of authentication and meaning for social and political existence. It is the basis for states as well as a source of civil society. It is invoked to give legitimacy to systems and regimes and to provide revolutionary fodder to challenge the legitimacy of states, systems, and regimes. Jerusalem represents the locus where all three Abrahamic faiths have come together in the past and remains the subject of common and at times competing claims. The challenge for the religious politics of the Middle East in coming years, as with the issue of Jerusalem, will be to develop a pluralistic mode of existence based on the recognition of shared principles, values, and interests amid acknowledged religious and political differences.

Source: Adapted from "Religion in the Middle East" (by John Esposito with Muqtedar Khan). In Deborah J. Gerner, ed., *Understanding the Contemporary Middle East* (Boulder, CO: Lynne Rienner, 1999).

The existence of the state of Israel represents for many Jews a redemption from 2,000 years of powerlessness, persecution, and exile. The state of Israel represents, for Jews, a new age of politics, power, and a capacity for self-defense in a world that has often been bent on subjugating or destroying them. Today, Jews continue to struggle to find a way to live constructively with their own diversity in the Diaspora. And they struggle as well to maintain the autonomy of the state of Israel, while seeking a just and lasting peace in the Middle East.

Conclusion

What we learn from the study of the diverse ways of being Jewish is that religion can either reject the secular or accommodate it. What form shall the life of the people Israel take in the modern world? That is the issue being debated among Jews as they move into the future. Those like the ultra-Orthodox, who reject the secular, see religion as being about a sacred, eternal, and unchangeable way of life that must not be profaned by accommodation with the world. Consequently, they are segregationists. The ultra-Orthodox, like fundamentalists everywhere, see modern secular society as profane—a contradiction of the sacred order embodied in premodern religious forms. All modern and postmodern/post-Holocaust religious forms of Judaism, by contrast, see the holy and the secular less as opposites than as complementary, and they tend to see historical change as the medium through which God reveals himself in time.

For modernist and post-Holocaust Jews, knowledge of the historical development of Judaism (in varying degrees) became an inherent component in their self-understanding and has made it possible for each person to admit new levels of diversity and change into the tradition. The modernist forms of Judaism (Reform, Conservative, and Orthodox) tend to regard diversity as competition in which one is "more right" than the others although all are Jews. The postmodern Judaism of Holocaust and Redemption envisions the diverse forms of Judaism as equal and mutually supporting. To the ultra-Orthodox, by contrast, diversity is apostasy, and segregation from the non-Jewish modern world and from all forms of Judaism that compromise with that world is the only path to being the true Israel or covenant people.

For most ultra-Orthodox, to admit any change is to condone relativism, and with it unbelief. For modernist and post-Holocaust Jews, to admit change is a matter of intellectual integrity: Since time cannot be stopped, some change is inevitable. Jews at the two ends of the spectrum disagree over how much change is permissible, with the Orthodox demanding a return to the fundamental truths and practices of premodern Judaism and the secular Judaisms accepting at least some integration with the non-Jewish world. For Reform, Conservative, and Holocaust and Redemption Jews, God reveals himself in the continued unfolding of history. For ethnicists, socialists, and Zionists, meaning is to be found not in the God of history but in the history itself. Such "secular" Jews are not "religious" in the traditional sense of biblical theism, but they do display one type of religious behavior commonly found in the history of religions—reverence for the ways of the ancestors, ways that are held sacred.

All but the ultra-Orthodox are convinced that to be the true Israel not only does not require Jews to go back but allows them to go forward. The strength of the modern/postmodern forms of Judaism is in their ability to adapt Jewish life to new environments and situations. The strength of the Orthodox and ultra-Orthodox is in challenging those who would adapt not to sacrifice the heart of Jewish religious existence as a people—God, Torah, and Israel. They would argue that history and Jewish ethnicity are not an adequate substitute.

The adventure continues as Jews everywhere wrestle with each other and with the world around them over what it means to be a Jew—especially in the state of Israel, where there can be no peace unless accommodation both among Jews and with their Christian and Muslim neighbors is found. And yet the very struggle of Jews everywhere, whether secular or religious, among themselves and with the non-Jewish world around them, is very Jewish. We need only recall the story of how Jacob's name was changed to Israel (Genesis 32:23–32): Jacob wrestled with the stranger who would not tell Jacob his name but instead blessed Jacob and changed Jacob's name to Israel, meaning "he who has wrestled with God and human beings and prevails." Throughout history, the drama of Judaism has been to wrestle with God and the stranger. Today, whether secular or religious, Jews are still deeply shaped by the stories of Israel, they still wrestle with the stranger, and they still prevail.

> Jacob was left alone; and a man (a stranger) wrestled with him until daybreak. . . . Then he said, "Let me go, for the day is breaking." But Jacob said, "I will not let you go, unless you bless me." So he said to him, . . . "you shall no longer be called Jacob, but Israel, for you have striven with God and with humans, and have prevailed. . . . So Jacob called the place Peniel, saying, "For I have seen God face to face and yet my life is preserved."
>
> —NRSV, Genesis 32:24–30

Discussion Questions

1. What does it mean to say that Judaism is a form of the "myth of history"? Give examples from both the biblical and postbiblical periods.

2. At what point in biblical history did the fundamental pattern of Jewish experience emerge, and what shape did it take? Give two examples from the history of Judaism, one secular and one religious.

3. What is the Talmud, and what is its significance for the religion of Judaism?

4. Compare and contrast Enlightenment Judaism (Haskalah) and Hasidic Judaism.

5. Whom would you nominate as the three most important postbiblical figures in the history of Judaism, and why?

6. In what ways have secular forms of Judaism transformed the shape of contemporary religious forms of Judaism? Give examples and explain.

7. How does the history of anti-Judaism in Western Christianity and Western civilization relate to the Holocaust?

8. What was the impact of the Holocaust on the shape of modern and postmodern forms of Jewish life, religious and secular?

9. What is the Judaism of Holocaust and Redemption, and how does it relate to modern and premodern forms of Judaism? Also, why might it be seen as the alternative to ultra-Orthodoxy?

10. Is Zionism a secular form of Judaism or a religious form, or both? Explain, with historical examples.

Key Terms

Ashkenazi	Hasidism	synagogue
bar mitzvah	Holocaust	Talmud
bat mitzvah	Israel	Tanak
circumcision	Kabbalah	Tannaim
covenant	kosher	temple
Diaspora	Marranos	Tisha B'Av
dual Torah	Mishnah	Tzaddik
Gemara	*mitzvot*	Zionism
gentile	Rabbinic	*Zohar*
halakhah	Sephardic	
haredim	*Shema*	

Suggested Readings

Fasching, Darrell J. *Narrative Theology After Auschwitz: From Alienation to Ethics* (Minneapolis: Fortress Press, 1992).

Greenberg, Irving. *The Jewish Way* (New York: Summit Books, 1988).

———. *For the Sake of Heaven and Earth: The New Encounter Between Judaism and Christianity* (New York: Jewish Publication Society of America, 2004).

Isaacs, Ronald H., and Kerry M. Olitzky, eds. *Critical Documents of Jewish History: A Source Book* (London: Jason Aronson, 1995).

Johnson, Paul. *A History of the Jews* (New York: Harper & Row, 1987).

Keppel, Gilles. *The Revenge of God: The Resurgence of Islam, Christianity, and Judaism in the Modern World* (University Park: Pennsylvania State University Press, 1991, 1994).

Lawrence, Bruce B. *Defenders of God: The Fundamentalist Revolt Against the Modern Age* (Columbia: University of South Carolina Press, 1995).

Neusner, Jacob. *The Death and Birth of Judaism* (New York: Basic Books, 1987).

———. *Self-fulfilling Prophecy: Exile and Return in the History of Judaism* (Boston: Beacon Press, 1987).

Schwartz, Barry. *Judaism's Great Debates: Timeless Controversies from Abraham to Herzl* (Lincoln: University of Nebraska Press, 2012).

Notes

1. Jacob Neusner, *The Death and Birth of Judaism* (New York: Basic Books, 1987), p. 116.
2. Elie Wiesel, *A Jew Today* (New York: Random House, 1978), p. 146.

Additional Resources

The Chosen (1981, feature film). Set in 1940s Brooklyn and based on a novel by Chaim Potok (published in 1967 by Simon and Schuster), this film presents the story of two young men, one from an ultra-Orthodox Hasidic family and the other from a more "modern" Orthodox family at the time of the Zionist struggle of Israel for statehood. A dramatic examination of the conflict between different ways of Jewish life and thought responding to the "modern" world at a critical moment in Jewish history. Color, 107 minutes, dir. Jeremy Kagan.

Genocide (1981, documentary). Academy Award–winning documentary on the Holocaust narrated by Elizabeth Taylor and Orson Welles. An Arnold Schwartzman production available from the Simon Wiesenthal Center (http://www.kintera.org).

Heritage: Civilization and the Jews (1984, documentary). A nine-part PBS video series on the history of the Jews narrated by Abba Eban. Available on interactive DVD-Rom from PBS. There is also an accompanying PBS website, including timeline and lesson plans. Here you will also find links to a wealth of web resources on the history of the Jews (http://www.pbs .org/wnet/heritage/HeritageGuide.pdf).

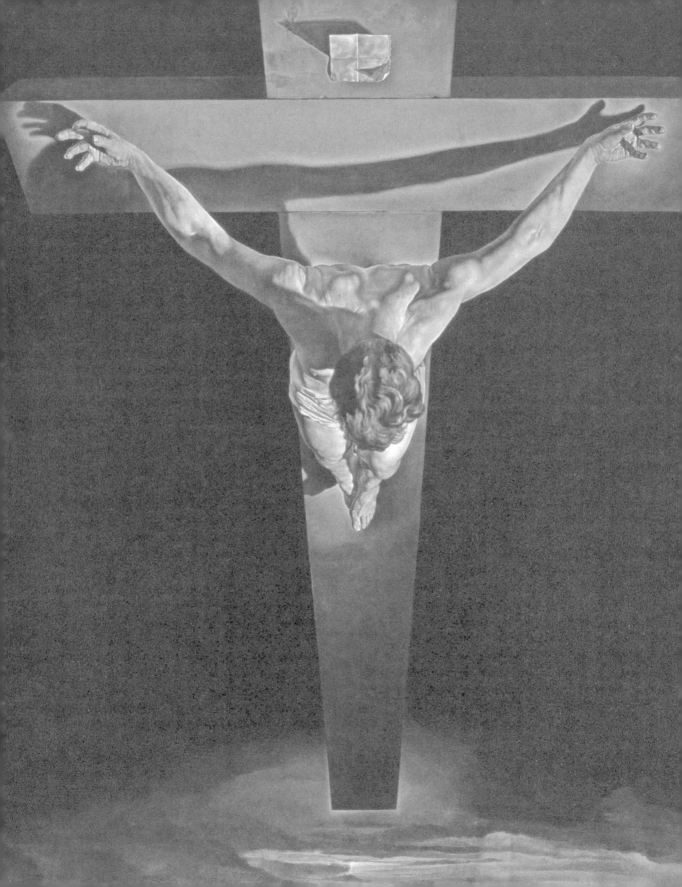

CHRISTIAN DIVERSITY 4

and the Road to Modernity

Overview

Somewhere in rural India, a small group of Christians, virtually indistinguishable from their neighbors, who are Hindus, gather to pray and offer flower petals before a statue of Jesus. In yet another place, somewhere in Africa, villagers gather to dance and sing tribal chants in praise of the risen **Christ**, even as in a small unadorned room in England, a dozen Quakers sit in wordless prayer, waiting for the Holy Spirit to inspire one of them to speak a message to the rest. At the same time, if we turn to the United States, we find a woman priest consecrating bread and wine as the body and blood of Christ at an inner-city Episcopal church in the Northeast. Southward, in a small village in Latin America, a dozen peasants sit in a circle on a hillside under the morning sun, preparing to share the bread and wine as the body and blood of Christ and studying the Gospel of Luke. Remembering that the word *gospel* means "good news," they are encouraged by Jesus' words of hope to the poor and the downtrodden. At the same time, televangelist Joel Osteen tells an American television audience of millions that Christ's message is that God has good things in store for them.

Elsewhere, in a storefront church in the Midwest of the United States, Christians—male and female, black and white—stand and raise their arms above their heads, their hands extended toward heaven. The eyes of many are closed; soon some begin to speak in an unknown language. These worshippers are **Pentecostal**, or charismatic Christians who believe they have gifts or abilities to speak a special spiritual language, known as *speaking in tongues*. They believe that the Holy Spirit of God has descended

Christ: title Christians apply to Jesus of Nazareth; from the Greek translation of the Hebrew word meaning "anointed one" or "messiah"

Pentecostal: churches that emphasize possession by the Holy Spirit and speaking in tongues

147

For some Christians, worship is a powerful and physically involving emotional experience, as in this contemporary charismatic service in a stadium in Anaheim, California.

Catholic: churches that define their Christian authenticity through apostolic succession

on them and speaks through them, even as this Spirit guides their daily walk with Christ. Meanwhile in Rome, the pope, leader of the largest Christian denomination in the world, the Roman **Catholic** Church, processes into the great Cathedral of St. Peter escorted by a long line of men in flowing robes. The procession makes its way between the majestic rows of stone pillars led by one man carrying a processional cross. Incense bearers follow, swinging pots of richly aromatic incense whose smoke wafts through the air as if carrying the sounds of organ music and chanting up to heaven. Soon the pope will arrive at the altar to celebrate Mass.

Despite their incredible diversity, all these believers are Christians engaged in Christian prayer and worship. The challenge before us is to understand the unity and diversity among Christians, especially in the contemporary world. In addition, in this chapter we will need to get a more complete picture of the history of the process of modernization and globalization that began in Western culture in an ambivalent relationship with Christianity. This will also give us the background necessary to better understand the reaction of other religions to modernization.

Like Jews and Muslims, Christians believe that there is but one God, the God who made all things and rules over history. This God is the highest reality, and to act in harmony with the will of this God is the highest goal of life. Christians are unique, however, in believing that God is one God yet three persons (Father, Son, and Holy Spirit) and that the reality of this God is uniquely revealed in the life and person of Jesus of Nazareth. Christians believe that the eternal Word of God was united to humanity through the person of Jesus, who suffered and died on the cross for the sins of the world. They believe that Jesus was raised from the dead three days later and after forty days ascended to heaven, where he will reign until he comes again at the end of time to judge the living and the dead at the final resurrection.

Like Jews and Muslims, Christians believe that the gravest problem in human life is sin—the failure to live in harmony with the will of God. Sin has two dimensions: idolatry and injustice. Idolatry is more than worshipping the images of false deities; it is treating anything that is not God as if it were more important than God. Idolaters shift the focus from the God who seeks the good of all to their selfish desires, thus sowing the seeds of injustice, for if nothing is more important than achieving such selfish goals as wealth and power, treating other human beings unjustly can be seen as necessary to ensure that these ends are met.

However, Christians differ from Jews and Muslims in their view of sin and how it is to be overcome. Most Christians define *sin* in terms of the concept of **original sin**, which says that the will to do good in all human beings was corrupted by the first human beings—Adam and Eve, who, through their disobedience to God's will, brought sin and death into the world. Thus, most Christians believe that while human beings were created good, their good will (the desire to do what is good) was corrupted by the inherited consequences of the sin of Adam and Eve, so humans feel compelled to act selfishly. Humans are enslaved to the power of sin and not fully capable of obeying the will of God. Out of compassion for human beings, God chose to send a savior, Jesus Christ, to redeem them by dying in reparation for their past sins and restoring human nature (re-creating a good will in them) in order for obedience to the will of God to be possible and in order to restore human destiny to its true goal of eternal life with God.

God sent into the world his only son, to become incarnate—that is, fully embodied—in the person of Jesus of Nazareth. In doing so, God united his divine nature to human nature, healing its flaws. The primary means for Christians to overcome sin and live in harmony with the will of God is to die spiritually and be reborn through faith in Christ. The Christian who has undergone this conversion experience believes he or she has become a new person, one who is free to obey the word of God as revealed in the scriptures. Christians believe that during their earthly lives they are called to help bring about the **Kingdom of God**—the beginning of a new creation of love, compassion, and justice in which death will finally be overcome, even as Jesus overcame death on the cross.

In century after century, Christians have sought this Kingdom of God, also referred to as the *kingdom of heaven* in scriptures. Constantly they have struggled to establish it. This goal has forced Christians to try to understand the relationship between the church and the world and how their faith and way of life should be related to the non-Christian world around them. Both Catholic Christianity, which took definitive shape in the early and medieval church, and the sixteenth-century **Protestant** movement to reform Catholicism have struggled with this question in every age, including the present one.

Despite the explanation of Christianity just given, it would be misleading to think that all Christians in all times and places would agree with it. Like all religions, Christianity is more than one thing. It has taken many forms and been many things

original sin: sin of Adam and Eve, who disobeyed God when they ate the fruit of the tree of knowledge of good and evil. This sin was said to weaken the will to do good of all humans born after them

Kingdom of God: occurs whenever humans live in accord with the will of God

Protestant: churches that emphasize direct personal relationship with God in Christ (rather than through the mediation of the Church established by apostolic succession) as necessary for salvation to many people. In the remainder of this chapter we shall try to understand both the unity and the diversity of Christianity.

Today Christianity is the largest religion in the world. With over 2.2 billion adherents, of whom about 1.1 billion are Roman Catholic, all together Christians represent approximately one-third of the world's population. Approximately 37 percent of Christians are Protestant, and 12 percent are either Greek or Russian Orthodox. Other minority Christian communities make up 1 percent of the global Christian population. Our primary task in this chapter is twofold: (1) to understand Christianity in all its diversity and (2) to appreciate the unique role that this religion has played in the development of the modern society that presented such a formidable challenge to it and all other faiths. So, unlike in our other chapters, here we will focus not just on religion but also on the emergence of the modern world out of the ancient world. So this chapter will trace important aspects of the social, intellectual, and political history of modernization as it emerged in the West. Since modernity grew up within the womb of Western Christian civilization, we will

Christianity Timeline

31 CE	Crucifixion of Jesus of Nazareth
48–60	Letters of Paul of Tarsus
70	Fall of the Jewish temple in Jerusalem to the Romans; Gospel of Mark written
80–100	Gospels of Matthew and Luke and John written
313	Edict of Milan by Constantine permitting Christianity in Roman Empire
325	Council of Nicaea declares Word of God to be same as (*homoousios*) God
380	Christianity declared the official religion of the Roman Empire by Emperor Theodosius
451	Council of Chalcedon, doctrine of two natures in the one person of Christ
500s	Development of Benedictine monasticism in the West
590–604	Pontificate of Gregory the Great, first great pope of the Middle Ages
732	Muslim invasion of Europe stopped at Tours by Charles Martel
800	Coronation of Charlemagne
1095	First Crusade against Muslims and mass violence against Jews
1184	Inauguration of church inquisitions by Pope Lucius III
1198–1216	Pontificate of Innocent III, most powerful pope in history
1224–1274	St. Thomas Aquinas, greatest theologian of Middle Ages
1414	Council of Constance—papal decadence and the declaration of conciliar rule in the church
1517	Luther's Ninety-five Theses posted on church door at Wittenberg, beginning of Protestant Reformation
1545–1563	Council of Trent, Catholic Counter-Reformation
1555	Peace of Augsburg—first attempt to end religious wars of the Reformation

have to understand not only the history of Christianity as a religion but the way it has influenced and been influenced by social, political, and intellectual trends in Western history.

As with Judaism and the other religions found in the modern world, pluralism presents a challenge. Some Christians believe there should not be diversity among Christians and blame modernization for this development. So some Christians, who identify themselves as **fundamentalists**, have argued that the alliance of Christianity with modernization is a mistake. This mistake could be corrected by returning to the "fundamentals" of the faith as they believe these fundamentals were understood and practiced before the emergence of the modern scientific and secular view of the world. Others (*modernists*) have argued that the historical evidence shows there has always been diversity within Christianity. For them modernization is not a problem but is itself evidence of the power of the Christian **Gospel** to transform the world. In their view, Christians should embrace modernization as the path to human dignity and liberation.

fundamentalist: the most conservative wing of Evangelical Protestants, who believe modern interpretations threaten certain Gospel truths

Gospel: literally "good news"; refers to Jesus' message of salvation in the New Testament

1648	Peace of Westphalia—end of religious wars, quest for religious tolerance
1703–1791	John Wesley, founder of Methodism
1768–1834	Friedrich Schleiermacher, father of modern theology
1791	First Amendment to U.S. Constitution, guaranteeing religious freedom for all
1813–1855	Søren Kierkegaard, Christian existentialism
1851	Karl Marx publishes *Communist Manifesto*
1859	Charles Darwin publishes *On the Origin of Species*
1869–1870	First Vatican Council
1910–1915	Publication of *The Fundamentals* begins fundamentalist/modernist controversy
1939–1945	World War II and the Holocaust
August 6, 1945	Atomic bomb dropped on Hiroshima, Japan, leading to end of World War II
1947	India achieves independence; Church of South India is formed
1950s, 1960s	Emergence of civil rights movement under Martin Luther King Jr.; Pope John XXIII and the Second Vatican Council
1970s–1990s	Religious resurgence of evangelical fundamentalism and emergence of liberation theology movements
2005	Death of Pope John Paul II and election of Pope Benedict XVI
2013	Pope Benedict XVI resigns (the first resignation since the thirteenth century) to permit the election of a new Pope, which occurred on March 13, 2013, when Jorge Mario Bergoglio, an Argentinean Jesuit, became Pope Francis

The Christianity of yesterday helped give birth to the modern world in all its diversity; and to understand the latter we need also to understand the former. We shall begin with the Protestant encounter with modernity and then look at Catholicism's struggle with the modern world. Then, to see how things came to be the way they are today, we shall return to the beginning in the first century and journey forward.   ○ ● ○

Encounter with Modernity: The Fundamentalist–Modernist Controversy (1859–)

The Protestant Confrontation with Modernity

When the first followers of Jesus of Nazareth looked up into the night sky in the first century, they did not see what modernists did when they looked upward in the nineteenth century. For modernists saw a cosmos with stars and planets scattered in infinite space. They knew that the earth is not at the center of the universe but just one of the planets circumnavigating a star (the sun) in one of many galaxies. When individuals in the first century looked up they saw a world shaped not by the modern scientific imagination but by the imagination of the ancient Greeks. They accepted the Greek view that the earth was at the center of seven spheres. The higher spheres of the stars and the planets embodied spiritual beings (Paul of Tarsus called them the "principalities and powers") that governed the universe. Everything above the moon, they believed, belonged to the realm of the spiritual and eternal. Everything below the moon belonged to the realm of the physical and temporal. The Greeks thought that the souls of all humans had their origin in the spiritual realm and had descended into the material or bodily realm. But the spiritual goal, each individual's hope of salvation, was to return to the eternal realm above, beyond time, decay, and death.

In addition to the legacy of the Greeks, the worldview of the first Christians owed a debt to the Hebraic tradition of ancient Israel, namely, that creation is a story unfolding in time. In the beginning God spoke and the story began. The story has many dramatic ups and downs as it unfolds, but at last God will bring the present world to an end, judge it, and transform it into a new creation. Today "modern" believers wrestle with the question of whether being a Christian requires adherence to the ancient worldview or can accommodate changing worldviews, including the modern scientific one.

The nineteenth century marked a critical turning point in the history of Christianity as it sought to coexist with an increasingly "modern" secular and scientific world whose views challenged many of the fundamental truths and practices of Christians.

The central issue in modern Christianity has been the struggle between modernism and fundamentalism. Indeed, the term *fundamentalism* originated with the American Protestant encounter with *modernism.*

Modernization in nineteenth-century America was fueled by the growth of science, industrialization, and concomitant urbanization. In this period the United States was becoming increasingly secular, especially in the area of higher education. This was a major cultural shift, for in the mid-1800s most colleges were under **evangelical** Protestant leadership. This form of Christianity emphasized the centrality of the powerful "born-again" experience of spiritual transformation and the primacy of the Bible as a source of true knowledge. By the end of the century higher education was more and more in the hands of universities modeled on the German scientific ideal of scholarship, in which each discipline has its own rational and empirical standards that make no direct appeal to the Bible or Christian beliefs. In this context, Charles Darwin's theories on the biological evolution of humanity from lower primates had caught the popular imagination. Less generally known but very much on the minds of evangelical preachers was the new "biblical criticism" that had come out of Germany. Although by *criticism* proponents meant "analysis," not "finding fault," this new scholarship, which looked on the Bible as a historical, humanly created document, challenged many pious beliefs about its teachings.

evangelical:
Christian movements that emphasize the emotional power of conversion as a spiritual transformation

The challenges stemming from Darwinism and biblical criticism were a double blow to Christian beliefs and elicited two opposing responses: the modernism of liberal Christian evangelicals on the one hand and the fundamentalism of conservative Christian evangelicals on the other. Liberal evangelicals developed a new theology to show how modernism and Christianity were compatible. They saw God at work in evolution and in history and embraced a "Social Gospel" oriented to making this world a better place for all. Christians, they argued, have an ethical calling to cooperate with God's will, operative in evolution and history, to transform this world into the Kingdom of God. By the end of World War I, liberal evangelical Christianity dominated the northern Protestant churches. However, in the eyes of many other evangelicals, the attempt to adapt Christianity to the modern world was doomed to failure. What one ended up with was a Christianity emptied of everything that made it Christian and filled with everything that was secular and modern.

It was modernization that split evangelical theology in two: opposing the liberal Social Gospel was Protestant fundamentalism. Whereas the theologians of the Social Gospel believed they represented the next logical stage in the historical development of Christianity, evangelicals who responded in a fundamentalist mode were convinced that there could be no historical development in this respect. If there was a conflict between the scriptures and modern science, then it must be modern science, not the Bible, that was in error.

In a series of twelve paperback books entitled *The Fundamentals,* published between 1910 and 1915, champions of the fundamentalist movement spoke in defense of Bible-based religion and against the apostasy, as they perceived it, of modernism. Convinced that liberal theology and Darwinism were undermining American civilization, they took their stand on the inerrancy of the Bible, pure and simple. If you did not share this belief, the fundamentalists did not consider you to be a true Christian.

The development of two American schools of evangelical Christianity was paradoxical. Evangelical Christianity had originated as a strategy for transcending the theological disputes and religious wars that occurred in the aftermath of the Protestant Reformation. The original evangelicals, in Europe, believed that a true Christian was identified not by acceptance of the right doctrines but by being "born again"—an emotional transformation undergone through a spiritual surrender to Christ that produced a life of love and compassion and enabled Christians to accept each other, despite disagreements over fundamental beliefs. One of the most influential proponents of evangelical Christianity, John Wesley (the founder of Methodism), was famous for insisting that doctrinal differences should not separate Christians who are truly united in their love of God and their neighbor.

Many later evangelicals, however, feared that the shock of modernism threatened Christian faith to the core, and by the 1920s the movement dubbed *fundamentalism* by the popular press was understood to refer to militantly antimodernist evangelical Protestants. The event that decisively formed the public image of Christian fundamentalism in America was the Scopes trial held in Dayton, Tennessee, in 1925. John Scopes, a high school teacher, had been accused of breaking a law that banned the teaching of evolution in the state's public schools. Three-time candidate for president of the United States William Jennings Bryan appeared for the prosecution. The defense was led by the legendary Clarence Darrow, a favorite of the international press corps that attended the trial. Although Bryan won the case in court, he lost the cause in the media, which portrayed fundamentalism as the philosophy of ignorant backwoods hicks. Fundamentalism then lost popular support, and Protestant liberalism, which sought to embrace modernity, held sway largely unchallenged until the surprising resurgence of fundamentalism in the last quarter of the twentieth century.

The Catholic Confrontation with Modernity

In 1864 Pope Pius IX issued a Syllabus of Errors listing eighty "modern" teachings that challenged the control of all knowledge and politics by the church. Pius IX thought that modern ideas could only lead to a godless society that would no longer heed the eternal and unchanging fundamental truths of the one true church, and he admonished Catholics to reject them. In 1869 Pius IX called the First Vatican Council of cardinals and bishops to shore up the teachings of the church against the threat of modernism. In 1870 the papacy was besieged not only by modern ideas but by modern secular politics. In that year the new secular kingdom of Italy seized the papal estates from Pius IX and the Vatican lost the political power it had enjoyed for centuries.

Thus Vatican I, as the council is now known, was in session precisely at the time when the intellectual and political authority of the papacy was at its weakest and most vulnerable. In 1870, at the insistence of Pius IX, Vatican I declared the pope to be infallible. This meant that a pope's official declarations on faith and morals could not be altered, even with the consent of the church, including any future councils.

There is a striking similarity between Protestant and Catholic antimodernist responses. Both attempted to prevent modernization and historical change from entering the church by an appeal to an infallible or inerrant authority that they believed was higher than scientific and secular authority. However each responded by appealing to a different form of authority. For Protestants it was the Bible; for Roman Catholics it was the pope, as the final authority on how the Bible was to be interpreted.

It is all the more remarkable, therefore, that almost a century later a new pope would seek to reverse many of the decisions of Vatican I and come to terms with the modern world. When Pope John XXIII called the Second Vatican Council in 1962, in one dramatic gesture he sought to reverse the more than four centuries of church attempts to reject the emerging modern world. And he sought to heal the bad feelings generated by religious divisions in Christianity going back to the Protestant Reformation and even earlier. Moreover, in its Declaration on the Relationship of the Church to Non-Christian Religions, the council expressed a new openness to the teachings of other world religions. Indeed, it declared: "The Catholic Church rejects nothing which is true and holy in these [non-Christian] religions."

The Second Vatican Council's meetings lasted from 1962 to 1965. John XXIII did not live to see them completed, but in his brief papacy (1958–1963) he unleashed a spirit that transformed the Catholic Church from a world-shunning institution into one that was open to the modern world. In the decades since Vatican II, Catholics have wrestled with their future, with some wanting to return to the fundamentals of the Catholicism of Vatican I, and others wanting to follow the road to modernization.

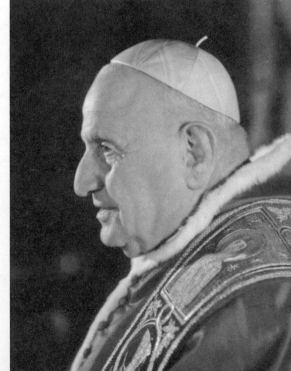

Pope John XXIII, who opened the doors of the Roman Catholic Church to modernity by calling the Second Vatican Council, in a portrait from 1963.

The Nineteenth-Century Historical and Social-Scientific Revolution

In the confrontation with modernity, both Catholics and Protestants responded to the scientific revolution in human thought that had marked the nineteenth century. This revolution was precipitated by the emergence of new academic disciplines, representing the final shock wave of modern consciousness.

The first wave had been created by the natural sciences. Copernicus had outraged the European world when he suggested in 1543 CE that the earth was not the center of the universe. Later, geologists had concluded that the earth was far older than had been calculated by anyone who used the Bible as a guide. Then in 1859 Charles Darwin published *On the*

Origin of Species, rendering completely implausible the biblical account according to which human beings appeared on earth on the sixth day of creation. Darwin claimed that evolution had been proceeding for many hundreds of thousands of years and was the result of a struggle between members of the various species culminating in the survival of the fittest.

The social sciences delivered the second shock wave, especially critical historiography, which showed that popular legends about the past often did not accurately describe the events they purported to chronicle. The other social sciences did little to ease the shock. Sociologists and anthropologists who studied societies comparatively suggested that humanity had invented gods to make the ways of life of various cultures seem sacred. This view was reinforced by Sigmund Freud's suggestion that God was a projection or instance of wish fulfillment—an illusion that human beings needed to create to give them a feeling of security in a dangerous world. Now human beings were asked to think of both society and human identity as created by human choices rather than by divine actions and decisions, as claimed by traditional teachings.

This new awareness created a profound problem. The question that came to divide modern Christianity was whether to reject the developments of modernity, as did Protestant evangelical fundamentalism and Vatican I Catholicism, or to accept them, seeing God at work in evolution and historical change, as did Protestant evangelical liberalism and Vatican II Catholicism—or strike some kind of compromise in between. Paradoxically, although modernity appeared to be a threat to Christianity, it had been nurtured, in significant part, by Christianity itself. Our task now is to return to the beginning of Christianity so that we can better understand the historical circumstances that led its adherents and its institutions, the churches, to contribute to the development of the modern world. In this we will focus entirely on tracing the role of Christianity in relation to the emergence of modernity in Europe and the role that Christianity has played in promoting European colonialism. Then we will further trace the new developments coming out of African and Asian Protestantism and Vatican II Catholicism. These trends seem to be leading to a post-European diaspora form of Christianity open to religious pluralism in an age of globalization.

Premodern Christianity: The Formative Era (31–451 CE)

The New Testament and the Life of Jesus

The journey of Christianity from the ancient to the modern world begins in the first century with the life and teachings of Jesus of Nazareth as communicated in the Gospels of the New Testament. Being a Jew, Jesus participated in a religious tradition that went back 2,000 years before his time. This is acknowledged in the Christian Bible, which is made up of two parts. What Christians call the Old Testament is basically an adoption of the Pharisaic and Hellenistic Jewish collections of sacred writings that have been the official scriptures of Judaism since the end of the first century of the common era (CE). The scriptural writings of Christians called the New Testament did not assume the form of the twenty-seven books we have now until the year 367 CE—more than 300 years after the death of Jesus. During those centuries there were in circulation many stories of the life and sayings of Jesus (other gospels such as the *Gospel of Thomas* and the *Acts of John*), most of which do not appear in the New Testament. Even after 367, extending into the sixth century, some of these "other gospels" appear in "new testament" Bibles.

What is striking is that the tradition did not settle on a single story of Jesus for its Bible but actually included four distinct yet overlapping stories—the Gospels of Matthew, Mark, Luke, and John. To these were appended letters by the apostle Paul and others, a short history of the early church (the Acts of the Apostles), and a vision of the end of time (the book of Revelation). Christians believe that these scriptures show that Jesus of Nazareth is the Christ—the anointed one, or messiah—whose coming was foretold by the Hebrew prophets.

According to tradition, the Gospels were written in the order of their appearance in the New Testament: Matthew, Mark, Luke, and John. After careful scrutiny of the literary structure and probable historical context of each Gospel, however, many modern scholars concluded that Mark's Gospel probably was written first (at the time of the fall of the temple in 70) and that both Matthew and Luke used Mark's material as a model in writing their versions (sometime between 80 and 90). The Gospel of John (written after 90) is so different in literary tone, content, and structure that it seems to have been a largely independent creation.

Also, according to tradition, the Gospels were written by disciples (or disciples of disciples) of Jesus. Taking advantage of historical and archaeological findings that shed additional light on the biblical period, modern scholars do not believe any Gospel had

Christians in every culture tend to imagine the birth of Christ in terms of their own culture, as in this Chinese painting.

a single author. Rather, each one began in shared oral traditions as told in different communities of believers after Jesus' death on the cross and attested resurrection. These traditions were eventually written down and edited to place the sayings of Jesus in the context of different remembered events from Jesus' life.

As we have noted, the sacred scriptures of Christianity were first examined critically in the nineteenth century. Within Christianity the validity of this modern approach is in dispute. Fundamentalists reject it, while other Christians see it as helpful for understanding the development of faith in the early church. And yet for all their differences, and quite apart from historical questions of "what really happened," all forms of Christianity share a common reverence for the stories of Jesus as they are found in the New Testament.

The Stories of Jesus

The power of the Christian message is revealed in the stories of Jesus. What the stories of Jesus tell is that God's true being manifested itself in the life of a human being, Jesus of Nazareth. Ancient philosophies often denigrated the human body as a prison to be escaped from and unworthy of association with God, who was pure spirit. The story of Jesus, in whom God's word was made flesh, affirmed that being human was not to be belittled, for God embraced it.

Jesus was born roughly at the beginning of the first century and grew up in Nazareth in ancient Palestine, then under Roman rule (see Map 4.1). Little is known of his youth, but according to the gospel stories he was raised by Joseph, a carpenter, and his wife, Mary, the child's mother. The birth of Jesus was said to have been miraculous, for Mary became pregnant through the power of God as announced by an angel rather than through marital relations with Joseph.

Around the age of thirty, Jesus had a traumatic experience. Someone he knew, admired, and was related to—John the Baptist—was arrested on orders from Herod and eventually beheaded. To everyone's surprise, soon after John's arrest Jesus began teaching the very message that had gotten John in trouble with Herod—"Repent, for the kingdom of heaven is at hand" (Matthew 4:17).

While his family and childhood friends at first thought he had gone mad, Jesus soon attracted followers who thought otherwise and called him rabbi, which means "teacher." The power of the Christian story is especially revealed in the Sermon on the Mount (Matthew 5–7), with its message of loving all persons, even your enemies. It is that message of compassion and forgiveness that has moved millions.

In addition to preaching repentance and love, according to the scriptures, Jesus began working miracles—healing the sick (Mark 1:40–45; Matthew 9:18–22), walking on water (Mark 6:45–52; John 6:16–21), casting out evil spirits (Mark 1:23–28; Matthew 8:28–34), and miraculously multiplying a few loaves and fishes to feed a multitude, a story recounted in all four Gospels. As the fame of Jesus spread, some of the Sadducees and Pharisees (see Chapter 3), according to the stories, grew jealous of him and began to plot his demise. They had him handed over to the Romans who had heard some call him "messiah." While the Gospels typically make it appear

"Love your enemies and pray for those who persecute you, so you may be children of your Father in heaven; for he makes his sun rise on the evil and on the good, and sends rain on the righteous and on the unrighteous."

—NRSV, Matthew 5:44–45

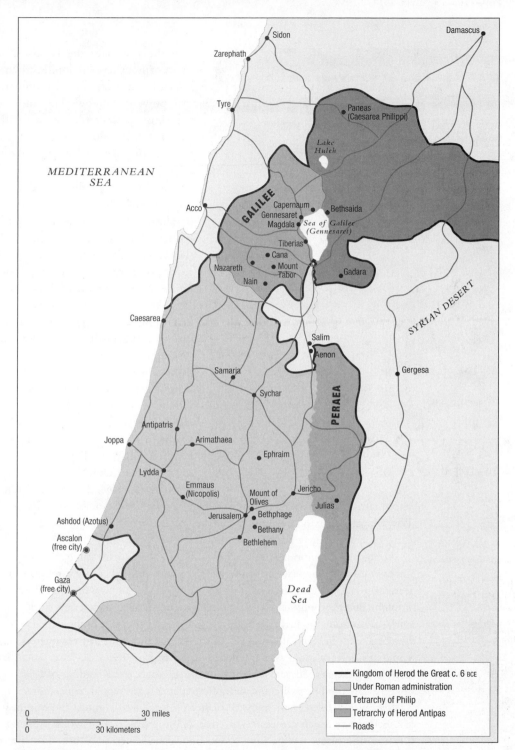

Map 4.1 Palestine at the time of Jesus.

Illustration of Jesus healing a leper from a biblical manuscript found at Mount Athos Monastery in Greece.

Second Coming: belief that Jesus will return at the end of time to establish a new heaven and a new earth

as if the Jews, not the Romans, are the cause of Jesus' crucifixion, historians have pointed out that only the Romans had that power. Moreover, for the Romans the term *messiah* was associated with their enemies the Zealots. A militaristic sect of Judaism that engaged in guerrilla warfare against the Roman legions, the Zealots openly announced their expectation that God would send a messiah, a political revolutionary who would overthrow the Roman Empire. Historically, the reason the Romans condemned Jesus to die nailed to a wooden cross was that they thought of him as such an enemy of the state.

Whatever the political facts, the followers of Jesus came to find deep spiritual meaning in the Crucifixion. What is striking about Mark's account (15:34) of the event (found also in Matthew 27:46) is the bleakness of Jesus' final words: "My God, my God, why have you forsaken me?" This is very different from the final words of Jesus reported in other Gospels: "Father, into your hands I commend my spirit" (Luke 23:46) and "It is finished" (John 19:30). Mark presents a Jesus with whom even a hearer in the depths of despair can identify. And yet the Gospels do not allow despair to be the final word. For they offer the hope that just as Jesus was raised from the dead, so may be those who have faith in him.

As the story continues (John 20), some of the disciples came to Jesus' grave on Sunday morning, the first day of the week, only to find an empty tomb; later Jesus appeared among them, displaying his wounds to prove it truly was he, risen from the dead. Now the disciples, who had been afraid, began to be filled with a new spirit—the Holy Spirit of the God who had raised Jesus from the dead (Acts 2). Emboldened by this spirit they began to proclaim the message of the risen Lord who had conquered death and would return very soon. At this **Second Coming**, or Parousia, Jesus would raise the dead, judge the heavens and the earth, and inaugurate the Kingdom of God, in which all injustice would be overcome and suffering and death would be no more.

In a world filled with injustice, suffering, and death under the oppressive rule of the Romans, such a message inspired hope and joy. The world was not a cold and uncaring place, for the love of God nourished every creature. The life of Jesus presented people with a story of suffering and tragedy that was real yet not final, for suffering and death were overcome in the resurrection. In the life of Jesus, people could see their own lives reflected, leading to the hope that their own tragedies would not be final and that they too would be resurrected. To understand these things is to understand some of the reasons why Christianity is the religion of one-third of the world's population.

Apocalypse: The Book of Revelation

The New Testament not only describes the life, death, and resurrection of Jesus but also offers a vivid description of how Jesus will return as Messiah to judge the heaven and the earth and bring about a new creation. In the Book of Revelation he is described as leading a battle against Satan or the Devil, banishing him to a "lake of fire" along with all sin and death, so that all remaining can share in the eternal life of God.

The *Apocalypse* or *Book of Revelation* is the last book of the New Testament. It is perhaps the most controversial and confusing book of the Christian bible (*Apocalypsis*, a transliteration of the Greek word for "revelation," leads to the familiar English title, *Apocalypse*). According to the opening chapter of the Book, it is written by a man named John who had visions given to him on the island of Patmos. These visions showed how God would soon bring about the destruction and recreation of the world. This would entail a final judgment, the end of the world as it had existed, and the establishment of a new creation in which all sin and death would be conquered in a final resurrection and the survivors would share eternal happiness with God.

Scholars disagree on the date the book was written. Some scholars say shortly before the year 70 CE when the Jewish Temple in Jerusalem was destroyed by the Romans. This might be consistent with the Gospel of Mark, Chapter 13, where Jesus predicts the destruction of the Temple as coming soon, and the world coming to an end. Others, noting that the end of the world did not follow upon the destruction of the Temple, think that it was written some twenty years later during the persecutions in the reign of the emperor Domitian and predicting a destruction to come at some later time. This has some plausibility since the Roman Empire is painted as the instrument of Satan and the enemy of the Gospel in the book.

A helpful way of reading the book is to see it organized around five sections, each describing a series of seven events, preceded by an introduction and followed by a conclusion.

Introduction (1:1–20)
    Seven Letters to the Churches (2:1–4:11)
    The Opening of the Seven Seals (5:1–7:17)
    The Sounding of the Seven Trumpets (8:1–14:5)
    The Casting of the Seven Bowls (14:6–18:24)
    The Seven Visions of New Creation (19:1–22:5)
Conclusion (22:6–21)

God and Satan: Zoroastrianism and the Biblical Tradition

In the time of Moses (ca.1280 BCE), the religion of Israel was technically not yet monotheistic but rather henotheistic, which means the worship of one God above all others. The first commandment given to Moses by this God is: "I am the Lord Your God, you shall have no other gods before me." It does not say there are not other Gods, but rather that the God of Israel is a jealous God who will not tolerate the tribes worshipping these other gods. It was only in the time of the Prophets, between 1000 and 400 BCE that tribal henotheism was transformed into a true monotheism, asserting that there is only one God and all others are false gods.

After the time of King David, Prophets like Amos and Hosea, Jeremiah, and Ezekiel and Isaiah proclaimed the God of Israel to be the one creator of the world and so of all peoples. This God, according to exilic prophets like Ezekiel and Isaiah, determined the destiny of all peoples and shaped the direction of history. As such, God was the source of all good and evil (Isaiah 45:7–8). When Solomon's temple was destroyed and the people of Israel were conquered and taken into slavery in Babylon (586 BCE), the Babylonians were said to be the instruments of God's will, punishing the Israelites for their sins. In the same way, Ezekiel promised that one day God would forgive and restore the people of Israel to their land. Indeed, Isaiah actually sees the King of Persia, Cyrus, who conquered the Babylonians, as a "messiah" or "anointed one" (Isaiah 45:1) sent by God to restore the people of Israel to the land of Israel (538 BCE) and even rebuild their temple. And both Ezekiel and Isaiah promised a resurrection of the dead—a new idea not part of the earlier biblical beliefs in the era from Moses to David. In Isaiah's view, there would be a coming Day of the Lord, when all nations would be gathered in Jerusalem (Isaiah 66:18ff), leading to a final judgment of all nations and a resurrection of the dead.

By the time Christianity emerged from Judaism in the first century, a new view of God and evil had emerged. Early Christianity adopted the Septuagint or Greek translation of the Bible used by Hellenistic Jews. This Septuagint included apocryphal books, meaning books containing "hidden meanings." The genuine biblical status of these books was often challenged, but they are of great historical value in assessing historical developments in Jewish and Christian beliefs. Many of these, such as the Book of Enoch, reflect a changing view of the Devil during the period in which Christianity was emerging from Judaism. In this new view it was not God who was the source of evil, but the Devil. An elaborate cosmology emerged in which there were minions of angels serving God in the heavens, and some of these, led by Satan, rebelled and sought to oppose God's plan for creation. The devil's minions or demons sought to enlist humans in this rebellion against God by seducing them into embracing selfishness and sin.

In the earlier biblical tradition, Satan, as we see in the Book of Job (chapters 1 and 2), is a member of God's court who acts as an *adversary* (the meaning of the word *satan*), who can do nothing without God's permission. God gives Satan permission to send misfortune into Job's life but forbids him from taking his life. God does this to test Job's faithfulness but in the end rewards Job for remaining faithful. By the time of the emergence of Christianity in the first century, the new popular mythology of evil asserted that Satan, acting in rebellion, seeks to defeat God and God's saving intentions for the history of the human race. In the Christian Gospels, we see Satan portrayed as the enemy of the Kingdom of God or Kingdom of Heaven. He tempts Jesus (Matthew 4:1–11) and incites his enemies. Jesus, himself, is portrayed as an exorcist who can cast out those demons who serve the Devil's purposes. Indeed, in the final book of the Christian bible, *The Book of Revelation*, the resurrected Jesus is portrayed as returning to earth as Messiah for a final battle with Satan in which he casts Satan and those who serve him into a lake of fire, and then a new earth comes down from heaven in which all evil and death are eliminated, bringing a final resurrection (Book of Revelation, chapter 20).

Where did this newer view of Satan as a powerful adversary and enemy of God come from? According to historians of the biblical literature, it seems likely that biblical thought was deeply influenced by the emergence of Zoroastrianism in Persia. For it was the Persians who conquered the Babylonians in 538 BCE and allowed all who had been enslaved by the Babylonians to return to their original homelands, including the people of Israel. Thereafter the imagery of Zoroastrianism seemed to inspire new more dramatic accounts of the nature of evil.

Zoroastrianism emerged as a religious phenomenon in Persia in the time approximately parallel to that between Moses in the thirteenth century and the Babylonian Exile in the sixth century BCE. Its teachings are attributed to a prophet/teacher known as Zoroaster or Zarathustra, depending on the transliteration. The revelations given to Zarathustra are contained in scriptures called Gathas, which also contain other later materials from the Zoroastrian tradition offered by the *magi*—its hereditary priestly caste (reference to the magi is found in the birth story of Jesus in the Gospel of Matthew 2:1–12).The complete book of Zoroastrianism is known as the Avesta and includes the Gathas, as well as the rituals and laws of the Zoroastrian tradition. The Gathas reveal the wisdom and benevolent power of Ahura Mazda, the "Wise Lord" and his attributes the "Amesha Spentas" or "bounteous immortals," which are aspects of God's power in the universe, later personified as angelic powers.

The beneficent power of Ahura Mazda is opposed by another power, that of Angra Mainyu. If the first represents the highest power of Good in the universe, the latter represents the opposing power of Evil. The view developed that the universe was caught in a cosmic struggle between these two powers of Good and Evil. Zoroastrians saw the universe as a struggle in time between Good and Evil—the holy spirit and the evil spirit—which will end with the final victory of Good over Evil at the end of time. As Zoroastrian cosmogony developed, human history was said to be predetermined to last 12,000 years. Zoroastrians developed a view of final judgment for each person leading to either a heavenly existence or punishment in a hell-like state until the end of time, when evil will be overcome and all will be redeemed. This struggle between good and evil culminates in the last 3,000 years in which a savior figure is born for each thousand-year period and ending finally in the resurrection of the dead, the exile of Evil, and the creation of a new world and eternal life.

Zoroastrianism was eventually challenged in Persia by the seventh century CE emergence and spread of Islam. Islamic persecution of Zoroastrians followed, and many Zoroastrians sought refuge in other lands. By the tenth century CE, the most significant diaspora community existed in India, where Zoroastrians are known to this day as Parsis (Persians), who continue to practice the rituals of their fire ceremony as a celebration of beneficent divine power in the universe. The obvious parallels between Christian beliefs and Zoroastrian beliefs about good and evil; divine and angelic powers; and heaven, hell, and final judgment suggests that much of the belief of New Testament–era Christianity was influenced by Zoroastrian cosmology. There are some similar parallels in Judaism and especially in Islam. The influence of Zoroastrianism on all three traditions is plausible because Zoroastrianism predates the biblical religions of Judaism, Christianity, and Islam. However, this influence is complicated by the fact that they all coexisted and seemed to have influenced each other over centuries. So the biblical religions influenced Zoroastrianism as well. Today, the total world population of Zoroastrians is very small, estimated at about 200,000.

Joyful Iranian Zoroastrians celebrate the ancient mid-winter Sadeh festival around a ritual fire near Tehran in January 2012.

The plot of the book reveals that God is bringing time to an end in a final resurrection of the dead and a final judgment, and the churches must remain faithful and be prepared. First there will be a reign of 1,000 years of peace. Then there will be a great battle between the forces of good (led by the Messiah) and the forces of evil (led by Satan). After a battle led by the Messiah against Satan and his minions, the forces of evil will be defeated and cast into a lake of fire. Then all suffering, death, and injustice will be destroyed; the dead will be raised; and the New Jerusalem will appear, where all will live with God in eternal happiness.

In the history of Christianity the book has been very controversial. Although some thought the author, John, must be the same as the author of the Gospel of John, modern biblical scholars find that unlikely. Its style and vocabulary are too different from that of the Gospel's author. Many communities in the early church did not accept the book as genuine revelation, especially among the Eastern Greek-speaking churches. Eventually the Latin churches of European Christianity accepted it, but even as late as the Protestant Reformation in the sixteenth century, Luther questioned whether it really belonged.

In the New Testament itself, Jesus is quoted as saying that no one knows the day or hour of the coming end of time, not even he, only his Father in heaven (Matthew 24:36). Despite this, the Book's vivid and often violent descriptions of signs of the coming end of the world have led many Christians in later centuries to believe its descriptions suggested the end was coming in their own time. All such expectations have been disappointed.

Famous passages in the Book of Revelation include the opening of the first four seals of a seven-seal scroll that reveal the four horses of the apocalypse, bringing war, famine, economic disaster, and death. The sounding of seven trumpets announces the coming judgment of the earth. The pouring of the seven bowls of judgment brings partial destruction to the earth, especially to the city of Babylon, which embodies the evil of all the cities of the world, and the battle between the Messiah and Satan, described as a defeated dragon who is, along with the two beasts who assist him, cast into the lake of fire. Finally, seven visions are presented of the coming of a new Jerusalem, a new heaven, and a new earth in a new city of God that has no temple but only the living presence of God. In this city all suffering and death are overcome and all the nations live by the light of God.

The Book of Revelation has struck both fear and hope in the hearts of its readers over the centuries as they have puzzled over the possible meanings of its mysterious symbolism and whether it is to be read literally or symbolically.

Christianity's Emergence from Judaism

Jesus was born a Jew; lived as a Jew, participating reverently in traditions that had originated as long as 2,000 years before his birth; and died as a Jew. His gentile followers, however, thought that Jews did not understand his message. As a consequence, what began as a way of understanding Judaism was embraced almost exclusively by gentiles (non-Jews), who thought of themselves as practicing a new and improved faith—Christianity. These gentile Christians came to teach what some scholars have called the myth or story of supersession—that God had rejected the Jews and chosen gentiles instead. It was a myth that would endure until the twentieth century.

Christianity, in fact, began as a Jewish sectarian movement. After 2,000 years of biblical history, especially after the Babylonian exile (586–538 BCE), a variety of movements (such as those of the Sadducees, Pharisees, Hellenists, Zealots, Samaritans, Essenes, and Nazarenes, discussed in Chapter 3) developed in Judaism. There was no agreement on a common set of sacred writings among them. Only at the end of the first century of the common era did the Hebrew Bible as we know it come into existence, largely owing to the influence of the Pharisees and the Hellenists. At the beginning of the century, however, these groups and others were engaged in an ongoing argument about the right way of life for the people of Israel.

Naturally, each movement saw itself as the model for the right way of life and all others as deviant. The result was a diverse set of sectarian movements, each proclaiming a message something like this: "We are the true Israel (i.e., the true Jews); you are not. The end of the world is at hand when God will come to judge the heaven and the earth. Jews who have strayed, who are thus no better than pagans, must repent and be ritually immersed. Then they will become true Israel again—true Jews who, by definition, live the way we do." The "we" here naturally was a different "we" depending on who was preaching the message. Of course any Jews who were not part of that "we" were likely to find the message an insult, for traditionally the baptismal rite of ritual immersion and purification was required only of non-Jewish converts to Judaism (along with circumcision for males).

Essential to the emergence of Christianity from Judaism is the preaching and teaching of Paul. Without Paul of Tarsus, a Pharisee and Hellenistic Jew, Christianity would not be the religion we are familiar with today. It is one of the paradoxes of Christianity that the one person, after Jesus himself, who has most deeply influenced the Christian tradition is a man who began as a persecutor of it. Paul of Tarsus at first treated the movement that began with the rabbi Jesus as a heretical form of Judaism. Yet he eventually came to argue that Christianity was not really a heresy but a way for gentiles to share in the promises made by God to the Jews. Paul, who came to be known as an apostle of Jesus, was not one of the original twelve apostles selected by Jesus and never met Jesus before his crucifixion. He came to know Jesus as the risen Lord after an extraordinary encounter on the road to Damascus, an experience that led to his conversion. Paul became the first great missionary of the Christian movement, and we know of Paul's thoughts and actions primarily from his letters to the churches that he founded in places like the ancient Greek cities of Corinth and Ephesus. The letters form approximately one-fourth of the New Testament. Other accounts of Paul's ministry appear in the Acts of the Apostles, in the New Testament, a book attributed to the author of the Gospel of Luke.

Throughout history the Crucifixion has captured the imagination of great artists such as Matthias Grünewald, creator of this sixteenth-century altarpiece now in Isenheim, Germany.

"God has imprisoned all (both Jews and gentiles) in disobedience so that he may be merciful to all."

—NRSV, Romans 11:32

Paul was born in what today is Turkey and educated in Jerusalem. Hellenistic Jews were very successful missionaries to the gentiles in first-century Judaism. They presented Judaism as open to Greek patterns of thought and behavior. When Paul became a convert to the Nazarene movement, as a Hellenistic Jew he continued this Hellenistic missionary activity but with a new twist: He argued that the task of the followers of Jesus was to bring the gentiles into Judaism as a "wild olive branch" grafted onto a cultivated olive tree of Judaism (Romans 11:16–18). Neither Jews nor gentiles were perfect but God did not hold their faults against them. Through Jesus, Paul taught, the gentiles were now called to share with the Jews in the promises made to Abraham (Ephesians 2:11–22). After the fall of the Jewish temple in Jerusalem (ca. 70), this teaching was ignored in favor of the view that Christians supersede or take the place of the Jews as God's chosen people. Tradition says that Paul was martyred in Rome, probably around the year 60 CE.

The Fall of the Temple

The whole picture of diversity in first century Judaism changed dramatically in the year 70 CE, when the Romans marched into Jerusalem with thousands of troops, burned down the temple, and drove the Jews out of their holy city. In the aftermath of the fall of the temple, two movements emerged to shape Western religious history: the Pharisaic movement, which became Rabbinic Judaism, and the Nazarene movement, which became gentile Christianity.

The Pharisees survived the destruction of the temple because they were able to provide flexible Jewish leadership under dramatically new conditions. Unlike Pharisaic Judaism, the Nazarene movement never had a large following among Jews. Its greatest success was a missionary movement for the conversion of gentiles. The Nazarenes were an apocalyptic movement, believing that the end of time was at hand and that their special mission was to convert the gentiles before the final judgment. In this they were inspired by the prophecies of Isaiah that in the last days all nations would be gathered into Jerusalem (Isaiah 66:18–20).

A critical issue for the Nazarenes was the status of new gentile converts. This was taken up around the year 48 at a meeting in Jerusalem. The Christian tradition refers to this meeting as the first church council or the "Council of Jerusalem." The conservatives from Jerusalem argued that gentile converts had to be circumcised and obey the whole Mosaic law, as required of other Jews. Paul of Tarsus came to this meeting from Antioch, where he and other Hellenistic Jews were converting large numbers of gentiles. Hellenistic Jewish missionaries believed in adopting Greek culture and language to make Judaism attractive to gentiles. Paul and others sympathetic to the Hellenistic mission argued that gentiles should be exempt from the requirement of circumcision and from most of the ritual obligations, focusing instead on obeying the moral commandments of the Mosaic covenant. The faction led by Paul won the argument, and a letter urging these changes went out to all the mission communities (Acts 15:19–21).

This ruling was decisive for the growth of the Nazarene movement among gentiles. Released from those Jewish practices that gentiles were most reluctant to embrace (circumcision, kosher food restrictions), they flooded into the movement. By the second century Jewish-born people made up a smaller and smaller proportion of the total membership. And as the leadership fell more and more into the hands of gentiles, the movement lost its sense of identity as a Jewish movement and began to take on a separate identity as a new religion—Christianity.

The Origins of Christian Anti-Jewish Sentiment

We are now in a position to discuss a problem that has plagued the relationship between Jews and Christians throughout the history of Western civilization. The New Testament reflects the context of the Jewish sectarian arguments that had been going on in the first century, in which groups like the Zealots, the Essenes, and the Nazarenes were saying to each other: "We, not you, are the true Israel, the true Jews. Therefore repent, be baptized, and become Jews the way we are, for the end of time and God's judgment are at hand."

TEACHINGS OF RELIGIOUS WISDOM: Paul on Faith, Hope, and Love

With the possible exception of Jesus' Sermon on the Mount, no teaching of Christianity is better known than the apostle Paul's teaching on faith, hope, and love from his letter to the Corinthians (1 Corinthians 13:1–13, New American Bible*) These three—faith, hope, and love—came to be known as the "three cardinal virtues" of Christianity.

If I speak in human and angelic tongues but do not have love, I am a resounding gong or a clashing cymbal. And if I have the gift of prophecy and comprehend all mysteries and all knowledge; if I have all faith so as to move mountains but do not have love, I am nothing. If I give away everything I own, and if I hand my body over so that I may boast but do not have love, I gain nothing.

Love is patient, love is kind. It is not jealous, (love) is not pompous, it is not inflated, it is not rude, it does not seek its own interests, it is not quick-tempered, it does not brood over injury, it does not rejoice over wrongdoing but rejoices with the truth. It bears all things, believes all things, hopes all things, endures all things.

Love never fails. If there are prophecies, they will be brought to nothing; if tongues, they will cease; if knowledge, it will be brought to nothing. For we know partially and we prophesy partially, but when the perfect comes, the partial will pass away. When I was a child, I used to talk as a child, think as a child, reason as a child; when I became a man, I put aside childish things. At present we see indistinctly, as in a mirror, but then face to face. At present I know partially; then I shall know fully, as I am fully known. So faith, hope, love remain, these three; but the greatest of these is love.

These first-century Jewish sectarian arguments were incorporated into the sacred writings of Christianity found in the New Testament. However, when these statements were read and repeated by the leaders of the "Christian" movement in the second and later centuries, they were no longer seen as exhortations from one Jewish group to another. Now gentiles who had come to identify themselves as Christians took up the refrain: "We are the true Israel; you are not." And thus was born the Christian myth of supersession, or divine rejection. Christians now argued: "We Christians have replaced you Jews as God's chosen people. Because you did not recognize Jesus as messiah and had him crucified, God has rejected you and chosen us to supersede you." In the next chapter we will see that in the seventh century CE, Islam emerged with Muhammad's similar teaching of supersession: namely, that Muslims replace both Jews and Christians as God's chosen people.

In Christianity the teaching of supersession took an especially violent turn. Soon this logic was disastrously extended to include the claim that since "the Jews" had brought about the death of the very son of God who was sent to save them, not only had God rejected the Jews for all time, but it was the Christians' duty to punish them. It was a view that played a tragic role in the persecution of Jews throughout much of Western history. It was not until the time of Vatican II (1962–1965) that a commission created by Pope John XXIII condemned the teachings of supersession and divine rejection of the Jews and affirmed Paul's view, that gentiles are like a wild olive branch grafted onto the tree of Judaism to share in God's promises to Abraham. By the end of the twentieth century, most Protestant churches had renounced the teachings of supersession as well.

Jesus as Son of God

In the first four centuries after the time of Jesus, as gentile Christianity separated itself from Judaism, Christians struggled to formulate an authoritative understanding (dogma) of who Jesus is and what his significance is. The essential problem that faced the early followers of Jesus, who, like the apostle Paul, believed that they had a special mission to convert the gentiles, was how to translate an essentially Jewish message about a coming "messiah" into terms non-Jews could understand. These missionaries did not want pagans to confuse Christian claims about Jesus being **Son of God** with pagan myths in which divine beings come down to earth in humanlike bodies. The challenge was to speak correctly and clearly about the being and meaning of Jesus of Nazareth without claiming either too little (that Jesus was just a good man) or too much (that Jesus was not really human but rather a supernatural being like the gods of pagan mythology). For about 300 years, Christians debated the various possible ways of thinking and speaking about Jesus and held several church councils. By the time the argument was settled, both extremes had been deemed **heresy**.

The most important councils were those of Nicaea in 325 and Chalcedon in 451. Some bishops and theologians argued that Jesus was a divine being with neither a mortal mind nor a body. Some argued that Jesus had a human body and a divine mind, others said that although his mind too was human and mortal he had a divine will, and so on. Such views made Jesus a kind of half-man and half-god, not unlike other characters in pagan mythology. The Council of Chalcedon rejected all such views, insisting that Jesus had a human body and a human mind. He was fully and completely human, with a birth and a death like every other person. Jesus' humanity differed from that of others in only one way—he was without sin. Moreover, in this man Jesus, God was wholly present. The formula arrived at to reconcile the apparent paradox was that in the "one person" of Jesus there were "two natures" (divine and human) united "without confusion" or mixture. That is, in the person of Jesus divinity and humanity were united yet completely distinct.

Two beliefs had to be held together in this formula, that of Nicaea—that the Word through which all things were created was the "same as" (**homoousios**) God (i.e., eternal)—and that of Chalcedon—that the man Jesus was a mortal human being to whom was united that eternal Word (which had existed before its incarnation in the man Jesus). If the Word was not eternal, it could not confer eternity; and if Jesus was not mortal, his resurrection offered no hope to other mortals. This formula was meant to combat Gnostic Christian views, eventually declared heretical, to the effect

---

"We all with one accord teach . . . the same Christ, Son, Lord, Only-begotten, recognized in two natures, without confusion, without change, without division, without separation; the distinction of natures being in no way annulled by the union . . . coming together to form one person."

—Church Council of Chalcedon

Son of God: title applied to Jesus of Nazareth

heresy: negative term in Christianity for choosing to believe in doctrines viewed as erroneous by more orthodox believers

homoousios: Greek term for the belief that the Word of God through which all things were created is "the same as" God

that Jesus was a divine being (i.e., pure spirit)—a god who only appeared to be a "flesh and blood" human being and therefore could not really have died on the cross, nor would it have been necessary for him to arise from the dead.

The formula of two natures in one person developed at Chalcedon was complemented by another unique doctrine or belief of Christians—the belief in a triune God, which had been affirmed earlier at the Council of Constantinople in 381. The doctrine of the **Trinity** asserts that God is one essence but three persons. The formula "three persons in one God: Father, Son, and Holy Spirit" is not really about mathematics. Rather, it means that God, the creator of the universe, can at the same time be present in the life of Jesus and in all things in the world through God's Word and Spirit—without ceasing to be transcendent or beyond the universe. The doctrine of the Trinity states that God is *in* all things without accepting the pantheistic notion that God *is* all things.

Jews and Muslims, with their theology of a prophetic monotheism, according to which God is one and not three, have typically misunderstood the meaning of the doctrine of the Trinity. But then so have many Christians. Nevertheless, the intent of both the "**two natures, one person**" doctrine concerning Jesus and the doctrine of the Trinity concerning God is to affirm the uniqueness of a God who is both present in and transcendent to the cosmos. This is the true God who has no equals—the God of Abraham—the very same God affirmed by Jews and Muslims.

Constantinianism: The Marriage of Christianity and Empire

Perhaps the single most important political event in the history of Christianity was the conversion of the Roman emperor Constantine, the first monarch to champion the rights of Christians. Constantine, who issued the Edict of Milan in 313, was baptized on his deathbed. With his imperial declaration, Christianity went from being an often-persecuted religion to a permitted (and eventually the favored) religion in the empire.

Up until this point, many Christians had tended to look at Roman civilization, with its imperialism and colonial domination of foreign territories, as the work of the devil. That is how it is portrayed in the book of Revelation, for instance. After Constantine, Christians began to see Roman imperialism as a good thing, as a way of spreading the Gospel throughout the world. This was a decisive step in shaping the Western religious vision of a Christian civilization. The **Constantinian** vision achieved the status of official political policy in 380, when Christianity became the official religion of the Roman Empire under Emperor Theodosius. Within ten years, pagan worship was declared illegal and all pagan temples were closed. Only Judaism was permitted as an alternative to Christianity, and it existed under severe legal restrictions, with Jews losing many of the freedoms they had had under pagan Rome.

Trinity: God as Father, Son, and Holy Spirit; God is not many gods but one God in three persons

two natures, one person: doctrine that in the one person of Jesus are two natures (divine and human) coexisting in unity but without mixture

Constantinian: under first Christian Roman Emperor, Constantine, the view that the Emperor rules over both the church and the state, and protects the church as the official religion of the Roman Empire

The Greek-speaking churches of the East took Constantine's relationship to the church as a model of how things should be. There were four great centers of Orthodoxy: Constantinople, Alexandria (Egypt), Antioch (Syria), and Jerusalem, each ruled by a patriarch. In the Eastern Byzantine part of the Roman Empire, centered in Constantinople, church and state existed symbiotically. The Christian emperor called church councils and even appointed the bishops. The emperor ruled over both church and state in the name of Christ.

However, the pattern of Western civilization that shaped the road to modernity was not that of Orthodox Christianity from the East but an important modification of it that put church and empire in a precarious relationship combining cooperation and antagonism. The Constantinian model thrived in Byzantium until the fifteenth century; but in the West, Roman political rule collapsed after the time of Theodosius. The political vacuum created by the absence of an emperor in the West allowed the bishops of the Latin-speaking churches to assume much greater independence with respect to the state. This was especially true of the bishop of Rome, whose power and authority grew as secular Roman political power and authority collapsed, leading to the idea of the primacy of this bishop of Rome as *pope* (father) over all other bishops. In the Latin church the idea of separation between church and state developed. The chief architect of this alternative vision was Augustine of Hippo.

The Constantinian unification of church and state is illustrated in this Roman mosaic showing the Roman emperor at the center as the unifying ruler of both the state (on his right) and the church (on his left).

Augustine, Architect of Western Christianity

From the fifth century on through the Protestant Reformation and the emergence of modernity, the West has been deeply influenced by the theological thought of Augustine of Hippo, whom Christians typically refer to as *St. Augustine*. After Jesus and the apostle Paul, probably no other individual in history is more responsible for the shape of Western Christianity. Augustine's vision deeply shaped the development of Roman Catholicism from the fifth through the twelfth centuries. Then he was eclipsed by Thomas Aquinas, only to be recovered by the Protestant reformers Luther and Calvin in the sixteenth century, who drew heavily on the writings of Augustine.

Constantine died in 337. Augustine, who was born in 354 and died in 430, lived through the time of Theodosius and witnessed firsthand the transformation of the Roman Empire from a pagan empire into a Christian one. This stunning transformation could not fail to impress contemporary observers. They could not believe that the pagan Roman Empire had become Christian through chance or good luck. They concluded instead that God intended to use the Roman Empire to provide the political unity and stability needed to spread the Gospel to the ends of the earth.

In century after century, Christians turned to Augustine's spiritual autobiography, *The Confessions* (400), as a model of conversion and piety. And in century after century, rulers of church and state turned to his book *The City of God* (423) as a model for the political order. Indeed, the first great medieval pope, Gregory I, used Augustine's vision to justify his exercise of power over the political order, and Charlemagne, who on December 25, 800, became the first Holy Roman Emperor, is said to have slept with a copy of *The City of God* under his pillow. The influence of *The Confessions* and *The City of God* on the history of European Christianity and European society is so vast and profound that it is almost impossible to calculate.

The Confessions: *Faith, Reason, and the Quest for Wisdom*

> "I was not encouraged by this work of Cicero's to join this or that sect; instead I was urged on and inflamed with a passionate zeal to love and seek and obtain and embrace and hold fast wisdom itself, whatever it might be."
>
> —Augustine, *Confessions*, Book III

A key turning point in Augustine's life, as he relates it, was the awakening of his mind and heart to a passion for wisdom when he was nineteen years old. Before that event, the young man had devoted himself to fulfilling selfish desires (*cupiditas*) for wealth, fame, power, and sexual pleasure. About the time Augustine was completing his studies in Carthage in Africa, he came across a book entitled *Hortensius*, by the pagan author Cicero. This book, says Augustine, set him on fire with a new kind of desire (*caritas*)—the selfless desire for wisdom.

And so Augustine resolved to follow his doubts and questions wherever they might lead him. Augustine doesn't say that *Hortensius* changed his thinking but, rather, that it "altered my way of feeling . . . and gave me different ambitions and desires" (III, 4). Augustine's wording here is very important. His experience changed his feelings and desires, which in turn changed his thinking and eventually led to his full conversion. Christianity is a religion of the transformation of the heart as the symbolic location of the emotions. In the first century of the common era, Jesus had called his hearers to undergo a change of heart, and virtually every great reform and renewal movement in Christian history has returned to this theme.

Augustine's story of his conversion became a model for understanding the relationship between faith and reason. Theology, he said, is "faith seeking understanding." Some interpretations to the contrary, this does not mean "you first have to believe to be able to understand." Rather, you will be led to deeper understanding if you have faith and trust that God is working through your very doubts to lead you to deeper understanding. In his *Confessions* Augustine says that only after his full conversion did he come to realize that when he had the faith to doubt, he already had an implicit faith in Christ, who was leading him to doubt and so to find true wisdom.

The City of God: *Augustine's Tale of Two Cities*

In the same way that *The Confessions* provided a model for faith and reason, *The City of God* provided a model for church and state. The meaning of history is unraveled for Augustine by a symbolic reading of the biblical stories as a history of two cities that exist side by side in history—the human city and the city of God. These two cities are guided by two different loves, *cupiditas* (selfish love) and *caritas* (selfless love), respectively. These, of course, are the same two loves Augustine saw at war in his own life in his *Confessions*. Augustine's formulation of the appropriate relationship of these cities provided the decisive model of relations between church and state, religion and politics, and sacred and secular for most of Western history.

For Augustine the story of the human city was the story of the history of civilizations going through endless cycles of progress and decline—a story without any clear purpose or meaning. But hidden within that history was another story—that of the city of God. This story, which is revealed in the Bible, has a clear purpose and direction. It is the story of a journey with God through time toward a final resurrection and eternal life for all who belong to the city of God. The city of God, however, was not identical with the church. In his view, some within the institution were not faithful believers and some outside of it were. Only at the final judgment will human beings come to know who truly belongs to the city of God.

In defining the relationship between the two cities Augustine argues that both state and church exist through God's will to serve God's purposes. God uses the state to establish the peace necessary for the spread of the Gospel by the church. In the journey through history each entity should serve the other. The state should be subject to the church in spiritual matters, and the church should be subject to the state in earthly matters. Neither should seek to dominate the other. However, in actual history the sides could never fully agree on where to draw the line between earthly matters and spiritual matters. And too often each side forgot the part about not dominating the other. Indeed, throughout most of Western history both popes and emperors maneuvered to upset the balance between the two by trying to dictate to the other.

This fifteenth-century miniature painting by Nicola Polani depicts Augustine writing *The City of God*.

Augustinian: views of St. Augustine emphasizing the separation of church and state, pope and emperor, rather than a Constantinian unity of both in the emperor

While our main emphasis is on Latin (Western) Christianity, because that is the form of Christianity that fostered the emergence of modernity, the Eastern churches have great historical and cultural significance. The earliest churches of Christianity were in communities that spoke Greek, not Latin. By the fourth and fifth centuries the Latin-speaking churches grew in number and influence to rival the Orthodox churches and declared the bishop of Rome to have unique authority among all bishops and came to treat him as "the holy father" or "pope." While the Greek churches followed the Constantinian model and gave ultimate religious authority to the emperor, the Roman churches came to reject that model. The Greek churches, by contrast, did not accept the central authority of one bishop that the Roman churches affirmed. All the bishops answered to the emperor, but internally these churches were conciliar, placing ultimate authority not in a single bishop (a pope) but in church councils as meetings of all the bishops.

Eastern Orthodox Christianity was distinctive for its mystical emphasis: Christ became human, it is said, so that humans could become divinized and share mystically in the eternal life of God—a process known as *theosis*. Orthodoxy is also distinctive for its understanding of sin as ignorance rather than as corruption of the will through original sin as put forward in Latin-Augustinian Christianity. For the Orthodox churches, Christ is the great teacher who comes to dispel human ignorance of oneness with God and to restore humans to mystical unity with the creator. The emphasis is not on Christ as the lord of History but on the cosmic Christ through whom all things are created, held together, and brought to fulfillment. From the beginning there was tension between the Eastern and Western churches, but a formal split did not occur until 1054.

The pure Constantinian vision of the Eastern churches sees the church as a branch of the state and the emperor as both the religious and political leader of the state. The **Augustinian** vision separates church and state by expecting there to be two ultimate authorities, both a pope and an emperor, each with their separate spheres of authority. Yet Augustine's vision is not yet the modern one that insists on a secular, or nonreligious, state that promotes religious pluralism and "freedom of religion." On the contrary, he assumes that the two powers will work together to achieve a worldwide Christian civilization. Since the time of Augustine, most Christians have assumed that the task of Christianity is to transform every society into a "Christian society" comprising two branches: church and state. This pattern continued even after the Holy Roman Empire collapsed and the Protestant Reformation helped usher in the modern era. In more recent times, modern European culture replaced Roman civilization as the political order thought to be willed by God for the purpose of spreading Christianity around the world. Only gradually, after the religious wars the Protestant Reformation provoked, did Christians begin to explore an alternative— the modern idea of a secular, or nonreligious, state as the guarantor of freedom to worship in a religiously pluralistic world. We will return to this observation when we discuss modernization.

Premodern Christianity:
The Classical Era (451–1517 CE)

In 476 Romulus Augustulus, the last Roman emperor in the West, was deposed. Less than a century after the time of Augustine of Hippo, the Roman Empire and its civilization collapsed in the West. Most commerce ceased, for example, and the Roman money economy was replaced by a barter system. Over several centuries Europe was invaded by tribes from the north; and as tribal leaders upgraded themselves into lords of their domains, feudalism began to take shape. The feudal system was a network of loyalties established between a landholder (a king or a nobleman) and those who served him and his estates. It was a hierarchical arrangement, with the nobility on the top, subordinates called vassals in the middle, and serfs and slaves at the bottom. The nobles were members of either a secular warrior aristocracy or the religious aristocracy consisting of bishops and abbots (the heads of monasteries), for the church was a major landholder and church officials too could be feudal lords.

The Middle Ages roughly span the sixth through the fourteenth centuries. It was a world without printing presses, and so the few existing books were handwritten. Only the elite among the clergy and the nobility could read, in any event. The average Christian got his or her religious view of life from sermons delivered by priests and from images depicted in the stained glass windows and on the walls of the churches and cathedrals.

In this new world, the church carried civilization forward into Europe, accomplishing this primarily through the spread of Christian monasteries. It was monasticism that provided the bridge of civilization between the ancient world and the modern world, bringing technological development and the light of learning to a European period that has been otherwise described as the Dark Ages.

Monasticism was the first serious reform movement in the church. Once Christianity became the official religion of the Roman Empire, many who became Christians did so for reasons of expediency rather than piety. The practice of Christianity came to be more about social acceptability and worldly success for them. By the late third century, members of the Eastern (Greek) churches who wanted to lead an exemplary

Before the printing press was invented, all books were written by hand. Depicted is a medieval monk transcribing a text at his desk.

"Idleness is the enemy of the soul; and therefore the brethren ought to be employed in manual labor at certain times, at others, in devout reading."

—*The Holy Rule of St. Benedict*, chapter 48.

SOURCE: Rev. Boniface Verheyen, OSB, trans. *The Holy Rule of St. Benedict*, 1949 edition.

Christian life often felt they had to separate themselves from the corrupt world around them, moving into the desert to live simply, with much time for prayer. The first monks tended to be hermits, but gradually many of these solitary men began to form monastic communities. The most outstanding of these monks, called the *desert fathers*, had a powerful influence on the church throughout the Middle Ages. For example, Gregory I, the first medieval pope, was born to aristocracy but abandoned his privileges to become a monk in the desert. It was the beginning of a pattern. Whenever Christianity tended to grow corrupt with worldly power and success, it was monasticism that provided reform movements to call the church back to its spiritual mission.

By the late fourth century, monasticism had spread to the Western (Latin) churches. Whereas Greek Orthodox monasticism was supported by church and state, the Latin communities, set up according to the model of Benedict of Nursia (480–543), were self-supporting communities of work and prayer under the leadership of an abbot. In the ancient world work was viewed as a task for slaves, but Benedict taught that "to work is to pray" and integrated physical labor into the daily schedule of group prayer and private devotions. Consequently, the Benedictine monasteries preserved and developed not only spiritual knowledge but also ancient learning and technology. The Benedictines were the great engineers of the Middle Ages, who developed impressive waterwheel and windmill technologies to improve the monks' productivity. The goal was to make work more efficient so that there would be more time for prayer. Thus, the monasteries brought to the West not only spiritual renewal but also intellectual and technological advances, making profound contributions to the full flowering of technological civilization in the modern period.

The Medieval Worldview: Sacraments and Festivals

In the medieval world, life on earth was seen as a test and a place of waiting to enter one's true home in heaven, if one passed the test. Christians believed that when they died their souls would be separated from their bodies and would come before God for individual judgment. In the future (at an unknown time) the world would come to an end and Jesus would return to raise the bodies of the dead and unite them with their souls. Those who had been faithful and good would be rewarded for all eternity in heaven, enjoying the "beatific vision" or presence of God; the rest would be consigned to eternal punishment in hell.

The church was God's gift to this world to help Christians prepare for their final judgment. The church was founded by Jesus Christ, the Son of God, who had passed on leadership of the church to his chief apostle, Peter (Matthew 16:18). This apostolic succession was continued by the popes, who were seen as the direct successors of Peter, guaranteeing that the church would be divinely guided because the pope speaks with the authority of Christ on earth. The Catholic Church claimed that apostolic succession proved that it alone was the one true church and that its task was to confer God's guiding and protecting grace upon all believers through the sacraments.

Sacraments

Through the descending hierarchy of the pope, the bishops, and the lower clergy, as Christ's priesthood, the **grace** of God was conferred on humankind, mediated to every Christian through seven **sacraments** that guided and assisted them from birth to death and beyond. These sacraments were baptism, confirmation, Holy Eucharist (communion), marriage, ordination (holy orders), confession, and extreme unction. These sacraments were taken to be the outward and visible signs of God's inward, invisible grace (forgiveness and assistance), helping Christians grow spiritually and morally toward holiness or saintliness. Grace, considered an undeserved gift from God, was also seen as an invitation to a renewed spiritual life that required human cooperation, accepting the aid offered by God and consciously trying to use that aid for spiritual and moral improvement. Because the sacraments could be administered only by ordained clergy, every Christian was dependent on the priests and bishops of the church, under the rule of the pope, to be in a right relationship to God. Outside the institutional church, it came to be thought, there was no salvation.

grace: the idea of unmerited divine love and assistance given to humans

sacraments: ritual materials and actions (such as pouring water over infant at baptism), usually through mediation of ordained clergy, said to impart the grace of God to Christians

Festivals

If the sacraments carried Christians from cradle to grave, the annual cycle of religious festivals carried them through the seasons of the year and created for them a world of stories in which to dwell. The early church saw itself as living in the time between Easter and the *advent*, or "Second Coming" (Parousia) of Jesus Christ to raise the dead and judge the heavens and the earth. By the Middle Ages a church calendar had developed to immerse the faithful in a cycle of festivals and stories that reminded Christians of their origin and destiny. The church year began with Advent, whose stories evoke hope for the Second Coming. Gradually a concurrent theme of Advent as preparation for Christmas developed, overshadowing the earlier theme. Christmas and Epiphany were festival seasons designed to celebrate the stories of the birth of Jesus, the visit of the wise men from the East, and the baptism of Jesus. No one knew the date on which Jesus was born; December 25 was chosen to compete with a popular pagan festival honoring the sun god.

Children reenacting the nativity story.

The season of Christmas/Epiphany is followed by Lent, a time of penitence, fasting, and prayer in preparation for Easter. Its stories recall the temptations, healings, and teachings of Jesus. Lent culminates in Holy Week, in which the stories of Jesus' trial and death are recalled. In the Easter season, the church retells the stories of the resurrection and the subsequent appearances of Jesus to his disciples. The final season of the church year, Pentecost, recalls the descent of the Holy Spirit upon the apostles and the birth and growth of the church. After Pentecost, of course, comes Advent again and a new year of hope and expectation. Thus, for many centuries the cycle of festivals has allowed Christians to dwell in a world of stories that tie and bind them into the great cosmic drama in which God is bringing salvation to the whole world.

Medieval Christians were grounded in the sacraments and oriented by the festivals, and their stories also sought divine aid through prayers to the saints and angels in heaven. That is, they prayed that exemplary Christians (*saints*) who had died and other spiritual beings, known as *angels*, would present their petitions to God in heaven. This was, after all, how things got done in medieval feudal society. If you wanted a favor from a member of the nobility or the king, it was best to ask someone at court to intercede for you. Hierarchies of saints and angels were believed to exist in heaven and to work in a similar fashion. On the other hand, it was believed that some angels who rebelled against God, the devil and his minions, exercised an evil influence over human beings that must be resisted through the power of prayer and the sacraments.

In this medieval worldview, we have the full integration of the biblical worldview of life, death, and resurrection of the body with the Greek metaphysical worldview

wne des haultes œuures du noble Charlemaine ror de franc

De plusieurs batailles que Charlemaine eut alencontre

A depiction of the coronation of Charlemagne as the first Holy Roman Emperor by Pope Leo III on Christmas Day in the year 800 CE.

of the cosmos as a hierarchical order. It forms the essence of the Catholic worldview. Lacking the historical consciousness that came after the Renaissance, medieval Christians thought this amalgamated worldview was exactly what Jesus had proclaimed in the Gospels.

The Two Cities Revisited

Throughout the Middle Ages there was a struggle between the two cities that Augustine had described. From the time of the Holy Roman Emperor Charlemagne (800–814), the emperors sought to dominate the church and the popes sought to dominate the state. A turning point in the development of the power of the papacy was its emulation of a monastic model of church discipline that originated in France. Because Benedictine monasticism had a strong work ethic, many monasteries became great centers of wealth, which in turn led to abuses. In 910 a new reform movement swept through monasticism, and a new monastery was founded at Cluny, in east central France. The Cluny reforms aimed at spiritual renewal and reorganization.

In addition to their emphasis on spirituality, the Cluniac monasteries provided an important organizational model for the development of colonialism, first adopted

RITUALS AND RITES: The Seven Sacraments and the Life Cycle

The seven sacraments, which Catholicism (both Orthodox and Roman) developed by the late Middle Ages, provided ritual assistance to the Christian at every stage of life, from birth to death. The word *sacrament* comes from a Latin translation of the Greek word for "mystery," a term borrowed from first-century pagan cults known as *mystery religions*, whose rituals were performed in the hope of achieving immortality.

The sacraments of Christianity, by uniting humans to God and eternal life, were said to guarantee salvation from sin and death. With the coming of the Protestant Reformation in the sixteenth century, only baptism and communion retained the status of sacraments. The other five rituals were rejected by Protestants on the ground that they could not be found as such in the New Testament. However, many of these "rejected" practices are observed in some Protestant denominations as rituals but not as sacraments in the full sense.

Baptism

The early Christians followed the Jewish practice of ritual immersion for new gentile converts in which the person's whole body was submerged in a river, lake, or special pool. For Christians, however, full submersion was seen as participation in Christ's death in the tomb; the emergence of the body from the water was equated with Christ's resurrection and departure from the tomb. The submersion was accompanied by the words "I baptize you in the name of the Father, the Son, and the Holy Spirit." As the practice of infant baptism developed in later generations, pouring of water over the baby's forehead was adopted as an alternative. Both types of baptism are still performed today.

This ritual is believed to flood the soul with divine grace (divine love, forgiveness, and assistance), erasing all stain of original sin, the sin of Adam and Eve that is said to mark every newborn child. Baptism changed one's destiny from death to eternal life.

Communion

Equal in sacramental importance was the Eucharist, or Holy Communion. This practice seems to have been an adaptation of the Jewish blessing of the bread and wine at meals, especially as it was practiced at Passover, the Jewish remembrance of the people's deliverance by God from slavery in Egypt. In the Gospels, at Jesus' last Passover, he broke the bread, blessed it, and said, "This is my body." He blessed the wine, too, and told his disciples, "This is the cup of my blood, shed for you and for many for the forgiveness of sins." By eating the bread and drinking the wine consecrated by a priest or minister who represents Jesus, Christians believe they are partaking of the body and blood of Jesus (for some literally, for others spiritually), who died for their sins on the cross and brought them to eternal life. Both baptism and communion were established well before the Middle Ages. However, to these, five other sacraments were added in the Catholic traditions.

Confirmation

The first converts to Christianity were adults who made a conscious decision to be baptized and to follow

Anglican Bishop Desmond Tutu, a Nobel Peace Prize winner, gives children communion during mass in Saint-Barnabas Church in South Africa.

Christ. As the practice of infant baptism developed, so did a controversy over whether this was appropriate, since the infant was too young to make such a choice. Infant baptism, it was decided, signifies that God is choosing the child rather than that the child is choosing God. At some point, however, a young Christian was expected to make a conscious choice to live for Christ. In the ritual of confirmation, young people at about the age of thirteen demonstrated their knowledge of the faith, were anointed on the forehead with oil, and made a public declaration of commitment to Christ. Thus, young adults were *confirmed* in the faith, accepting responsibility for the commitment made for them at baptism.

Marriage

During the Middle Ages, marriage was transformed from a civil proceeding into a sacrament. The union between a man and a woman came to be compared to the union between Christ and the church. As such it became more than a union between the couple for the purpose of raising a family. It became a ritual for uniting the spouses to each other in Christ. The husband and wife promised to love and care for each other as Christ loved and cared for his church.

Holy Orders

In the Middle Ages, a ritual also developed for inducting men into the priesthood. Bishops, Christ's representatives in the community of the faithful, ordained others, priests, to assist them in their pastoral work. In the ritual of ordination, bishops anointed the new priests' hands with oil to symbolize their sacred role in conferring the grace of God upon their parishioners through the administration of the sacraments. Bishops themselves were consecrated to their new office by the laying on of hands by other bishops.

Until the late Middle Ages, ordained priests could also be married. In the Western church, later reforms established the requirement that priests remain unmarried, or celibate. From this point on a man had to choose between the sacrament of marriage and that of ordination. In the Eastern church priests have always been allowed to marry, but bishops must be celibate.

Confession and Extreme Unction/ Anointing of the Sick

Two additional sacraments were developed during the Middle Ages: confession, to mediate God's forgiveness for sin, and extreme unction anointing of the sick, to confer God's power of healing in times of illness. In the early church it was common for people to put off baptism until death was near, for fear that sins committed after baptism could not then be washed away. To encourage baptism in infancy, the church developed a sacrament for the forgiveness of sins: The penitent would confess his or her sins and express true sorrow for them to a priest, who would then absolve the person, that is, forgive the sins of each in the name of Christ, thereby reconciling the sinner with God. The priest would also assign an appropriate penance for the absolved sinner to complete in reparation for his or her sins. Penance varied depending on the seriousness of the sin but most frequently required the penitent to repeat certain prayers or make a pilgrimage to a sacred place and resolve not to fall into sin again.

Closely associated with the practice of confession was the anointing of the sick with oil. In cases of serious illness, a priest would be called to anoint the Christian with oil in hopes of mediating God's grace to heal the person. Since this ritual of healing was administered to a person who was near death, it was called *extreme unction* and came to be thought of as the sacrament of the dying.

by the church and later emulated by such secular institutions of modernity as the multinational corporation. Whereas each Benedictine monastery was a world unto itself, under its own abbot, all the Cluniac monasteries, regardless of location, were answerable to a central command—the monastic headquarters in Cluny. Under Pope Gregory VII (1073–1085), Rome adopted this form of organization, thus imposing papal authority centered in Rome over all the bishops in the church.

The height of papal power occurred under Pope Innocent III (1198–1216), who forced the kings of England and France into submission, authorized the Fourth Crusade, and carried forward an immensely punitive inquisition against all heretics without interference from civil authorities. Innocent actually had both absolute spiritual power over the church and temporal political power over the state, to which the papacy had long aspired. The weakest moment of papal power, by contrast, occurred, as we have noted in connection with the First Vatican Council, under Pius IX in the late nineteenth century, when the church lost most of its temporal power.

The Promise and Threat of Christian Mysticism

Like every great religion, Christianity has a long tradition of mysticism—referring, in this context, to beliefs and practices thought to lead to a direct and immediate experience of God in Christ. The meaning of this experience is communicated through the biblical claim that human beings are created in the image and likeness of a God who is without image. The closer one comes to being like God, the more one is emptied of ego-identity.

Christian mysticism expresses itself in two dramatically different forms—the mysticism of love and union (the divine–human marriage) and the mysticism of identity. The former is exemplified by Spanish mystics of the sixteenth century, Teresa of Avila and her student, John of the Cross; the latter by the German mystic Meister Eckhart. Unlike early Christian theology, Christian mysticism has for centuries been enriched by the contributions of women: Teresa of Avila, Catherine of Siena, Therese of Lisieux, and Julian of Norwich, to name a few. In part this is because mystical experience is viewed as a gift from God that cannot be institutionally controlled. Consequently, it unleashes a powerful impulse toward equality. The mystical experience is accessible to male and female without distinction—all are equally in the image of the God without image.

As with the Jewish tradition, so too in Christianity, mysticism has been viewed ambivalently. This is because some mystics seem to speak as if they are not just in union with God but, in some sense, *are* God. This sometimes seems to be the case for the mysticism of identity. Yet despite this strain of what some consider to be blasphemy, Christianity has continued to affirm the validity and importance of mysticism.

"Christ has no body now but yours. . . . Yours are the feet with which he walks to do good. Yours are the hands through which he blesses all the world."

—St. Teresa of Avila

Christianity, Judaism, Islam: Crusades and Inquisition

Islam, which seemed to appear abruptly in the Arabian desert in the early 600s, grew within the span of a century into a civilization larger than the Roman Empire had been. For a time the Muslims seemed poised to proceed east of Spain to conquer most of Europe. But Charles Martel, whose initiative led to the formation of the Carolingian dynasty and the Holy Roman Empire, turned the Muslims back at Tours in 732. Europe remained Christian, but its holy sites, in Palestine, were in the hands of Muslims.

The Crusades were meant to change that. There were four main Crusades, in 1095, 1147, 1189, and 1202. Armies were organized to march to the Holy Land (Jerusalem and surrounding territories) and free it from the Muslims. But as the crusading armies marched through Europe they unleashed devastating violence on the Jewish communities they encountered along the way, fed by ancient Christian stereotypes of Jews as a "rejected people," killing an estimated 10,000 Jews in Germany alone during the first expedition.

As the Crusaders advanced toward Jerusalem, considerable violence was done even against Orthodox Christians, who were considered semi-heretics by the papal troops. The Muslims were the Crusaders' primary targets, however, for the Muslims held the Holy Land in their possession and threatened the Eastern church, whose main center was Constantinople. Thus the Crusades were ostensibly for the purpose of driving back the Muslims, reclaiming Jerusalem, and reuniting the Eastern and Western branches of the church. Pope Urban II, who preached the First Crusade, promised that all soldiers who participated would have their sins forgiven and would enter heaven. In addition, Crusaders were promised that they could keep the lands they conquered. The Crusaders laid siege to Jerusalem in June 1099, and the city fell on July 15. Muslim men, women, and children lost their lives in a bloody massacre.

The Crusades brought dramatic changes to Christendom, opening up new trade routes and fostering interactions between cultures, all of which stimulated

This fourteenth-century manuscript painting depicts the Crusaders at the gates of Jerusalem.

economies. As a result of their exposure to new ideas and attitudes and new religious beliefs and practices, some Europeans embraced new forms of ancient "heretical" beliefs. For example, a religious movement known as the *Cathari* or Albigensians took root in southern France and began to spread. The Cathari believed in reincarnation, and their goal was to liberate the spirit from the evil of a fleshly body. This led Pope Lucius III (1184) to initiate the Inquisition, an effort to stamp out heresy. The Fourth Lateran Council in 1215 authorized the punishment of all heretics by the state and also prescribed distinctive dress for Jews and Muslims (e.g., pointed hats or yellow badges) and restricted Jews to living in ghettos. Soon, inquisitions under church auspices would become infamous for their cruelty.

There were positive consequences of the Crusades as well. Most of Aristotle's work, lost to the West, had been preserved by Islamic scholars. The rediscovery of Aristotle led to new and controversial ways of thinking in the new universities of Europe in the twelfth and thirteenth centuries. And for a brief time Jewish, Muslim, and Christian philosophers, such as Maimonides (1135–1204), Averroes (Ibn Rushd, 1126–1198), and Thomas Aquinas (1224–1274), all used a common philosophical language to learn from each other's traditions, even if only, in the end, so that each could argue for the superiority of his own.

Christianity and Modernity (1517–1962)

The Emergence of Modernity

By the year 1500, Europe had been transformed from a primitive land of farms and undeveloped regions into a network of significant urban centers. In these cities, incorporation, a form of legal agreement that gave citizens the right of self-governance in exchange for taxes paid to the nobility, facilitated the emergence of individualism, an independent economy, and democratic self-governance. With increased craftsmanship and trade, corporate charters were also granted to the new craft guilds or "universities." These corporations mark the beginnings of the secularization of social institutions. Indeed, one of the defining characteristics of modernization is the existence of self-governing institutions that operate independent of direct religious authority (pope and bishops) and also of traditional medieval political authority (kings and lords). Education, too, declared its independence from the monasteries and cathedral schools, as scholars banded together to form their own universities. It was in these institutions of learning that intellectual secularization first appeared, as scholars began to think about their subject matters with a sense of independence from direct church authority. These changes facilitated the development of the institutional and intellectual diversity characteristic of modern secular societies. And in this environment three trends converged to shape the modern West: the millennialism of historical progress, the *via moderna* of autonomous reason, and the *devotio moderna* of emotional transformation.

Millennialism: History as Progress

One strand of modernity had its roots in the apocalyptic visions of Joachim of Fiore (1132–1202), a monk and abbot from southern Italy whose vision of history deeply influenced the modern age. Joachim's *"everlasting Gospel"* suggested that history can be divided into three ages corresponding to the three persons of the Trinity: the age of the Father (beginning with Abraham), which was superseded by the age of the Son (beginning with Christ), which would in turn be replaced by a third and final age, that of the Holy Spirit. Joachim thought of himself as living at the beginning of the *millennium*, the final age of the Spirit, in which there would no longer be any need for the institutional church and its clergy—nor for any other institution, including the state. Joachim, a mystic, expected the Holy Spirit to inspire a natural spontaneous harmony between all individuals, rendering existing institutions superfluous. This third age, which Joachim believed was predicted in the book of Revelation, would be the beginning of the Kingdom of God on earth, an age of perfect freedom and harmony that was destined to last a millennium, that is, a thousand years.

Joachim's version of the myth of history as proceeding through three ages profoundly shaped the modern view of history as a story of progress—history was seen as moving forward from the ancient period through the medieval, culminating in the modern age. For Joachim the third age was identified with the triumph of mysticism over the institutional church. But his three ages became increasingly secularized in the eighteenth century, during the Enlightenment in western Europe. As a result, while the three-age model persisted, the Holy Spirit was no longer identified as the force behind the millennium. For instance, Gotthold Lessing, the great Enlightenment scholar, held that the education of the human race passed through three phases: childhood, adolescence, and adulthood. The last, or third, age he identified with the Age of Enlightenment, in which the autonomy of reason (instead of the Holy Spirit) would lead to a natural and rational harmony among human beings. This vision of three ages was carried forward into the nineteenth century. Auguste Comte, the founding father of sociology, divided history into the ages of myth, philosophy, and science. One can find further parallels in the visions of other nineteenth-century philosophers, such as Hegel and Marx.

The Via Moderna and Devotio Moderna

According to Thomas Aquinas, the greatest of the medieval theologians and also generally regarded as the most influential Roman Catholic theologian, faith complements and completes reason. For Aquinas the Prime Mover known through Greek philosophy (especially Aristotle) is the same as the God of the Bible. One can have some knowledge of God through reason, independent of faith, but scripture enriches this knowledge immeasurably. Faith and reason, rightly used, can never contradict each other. However, the generation of theologians that followed Aquinas, known as *nominalists*, radically disagreed with him. William of Ockham (1287–1347) and other nominalists rejected this view as "ancient" (they called it the *via antiqua*) and outmoded. Espousing instead a *via moderna,* or modern way, these later theologians argued that reason was of little help in discerning the will of God. The split between faith and reason had made its appearance.

The "modern way" secularized the world by separating faith and reason. The only way to know what God wills is through faith as a deep emotional trust in God and a fervent reading of scriptures as the revealed word of God (the *devotio moderna*). The only way to know the world God has created is through rational empirical investigation of the world God has actually created. Thus, when it comes to knowledge of the world, faith requires the secular *via moderna* of rational scientific or empirical inquiry. And when it comes to knowledge of God, only revelation understood through "faith alone" will do. Protestantism and modernity are like two sides of the same coin, arising out of the *via moderna* and *devotio moderna* of the late medieval theology to flourish in the Renaissance and the Reformation. Therefore, unlike all other religious traditions, Protestantism did not, at first, experience modernization as the intrusion of an outside force but rather as a form of experience nurtured from within. It was only as modernization and secularization took on lives of their own, independent of the Protestant Reformation, that they began to appear threatening.

The Renaissance and the Reformation are siblings that grew up together. The intent of the first Renaissance thinkers was to recover the pre-Christian wisdom of the ancient world of Greece and Rome. The Reformation, in a parallel fashion, sought to reach back into antiquity and recover the original New Testament Christian vision as it existed before medieval theologians integrated it with Greek metaphysics. The new ideas of modernity were greatly facilitated by new technology, the printing press. With the introduction of movable type in 1454, a growing popular literacy made possible the rapid and wide dissemination of new ideas. The printing press also greatly accelerated the development of national identities by promoting a common language and shared ideas within a geographic area.

The initiator of the Protestant Reformation was Martin Luther (1483–1546), an Augustinian monk who embraced the new, modern way of thinking. While Luther thought that reason could be useful in secular matters, when it came to matters of faith, Luther called reason a "whore" that could not be trusted to lead one to God. Knowledge of God, rather, can be obtained only through faith and scripture undistorted by reason. "By faith alone," in fact, became the central doctrine of the Protestant Reformation, also embraced by the second major figure of the Protestant Reformation, John Calvin (1509–1564).

The Renaissance and the Reformation fostered a new individualism in the new, free cities by encouraging people to affirm their individuality and to have a sense of personal dignity and equality with others. This way of thinking could not be sustained without a shift from the medieval hierarchical view of authority to a democratic view. Knowledge through empirical inquiry and political authority based on the consent of the governed lie at the heart of the revolution called *modernization*. It is the encounter with these modern notions of knowledge and power, throughout the nineteenth and twentieth centuries, that has placed anxiety in the hearts of traditional or premodern societies around the globe. Such societies, like those of premodern Europe, typically are imbued with a sense of sacred, cosmic hierarchical order in which those in power ruled with sacred authority from above. As suggested earlier, Protestantism was unique in that from the beginning it was part of the revolutionary shift away from divinely decreed hierarchies toward individuality, equality, and dignity.

Devotio Moderna and the Protestant Reformation

The *devotio moderna* is exemplified in Martin Luther's emotional experience of being "born again." Luther grew up in a medieval Catholic world in transition toward the modern world of the Renaissance. At the insistence of his father he began to train in law as a young man, but after nearly getting hit by lightning in a rainstorm, he abandoned that path, became an Augustinian monk, and was ordained as a priest as well. His quest for moral and spiritual perfection drove him into feelings of great anxiety and hopelessness, for he felt that he could never live up to what was expected of him by God. Then, somewhere between 1511 and 1516, he had a powerful spiritual experience. While studying Paul's letter to the Romans, he suddenly came to see the meaning of the phrase often translated as "The just shall live by faith" (Romans 1:17).

What Luther came to realize, he said, was that he was acceptable before God with all his imperfections, as long as he had faith in Christ, who had died for his sins. There is nothing one can do to be saved. God has done everything. Salvation is a gift of grace. All sinners must do is have faith; and because of that faith, God will treat sinners as if they were saints, as if they were without sin. As this realization came over him, Luther said he was overcome by a liberating and exhilarating experience of having been in the immediate presence of a forgiving and compassionate God.

In this portrait of Martin Luther, by the sixteenth-century painter and eyewitness Lucas Cranach the Elder, the fiery reformer, once an Augustinian monk, appears peaceful and contemplative.

And Luther now knew that *justification* (i.e., being considered to be just and good) before this God was not by a person's works but by God's grace. One cannot will faith; it is received as a gift from God or pure grace. So salvation is by faith through grace—faith alone understood through scripture alone—not, as the Catholic Church had insisted, through grace *and* works, faith *and* reason, scripture *and* (hierarchical) tradition. This understanding of **justification by faith** is the cornerstone of the Protestant Reformation.

In 1516, Pope Leo X authorized the selling of indulgences to raise funds to re-build the Cathedral of St. Peter in Rome. That is, the pope promised that the sins of generous donors would be wiped away so that after death, they would avoid all punishment due them for their sins. For Luther, this was the last straw. Salvation was not to be purchased, since it comes by grace and faith alone. On October 31, 1517, Luther posted *Ninety-five Theses Against the Sale of Indulgences* on the church door of Wittenberg Castle, calling for public debate. That event marks the beginning of the Reformation.

Luther's problem was how to reform a church tradition gone corrupt. His solution was to criticize the tradition by raising faith and scriptures to a higher level of authority than church tradition, using scripture to judge and reform the tradition. This was an option open to him that was not available to Christians before the *canon*, or list of books in the New Testament, had been agreed on (after 387). It was the Catholic tradition that picked the scriptures and created the Christian Bible, as Catholics would say, "under the guidance of the Holy Spirit." Without the success of Catholicism, Protestantism's "faith alone, scriptures alone" would not have been possible, and without the failures of Catholicism, Protestant reform would not have been necessary.

Luther started out protesting abuses in the church, but he quickly moved on to challenge the entire mediating role of the church, the sacraments, and the papacy. Luther did not start out to create a new form of Christianity, only to reform the existing tradition. But events took on a life of their own that very quickly turned a reformation into a revolution, and Protestant Christianity was born in a radical break with the ancient, medieval way. In addition to the ancient Catholic way of faith *and* reason, scripture *and* tradition, guided by papal authority, there would be the new, modern Protestant way of faith alone, through scripture alone, and the individual alone before his or her God.

Calvin and the Protestant Ethic

Protestantism was unique in that from the beginning it was part of the revolutionary shift away from sacred hierarchy toward not only secular rationality but also individu-ality and equality. In this, Protestantism, in conjunction with Renaissance humanism, laid the groundwork for the emergence in the West of the idea of human dignity and human rights. And yet, in the relation of Christianity to the state and to society, the

justification by faith: doctrine that humans are saved by faith as a gift from God rather than through works of obedience

"Thereupon I felt myself to be reborn and to have gone through open doors into paradise. The whole of scripture took on a new meaning."

—Martin Luther

basic assumptions of the Constantinian/Augustinian visions of the unity of church and state remained operative, at least for the major strands of the Protestant Reformation. The state should be a Christian state, only now that meant Protestant.

Next to Luther, John Calvin was the greatest of the reformers. Calvin spent his life transforming the city of Geneva in Switzerland into a model for Protestant civilization. Arguing that human sinfulness requires that all power be limited, he created a Christian democratic republic with a division of powers among its representative bodies. This institutional strategy served as a model for later secular democracies.

The Protestant work ethic associated with Calvinism really represents the secularization of the Benedictine motto "to work is to pray." Indeed, a major teaching of Luther and Calvin is the idea that work in the world (whether as a shoemaker or doctor, etc.) is as holy a task as praying in a monastery—indeed, a holier task. What makes work holy is not where it is done but doing it as a result of God's call. The **Protestant ethic** demanded that one live simply and work hard: "earn all you can, save all you can" to be able to "give all you can" for the greater glory of God. The early twentieth-century sociologist Max Weber suggested that this ethic helped to fuel the emergence of capitalism in Europe by encouraging both hard work, which allowed individuals to prosper, and savings, which were needed for investment.

> **Protestant ethic:** sociologist Max Weber's observation that Calvinist beliefs about holiness and work contributed to accumulation of wealth and facilitated the growth of capitalism

Calvinistic concepts are important to note here because in Europe and North America, it was Calvin's rather than Luther's vision of Protestant civilization that most influenced the future, not only of democracy but also of Western capitalism and colonialism.

Other Reform Movements

If the *via moderna* split faith and reason apart and confined reason largely to the secular parts of life, the *devotio moderna* of mystical piety played a parallel role, restricting faith to the domain of spiritual emotions. By the fourteenth and fifteenth centuries, a new kind of "this-worldly" mysticism—the *devotio moderna*—was creating popular pietistic movements for spiritual renewal that grew up spontaneously and without official church approval. These "grassroots" movements focused on personal piety founded on intense, emotionally transforming religious experiences. The experiences fostered a new, democratic spirit by emphasizing the equality of all before God and the spiritual benefits to be obtained from living simply. They were typically critical of the medieval Catholic Church, its wealth and its hierarchical order.

The Anabaptist Rebellion Against Both Church and State

We have described the Lutheran and Calvinist center of the Protestant Reformation. However, there were wings to the left and right of this center as well. On the left were the radical reformers and on the right the Anglicans. The radical reformers have deep roots in the mystical and millennial "grassroots" movements of the late Middle Ages.

The Anabaptists were Christians who denied baptism to infants because the practice is not mentioned in the New Testament and because they believed that only those who freely choose to join the church should be baptized. The views of the Anabaptists alienated them from Protestantism and Catholicism and led to their severe persecution by both traditions. By 1535 over 50,000 Anabaptists had been martyred.

Interestingly, the pacifist strands of this movement stand out in the history of Christianity because the Anabaptists do attempt to break with the Constantinian vision of a Christian civilization, rejecting both the authority of the hierarchical church and the authority of the state. This meant that pacifist Anabaptists refused any role in public service on the grounds that the state condones killing and that taking an oath of office goes against one of Jesus' statements in the Sermon on the Mount: "No one can serve two masters" (Matthew 6:24). The Hutterites, the Mennonites, and the Amish are all products of the Anabaptist wing of the Reformation. The most pious of their twentieth-century descendants among the Amish are distinctive for refusing to compromise their principles by taking advantage of modern conveniences such as electricity and motor vehicle transportation.

The Anglican Reformation and the Puritan Revolt

At the other extreme, the English Reformation was initiated by the state rather than by Christians in the churches. Initially the English monarch championed Catholicism against Luther's views as "heretical." Indeed, Pope Leo X conferred the title "Defender

The struggle to keep the premodern traditions pure is difficult. But note that this Amish woman is using in-line skates while pushing a baby stroller to reach her destination faster without utilizing gas or electricity.

of the Faith" on King Henry VIII. Problems arose, however, when Henry, who had no male heir to the throne, wanted to divorce his first wife, Catherine of Aragon, and remarry in hopes of fathering a son. Pope Clement VII refused to give his permission. So in 1534, Henry VIII nationalized the church, making himself the head of what was now the Church of England. Then the archbishop of Canterbury declared the marriage to Catherine invalid. Nevertheless, apart from breaking with the papacy, the English church remained essentially Catholic, and Henry continued to oppose and often punish those he considered to be heretics. Only after Henry's death were Protestant reformers safe in England.

As Protestants made inroads in Britain, the Church of England's doctrine did not seem pure enough for the Puritans, Calvinist radicals who were intent on returning to a New Testament Christianity shorn of all "popery." After a short period of dominance under their military leader, Oliver Cromwell, Puritans became the object of persecution. Puritanism was a diverse and fragmented movement that had splintered into Congregationalists, Presbyterians (who prevailed in Scotland), Separatists, and Nonconformists, including Baptists—all rejecting the thirty-nine Articles of Religion, the official statement of doctrine of the Church of England. In 1620, 101 Pilgrims sailed for North America. Over 40,000 Pilgrims fled England in the next two decades, bringing to the new colonies their propensity for sectarian diversity.

The Catholic Counter-Reformation

The Council of Trent was a series of meetings held between 1545 and 1563 for the purpose of responding to the reformers. The positions hammered out in these meetings reinforced the absolute power of the pope and made the medieval theology of Thomas Aquinas normative for the Catholic Church. Trent, for the most part, froze Catholicism in its late medieval form. It affirmed that the Catholic "tradition" was equal in authority to scripture and that Latin should remain the language of the Bible and of worship. It also retained the seven sacraments (which Protestantism had reduced to two, baptism and communion) and the importance of the saints, relics, and indulgences. Indeed, the buying and selling of indulgences was not even discussed. At the conclusion of the meetings of the Council of Trent, Pope Pius IV declared that there was "no salvation outside the Catholic faith."

Religious Diversity: Church and State in War and Peace

The Reformation led to political divisions and open warfare between Catholics and Protestants throughout Europe. Like Catholics, all Protestants except the Anabaptists assumed that the goal of Christianity was a Christian civilization. For the most part, however, neither side considered the other side Christian. Each tended to think the other was doing the work of the devil. Consequently, Christians resorted to warfare to settle whose religion would shape the public order. In Germany, a series of wars between Protestants and Catholics ended in the Peace of Augsburg in 1555, with its compromise statement *"cuius regio, eius religio"* (the religion of the ruler shall be the religion of the land). As a consequence, the splintering of the church seemed to match the splintering of Europe into nation-states. Another series of battles, known as the Thirty Years War, erupted but was brought to a conclusion with the Peace of Westphalia in 1648. This was a general settlement that reestablished the conditions of the Peace of Augsburg, with additional protections for minorities and encouragement of religious toleration (see Map 4.2).

Clearly the Protestant Reformation created not a new and purer unity but a new and chaotic diversity. The more people learned to read the Bible for themselves, the more a diversity of interpretations emerged, leading in turn to more and more diverse forms of Christianity. The Protestant Reformation and the religious wars that followed had relativized and privatized religion, making the very act of interpreting the Bible seem more and more private and subjective. Thus, the Reformation helped to create a key element of modern consciousness, the awareness of the relativity of one's understanding of the world and the need to choose one's identity. The result, after much bloodshed, was the gradual transformation of both Protestantism and Catholicism into denominational religions. Whereas in medieval Catholicism and the early sectarian movements of Protestantism, each group had seen itself as the sole repository of truth to which all in society should conform, denominational religions accept the establishment of religiously diverse communities, each expressing the private views of their adherents.

With the emergence of denominationalism, Christianity was on a path leading to a new relationship to the public and political order of society. In North America first and then in Europe, a new understanding of the state emerged—the state as a secular and neutral political institution that favored no one religion. Hence, after the French and American revolutions, the secular, democratic nation-state that functioned by privatizing religion (restricting it to peoples' personal/denominational lives) increasingly became the normative model for the modern Western world. Paradoxically, this development coexisted with the continued assumption by many Christians that the task of Christianity was to Christianize the world. Consequently, as Europe's public order was becoming more and more secular in the nineteenth and twentieth centuries, European Christians were setting out to Christianize the world in concert with Western colonialism's political and economic attempts at global conquest.

Enlightenment Rationalism and Christian Pietism

Pietism and rationalism, two responses to the doctrinal, social, and political divisions created by the Reformation, were rooted in the split between faith and reason that we have already described. And both contributed to the development of Western notions of universal human rights.

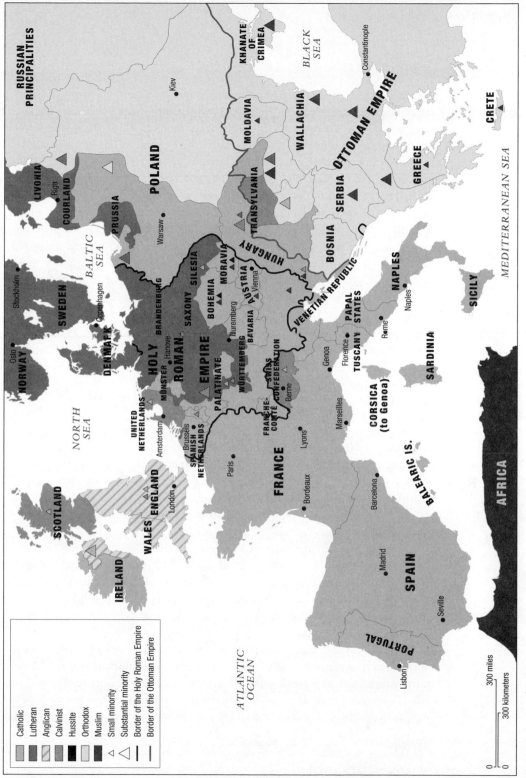

Map 4.2 Europe after the Peace of Wesphalia.

Rationalism

The rise of modern science and technology was dramatic and impressive. Science came to express the most public and certain knowledge that people believed they had about their world. And the more public and certain scientific knowledge appeared to be, the more private and uncertain religious knowledge seemed to be. As science developed, scientists came to believe that they had less and less need to bring God into their explanations. In the nineteenth century, the French astronomer Pierre Laplace announced that he had no need of the "God hypothesis" to explain the world scientifically.

We have seen that in the view of Enlightenment philosopher Gotthold Lessing human beings were entering the third age of history. Lessing called this era the *age of reason*, or the adulthood of the human race. People no longer needed to be told what to believe. To be "enlightened" was to "think for oneself, using one's capacity to reason." Enlightenment rationalism became the foundation of all scientific and public knowledge. The Enlightenment was built on four key concepts:

1. use of one's own reason,
2. freedom from tradition through the rational critique of the past,
3. a view of nature as a finely tuned machine whose mechanisms can be rationally understood, and
4. the belief that history is guided by hidden laws of progress.

deism: enlightenment view that God created the world as a watchmaker does a watch, leaving it to run without interference

The power of reason was assumed to be capable of freeing human beings from the irrationality of the past (including the irrationality of much of religion), of discovering how the universe really works, and of introducing a golden age of progress.

Enlightenment rationalism fostered the emergence of **deism**, which likened the world to a clock and God to a divine clockmaker. Just as a clockmaker makes a perfect machine that runs on its own without assistance from its maker, so God, as creator, does not actively guide or influence events in the world.

The Enlightenment promised to overcome the divisions among human beings that had generated the religious wars of the Reformation by reducing religion to its rational elements. By thus eliminating the emotion-laden "superstitions" of traditional religions, rationalists believed they would create a more tolerant world. Enlightenment rationalists, who identified reason as the one universal that all humanity shared, expected the exercise of universal reason to lead people of every religion and culture into greater harmony. Such an enlightened deism was characteristic of denominations such as the Unitarians and the Universalists and played an important role in championing universal rights. Enlightenment morality contributed to the emergence of a modern ethic of human dignity and human rights by stressing the fundamental unity of the human race. And indeed, in England and elsewhere laws of toleration began to be passed.

Pietism

What was missing in the clockwork universe of deism was warmth or emotion. The alternative to the cold rationality of both Enlightenment rationalism and Protestant rationalism was supplied by Pietism, a new movement that gave rise to evangelical Christianity. In their search for a way of uniting people of faith, who had been divided since the Protestant Reformation, the Pietists explored the nonrational aspects of religion, those in the realm of emotion. Indeed, Pietism was a movement to recover the *devotio moderna* of the late medieval and Reformation periods.

Pietists sought to transcend religious differences by minimizing the role of sectarian dogma, which seemed to divide Christians, and maximizing the role of religious emotion, which they hoped would be a unifying factor. The true test of Christian faith, Pietists argued, is found not so much in right belief or dogmas as in a changed heart. Thus the goal of evangelical piety was in the beginning antisectarian and antidogmatic. One of its greatest representatives, John Wesley (1703–1791), believed passionately that doctrinal differences should not separate Christians. He saw the deep emotion of faith as the way to Christian unity.

The first wave of Pietism came in the seventeenth century. It included such groups as the Moravians and the Quakers. The greatest and most far-reaching expression of Pietism in the eighteenth century was the Methodist movement begun by John Wesley, who was deeply influenced by the Moravians as well as by Catholic and Anglican mystics. Wesley, whose conversion had "strangely warmed" his heart, rejected some of Calvin's ideas and questioned the doctrine of original sin by emphasizing freedom of choice, suggesting that humans were capable of achieving spiritual and moral perfection.

Wesley's message was aimed primarily at the new working class created by the Industrial Revolution. Factory owners did not always pay just wages, and working conditions and hours were often inhumane. The Methodist movement was one of the first constructive responses of Christianity to these changing conditions. Methodist communities were committed to a morality of perfecting both self and society. Mystical piety is a great equalizer in social experience because it is contagious and can overtake anyone, without regard to social status, race, gender, or creed.

Methodism's most striking accomplishments include leading roles in the abolition of slavery in England (1833) and in introducing women into the ministry. Both exemplify the importance of evangelical piety in the development of the modern commitment to human dignity, equality, and rights.

The tremendous power of the Methodist and other evangelical movements tapped a long tradition in the history of Christianity. This is the tradition of combining a simple regimen of prayer and devotion with life in small communities of discipline and mutual encouragement oriented toward improving the world. This formula fueled the monastic movement that missionized the tribes of Europe and brought learning and the heritage of Greek civilization to Europe. This same spirit was carried forward in Calvinism and was transferred to evangelical Christianity, primarily (but not exclusively) through Methodism. In these Protestant formulations, it would be

John Wesley, the founder of Methodism, often preached to the men, women, and children of the new working class during the Industrial Revolution.

carried around the world in the global missions of the nineteenth century. Thus, paradoxically, the Augustinian vision of a mission to Christianize the world that had had such consequences as the Inquisitions and the excesses of the Crusades also afforded a model for promoting human dignity and equality. The arrogant side of Western colonialism brought with it the seeds of its own demise as it spread around the world. Today, the base communities of liberation theology and the communities of indigenous (non-European) spiritual renewal among African and Asian Christians are touched by a postcolonial form of the evangelical missionary message.

Nineteenth-Century Romanticism and Existentialism

The rationalism and pietism of the Enlightenment shared a faith in the progress of the human race. Drawing on the myth of the three ages as formulated by Joachim of Fiore in the thirteenth century, members of these groups shared a millennial faith that they lived in the final age of history, when people would throw off the authoritarianism of past tradition and institutions and instead be guided by a direct inner light that would bring with it progress and harmony. For this to come about, the rationalists relied on the *via moderna* of the light of reason. For the Pietists it was the *devotio moderna*—the warm emotional light of spiritual illumination that comes from being born again. Thus both share the millennial mysticism (of Joachim of Fiore) that has driven the modern spirit of progress. But the progress and harmony they expected from piety and from reason did not come.

The French Revolution in the Wake of the Failure of Reason

At the end of the eighteenth century economic conditions grew very bad in France, and they were not helped by the extravagance of the court of King Louis XVI. This led to a massive revolt, the French Revolution, which began in 1789. In addition to replacing the government, the new leaders created a revolutionary religion featuring a "Cult of Reason" and later a "Cult of the Supreme Being" (deism). The churches were transformed into "Temples of Reason," and statues of the Virgin Mary were replaced by icons of "nature goddesses" and "the goddess of reason." King Louis and his wife, Marie Antoinette, were executed in 1793, and in the Reign of Terror that followed, thousands of clergy and nobility were arrested and beheaded.

The bloody events of the 1790s brought about considerable disillusionment with reason. Reason had been embraced at the beginning of the Enlightenment as the way of avoiding fanaticism, dogmatism, violence, and intolerance. And yet in the French Revolution reason had shown itself to be fanatical, dogmatic, violent, and intolerant. People grew weary of the violence and complexity of urban life and longed for the simplicity of nature uncorrupted by civilization. With the failure of reason, many people turned to emotion as the foundation for renewal of life. If the Enlightenment was rationalistic and mechanistic, the Romantic period that followed was emotional and organic. If the Enlightenment had sought to escape the suffocation of past tradition

GENDER FOCUS: Women in Christianity

Christianity (like Judaism, Islam, and the religions of Asia) arose in *patriarchal* (male-dominated) societies. Historically, women have played the greatest roles in forms of Christianity that valued direct and immediate religious experience (mystical piety) as more authoritative than the institutional authority of the bishops. Thus in the early church women played a greater role in Gnostic (mystical and otherworldly) and Montanist (apocalyptic and ecstatic) Christian movements than in Catholicism, which was institutionally hierarchical. And yet there were always some women who were exceptions to the rule. According to the letters of Paul, women had leadership roles in some of the early Christian communities. As the early church became institutionalized, however, prevailing customs of male dominance seemed to reassert themselves, and the pattern of excluding women from roles as priests and bishops took hold.

During the Middle Ages women found ways to exercise autonomy and independence by founding female monastic orders. With the Protestant Reformation, however, even that option was taken from them, and women were largely confined to the home and child rearing. This began to change in the nineteenth century, when the evangelical missionary movements with deep roots in the mystical traditions of piety (*devotio moderna*) offered new opportunities for women in leadership roles. The role of women in these missions played an important part in the political development of the woman's movement for independence and the right to vote. Also, among the more unusual forms of Christianity, with mystical or Gnostic roots, women founded new traditions. For example, the Shakers, the Unity School of Christianity, and Christian Science were begun by Ann Lee, Emma Curtis Hopkins, and Mary Baker Eddy, respectively.

Another major source of women's autonomy was the *via moderna* as expressed in the denominations influenced by Enlightenment secularization

A civil rights activist who marched with Martin Luther King Jr. in Selma, Barbara Harris was ordained a bishop in the Episcopal Church in 1980.

and rationalism. Consequently, in the nineteenth century women began to be ordained in some Protestant denominations. The Congregationalists led the way in 1853. They were followed by the Universalists, the Unitarians, and other denominations. The mainline Protestant churches (e.g., Methodist, Presbyterian, Episcopal, and Lutheran) did not follow suit until the twentieth century. The Roman Catholic and the Orthodox churches still do not ordain women, arguing that the maleness of Jesus and the apostles reveals the divine intent for an all-male priesthood.

The last four decades of the twentieth century saw the rise of a theologically based feminism. The issue that divides feminists and fundamentalists is whether God created a sacred natural order in which men's and women's roles are eternally defined. Fundamentalists say yes, feminists say no. Feminists say that fundamentalists confuse the cultural attitudes and common practices of premodern societies with the will of God. Fundamentalists turn this argument around, saying that feminists and other liberation advocates confuse the cultural attitudes and common practices of modern societies with the will of God.

and enter a bright new future of scientific advances, Romanticism sought to return to the organic, familial, and deeply emotional connections of traditional agricultural or village society. An ambivalent struggle between these alternative visions is still very much a part of our contemporary culture.

From Reason to Emotion: The Romantic Alternative to Enlightenment Rationalism

"The sum total of religion is to feel that, in the highest unity, all that moves us in feeling is one; . . . that is to say, that our being and living is a being and living in and through God."

—Schleiermacher

The German philosopher Immanuel Kant (1724–1804), the greatest of the Enlightenment philosophers, argued for religion within the limits of reason that focused on ethics, on the grounds that there is no rational way at arriving at belief in God. Friedrich Schleiermacher (1768–1834), considered to be the father of modern Christian theology, offered the Romantic solution to Kant's rationalist challenge, suggesting that knowledge of God comes to people not through reason (the *via moderna*) but rather through emotion (the *devotio moderna*). Consequently, knowledge of God can coexist with scientific knowledge of the world: There is no conflict because the outer, secular, public sphere of reason is separate from the inner, private sphere of faith.

Moreover, Schleiermacher disputed the opinion of some Christians that the affirmation of faith in the resurrection of Jesus Christ depends on historical proof. When a person does not believe in the resurrection one day and then confesses such faith the next day, the theologian argued, the altered conviction was not the result of that person's having learned a new historical fact but of that person's having had a powerful transformative emotional experience. This emphasis on transformative emotion places Schleiermacher directly in the tradition of the *devotio moderna* and evangelical Pietism.

Kierkegaard and the Existentialist Response to Cultural Relativism

"To have a self, to be a self, is the greatest concession made to man, but at the same time it is eternity's demand upon him."

—Kierkegaard

Another important development in modern Christianity was existentialism, marking the start of the postmodern exploration of the implications of cultural relativism. Existentialism was responding to the new thinking that accompanied advances in historical and social scientific consciousness. The results of both historical and ethnographic studies made people aware that various cultures interpreted "human nature" differently. Cultural relativism entails the acknowledgment and examination of these differences.

According to the existentialists, one is not born with an essential human nature. Rather, "existence precedes essence"—that is the core insight of existentialism. When you plant an acorn, you know you will get an oak tree. The essence of the tree is there from its beginnings. But when a human child is conceived, biology is not definitive because human freedom enters into the equation. No one can predict who or what that child will become. The life task of a human being is to create a self through his or her choices.

Søren Kierkegaard (1813–1855) invented what came to be called *Christian existentialism*. Kierkegaard argued that if we have no innate human nature, each person must make a "leap of faith" inspired by faith in Christ to trust God to help him or her construct an identity as a loving and compassionate human being. Like Schleiermacher, Kierkegaard wrote that such faith depends neither on logical reasoning nor on historical proof but on a personal choice driven by powerful emotions that lead one to make the leap of faith.

From the Holocaust to Hiroshima: The Global Collapse of the Modern Myth of History as Progress

The existentialist response to the social sciences and cultural relativism led some philosophers, such as Friedrich Nietzsche (1844–1900), to conclusions quite the opposite of Kierkegaard's namely, that history and ethnography show "God" to have been a human invention, who is now dead, a circumstance that obliges us to invent our identities without God.

Christian faith is proved not by scientific and/or historical facts, nor by metaphysical arguments, but by the emotional, moral, and spiritual transformation of the individual. In making this argument, Friedrich Schleiermacher became the founder of modern Protestant theology.

For Nietzsche, the modern world was incompatible with belief in the biblical God: History had demythologized the sacred stories of the Bible and shown them to be false even as science had demythologized the biblical view of creation and replaced it with Darwin's theories of evolution. As Nietzsche saw it, European Christians who acted as if Christianity and modernity were compatible would one day realize that in embracing modernity they had killed God. Recalling the argument between fundamentalists and modernists at the beginning of this chapter, we can now see that Nietzsche and fundamentalists shared at least one conviction—that belief in God is incompatible with modernity. But for fundamentalists this meant that Darwin's theories had to be rejected, whereas for Nietzsche it meant belief in God had to be rejected.

Nietzsche, having rejected the God of the Bible, believed that history is guided by a struggle for existence that takes the form of a "will to power." Like Kierkegaard, he argued human beings must choose who they will become, but he believed their choices should be preceded by a rejection of Christian values and beliefs. The problem with Christianity, said Nietzsche, is that biblical morality teaches "weak values" such as forgiveness and pity that ultimately lead to resentment against persons who are strong and courageous. They lead, the philosopher believed, to an ideal of "equality" that rewards mediocrity. Nietzsche therefore called biblical values bad for civilization. The future, he believed, should belong to the strong—those superior and creative individuals who had the courage to "transvalue all values" and to make their own morality.

Little more than half a century after Nietzsche announced the death of God, the Nazis came along to embrace Nietzsche's vision of a will to power. Nietzsche's model for a world ruled by superior persons was not that of the Nazis, who distorted the philosopher's ideas when they cast themselves as those superior human beings destined to re-create the world. What Nietzsche's vision did have in common with that of the Nazis was contempt for the ideals of equality and democratic rule that Nietzsche associated with Christianity.

Nietzsche, who had characterized Christians as weak because their religion taught them to show compassion and pity, might have been surprised by the number of churchgoers who showed themselves quite willing to abandon their weak values of compassion in exchange for the Nazi ideals of elitism and the will to power. Between 1933 and 1945, Hitler and the Nazi Party ruled Germany and drew Europe and America into World War II (1939–1945).

One of the key factors in Hitler's rise to power was his successful appeal to anti-Semitism in German and Austrian culture. Hitler was able to achieve power, in large part, by appealing to long-standing prejudice against the Jews created by the churches over the centuries. By the time of the Middle Ages, Christians viewed Jews as deserving to suffer for rejecting and crucifying the messiah, the Son of God. Consequently, the Nazis were able to strip the Jews of their citizenship, confiscate their property, and send them off in boxcars to concentration camps without serious resistance from the churches and often with their assistance. Over 6 million European Jews are estimated to have been killed, mostly in the gas chambers of the Nazi concentration camps.

The Christian churches might have been a powerful force against the Nazi attempt to exterminate the Jews, but they were not. In Germany, by some estimates, only 20 percent of the Protestant churches resisted Hitler and the Nazi message, as the famous Protestant theologian and martyr Dietrich Bonhoeffer did. Even fewer took issue with the treatment of the Jews. Pope Pius XI signed a concordat with Hitler in hopes of protecting the autonomy of the German Catholic churches. Most Christians passively acquiesced in the Nazi program of genocide, and many actively cooperated.

A minority of Christians held fast to what Nietzsche called the "weak values" of Christianity (love and compassion) and rescued Jews, but with a few important exceptions they were lone individuals of conscience. Christians in Denmark were one notable exception, and most of Denmark's Jews survived because of collective resistance by church and state. Le Chambon sur Lignon in France is another such exception: This small village of mostly French Protestants saved over 5,000 Jewish lives. Wherever the churches led resistance to the Nazis, Jewish lives were saved. Unfortunately, that did not happen often. As the church historian Franklin Littell has noted, the irony is that more priests and ministers died in Hitler's armies than died resisting Hitler.

Reflection on the lessons of the Holocaust brought unprecedented change to Christianity in the last decades of the twentieth century. Since Vatican II and in response to the Holocaust, not only the Catholic Church but also the main Protestant denominations have sought to correct past teachings about the Jews as a rejected people (the myth of supersession) and have replaced these teachings with an affirmation that the Jewish covenant is an authentic covenant with God—one that exists both prior to and apart from the Christian covenant. This public acknowledgment of the Jewish people as chosen by God and of the religion of Judaism as a valid expression of monotheism is unprecedented in the history of Christianity.

> "Being a Christian is less about cautiously avoiding sin than about courageously and actively doing God's will."
>
> —Dietrich Bonhoeffer

The horrors of World War II made Nietzsche's claim that God was dead seem more plausible. The killing of millions on the battlefields and in the camps, achieved by means of the latest science and technology, represented the death of what "God" had become for many in Western civilization, namely, the "God of progress." The millions upon millions of dead and the shameless reality of the Nazi death camps gave modern persons good reasons to question whether modernity and "progress" were truly worthy human ideals. Science and technology had become essential instruments in the propagation of mass death.

Finally, with the dropping of the atomic bomb on Hiroshima, Japan, at the end of World War II and the accumulation of nuclear weapons by the USSR and the United States in the second half of the twentieth century, a turning point may have emerged. The possibility of a nuclear war that would destroy the planet made belief in the progress of history and a better future through science and technology seem far from inevitable. As the world moves beyond its modernist phase, many Christians are beginning to explore the possibility of separating the church's message from the myth of history as progress and from the assumptions of the cultural superiority of the West that reinforced colonialism.

> "The madman jumped into their midst and pierced them with his eyes. 'Whither is God?' he cried; 'I will tell you. *We have killed him*—you and I. All of us are his murderers.'"
>
> —Friedrich Nietzsche, "The Parable of the Madman"
>
> SOURCE: Friedrich Nietzsche, *The Gay Science* (1882, 1887) para. 125; Walter Kaufmann, ed. (New York: Vintage, 1974), pp. 181–82.

Christianity and Postmodern Trends in a Postcolonial World (1962–)

From Colonial to Postcolonial Christianity

For most of its history Christianity has been predominantly a European religion. The Christianity that fostered the rise of modernization and the myth of progress was not that of the Eastern Orthodox churches, which saw Christian civilization as a sacred unity of church and state. It was Western Augustinian Christianity, with its model of two cities, one sacred and the other secular.

Europe gave birth to Roman Catholicism during the Middle Ages and to modern Christianity with the Protestant Reformation. In 1600 the overwhelming majority of Christians in the world lived in Europe. However, the invention of the modern three-masted sailing ship (ca. 1500) unleashed massive changes that began when the countries of Europe acquired their first colonies and seems to be culminating in the birth of a global civilization. Colonial expansion was accompanied by worldwide missionary activity, led first by Catholic countries such as Portugal and Spain and later by countries with new Protestant centers of power, especially England. By 1900 only half of all the Christians in the world lived in Europe, and by the end of the twentieth century the majority of the world's Christians resided elsewhere, in Latin America, Africa, and Asia. Thus, postcolonial Christianity is decisively non-European.

Even as church membership was waning in Europe, it was planting the seeds of its possible transformation and renewal in postcolonial forms elsewhere in the world. On the one hand, while birthrates among Christians declined in Europe, the number of children born to Christians elsewhere increased dramatically. On the other hand, the secularization of Europe led to a large decline in the practice of Christianity there. Paradoxically, at the same time, through European colonial expansion, Protestant evangelical Christians engaged in a massive missionary enterprise whose aim was the Christianization of every part of the world touched by colonization (see Map 1.3 in Chapter 1). This plan was justified by the assumption that the political and economic colonization of the world by Europe was part of God's plan to make possible the spread of the Gospel to the very ends of the earth.

The feeling of the superiority and global destiny of European civilization that accompanied colonialism communicated itself through an attitude of paternalism. At first many in the premodern cultures were impressed with the wonders of Western science and technology. Before long, however, indigenous peoples came to feel demeaned and diminished by the Westerners' attitude toward them.

In former colonial areas, whether in Africa, Asia, or the Americas, resentment against western Europeans inevitably led to a political backlash that typically coalesced around liberation movements. Activists called for rejection of some Western values, such as capitalism and individualism, in favor of political and economic independence and restoration of traditional values and customs. Paradoxically, at the same time, other values espoused by the West, such as dignity and equality, lent support to these indigenous liberation movements. We see this paradox, for example, in Gandhi's campaign to liberate India from English colonial domination, which appealed both to Hindu values and to modern Western values in just this way.

If colonialism brought modernity to the non-European world, the rejection of Western colonialism can be said to mark the beginnings of postcolonial and postmodern trends in Christianity. It is among postcolonial Christians that we might find the beginnings of a new postcolonial and non-Eurocentric form of Christianity, more open to coexistence with other religions and cultures.

Latin America

liberation theology: liberation theology emerged in Latin America in the twentieth century; the goal was to show that the Gospel was more radical than Marxism in its promotion of justice for the poor

Latin America was colonized in the sixteenth century by Spain and Portugal, two Roman Catholic countries untouched by the Protestant Reformation. Thus the Spanish and the Portuguese brought to the New World medieval patterns of social order that were hierarchical and antidemocratic. By the mid-twentieth century, however, the forces of secularization and Marxism had taken their toll, and while 90 percent of Latin Americans were baptized, only about 15 percent were estimated to be practicing their faith. This situation set the context of the emergence of postcolonial movements of **liberation theology** and evangelical–charismatic Christianity.

In the last decades of the twentieth century, Latin American Christians (mostly Catholics) exposed to the Marxist analysis of European colonial exploitation criticized the traditional hierarchical order of society that reinforced privileges for the few and ensured poverty and oppression for the many. Their response was called liberation theology. These ideas, in turn, produced a backlash among some branches of Evangelical and Pentecostalist Protestant Christianity, the movements that had inspired the missionary zeal of the nineteenth century. These evangelical and Pentecostal Christians saw liberation theologies as a new form of the social gospel and its ultimate sellout of Christianity to modern culture. In an effort to return to the premodern spiritual foundations of their faith, Pentecostalists and others downplayed issues of cultural and economic oppression. Rather, they focused on issues of personal conversion (being born again) and/or ecstatic experience (e.g., speaking in tongues). Their idea was to transform society through personal virtue that could be cultivated by spiritual means within the parameters of any social system in which individual Christians happened to live.

For Christians in the liberation movements, the heart of the Gospel is love for the poor and the struggle for social justice. For evangelical Christians it is personal conversion, personal regeneration in the Spirit, and the shaping of a public order that will give priority to these goals. Despite their differences, however, both parties regard Christianity as the only appropriate means of shaping the public order of political and economic life.

For some Christians, worship inspires hope for a world of justice and compassion. A liberation theology base community meets in Panajachel, Guatemala, to hear the good news from scripture that Jesus Christ has come to liberate the poor and the oppressed.

N. S. de Guadalupe, Patrona de Mexico y de la Nueva España, retocada del Sagrado Original, el día 6 de Marzo, de 1766. Adem.º de D.ᵉ Blas Antonio de Orta.

(above) Painting of the Virgin of Guadalupe, who is said to have appeared to a peasant in Mexico in 1531. The Virgin Mary, mother of Jesus, conveys God's love and compassion to Catholic believers around the world.

Africa

For models of Christianity that break with both the premodern and modern visions of a "Christian civilization" one must look primarily to the African and Asian churches, where we see the emergence of a "diaspora" model of Christianity. A diaspora religion is one whose adherents are "dispersed" as minority communities among many nations and cultures.

Except for the ancient Coptic Church in Egypt and the Church of Ethiopia, Christianity in Africa is the result of missionary efforts primarily from the colonial period. At the beginning of the twentieth century there were scarcely any Christians in Africa. At the end of the century it was the fastest-growing geographic area for Christianity, and more than a fifth of the world's Christians can be found there today. Almost half of the population of Africa is now Christian, with Islam a close second.

As the number of converts to Christianity grew, the people overcame the tight control missionaries had sought to maintain over African Christianity by developing indigenous forms. One of the most interesting of the African independent church movements is Isaiah

(right) In Africa and everywhere around the world, entry into the Christian faith is through the ritual of baptism, as shown here in Mozambique.

Shembe's Nazareth movement, whose members openly long for a black Christ. Shembe is described as having a miraculous birth and being born of the Spirit—as one who came from heaven so that native Africans might know that God is with them. In general in the twentieth century, even among the more traditional denominational native African congregations, Christianity became more and more African and less and less European. Such African churches involve strong **syncretistic** elements; that is, some of their beliefs and practices are Christianized versions of indigenous pre-Christian religious elements.

There is a liberation theology in Africa, but, as the leadership of retired Anglican bishop Desmond Tutu in South Africa illustrates, it is less on the model of Latin American Marxist theory and more on the model of the nonviolent civil rights movement in the United States. Indeed, the movement led by Martin Luther King Jr. is an interesting blend of the liberation passion for justice with an evangelical ecstatic piety that is revealed in his moving and passionate public speaking style that moves both heart and mind. This type of evangelical/Pentecostalist piety has also left its stamp on African Christianity, commingling with the experiential/ecstatic elements of traditional African tribal religions. In the twenty-first century, African Christianity is likely to be a major contributor to the development of a postcolonial Christianity. However, in Africa, Christianity's success tempts believers to envision a "Christian Africa."

> **syncretistic:** identification of the gods of one religion with the gods of another

Asia

European colonialism moved into Africa and Asia simultaneously. The British went into Ceylon (Sri Lanka), India, Burma (Myanmar), Malaysia, Singapore, Hong Kong, and various Pacific islands (also Australia and New Zealand). The French expanded into the Indochina peninsula, including Laos and Cambodia. As in Latin America and Africa, the spread of Christianity that accompanied this colonial expansion was driven by the same Augustinian sense of the providential link between the expansion of European civilization and the spread of the Gospel.

Asia presented Christianity with interesting new challenges. The expansion of a great world religion, it seems, can be stopped only by another great world religion, such as Hinduism or Confucianism. In Asia, Christianity is a distinct minority presence and seems unlikely ever to become the religion of civilizational order. Asia's contribution to the development of a postcolonial Christianity may well be the development of a diaspora model of Christianity,

Archbishop Desmond Tutu and Nelson Mandela triumphantly greet the crowds at the City Hall in Cape Town, South Africa, after Mandela's election as State President (May 11, 1994).

The Black Nazarene festival in the Philippines is illustrative of the indigenization of Christianity in local cultures.

one that will transcend traditional Western civilizational and denominational boundaries and be open to creative coexistence with other religions and cultures. We shall briefly survey this movement as it is unfolding in South and East Asia.

India

According to ancient Christian traditions, Thomas, one of the twelve apostles of Jesus, brought Christianity to India. In the sixteenth and later centuries Jesuits, Dominicans, and representatives of other Catholic orders spread their faith in India and elsewhere in Asia. As in Africa and Latin America, the major Protestant incursion was the wave of mission activity that accompanied nineteenth-century colonialism. Once India had won its independence from British colonial rule in 1947, there was increasing pressure on the churches in India to become less European and more Indian. In response, Indian Christians began to move beyond European denominational Christianity.

In 1947 Anglicans merged with Methodists and other Protestant bodies to form the Church of South India. Much later, the Protestant Church of North India was founded and also a Protestant Church of Pakistan (1970). With these changes there was also a shift of emphasis from conversion to dialogue, with the goal of showing the compatibility of Hinduism and Christianity. Christians have had to learn how to live as a diaspora religion in a largely Hindu culture, renewing efforts to indigenize Christianity with the appearance of Christian ashrams (both Protestant and Catholic) and syncretistic trends resulting in Hinduized forms of Christian worship.

China

Similar patterns of missionary activity by Catholics followed by Protestants occurred in China and Japan. Although Christian missionary activity goes back to the seventh century, it was aggressive colonial missionizing that led to backlash and persecution

Everywhere the story of Jesus has been told, believing artists have tried to present the events in terms of their own cultures. In this way the universal appeal of the story of Jesus is demonstrated, as in this depiction by the Indian artist Jamini Roy of the Holy Family's flight to Egypt.

in the nineteenth and twentieth centuries. Nineteenth-century colonialism brought the first large-scale attempts to convert the Chinese. China did not welcome the missionary movements and permitted them only under the military and economic duress that accompanied colonialism. After the Communists came to power in 1949, many missionaries were either imprisoned or expelled. Chinese Christians were persecuted and often forced to undergo "reeducation."

With the coming of Mao Zedong's Cultural Revolution in 1966, churches were closed, Bibles burnt, and Chinese priests and ministers sent to work camps. All public worship was banned. Nevertheless, Chinese Christians persisted by secretly worshipping in private homes (*house churches*). When Western relations with China improved in the 1980s, it was discovered that indigenous forms of Christianity had survived and were still being practiced in that country.

Today, Christianity, an estimated 5.1 percent of the population of China, is thriving and growing, with government tolerance—including house churches—so long as it appears indigenous and not the result of "foreign" missionaries. Government persecution seems to be focused on those Christian movements that advocate unpatriotic political issues, such as human rights, that threaten the Confucian ethos of Chinese society.

Japan

Until the nineteenth century Japan was largely closed to all Western enterprises, including missionary activity. While as early as the 1500s, the Jesuit Francis Xavier (1506–1552) had established a Catholic community in Japan, the Jesuits were driven out by severe persecution in the next century. Nevertheless, when missionaries returned in the mid-nineteenth century they found a thriving community of "hidden Christians" at Nagasaki. These believers were considered by Japanese rulers to be unpatriotic and subversive. Very quickly, Japanese Christians moved to assert their independence from Western forms of Christianity and to develop indigenous forms.

The Japanese Protestant leader Uchimura Kanzo is famous for having started the "nonchurch" movement. He saw Western church structures as culturally inappropriate to Japanese culture and sought to restructure Christianity on the Asian teacher–disciple model. He tried to demonstrate in his life that it was possible to be both a patriotic Japanese citizen and a Christian. Ironically, the atomic bomb dropped on Nagasaki destroyed the oldest center of Christianity in Japan. After the war, Japanese Christians turned strongly pacifist and sought to break with the Japanese state by resisting any move toward government involvement with Shintoism.

Korea

Korea is the great success story of Christian missionary activity in Asia. A Catholic presence in Korea goes back to the eighteenth century. Protestant missionaries came in the 1870s, but significant growth did not occur until Korea began signing trade agreements with the West in the 1880s. Korean interest in Christianity mounted after the Japanese victory over China in 1895, which Koreans rightly felt was threatening to their own autonomy. Christianity became identified not only with modernization and Westernization but also with anti-Japanese sentiments, which increased in 1910, when Japan annexed Korea.

After World War II, the victorious Allies divided the country into North and South Korea, and civil war followed (1950–1953). Communists in North Korea have driven out Christians there, although house churches may survive. South Korea has the highest percentage of Christians of any nation in Asia except for the Philippines. Nowhere in Asia (except for the Catholic Philippines) has Christianity played as strong a role in public life as it has in South Korea, whose first two presidents were Christians. Since the 1970s a highly political liberation theology similar to that developed in Latin America, known as *minjung* theology, has emerged. And as in Latin America, Africa, India, China, and Japan, Korea too developed its own indigenous forms of Christianity, the most famous of which is the Unification Church of Sun Myung Moon, who is heralded by his followers as a new messiah—in this case an Asian messiah.

Given that the majority of Christians in the world are now non-European, it is likely that much of postcolonial Christianity will draw on the experiences of the various Asian "mission churches." The question remains whether the dominant model will be an African model, aspiring against the odds to Christianize the continent, or an Asian model of diaspora churches, creatively relating to the consequences of globalization and a world that is religiously diverse.

North America—the United States

Although the first explorers and settlers in North America were the Vikings and then later and more successfully the Spanish, and although France extended its reach to the continent as well, the United States came to be primarily as a result of colonization by the British. Indeed, it was a revolt against British colonialism by the citizens of its colonies that led to the Declaration of Independence in 1776 and later to the Constitution of the United States of America as the foundation for a new nation as formulated in 1787.

The citizens of the thirteen colonies that became the United States of America were largely but not exclusively refugees from the political intolerance toward sectarian religious minorities experienced in Europe. At first the European pattern of sectarian rivalry continued in the New World, but it soon became clear to the colonists that the uniqueness of America as an alternative to Europe had to lie in toleration of diversity. Consequently, the very first amendment to the U.S. Constitution declares: "Congress shall make no law respecting an establishment of religion, or prohibiting the free exercise thereof." These words guarantee religious freedom to all Americans by forbidding the government to name any religion as the state religion. This amendment, which became effective in 1791, created a major break with the Constantinian and Augustinian models of Christian civilization and opened the door to diaspora models of Christianity. It was, however, a legal transformation that took on cultural embodiment only as non-Christian populations in America began to grow.

In the nineteenth and twentieth centuries Protestant denominationalism emerged as a new pattern for a culture characterized by religious diversity, and new denominations proliferated out of all proportion to Protestant divisions in Europe. Gradually, diverse religious communities in North America came to think of the church as an invisible reality embracing all Protestants and denominations as voluntary associations that one joined according to one's preferred style of being Protestant.

Enlightenment rationalism and evangelical Pietism, both of which de-emphasized dogmatic divisions, deeply influenced the emergence of denominationalism. But this new perspective was, at first, developed around the notion of America as a Protestant nation. Therefore, it was very traumatic when, beginning in the latter half of the nineteenth century, Catholic and Jewish immigrants poured into the United States and tipped the balance away from a Protestant majority. This led to a strong reaction of anti-Catholicism and anti-Judaism, which did not disintegrate until the last half of the twentieth century, when Protestant, Catholic, and Jew came to be seen as acceptable alternatives within the denominational pattern. In the twenty-first century, the modern equilibrium is being further challenged by influxes of immigrants from Asia and the Middle East. In an emerging global civilization, U.S. citizens who are Muslim, Hindu, or Buddhist are increasing in numbers and in prominence.

TALES OF SPIRITUAL TRANSFORMATION: Martin Luther King Jr.'s Kitchen Experience

Martin Luther King Jr. transformed the social and political landscape of America in the 1950s and 1960s by leading a movement of nonviolent protest against the practices of racial segregation in American life. The "civil rights movement," as it came to be known, led to equal rights under the law for people of all races and opened the way for the election of the first black president of the United States in 2008.

During the civil rights movement, King's life was threatened on a regular basis. There was a defining religious experience that lay behind his courage to continue despite these threats. King came home late from a bus boycott meeting when the movement was just beginning in Montgomery, Alabama. He was sitting in his kitchen when the phone rang. A voice said: "Nigger . . . we are tired of you and your mess now, and if you are not out of this town in three days, we're going to blow your brains out and blow up your house." Although he had received dozens of such calls before, this one got to him. Fear gripped him and he could not sleep, so he went to the kitchen for a cup of coffee. James Cone records King's telling of what happened.

> Something said to me, you can't call on daddy now; he's in Atlanta, a hundred seventy-five miles away. . . . You've got to call on that something, on

that person that your daddy used to tell you about, that power that can make a way out of no way. And I discovered then that religion had to become real to me and I had to know God for myself. And I bowed down over that cup of coffee. I never will forget it. Oh yes, I prayed a prayer. And I prayed out loud that night. I said, "Lord, I'm down here trying to do what's right. I think I'm right. I think the cause that we represent is right. But Lord, I must confess that I'm faltering, I'm losing my courage and I can't let the people see me like this because if they see me weak and losing my courage they will begin to get weak." . . . Almost out of nowhere I heard a voice . . . "Martin Luther, stand up for righteousness. Stand up for justice. Stand up for truth. And lo, I will be with you, even until the end of the world." After that experience . . . I was ready to face anything. (James Cone, *Martin and Malcolm and America: A Dream or a Nightmare* [Maryknoll, NY: Orbis Books, 1991], 124–125).

Three days later King's home was bombed. Fortunately no one was hurt. While some gathered with guns seeking to protect him, he urged them to remain nonviolent, and he reminded them that no matter what happened, God would be with them in their struggle.

Consequently, the decision of whether to be a Christian civilization or adopt a diaspora model of Christian life is playing itself out not only in the developing world but in North America as well. Fundamentalism wants to create a public order focused on creating a "Christian America," yet a North American form of liberation theology seems to be embracing a diaspora model of Christianity. The liberation movement sees itself as one force among many, seeking social justice for all in a pluralist society. The roots of North American liberation theology lie not so much in Marxist liberation theology as is the case in South America. Rather, North American liberation theology is shaped primarily by the civil rights movement, initiated by the Reverend Martin

Not all Christian houses of worship in America have that New England look. This adobe mission church is in Taos, New Mexico.

Luther King Jr., perhaps the most important figure for understanding postmodern Christianity in an age of globalization.

On December 1, 1955, Rosa Parks, a black woman in Montgomery, Alabama, refused to move to the segregated section at the back of a public bus. Her subsequent arrest aroused the churches in the black neighborhoods of Montgomery to organize a boycott of the buses and to demand repeal of the state's bus segregation laws. The Reverend Martin Luther King Jr., pastor of the Dexter Avenue Baptist Church, himself the son of a Baptist minister, was elected to lead the boycott. The boycott marked the beginning of the struggle to end segregation (ca. 1954–1966). The boycott came to a successful conclusion when the Supreme Court declared Alabama laws requiring segregated buses unconstitutional. The ruling, on November 13, 1956, took practical effect on December 21, 1956.

King introduced a diaspora model of Christianity into American social and political life. He was open to the wisdom of other religions, for he believed that God spoke to humanity in every time and in every culture. Indeed, he drew on the principles of nonviolence and civil disobedience first perfected by the great Hindu leader Mohandas K. Gandhi to bring about a nonviolent racial revolution

CONTRASTING RELIGIOUS VISIONS

As the following contrasting visions indicate, every religious tradition is capable of generating both visions that encourage peace and understanding and visions that encourage conflict and violence.

Martin Luther King Jr.— the Gospel of Divine Mercy

The single most important Christian example of postmodern Christianity, open to other religions and global diversity, is Martin Luther King Jr. It is he that others, such as Bishop Desmond Tutu of South Africa, took as their model. King lived and died by Jesus' teachings from the Sermon on the Mount, found in the Gospel of Matthew (chapters 5–7). Here Jesus tells his hearers to love their enemies, do good to those who persecute them, and, when struck, turn the other cheek. God's love, like the rain, says Jesus, falls on the just and the unjust alike. In addition, the apostle Paul explains that God's love of his enemies is expressed in the fact that Christ died for "the ungodly," all who were "still sinners" so that "while we were enemies we were reconciled through the death of his Son" (Romans 5:6–11, NRSV). For Martin Luther King Jr., these teachings of Jesus are the heart of the Gospel and therefore the heart of Christianity. Christians must follow these teachings and love their enemies.

For centuries Christians were inspired by these teachings yet sought ways to avoid having to put them into practice. It was typically argued that "in the real world" to love your enemies while "turning the other cheek" was the equivalent of turning the world over to the rule of those who were most violent and unjust, which would be disastrous. So early Christian theologians like Augustine of Hippo developed the idea of "just war" or the just use of violence to protect the weak and the innocent. It was Martin Luther King Jr.'s study of Gandhi's philosophy of nonviolence that enabled him to see that there was another alternative—nonviolent resistance to evil.

Martin Luther King Jr. transformed the social landscape of American society by integrating the Sermon on the Mount with Gandhi's techniques of nonviolence to further racial and social justice in the United States.

King argued that the way of violent retribution, "an eye for an eye," only escalates the violence (even in a "just war") and leaves everyone blind. With the strategy of nonviolent resistance, however, you do not simply hand the world over to those who are most violent. On the contrary, you create a mass movement of nonviolent noncooperation that brings the normal business of society to a standstill until your enemy consents to compromise and begins to act more justly. This was the strategy King used to organize the bus boycott in Montgomery, Alabama, in 1955–1956. A major portion of the users of the bus system were black, and when they stopped riding the buses the city could not bring in enough income to run the bus system, which many whites also needed to use. This in turn affected the amount of shopping that was being done in the city, which hurt the economy. Within a year the city was forced to rescind the law requiring racial segregation of the buses, and justice for all its citizens was increased without resort to violence by King's movement.

Tim LaHaye and Jerry B. Jenkins: *Left Behind*—the Gospel of Divine Judgment

Reportedly, more than 65 million books in the *Left Behind* series have been sold, and a children's series has sold more than 10 million copies. In addition there are a variety of related materials—movies, clothes, games, music, and so on. The series of novels on the coming end of the world is the core of a religious media sensation in contemporary American life and culture. In an interview for the television news program *60 Minutes* (broadcast April 14, 2004), the books' authors, Tim LaHaye and Jerry B. Jenkins, insisted that according to the Bible, when Jesus comes to judge the earth at the end of time he will not be forgiving his enemies. On the contrary, he will be God's warrior who comes to slay God's enemies in a final battle between believers and unbelievers, in which all believers will be "raptured" (lifted up into heaven) and all nonbelievers will be "left behind."

Martin Luther King Jr. put the emphasis on the Jesus of the Sermon on the Mount, who emphasizes that God who loves the "just and the unjust" alike, while the authors of the *Left Behind* series emphasize the Jesus who comes to judge the world at the end of time. In the *60 Minutes* interview with Morley Safer, *Left Behind* coauthor LaHaye explains: "Unfortunately, we have gone through a time when liberalism has so twisted the real meaning of scripture, that they have manufactured a loving, wimpy Jesus that would never

Not all Christians have embraced Martin Luther King Jr.'s nonviolent Christian message. In their best-selling "Left Behind" book series, Tim LaHaye and Jerry B. Jenkins portray the violence and terror of the God who comes to destroy his enemies at the end of time.

do anything in judgment, and that is not the God of the Bible." To this, coauthor Jenkins adds that they stay as close to the Bible as you can get. Jesus' "slaying the enemy . . . and the fact that the enemies' eyes melt in their head, their tongues disintegrate, their flesh drops off—I didn't make that up, that is out of the prophecy." For these authors, the Gospel's final message is not God's love for his enemies as found in Jesus' Sermon on the Mount but the violence and terror of the God who comes to destroy his enemies, which they believe can be found in the book of Revelation.

in the United States. Moreover, he worked to bring an end to the war in Vietnam that was raging in the 1960s by participating in a cooperative nonviolent protest movement with Jewish and Buddhist leaders such as Abraham Joshua Heschel and Thich Nhat Hanh.

Dr. King and the Southern Christian Leadership Conference, which he founded in 1957, were at the forefront of these efforts. In 1963, *Time* magazine named Martin Luther King Jr. "Man of the Year"—the first black American ever so designated. In June 1964 the Civil Rights Act was passed, and in December King became the youngest person ever to win the Nobel Peace Prize. Then in the spring of 1965, King, accompanied by Rabbi Heschel and others, led a successful march from Selma to Montgomery, Alabama, to emphasize the need for laws to protect the right to vote for all blacks. He compared it to Gandhi's march to the sea to protest the Salt Act. It was, indeed, a turning point, for on August 6, 1965, the Voter Rights Act was signed by President Lyndon Johnson. On April 4, 1968, at the age of thirty-nine, King was assassinated by a sniper in Memphis, Tennessee, but the civil rights movement went on to transform America to the extent that in 2008 the United States elected its first black President, Barack Obama.

Conclusion: The Challenge of Religious Pluralism

A significant gulf divides the fundamentalist and postmodern ways of affirming Christian faith. Modern Christians tended to privatize religion and segregate personal piety from public life. Religion is a personal and family matter: public life should be secular and therefore free of religion. Neither fundamentalist nor postmodern Christians are willing to accept that model. Both insist that their faith should affect public life. The question is how to do this in an age of global pluralism, for the form that public faith takes in each is very different. Fundamentalism champions either a Constantinian or an Augustinian vision of a global Christian civilization. Postmodern, postcolonial Christianity affirms a pluralistic world and a diaspora model of Christianity, in which those who believe in Jesus seek, as King did, to cooperate with others, religious and nonreligious, in achieving a compassionate social order with justice for all. We should not expect that Christians will eventually favor one view at the expense of the other. More likely, as in the past, there will be diverse expressions of Christianity in diverse social, historical, and political circumstances.

Discussion Questions

1. What were the issues that were resolved by the development of the doctrine of "two natures in one person" (Council of Chalcedon) and of the Trinitarian nature of God (Council of Constantinople)? Do these doctrines put Christianity into fundamental disagreement with the prophetic monotheism of Judaism and Islam? Explain.

2. What is original sin, and why does it lead to the need to expect a savior? Is original sin a universal belief among Christians? Explain.

3. Why are Jesus, Paul, and Augustine often thought to be the three most important figures in the history of Western Christianity?

4. It can be argued that Eastern Christianity, Western Christianity, and postcolonial Christianity offer three different models for understanding the relationship between church and state and the relation of Christianity to the non-Christian world: a Constantinian model, an Augustinian model, and a diaspora model. Explain these models, and identify their strengths and weaknesses.

5. The idea of "modernity" is deeply rooted in the Christian version of the myth of history as it was interpreted by Joachim of Fiore. Explain how this is so. Give examples.

6. What is secularization, and how is it related to the history of Christianity?

7. How did Luther's understanding of Christianity differ from that of the medieval church? What was the political and religious significance of this difference?

8. How did the emergence of Protestantism contribute to the development of the secular nation-state?

9. How did Western colonialism contribute to the emergence of a post-European or postcolonial Christianity? Define and explain.

10. What are the issues that separate premodern from modern and postmodern Christianity, and how do they exemplify the fundamentalist–modernist debate?

Key Terms

Augustinian	heresy	sacraments
Catholic	homoousios	Second Coming
Christ	justification by faith	Son of God
Constantinian	Kingdom of God	syncretistic
deism	liberation theology	Trinity
evangelical	original sin	two natures, one
fundamentalist	Pentecostal	person
Gospel	Protestant	
grace	Protestant ethic	

Suggested Readings

Bettenson, Henry, and Chris Maunder, eds. *Documents of the Christian Church*, 4th ed. (New York: Oxford University Press, 2011).

Fasching, Darrell J. *The Coming of the Millennium* (New York: Authors Choice Press, 1996, 2000).

Johnson, Paul. *A History of Christianity* (New York: Atheneum, 1976, 1979).

Keppel, Gilles. *The Revenge of God: The Resurgence of Islam, Christianity and Judaism in the Modern World* (University Park: Pennsylvania State University Press, 1991, 1994).

Lawrence, Bruce B. *Defenders of God: The Fundamentalist Revolt Against the Modern Age* (Columbia: University of South Carolina Press, 1995).

Littell, Franklin. *The Crucifixion of the Jews* (New York: Harper & Row, 1975).

Marsden, George M. *Understanding Fundamentalism and Evangelicalism* (Grand Rapids, MI: William B. Eerdmans, 1991).

McManners, John, ed. *The Oxford Illustrated History of Christianity* (New York: Oxford University Press, 2001).

Roof, Wade Clark, and William McKinney. *American Mainline Religion* (New Brunswick, NJ: Rutgers University Press, 1987).

Ruether, Rosemary. *Faith and Fratricide* (New York: Seabury Press, 1974).

———. *Liberation Theology* (New York: Paulist Press, 1972).

Stendahl, Krister. *Paul Among Jews and Gentiles* (Philadelphia: Fortress Press, 1976).

Tillich, Paul. *A History of Christian Thought*, Vols. 1 and 2 (New York: Harper & Row, 1967, 1968).

Von Campenhausen, Hans. *The Formation of the Christian Bible* (Mifflintown, PA: Sigler Press, 1997).

Additional Resources

Ad Hoc: Resources for Teaching and Research Relating to the History of Christianity. Yale University Library. (www.yale.edu/adhoc/research_resources/links.htm) This source provides links to a variety of scholarly online resources.

From Jesus to Christ: The First Christians. This four-hour PBS video series traces Christianity from Jesus to Constantine. The entire series can be watched online at http://www.pbs .org/wgbh/pages/frontline/shows/religion/watch/. Includes timelines, study guides, etc.

A History of Christianity: The First Three Thousand Years, by Oxford historian Diarmaid MacCulloch. DVD available from PBS. Episode 1: The First Christianity; Episode 2: Catholicism: The Unpredictable Rise of Rome; Episode 3: Orthodoxy: From Empire to Empire; Episode 4: Reformation: The Individual Before God; Episode 5: Protestantism: The Evangelical Explosion; Episode 6: GOD in the Dock.

The Longest Hatred. A documentary on anti-Semitism in Christianity and Islam. Two videos, total of 150 minutes (Copyright Thames Television 1993 and WGBH Boston 1993).

ISLAM

The Many Faces of the Muslim Experience

Overview

"Allahu Akbar. . . . There is no God but God. Come to prayer." Five times each day, Muslims throughout the world, in Algiers and Mindanao, London and Paris, Bosnia and New York, are called to prayer.

The images and realities of Islam and of Muslims across the world are multiple and diverse. Poor villagers and wealthy urban professionals from Nigeria, Egypt, and Saudi Arabia to Afghanistan, Pakistan, and Indonesia make their way to the Friday congregational (*juma*) prayer. At the same time, attacks by suicide bombers in Iraq, Afghanistan, or Pakistan kill other Muslims at prayer. On the streets of Cairo, Geneva, Kuala Lumpur, and Jakarta, Muslim women walk, some in stylish Islamic dress, some in dresses and veils that cover their faces and bodies. They join others adorned in Western fashions.

While in many Muslim societies women's status and rights are undermined by patriarchal cultures and reflect serious inequality in education and literacy, at the same time there are significant indications of change. On the one hand, in Yemen, women's literacy is anywhere from 26 percent to 47 percent (vs. 81 percent for men); in Pakistan, the rate is anywhere from 12 percent to 40 percent (vs. 69 percent for men). On the other hand, women's literacy rate in Iran is 70 percent and the rate in Saudi Arabia is 81 percent, and they are as high as 89 percent in Jordan and 85 percent in Malaysia. In the United Arab Emirates, as in Iran, the majority of university students are women. Educated Muslim women in some sex-segregated countries are not visible in the workplace, but in other countries they work as engineers,

Islam Timeline

ca. 570	Birth of Muhammad
610	Muhammad receives first revelation, commemorated as "Night of Power and Excellence"
620	Muhammad's Night Journey to Jerusalem
622	Emigration (*hijra*) of the Muslim community from Mecca to Medina; first year of the Muslim lunar calendar
632	Muhammad's final pilgrimage to Mecca, farewell sermon, and death
632–661	Rule of the Four Rightly Guided Caliphs, formative period for Sunnis
638	Muslim conquest of Jerusalem
661–750	Umayyad Empire
680	Martyrdom of Husayn and his followers at Karbala, Iraq
750–1258	Abbasid Empire: height of Islamic civilization, patronage of art and culture, development of Islamic law, and rising trade, agriculture, industry, and commerce
756–1492	Andalusia (Muslim Spain): period of interfaith coexistence of Muslims, Christians, and Jews
765	Death of sixth Shii imam, Jafar al-Sadiq; succession disputed, causing split between Sevener and Twelver Shiis
8th–9th c.	Formation of major Sunni law schools
1000–1492	Christian reconquest of Muslim-ruled territories in Spain, Sicily, and Italy
1095–1453	Crusades
12th c.	Rise of Sufi orders
1187	Saladin and Muslim forces reconquer Jerusalem
1281–1924	Ottoman Empire (Middle East, North Africa, and portions of Eastern Europe)
1453	Fall of Constantinople/Istanbul, capital of former Byzantine Empire, to Ottomans
1483–1857	Mughal Empire (South Asia)
1501–1722	Safavid Empire (Iran)
1876–1938	Muhammad Iqbal, Islamic modernist and ideologue for foundation of Pakistan
1897–1975	Elijah Muhammad, leader of the Nation of Islam in the United States
1903–1979	Mawlana Abu Ala Mawdudi, founder of the *Jamaat-i-Islami* in India/Pakistan
1906–1949	Hassan al-Banna, founder of the Muslim Brotherhood in Egypt
1906–1966	Sayyid Qutb, radical, militant ideologue of the Muslim Brotherhood in 1950s and 1960s
1975	Wallace D. Muhammad (name later changed to Warith Deen Muhammad) succeeds his father, Elijah Muhammad, and progressively brings his followers into conformity with mainstream Sunni Islam
1979	Iranian Revolution and foundation of Iranian Islamic Republic under leadership of Ayatollah Khomeini; seizure of the Grand Mosque in Mecca by Muslim militants; Soviet Union invades Afghanistan
1990	FIS (Islamic Salvation Front) wins Algerian municipal and regional elections
1993	Bombing of World Trade Center in New York City by Muslim militants
1995	Welfare (Refah) party wins parliamentary elections; Dr. Necmettin Erbakan becomes Turkey's first Islamist prime minister

1998	U.S. embassies in Tanzania and Kenya bombed by Muslim militants
September 11, 2001	Terrorist attacks against the World Trade Center in New York City and the Pentagon in Washington, D.C.; sparks U.S.-led war against global terrorism and the hunt for Osama bin Laden and al-Qaeda
2003	U.S.-led invasion of Iraq and overthrow of Saddam Hussein; Iran's Shirin Ebadi becomes first Muslim woman to win Nobel Prize for Peace; first female judge appointed to Egyptian Supreme Constitutional Court
2004	French Parliament bans Muslim headscarf in schools and public places; terrorist train attack by Muslim militants in Madrid, Spain
2005	Series of bombings on London subways and a bus kill fifty-one people; London bombings (also called the 7/7 bombings) were a series of coordinated terrorist attacks on London's public transport system during the morning rush hour.
2006	Hamas landslide victory in Palestinian elections; Bangladeshi economist Muhammad Yunus and his Grameen Bank win the Nobel Peace Prize. Yunus pioneered the concept of microcredit—giving unsecured loans to poor people
2007	Turkey reelects Prime Minister Erdogan and Justice and Development Party in parliamentary elections; Declaration on Muslim-Christian relations signed by some 138 Muslim religious leaders and authorities
2009	Popular protests in Iran following controversial presidential elections marred by corruption. Nicknamed the "Twitter Revolution" because of its use of social networking tools to organize nonviolent protests.
2011	Reelection of Erdogan in Turkey; beginning of the "Arab Spring," sparked in Tunisia and Egypt, largely through social networking tools, as series of nonviolent protests calling for greater levels of democracy, freedom, and an end to government corruption.
2011	Osama bin Laden, the founder and head of the Islamist militant group al-Qaeda, killed in Pakistan by American military
2011	Ennahda (the Renaissance Party), in Tunisia's first democratic election, wins a plurality of votes in the Constituent Assembly
2012	In first open democratic elections in Egypt, the Muslim Brotherhood wins a majority of the vote in the parliamentary election to the People's Assembly, and the Brotherhood's Mohammed Morsi is elected president
2013	Egypt's first democratically elected president, Mohammed Morsi, after widespread antigovernment demonstrations on July 30, overthrown in a military backed coup
August 14, 2013	Egyptian security forces use lethal force against Morsi supporter sit-in, killing more than 625 and injuring thousands. The interim government moved quickly to declare the Muslim Brotherhood a terrorist organization and attempted to totally suppress it, using mass arrests and military trials that drew sharp criticism from major international human rights organizations. The government cracked down and arrested foreign journalists and Egyptian critics and democracy activists.
January 27, 2014	Tunisian Assembly passes new constitution
March 24, 2014	An Egyptian court sentences 529 members of the outlawed Muslim Brotherhood to death, the largest mass death sentence in modern Egyptian history

doctors, scientists, teachers, and lawyers alongside their male colleagues. In contrast to those in many Muslim countries, Muslim women in America are as educated and earn as much as American Muslim men.

Islamic associations in the slums and lower-middle-class neighborhoods of Cairo and Algiers, Beirut and Mindanao provide families who cannot afford state services or who live under governments that do not provide adequate social services (such as the West Bank and Gaza) with inexpensive and efficient educational, legal, and medical social services. At the same time, the terrorist attacks of 9/11 signaled a decade of global terror from Morocco, Spain, Scotland, and Britain to Iraq, Saudi Arabia, Yemen, Pakistan, Afghanistan, Indonesia, and the Philippines.

If a militant minority has turned to bullets, many mainstream Muslims have turned to the ballot box when given the opportunity by their governments, many of which are authoritarian. Members of Islamic organizations have been elected to parliaments in Turkey, Algeria, Jordan, Egypt, Kuwait, Yemen, Pakistan, Thailand, and Malaysia. They have been elected prime minister of Turkey and served as president of Indonesia and Turkey and in cabinet-level positions in many countries. Others have been elected officials in professional associations of doctors, lawyers, engineers, journalists, and teachers.

Islam: submission or surrender to God

Muslim: one who follows Islam

This chapter will look at the history and heritage of **Islam** and impact on **Muslim** societies and world events today. It will explore the challenges and struggles within the global Muslim community in defining the meaning of Islam for modern and postmodern life.

Mecca is the holiest city of Islam: the birthplace of the Prophet Muhammad, where the earliest revelations occurred and toward which Muslims turn in prayer five times each day. Muslims on pilgrimage gather near Mecca's Grand Mosque following Friday dawn prayers.

The study of Islam and Muslim societies, yesterday and today, is a fascinating trip across time and space. It requires a bridging of the gap between religion, history, politics, and culture. Let us begin by briefly discussing what Islam is and where the Islamic world is.

The word *islam* means "submission" or "surrender." A Muslim is one who submits, who seeks to follow and actualize God's will in history. The Muslim community (**ummah**) is a transnational community of believers, God ordained and guided, whose mission is to spread and institutionalize an Islamic Order, to create a socially just society: "You are the best community ever brought forth for mankind, enjoining what is good and forbidding evil" (Q. 3:110).

> **ummah:** Muslim community of believers

Islam belongs to the Abrahamic family of great monotheistic faiths. Muslims like Jews and Christians view themselves as the children of Abraham, as proclaimed in each of their sacred scriptures: the Old and New Testaments and the Quran. Despite specific and significant differences, Judaism, Christianity, and Islam share a belief in one God, the creator, sustainer, and ruler of the universe who is beyond ordinary experience. And all believe in angels, Satan, prophets, revelation, moral responsibility and accountability, divine judgment, and reward or punishment. Yet while Jews and Christians claim descent from Abraham and his wife, Sarah, through their son Isaac, Muslims trace their religious roots back to Abraham (Ibrahim) through Ismail, his firstborn son by Hagar, Sarah's Egyptian servant.

> "Say: He is Allah, the One and only; Allah, the Eternal. He did not beget, nor is He begotten; And there is none like Him."
> —Quran, 112

Today, Islam is the world's second-largest religion. Its 1.5 billion followers can be found in some fifty-seven predominantly Muslim countries, extending from North Africa to Southeast Asia (see Map 5.1). Because Islam has often been equated simply with the Arabs, only about 20 percent of the worldwide Muslim community, few realize that the vast majority of Muslims live in Asia and Africa: Indonesia, Bangladesh, Pakistan, India, and Nigeria. Islam's presence and impact extend beyond countries in which the majority of the population is Muslim. In recent years, Islam has become a significant presence in the West as the second- or third-largest religion in Europe (in particular, France, Germany, and England) and in North America. Today the capitols or major cities of Islam are not only exotic-sounding places like Cairo, Damascus, Baghdad, Mecca, Islamabad, and Kuala Lumpur, but also London, Paris, Marseilles, Brussels, New York, Detroit, and Los Angeles.

A dynamic religion that interfaces and at times competes with other faiths, Islam has had a significant impact on world affairs. In contrast to the modern secular belief in the separation of church and state, Islam for many Muslims represents a more comprehensive worldview in which religion and society, faith and power, have been and are more closely bound. Throughout much of history, to be a Muslim was not simply to belong to a faith community or to worship in a given place but to live in an Islamic community or state, governed (in theory if not always in practice) by Islamic law. Historically, Islam has significantly informed politics and civilization, giving rise to vast Islamic empires and states as well as Islamic civilization.

From Islam's origins to the present, Muslims have been engaged in a continuous process of understanding and interpreting the word of God (**Quran**): defining,

> **Quran:** Muslim scripture

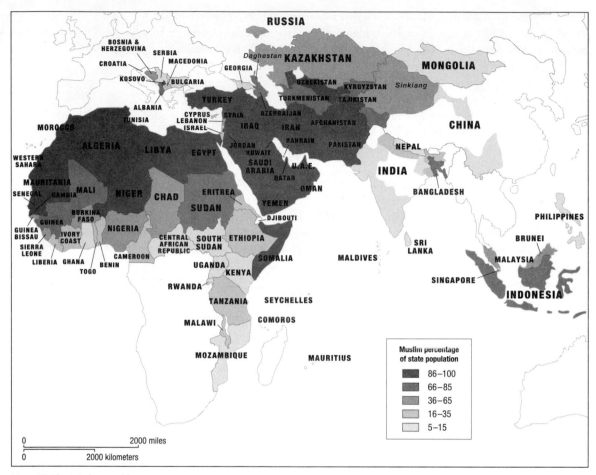

Map 5.1 The Muslim world.

redefining, and applying Islamic practices to the realities of life. Thus, while it is correct to say that there is one Islam, revealed in the Quran and the traditions of the Prophet, as we shall now see, there have been many interpretations of Islam, some complementing each other, others in conflict.

Muslims today, like other people of faith, struggle with the relationship of their religious tradition to modernity and postmodernity. How does a faith revealing a God-centered universe speak to a modern, post-Enlightenment, human-centered secular world that emphasizes reason and science? Like Judaism and Christianity, Islam contends with questions about a range of issues, from evolution, birth control, abortion, artificial insemination, and organ transplants to ecology, nuclear energy, chemical warfare, religious extremism, and terrorism. The questions are many: What is the relationship of Islam to secularization? Should Islam today be restricted to personal life,

Muslim dietary law, like Judaism's kosher law, requires the ritual slaughter of animals permitted to be eaten. Today across America, *halal* butcher shops may be found, providing these religiously pre-pared meats for their Muslim customers.

or should it be integral to the state, law, and society? Is Islam compatible with modern forms of political participation, such as democracy? In the twenty-first century, what should be the Islamic positions on treatment of religious minorities, non-Muslims, and women?

Encounter with Modernity: The Challenge of Western Colonialism

When Muslims were asked in the Gallup World Poll (2007) what they feared most, majorities cited intervention, invasion, or occupation by foreign powers. This concern can be seen in widespread opposition to the invasion of Iraq and Afghanistan by America, Britain, and other Western powers and the charge that this is but another form of Western colonialism. The Islamic world has witnessed upheaval and renewal since the nineteenth century as Muslims absorbed the impact of European colonialism. European colonialism challenged Muslim historical self-understanding and pride. A common belief throughout history had been that the early and rapid expansion of Islam and Islamic empires, extending from Africa to Asia and their continued success and power until the nineteenth century, were signs of God's guidance and pleasure with the Islamic community.

Yet by the nineteenth century, Europeans had colonized many Muslim areas: the French in North, West, and Equatorial Africa and the Levant (Lebanon and Syria); the British in Palestine, Transjordan, Iraq, the Arabian Gulf, and the Indian subcontinent; and in Southeast Asia, the British in Malaya (Malaysia, Singapore, and Brunei) and the Dutch in Indonesia.

Muslims found themselves on the defensive against a European imperialism that threatened their political, religious, and cultural identity and challenged time-honored beliefs and practices. Muslim responses to colonialism and Western culture and ideas varied from rejection and confrontation to admiration and imitation.

While many conservative religious leaders dug in their heels and resisted any significant change and new Western-oriented elites opted for a Western secular approach, Islamic modernist reformers staked out a middle path. They sought to restore the pride, identity, and strength of their debilitated community by bridging the gap between their heritage and modernity. They emphasized the compatibility of Islam with reason, modern science, and technology, reminding Muslims of the development of Islamic civilization and its contributions to philosophy, science, medicine, mathematics, and architecture. Reformers championed the need for *ijtihad*, the reinterpretation of Islamic law to meet the needs of the modern world. However, they failed (1) to produce a systematic reinterpretation of Islam; and (2) to develop effective organizations and institutions to preserve and propagate their reformist message. These two failures led to the emergence of modern Islamic activist organizations (sometimes referred to as fundamentalist movements), such as the Muslim Brotherhood in the Middle East and *Jamaat-i-Islami* (the Islamic Society) in South Asia. Both these organizations criticized Islamic reformers for tending to Westernize Islam. In particular, they condemned the tendency of most Muslim countries to adopt Western models of development uncritically. Islam, they insisted, is a total, comprehensive way of life that offers an alternative path to Western capitalism and communism/socialism. These movements and their many offshoots, from mainstream social and political organizations to radical revolutionary groups, continue to be major forces today.

During the post–World War II era, most of the Muslim world regained its independence. However, the boundaries of modern nation-states such as Lebanon, Syria, Sudan, Jordan, Iraq, Kuwait, Malaysia, and Pakistan were arbitrarily drawn by the European states that had colonized the areas. Indeed, many Muslim rulers were appointed by colonial governments; others, often military officers or former officers, simply seized power. As a result, instead of elected governments, much of the Muslim world received a legacy of autocratic rulers (kings, military and ex-military) not of their choosing.

The political legitimacy of rulers and issues of national identity and unity have plagued many of these nations to this day; governments have relied heavily for control and stability on internal security forces rather than elections. Because the West provided the models for development, it was widely supposed that modernization and progress would depend on Westernization and secularization. Iran's Islamic revolution of 1979–80 shattered this assumption.

ijtihad: interpretation or independent reasoning in Islamic law

The Islamic Resurgence

The Iranian revolution signaled the resurgence of Islam in Muslim politics. Although Iran drew attention to the reassertion and power of Islam in politics and society, Islam had already become a major factor in Muslim politics for more than a decade before 1979 in Egypt, Libya, and Pakistan. The crushing military defeat of combined Arab forces in the Six–Day War of 1967 and the consequent loss to Israel of major territories (the Sinai, the West Bank and Gaza, the Golan Heights, and especially Jerusalem, the third-holiest city of Islam) became "*the* disaster" in Muslim literature and consciousness. This key event triggered a period of doubt and self-examination.

Despite national independence, most Muslim countries had remained politically and economically weak, underdeveloped, and dependent on the West. What went wrong? To regain their past power and glory, many Muslims believed that they must return to the straight path of Islam. The 1973 Arab oil embargo and the later Islamic revolution in Iran reinforced the belief that Muslim economic and political power could be attributed to the resurgence of Islam in contemporary Muslim politics and society.

During the late 1960s and 1970s, Islam enjoyed a higher profile in personal and public life, demonstrated by greater religious observance and Islamic dress as well as the growth of Islamic political and social organizations and institutions: banks, publishing houses, schools. In addition, governments in Egypt, Libya, Sudan, and Pakistan as well as their opposition political parties turned to Islam in politics during the 1970s and 1980s to enhance their legitimacy and mobilize popular support. At the same time, Islamic activist organizations mushroomed in number and size throughout the Muslim world. Alongside Islamic organizations such as the Muslim Brotherhoods of Egypt, Syria, Jordan, and Sudan, there were violent revolutionary organizations with names like Jund Allah (Army of God), Hezbollah (the party of God), and Islamic Jihad.

Yet, by the late 1980s and 1990s, a quiet (nonviolent) revolution had also occurred. From North Africa to Southeast Asia, Islam was playing an increasingly more visible and important role in the socioeconomic and political life of society. In the twenty-first century, Islamic activists and parties are a significant factor in electoral politics in Egypt, Algeria, Morocco, Sudan, Lebanon, Jordan, Turkey, Palestine, Pakistan, Malaysia, and Indonesia. Many authoritarian rulers have experienced the power of religion in Muslim politics through ballots of Islamic supporters as well as bullets of the more radical groups.

Islam in the West

To speak of Islam in the twenty-first century is not only to speak of Islam and the West but also of Islam in the West. Islam is the fastest-growing religion in North America and in Europe, the second-largest religion in France, Holland, Belgium, and Germany, and the third-largest in Britain and the United States. Even without increases in Muslim immigration and conversions to Islam, in several decades Muslim projected birthrates will result in Islam's replacing Judaism as the second-largest religion in the United States.

Muslims in the United States, like other religious or ethnic minorities before them, face many questions about their faith and identity: Are they Muslims in America or American Muslims? Can Muslims become part and parcel of a pluralistic American society without sacrificing or losing their identity? Can people be Muslims in a non-Muslim state that is not governed by Islamic law? Is the U.S. legal system capable of allowing for particular Muslim religious and cultural differences?

In the West, it has sometimes been fashionable to speak of a post-Christian society; but for many Muslims, talking about a post-Islamic society is not relevant. For many Muslims, the debate is not over whether religion has a place and role in society, but rather what kind of Islam or Islamic presence should exist. Understanding Islam today requires an appreciation of the full spectrum of Muslim responses to the modern world, ranging from those who view Islam as a personal faith to others who wish to see it implemented more formally in state and society.

Throughout the ages, when Muslims have sought to define or redefine their lives, the starting point has always been an understanding of the past. Thus, we need to go back in order to go forward. To understand Islam's present and future, we must learn about the history and development of Islam and the Muslim community.

Premodern Islam: The Formative Era

Like all the world's religions, Islam places great emphasis on its early history. For Muslims, the formative period is the time of the Prophet Muhammad, a period that included the revelation of the Quran and Muhammad's founding of the first community. It is often seen as the "best of times," the time of the purest and most authentic Islamic community, a society that was to be emulated by future generations, a model to return to for inspiration and guidance.

At the core of Muslim belief and faith are the messenger and the message. As Christians look to Jesus and the New Testament and Jews look to Moses and the Torah, Muslims regard Muhammad and the Quran as the final, perfect, and complete revelation of God's will for humankind. Also, because of the remarkable success of Muhammad and the early Muslim community in spreading the faith of Islam and the rule of Muslims, an idealized memory of Islamic history and of Muslim rule became the model for success, serving as a common reference point for later generations of reformers.

Allah: God

The foundations of Islam are belief in God (**Allah**, Arabic for "The God") and in God's messenger, Muhammad. Though God is beyond our ordinary experience, or transcendent, Islam teaches that he can be known directly through his messengers and revelations. Thus, Muhammad and the Quran, the final messenger and the message/revelation, are key in the formation and development of the Islamic tradition, its beliefs, laws, rituals, and social practices. Learning more about the messenger and the message will increase our understanding of Islam today and our insights about the sources Muslims use to guide their lives in the twenty-first century.

Muhammad's Early Life

Few observers in the sixth century would have predicted that Muhammad ibn Abdullah and central Arabia would come to play pivotal roles in world history and world religions. Most would have seen as limited at best the future impact of an orphan raised in a vast desert region marked by tribal warfare and divisions and bounded by two great imperial powers, the Eastern Roman, or Byzantine, Empire and the Persian (Sassanid) Empire. And yet the message Muhammad brought from God and the force of his personality would quite literally transform Arabia and have a significant impact on much of the world, past and present.

Because Muhammad regarded himself as a religious reformer and not the founder of a new religion, it is important to understand pre-Islamic Arabian society and religion, which were tribal in structure and organization. Individuals lived in extended families; several related families constituted a clan; a cluster of several clans comprised a tribe. Al Ilah (Allah) was seen as the high god over a pantheon of tribal gods and goddesses who were believed to be more directly active in everyday life. Each city or town had its divine patron/protectors and shrine. Tribal gods and goddesses were respected and feared rather than loved, the focal points of the rituals of sacrifice,

Muhammad: The Final Messenger

No prophet has played a greater role in a world religion and in world politics than Muhammad. Both in his lifetime and throughout Muslim history, Muhammad ibn Abdullah has served as the ideal model for Muslim life. Some Muslims have called him the "living Quran," that is, the embodiment in his behavior and words of God's will. He is viewed as the last or final prophet, who brought the final revelation of God. He is so revered that the name Muhammad (or names derived from it—Ahmad, Mahmud) is the most common Muslim name. In some Muslim countries, every male child has the Prophet's name as one of his forenames. Thus, the Prophet and his example, or *Sunnah*, are central to Islam and Muslim belief and practice. Muhammad is not only the ideal political leader, statesman, merchant, judge, soldier, and diplomat but also the ideal husband, father, and friend. Muslims look to his example for guidance in all aspects of life: eating; fasting; praying; the treatment of a spouse, parents, and children; the creation of contracts; the waging of war; and the conduct of diplomacy.

prayer, and pilgrimage. The tribal polytheism of Arabia was embodied in a cube-shaped building that housed the idols of 360 tribal gods and was a center of pilgrimage. Located in the ancient city of Mecca, this cube, *Kaaba*, would be rededicated to Allah in the seventh century.

Tribal polytheism was a very "worldly" religion, with little concern about or belief in an afterlife, divine judgment, or reward or punishment after death. Individual identity and rights were subordinated to tribal and family identity, authority, and law. The key virtue, "manliness," included loyalty to family and protection of its members, bravery in battle, hospitality, and honor. There was little sense of moral responsibility and accountability beyond tribal and family honor. This era, in which justice was guaranteed and administered not by God but by the threat of retaliation by family or tribe, is referred to as the period of ignorance (*jahiliyya*) before Islam.

jahiliyya: unbelief; ignorance; used to describe pre-Islamic era

Forms of monotheism did exist in Arabia; both Arab Christian and Jewish communities had long resided in the region. The Quran also speaks of Arab monotheists, *hanifs*, descendants of Ibrahim (Abraham). In addition, Arab traders would have encountered Judaism and Christianity, since Jewish and Christian merchants regularly came to Mecca, a major center for trade as well as pilgrimage. However, monotheism's most powerful appeal to the Arabs came only when the Prophet Muhammad received his revelation from Allah, a message that would change the lives of hundreds of millions of people throughout Arabia and beyond.

There is little information about Muhammad's life before his "call" to be God's messenger; the portrait of his early years is drawn from early Muslim writers, legend, and Muslim belief. Muhammad ibn Abdullah (the son of Abdullah) was born in 570 into the ruling tribe of Mecca, the Quraysh. Orphaned at an early age, Muhammad was among the tribe's "poorer cousins," raised by an uncle and later employed in Mecca's thriving caravan business. Muhammad had one wife, Khadija, for twenty-eight years, until her death. Much is recorded about Muhammad's relationship with Khadija, who was his closest confidante and strongest supporter. The couple had six children, two sons who died in infancy and four daughters. After Khadija's death, Muhammad married other women, all but one of them widows.

By the age of thirty, Muhammad had become a prominent, respected member of Meccan society, known for his business skill and trustworthiness (he was nicknamed al-Amin, the trustworthy). Reflective by temperament, Muhammad would often retreat to the quiet and solitude of Mount Hira to contemplate his life and society. Here during the month of Ramadan in 610, on a night Muslims commemorate as the Night of Power and Excellence, Muhammad the caravan leader became Muhammad the messenger of God. Muhammad at the age of forty received the first message, or divine revelation, from a heavenly intermediary identified by later tradition as the angel Gabriel: "Recite in the name of your Lord who has created, / Created man out of a germ cell. / Recite, for your Lord is the most generous One, / Who has taught by the pen, / Taught man what he did not know."

Muhammad became a link in a long series of biblical prophets, messengers from God who served as a conscience to the community and as God's messenger. Like

Moses, who had received the Torah on Mount Sinai, Muhammad received the first of God's revelations on Mount Hira: "It is He who sent down to you the Book with the truth, confirming what went before it: and He sent down the Torah and the Injil ["Evangel," "Gospel"] before as a guidance to the people" (Q. 3:3). Also, like Amos and Jeremiah before him, Muhammad served as a "warner" from God who admonished his hearers to repent and obey God, for the final judgment was near:

> Say: "O Men I am only a warner." Those who believe, and do deeds of righteousness—theirs shall be forgiveness and generous provision. And those who strive against our signs to avoid them—they shall be inhabitants of Hell. (Q. 22:49–50)

Muhammad continued to receive revelations for more than two decades (610–32); together these revelations constitute the text of the Quran (literally, "the recitation or reading").

The first ten years of Muhammad's preaching were difficult. At first he revealed his religious experience to his wife and close friends only. When he finally began to preach God's message, critiquing the status quo, he encountered the anger of Mecca's prosperous, powerful political and commercial leaders. In the name of Allah, the one true God, Muhammad increasingly denounced polytheism and thus threatened the livelihood of those who profited enormously from the annual pilgrimage, which was the equivalent of a giant tribal convention. Equally problematic, Muhammad preached a message strong on issues of social justice, condemning the socioeconomic inequities of his time. The Prophet denounced the exploitation of the poor, orphans, and widows as well as prevailing business practices such as false contracts and usury. Muhammad claimed an authority and legitimacy, as God's prophet, that undermined the primacy of Mecca's rich and powerful masters. He called all true believers to join the community of God, a universal community that transcended tribal bonds and authority, a community led by Muhammad, not by the Quraysh.

As Muhammad continued to preach his message, the situation in Mecca became more difficult. After ten years of rejection and persecution in Mecca, Muhammad and his followers migrated to Yathrib, renamed Medina, "city" of the prophet, in 622. Invited to serve as arbiter or judge, for Muslim and non-Muslim alike, Muhammad became the political and religious leader of the community. Medina proved a new beginning, as the Muslim community prospered and grew.

After the *Hijra*

The emigration (*hijra*) from Mecca to Medina in 622 was a turning point in Muhammad's life and in Islamic history. The central significance of *hijra* and the birth of the Islamic community (the *ummah*) led to Muslims dating their calendar not from the birth of the Prophet or from the first revelation but from the creation of the Islamic

hijra: migration of Muhammad from Mecca to Medina; marks first year in Muslim lunar calendar

community at Medina. Thus, 622 CE became 1 AH, "after the *hijra*." Muslims, then and now, believe Islam is a world religion, a global community of the faithful, with a universal message and mission.

Muhammad did not intend to create a new religion; rather, he was a prophet and reformer. His message proclaimed an absolute monotheism, the unity (**tawhid**), or oneness, of God and God's final revelation. Polytheism and idolatry—putting anything in place of the one, true God—were to be condemned and suppressed. Islam was to be a corrective to Arabian polytheism, and, Muslims believe, the distortions of God's original revelation to Moses and Jesus by the authors/editors of the Bible that had occurred over time. Muhammad called all to repentance, to turn away from the path of unbelief and false practice and toward the straight path (**sharia**) of God. Thus, Muhammad (the last, or "seal," of the prophets; Q. 33:40) and the Quran (the complete, uncorrupted revelation) were a corrective, a restoration of the true faith and message of God.

Muhammad taught that submission (*islam*) to God was both an individual and a community obligation. Tribal identity must be replaced by identification with Islam, now the primary source of community solidarity. This belief was reinforced by the Quran's emphasis on social justice, social welfare, in particular protection of women, orphans, and the poor. Muhammad rejected or reformed some rituals and introduced

tawhid: oneness of God; monotheism

sharia: Islamic law

The courtyard of the Mosque of the Prophet in Medina, the first mosque in Islam, is among the most sacred sites in Islam. The original structure has been rebuilt and expanded several times.

others. He reinterpreted the pre-Islamic Arabian pilgrimage to the Kaaba at Mecca. The Kaaba was cleansed of its 360 tribal idols and rededicated to Allah. Pilgrimage to the Kaaba in Mecca, like prayer five times each day, became one of the Five Pillars, or required practices, of Islam.

During the short decade that Muhammad led the community at Medina, he, in light of continuing revelations, defined its mandate and mission. He forged its identity, consolidated its political base, and established its basic religious law and practice.

Muhammad skillfully employed both force and diplomacy to defeat the Meccans and then to unite the tribes of Arabia under the banner of Islam. In 624 Muhammad and his followers successfully engaged and defeated the far greater Meccan forces at the Battle of Badr. For Muslims, then and now, this battle has special significance, a "miraculous" victory in which the forces of Allah and monotheism were pitted against those of Meccan polytheism. Yet despite overwhelming odds, the army of God vanquished the unbelievers. The Quran itself tells of God's assistance (Q. 8:42ff, 3:123) in securing the victory. The Battle of Badr became a symbol of divine favor and intervention remembered and invoked throughout history, as witnessed in the 1973 Egyptian-Israeli war, when President Anwar Sadat used the code name Operation Badr to inspire and motivate his forces.

After a three-year series of battles, a truce was struck at Hudaybiyah. However, in 630, Muhammad, charging that the Meccans had broken the truce, led an army 10,000 strong on a march to Mecca; the Meccans surrendered without a fight. Muhammad proved magnanimous in victory, rejecting vengeance and plunder and instead granted amnesty to his former enemies. The majority of the Meccans converted to Islam, accepted Muhammad's leadership, and became part of the Islamic community.

In his early preaching, Muhammad had looked to Jews and Christians as natural allies. As "**People of the Book**" (*ahl al-kitab*) who had received prophets and revelation, they had much in common with Muslims, and so he anticipated the approval and acceptance of Islam by the Jews of Medina. Muhammad initially presented himself to the Jews of Arabia as a prophetic reformer reestablishing the religion of Abraham. However, the Jewish tribes of Medina, who had lived there a long time and had political ties with the Quraysh of Mecca, did not accept the reformer's message. While the majority of tribes converted to Islam, Medina's three Jewish tribes, half the population of Medina, did not. Until that time, Muslims had faced Jerusalem to pray and, like the Jews, fasted on the tenth day of the lunar month. However, when the Jews rejected Muhammad's claims and proved resistant to conversion, Muhammad received a revelation and changed the direction of prayer from Jerusalem to Mecca. Thereafter, Islam was presented as a distinct religious alternative to Judaism.

Because of the multireligious and multitribal nature of Medina, Muhammad promulgated the Charter or Constitution of Medina, which set out the rights and duties of all citizens and the relationship of the Muslim community to other communities. Jews were recognized as a separate community, politically allied to the Muslims but retaining internal religious and cultural autonomy. However, political loyalty and

People of the Book: those possessing a revelation or scripture from God; refers particularly to Jews and Christians

"In matters of faith, He has laid down for you the same commandment that He gave Noah, which We have revealed to you [Muhammad] and which We enjoined on Abraham and Moses and Jesus: 'Uphold the faith and do not divide into factions within it.'"

—Quran 42:13

allegiance were expected. The Jews' denial of Muhammad's prophethood and message and their political ties with the Meccans became a source of conflict. The Quran accuses some Jewish tribes of regularly breaking treaties: "Why is it that whenever they make pacts, a group among them casts it aside unilaterally?" (Q. 2:100). Muslim perception of intrigue, rejection, and betrayal by the Jewish tribes led first to exile and later to warfare. After the Battle of the Ditch in 627, the Jews of the Banu Qurayza, a Jewish tribe who lived in Yathrib at the time, were denounced as traitors who had consorted with the Meccans. In the end, Muhammad moved to crush the remaining Jews in Medina, whom he regarded as a political threat to Muslim consolidation and rule in Arabia.

Muhammad's use of warfare was not alien to Arab custom or to the Hebrew prophets' belief (Exodus 14:14, Deuteronomy 20:4, and 2 Kings 10:25–31) in God-sanctioned battle—the conquest and the punishment of "enemies of God" in which the men were often killed and the women and children were spared but enslaved. Both believed that God had sanctioned battle with the enemies of the Lord. However, it is important to note that the motivation for Muhammad's actions was political rather than racial or theological, a fact often overlooked by critics of Islam as well as militant Muslims.

In 632, Muhammad led the pilgrimage to Mecca. There the sixty-two-year-old leader delivered a farewell sermon in which he emphasized:

> Know ye that every Muslim is a brother unto every other Muslim, and that ye are now one brotherhood. It is not legitimate for any one of you, therefore, to appropriate unto himself anything that belongs to his brother unless it is willingly given him by that brother.[1]

This event continues to be remembered and commemorated each year by millions of Muslims who make the annual pilgrimage to Mecca, in modern Saudi Arabia.

The Message of the Quran

The Quran is the foundation and heart of Islam. Muslims believe that the Quran is the eternal, uncreated, literal, and final word of God revealed to Muhammad as guidance for humankind (Q. 2:185). Thus, for Muslims, Islam is not a new religion but rather the oldest, for it represents the "original" as well as the final revelation of God to Abraham, Moses, Jesus, and Muhammad. In fact, it has become common for many who convert to Islam to be referred to as "reverts" rather than converts.

The Prophet Muhammad is seen as a conduit, an intermediary, who received God's message and then communicated it over a period of twenty-two years. The text of the Quran is about four-fifths the length of the New Testament. The Muslim scripture consists of 114 chapters (**surahs**) of 6,000 verses, arranged by length, not chronology.

surahs: chapters of the Quran

The God (Allah) of the Quran is seen as the creator, sustainer, ruler, and judge of humankind. He is merciful and just, the all-knowing and all-powerful, the lord and ruler of the universe. The Quran teaches that God's revelation has occurred in several forms: in nature, in history, and in scripture. God's existence can be known through nature, which points to or contains the "signs" of its creator and sustainer (Q. 3:26–27). The record of humankind also contains clear examples and lessons of God's sovereignty and intervention in history (Q. 30:2–9). And finally, God's will for humankind has been revealed through a long line of prophets and messengers: "Indeed We sent forth among every nation a Messenger saying: 'Serve your God and shun false gods' " (Q. 16:36). As a result, throughout history, people could know not only that God exists but also his will, what God desires and commands, for humankind.

Muslims believe that the Quran, like the Torah and the Evangel (Gospel), is taken from an Arabic tablet, the source, or mother, of all scriptures, preexisting with God in heaven. From it, the teachings of the three Abrahamic faiths (Judaism, Christianity, and Islam) were taken and revealed at different stages in history. Indeed, many Muslims take their names from the biblical prophets Ibrahim (Abraham), Musa (Moses), Sulayman (Solomon), Dawud (David), Yahya (John), Maryam (Mary), and Issa (Jesus). Equally striking to many is the fact that the name of Mary, the mother of Jesus, is cited more often in the Quran than in the entire New Testament.

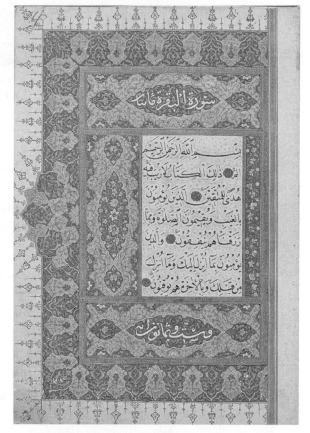

God's word, as revealed in the Quran, is the final and complete revelation. It provides the primary and ultimate source of guidance, the basis for belief and practice in Islam. Study, memorization, recitation, and copying of the Quran have been central acts of piety. The noble art of copying the Quran has produced a rich tradition of calligraphy. This manuscript page provides a beautiful example.

Throughout history, Jesus and Mary (Maryam), his mother, have been held in high esteem. Jesus enjoys a special place among the prophets in Islam. The Quran affirms the virgin birth of Jesus, the promised Messiah, who declared from his cradle: "I am God's servant; God has given me the Book, and made me a prophet" (Q. 19:30).

Because Arabic is the language of the Quran, all Muslims memorize, recite, and pray the Quran in Arabic, whether they understand it fully or not. Much as the Roman Catholic Mass until the middle of the twentieth century was always said in Latin, Arabic is viewed as the sacred language of Islam; in a very real sense it is regarded as the language of God. Whatever their local language, Muslims pray in Arabic five times each day. Whereas Christianity, at an early stage translated its scriptures into Latin and Greek and after the Reformation into local languages, Muslims maintain Arabic as the language of the Quran, the primary source for religious learning and of formal worship.

Because the Quran is regarded as God's sacred Word, it is handled with reverence. A devout Muslim will not write in a Quran that is used for spiritual reading or prayer. Memorization of the entire text of the Quran is a time-honored act of piety. For many Muslims the clearest evidence of the Quran's power and uniqueness is its impact on its hearers; indeed, many have been moved to conversion after hearing the beauty of a Quranic recitation. Recitation or chanting of the Quran is a major art form as well as an act of worship. Muslims gather in stadiums and auditoriums around the world to attend international Quran recitation competitions as many in the West might attend an opera. To win an international competition can be a source of great national pride.

A Golden Age of Expansion, Conquest, and Creativity

caliph: successor of Muhammad as political and military leader of the Muslim community

Sunnah: example set by Muhammad of living the principles of the Quran

Because Muslims believe that the Quran is God's Word or revelation, from an early age children are taught to recite the Quran.

The rule of Muhammad and his first four successors, or **caliphs**, is seen as the formative, normative, exemplary period of Muslim faith and history. After God sent down his final and complete revelation for humankind through his last prophet, the Islamic community/state was created, and the sources of Islamic law, the Quran and **Sunnah** of the Prophet, originated. Both reformers and Islamic revivalists today look to this period as the reference point for divine guidance and historical validation. Muslims believe that the revealed message of the Quran and the example of the Prophet and his successors were corroborated in the full light of history after "miraculous" victories at Badr and elsewhere, by the spread of Islam as a faith as well as its phenomenal geographic and political expansion, which produced *Islamic Empires*.

Through force and diplomacy, Muhammad united the tribes of Arabia under the banner of Islam. During the century after his death, the period of the four Rightly Guided Caliphs, Muslim armies were inspired by their new faith, material (bounty from richer societies) and spiritual rewards, especially paradise for those who died and were remembered as martyrs. These highly motivated armies overran the Byzantine and Persian empires, which had already been greatly weakened by internal strife and constant warfare between them.

Christendom experienced the early expansion of Islam as a threat to its religious and political hegemony. Muslim rule, and with it the message of Islam, quickly spread from the Byzantine and Persian empires to Syria, Iraq, and Egypt and then swept across North Africa and into Europe, where Muslims ruled Spain and the Mediterranean from Sicily to Anatolia (see Map 5.2).

For non-Muslim populations in Byzantium and Persia, who had been subjugated by foreign rulers, Islamic rule meant an exchange of rulers rather than a loss of independence. Many in Byzantium willingly exchanged Greco-Roman rule for that of new Arab masters, fellow Semites, with whom they had closer linguistic and cultural affinities and to whom they paid lower taxes. Upon declaration of their allegiance to the Islamic state and payment of a poll (head) tax, these "protected" (***dhimmi***) peoples could practice their faith and be governed by their religious leaders and law in matters of faith and private life.

dhimmi: "protected"; refers to non-Muslim peoples who were granted religious freedom under Muslim rule in exchange for payment of a tax

Islam proved more tolerant than imperial Christianity, providing greater religious freedom for Jews and indigenous Christians. Under Muslim rule, most local or indigenous Christian churches, persecuted as schismatics and heretics by the "foreign" Christian orthodoxy of their rulers, could practice their faith.

The rapid spread and development of imperial Islam produced a rich Islamic civilization that flourished from the ninth to the twelfth centuries. Urban cultural centers emerged in Cairo, Baghdad, Cordova, Palermo, and Nishapur. With significant assistance from Christian and Jewish subjects, Muslims collected the great books of science, medicine, and philosophy from the West and the East and translated them into Arabic from Greek, Latin, Persian, Coptic, Syriac, and Sanskrit. The age of translation was followed by a period of great creativity as a new generation of educated Muslim thinkers and scientists made their own contributions to learning in philosophy, medicine, chemistry, astronomy, algebra, optics, art, and architecture. Towering intellectual giants dominated this period: al-Farabi (d. 950), Ibn Sina (known as Avicenna, 980–1037), Ibn Rushd (known as Averroes, d. 1198), al-Biruni (973–1048), and al-Ghazali (d. 1111). Avicenna (Ibn Sina) exemplified these multitalented men of genius:

> I busied myself with the study of Fusus al-Hikam (a treatise by al-Farabi) and other commentaries on physics and mathematics, and the doors of knowledge opened before me. Then I took up medicine. . . . Medicine is not one of the difficult sciences, and in a short time I undoubtedly excelled at it, so that

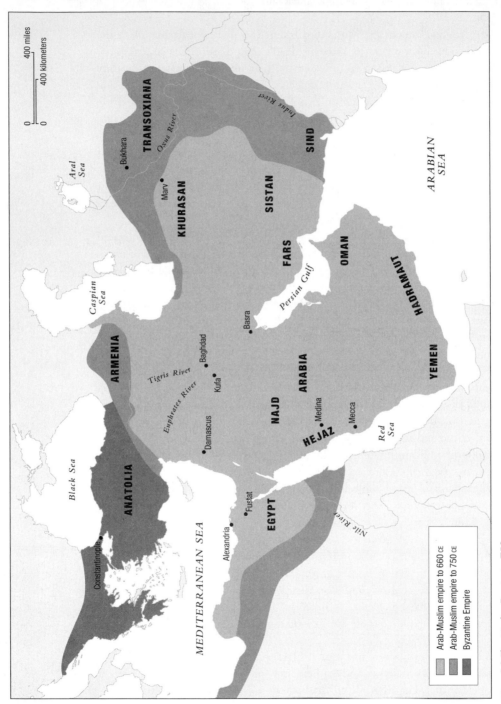

Map 5.2 The Muslim Empire to 750 CE.

Arab-Muslim empire to 660 CE
Arab-Muslim empire to 750 CE
Byzantine Empire

physicians of merit studied under me. . . . At the same time I carried on debates and controversies in jurisprudence. At this point I was 16 years old. Then, for a year and a half, I devoted myself to study. I resumed the study of logic and all parts of philosophy. During this time I never slept the whole night through and did nothing but study all day long. . . . Thus I mastered logic, physics, and mathematics. . . . When I reached the age of 18, I had completed the study of all these sciences. At that point my memory was better, whereas today my learning is riper.[2]

The cultural traffic pattern was again reversed when Europeans, emerging from the Dark Ages, turned to Muslim centers of learning to regain their lost heritage and to learn from Muslim advances. They retranslated the Greek philosophers and the writings of their great Muslim disciples: men like al-Farabi, who had come to be known as "the second teacher or master" (the first being Aristotle) and Ibn Rushd (Averroes), remembered as "the great commentator on Aristotle." Many of the great medieval Christian philosophers and theologians (Albert the Great, Thomas Aquinas, Abelard, Roger Bacon, Duns Scotus) acknowledged their intellectual debt to their Muslim predecessors.

The failures and reforms of Muslim societies today, as in the recent past, are often measured against this history, at times romanticized, of an earlier period of brilliant success.

Diversity, Division, and Dissent

The victories and accomplishments during the early history and spread of Islam were also accompanied by deep division and dissent. During the lifetime of the Prophet, the community had been united by Muhammad's prophetic claims, his remarkable leadership skills, and the divine revelations he continued to receive. However, Muhammad's death precipitated crises, dissent, and civil wars.

Given the pivotal role of Muhammad in the life of the community, his death in 632 was a traumatic event. What was the community to do? Who was to lead? Issues of political succession and secession or civil war were to plague and threaten its survival.

Muhammad's senior followers, known as the *Companions* of the Prophet, moved quickly to reassure the community. In proclaiming Muhammad's death to the faithful, the Companion Abu Bakr declared: "Muslims! If any of you has worshipped Muhammad, let me tell you that Muhammad is dead. But if you worship God, then know that God is living and will never die." The Companions selected Abu Bakr as caliph (*khalifah*, "successor or deputy"). As caliph, he was not a prophet but rather Muhammad's successor as political and military head of the community.

This next stage in the history of the Muslim community, the Caliphate (632–1258), has traditionally been divided into three periods: the time of the Rightly Guided Caliphs (632–661), followed by the Umayyad (661–750) and Abbasid (750–1258)

This enameled glass mosque lamp, made in the early 1300s, was dedicated to a Muslim ruler. Quotations from the Quran decorate the lamp.

dynasties. During these centuries a vast empire was created, with successive capitols at Medina, Kufa, Damascus, and Baghdad. Stunning political and military success was complemented by a cultural florescence, resulting in powerful Islamic empires and a brilliant Islamic civilization. However, it was the earliest period, that of the Rightly Guided Caliphs and the Companions of the Prophet, that was to become the example for later generations of believers.

Abu Bakr (632–34), the first successor of Muhammad, was tested almost immediately when some Arab tribes attempted to bolt from the community, declaring their independence. Abu Bakr crushed the tribal revolt, consolidated Muslim rule over the Arabian Peninsula, and preserved the religiously based unity and solidarity of the Islamic-community state.

Abu Bakr's successor, Umar ibn al-Khattab (634–44), initiated a period of expansion and conquest. During the reign of the third caliph, Uthman ibn Affan (644–56), from the Umayyad clan, tribal factionalism resurfaced with a series of rebellions that would plague the Islamic community's development.

A second crisis of leadership, with repercussions down through the centuries, occurred when civil war broke out during the reign of the fourth caliph, Ali. Although in 632 the majority of the community had supported the selection of Abu Bakr as caliph, a minority dissented, believing that leadership should stay in the family of the Prophet and thus pass to its senior male member, Ali. In addition to being Muhammad's cousin, Ali was the Prophet's son-in-law, having married Fatima, a daughter of Muhammad and Khadija. Shortly after Ali's accession to power, his authority was challenged by a triumvirate that included Muhammad's widow, Aisha, who was the daughter of Abu Bakr. This was followed by the rebellion of Muawiya, the governor of Syria. Arbitration proved inconclusive but did lead to two results that have had a profound impact on the history of Islam.

First, a group of Ali's followers, the Kharajites (those who "go out," or secede), broke away. They maintained an uncompromising faith, believing that Ali's failure to subdue his opponents rendered him no better than Muawiya. The Kharajites held both Ali and Muawiya to be unbelievers whose revolt against God was punishable by death. Second, Muawiya remained recalcitrant in Syria, biding his time until Ali was assassinated by a group of Kharajites. Muawiya then seized power and established a monarchy, the Umayyad dynasty (661–750).

The Umayyad dynasty was responsible for the rapid spread of Islam and the emergence of imperial Islam, with its capital in Damascus. However, opposition to what later Muslim historians would characterize as impious Umayyad caliphs also resulted in important movements for renewal and reform. Some movements, such as the Kharajites and the Shiah, were revolutionary, while others led to the development of Islamic law and mysticism (Sufism).

The Kharajites, who had broken with Ali, emerged as revolutionaries who, although unsuccessful in their own times, continue to inspire contemporary radical groups. Like some religious extremists today, the Kharajites interpreted the Quran and the Sunnah literally and sought to follow their beliefs absolutely and to impose them on others. They viewed the world as divided into belief or unbelief, into Muslims, defined as those who agreed with the Kharajites, and infidels, the enemies of God: those who differed with the Kharajites and therefore should be excommunicated, or cut off from the community.

Like extremist groups today, who have taken such names as Jihad, the Soldiers of God, and al-Qaeda, the Kharajites, claiming to follow the letter of the Quran and the example of the Prophet, adopted their own interpretation of Muhammad and the experiences of the early community. Seeing themselves as the instruments of God's justice, God's righteous army, they believed that violence, guerrilla warfare, and revolution were not only legitimate but obligatory in their battle against the usurpers of God's rule. Other Muslims, however pious, who committed an action contrary to the letter of the law, as interpreted or understood by the Kharajites, were guilty of grave (quite literally mortal) sin. According to the Kharajites, they were apostates and thus had committed treason against the Islamic community-state. If they did not repent, they were to be fought against and killed. Many of the components of this early Islamic worldview may be found in twentieth- and twenty-first-century Muslim extremist writings, including those of the Muslim Brotherhood's Sayyid Qutb, who will be discussed below, and in the ideology of groups such as Islamic Jihad, the Army of God, the Armed Islamic Group, Muhammad's Youth, Takfir wal Hijra (Excommunication and Flight), and al-Qaeda.

The Origins of the Sunni and Shiah Split

A second major revolutionary movement spawned by opposition to Umayyad rule was the rebellion by the followers of the fourth caliph, Ali. The results of this violent disagreement would lead to the two major branches of Islam, the communities of the **Sunni** majority and the **Shiah**, or Shii, minority.

Sunni: Muslims who accept the *sunna* and the historic succession of the Caliphs

The followers (*shiah*, "partisans") of Ali had been thwarted twice: when Muhammad's cousin was not appointed as the first caliph, and later when Muawiya seized the caliphate from Ali, who had been the Prophet's fourth successor. In 680, when the Umayyad ruler Yazid, the son of Muawiya, came to power, Husayn, the son of Ali, was persuaded by a group of Ali's followers in Kufa (a city in modern Iraq) to lead a rebellion. However, the support promised to Husayn did not materialize, and Husayn and his army were slaughtered by the Umayyad army at the city of Karbala (also in modern Iraq).

Shiah: followers of Ali, the cousin and son-in-law of Muhammad

The memory of Karbala and the "martyrdom" of Husayn resulted in a Shii worldview, a paradigm of suffering, oppression, and protest against injustice. The mentality encouraged by this paradigm was reinforced by the Shiis' minority status and discrimination against them through the centuries. It sustained the community throughout history and became a major source of inspiration and mobilization during Iran's "Islamic" revolution of 1978–79.

Sunni Muslims constitute 85 percent and Shiah approximately 15 percent of the global Islamic community. Although united in their common confession of faith in

The Blue Mosque, Shrine of Ali bin Thabit, cousin and son-in-law of Prophet Muhammad. Ali was the fourth caliph of Sunni Islam and the first imam of Shiah Islam. Built in the fifteenth century, the mosque has survived countless wars in near perfect condition. While some believe that it houses the tomb of Ali, most believe that he is buried in the Imam Ali Mosque in Najaf, Iraq.

imam: in Sunni Islam, the prayer leader and one who delivers the Friday sermon; in Shia Islam, refers to Ali's descendants, who are believed to be the legitimate leaders (not the Sunni caliphs) of the global Muslim community or *ummah*

God, the Quran, and the Prophet Muhammad, their notions of leadership and history differ. The reality of the dynastic Umayyad and Abbasid caliphates notwithstanding, in Sunni Islam, the caliph ideally is the selected or elected successor of the Prophet. He serves only, however, as political, military leader of the community, not as prophet. In Shiah Islam, the **imam**, or leader, is not selected from among the members of the community but must be a direct descendant of the Prophet's family. Moreover, he is the religiopolitical leader of the community. Though not a prophet, he is the divinely inspired, sinless, infallible, and final authoritative interpreter of God's will as formulated in Islamic law.

Sunnis and Shiah also developed differing interpretations of history. For Sunni, the early success of Islam and the power of its rulers were signs of God's guidance, rewards to a faithful community that were seen as historical validation of Muslim belief and claims. In contrast, the Shiah saw the same events as the illegitimate usurpation of power by Sunni rulers. For the Shiah, therefore, history is the theater for the struggle of a minority community, righteous but historically disinherited and oppressed, that must restore God's rule on earth under his imam. The early centuries of Islamic history would witness ongoing struggles between Sunnis and Shiah but also the remarkable development of religious thought (Islamic law, theology, and mysticism), institutions, traditions, and civilization.

Premodern Islam: The Classical Era

A critical issue faced by all religious believers today is the connection or continuity of current religious belief and practice with centuries-old sacred traditions. So, too, Islamic tradition and heritage become important reference points to justify contemporary beliefs and practices and as the basis for Islamic reform.

Law and Mysticism: The Outer and Inner Paths to God

Dissatisfaction with Umayyad rule, in which wealth led to abuse of power and corruption, resulted in the development of two nonrevolutionary reform movements or institutions: the **ulama** (religious scholars, or learned ones), with their Islamic law, and the Sufis, whose Islamic mysticism we shall discuss later.

In contrast to Christianity's emphasis on doctrine or theology, Islam, like Judaism, places primary emphasis on what believers should do, on religious observance of and obedience to God's law. Muslims are commanded by the Quran to strive or struggle (the literal word for struggle is **jihad**) in the path (*sharia*) of God, to realize, spread, and defend God's message and community. The faithful are to function as God's vicegerents (representatives or stewards) on earth, promoting the good and prohibiting evil (Q. 3:104, 3:110). All Muslims are responsible as individuals and as a community for the creation of the good society. Despite vast cultural differences, Islamic law has provided an idealized blueprint, a moral compass, that has provided a source of identity and guidance, a code of behavior, among Muslims throughout the ages.

Islamic law developed during the Umayyad dynasty in the eighth and ninth centuries as a response to real religious and political concerns and issues. Law was standardized by legal experts, with a view to limiting the power of the caliph or his appointed judges. Law continued to flourish during the tenth century under the Abbasid caliphs, who overthrew the Umayyads and legitimated their revolution by becoming the patrons of Islam and Islamic law. It is important to note that law did not develop primarily from the practice of courts or from government decrees but through the interpretation of scholars. In Sunni Islam, the *ulama* set out a religious ideal or blueprint based on four official sources of Islamic law: the Quran, the Sunnah, *qiyas*, and *ijma*.

The primary material source of Islamic law is the Quran, God's will for humankind: "Here is a plain statement to men, a guidance and instruction to those who fear God" (Q. 3:138). The Quran contains only eighty prescriptions that would qualify as law in the strict sense of the term; the majority of Quranic texts provide general principles and values, reflecting what the aims and aspirations of Muslims should be.

The Sunnah (example) of the Prophet comes from the Quran, early biographies, and especially prophetic traditions, the richest sources of information about Muhammad and his times. The Sunnah consists of volumes of hundreds of thousands

> **ulama:** religious scholars

> **jihad:** armed struggle in defense of Islam or the Muslim community; often, terrorists have also used this term to legitimate their actions

---

"Goodness is not turning your faces towards the East or West; goodness is to believe in Allah, the Last Day, angels, and the Book, and the prophets; to spend money, out of love for Him, for your kin, for orphans, for the needy, for the wayfarer, for those who ask, and for the freeing of slaves; to be steadfast in prayer, and pay the alms tax regularly; to fulfill contracts you have made; and to be firm and patient, in pain (or suffering) and adversity, and throughout all periods of panic. Those are truthful and God-fearing people."

—Quran 2:177

hadith: narrative report of Muhammad's sayings and action

of narrative stories or reports (**hadith**) about what the Prophet said and did. The material seemingly covers every situation. The centrality of the Prophetic traditions, yesterday and today, cannot be overestimated: "They are associated with the person who is 'alive' here and now and who is as revered and loved by all Muslims now as he was fourteen centuries ago."[3]

qiyas: legal term for analogical reasoning

The third source of law is analogical reasoning (**qiyas**). When confronted by a question or issue not addressed specifically and clearly, in the Quran or Sunnah, jurists looked for similar or analogous portions of scripture to identify principles that could be applied to a new case. For example, there is no specific text dealing with the use of mind-altering drugs, but from *qiyas*, jurists can justify the condemnation of such substances on the basis of sacred texts that plainly forbid the consumption of alcohol.

ijma: in Islamic law, consensus

Finally, consensus (**ijma**) is based on a statement traditionally attributed to the Prophet: "My community will never agree on an error." In reality, consensus has generally amounted to acceptance or consensus about an issue from the majority of religious scholars who represented religious authority.

ibadat: worship, ritual obligations

muamalat: social interactions

The two main divisions of Islamic law concern a Muslim's duties to God (**ibadat**), which consist of obligatory practices such as the Five Pillars of Islam, and duties to others (**muamalat**), which include regulations governing public life, from contract and international law to laws on marriage, divorce, and inheritance.

Islamic law is a source of unity and guidance, but individual jurists and legal scholars from diverse social backgrounds and cultural contexts have ever differed in their interpretation of texts, in their personal opinions, and in their notions of equity and public welfare. Diversity and disagreement in Islamic law are reflected in the acceptance of different law schools and the validity of their different (*ikhtilaf*) opinions.

fatwa: legal opinion or interpretation from a Muslim legal expert (*mufti*)

mufti: legal expert who issues *fatwas* to judges and litigants

We see these differences in official legal opinions or interpretations (*fatwas*) of Muslim jurists (**muftis**) who advised judges and litigants in recent times. In the Gulf War of 1991, some muftis supported Iraq, and others supported a U.S.-led armada that included troops from Egypt, Kuwait, and Saudi Arabia. Similarly, sharp differences have existed among religious leaders over the religious legitimacy or illegitimacy of suicide bombing in Israel-Palestine. But however different and contentious interpretations of Islamic law have been throughout Islamic history, the Five Pillars of Islam unite all Muslims in their worship and following of God.

The Five Pillars of Islam

If God, the Quran, and the Prophet Muhammad unite all Muslims in their common belief, the Five Pillars of Islam provide a unity of practice in the midst of the community's rich diversity. These are the Five Pillars:

shahadah: Muslim declaration of faith

1. *The Declaration of Faith.* A Muslim is one who bears witness that "There is no God but the God and Muhammad is the messenger of God." One need only make this simple statement, known as the **shahadah**, to become a Muslim.

The first part of the *shahadah* affirms Islam's absolute monotheism, an unshakable and uncompromising faith in the oneness or unity (*tawhid*) of God. The second part is the affirmation that Muhammad is the messenger of God, the last and final prophet, who serves as a model for the Muslim community.

The action, or doing, orientation of Islam is illustrated by the remaining four pillars or duties.

2. *Prayer.* Five times a day (dawn, noon, midafternoon, sunset, and evening), Muslims throughout the world are called to worship God. In many cities of the world, the quiet of the night or daily noise of busy city streets is pierced by the call of the **muezzin** from atop the tower (*minaret*) of the mosque: God is Most Great (Allahu Akbar)!, God is Most Great!

> I witness that there is no god but God (Allah) . . .
> I witness that Muhammad is the Messenger of God . . .
> Come to prayer . . . come to salvation . . .
> God is Most Great! God is Most Great! There is no god
>   but God!

Prayer (**salat**) is preceded by a series of ablutions to cleanse the body and to symbolize the purity of mind and body required for worshipping God. Facing the holy city of Mecca, Islam's spiritual homeland where the Prophet was born and received God's revelation, Muslims recall the revelation of the Quran and reinforce a sense of belonging to a single, worldwide community of believers. Muslims may pray in any appropriate place wherever they happen to be: at home, in an airport, on the road. They may do so as individuals or in a group. For Muslims, *salat* is an act of worship and adoration of God and remembrance of his word, not one of request or petition.

"Recite what has been revealed to you of the Book and perform prayer regularly: for prayer restrains from shameful and unjust deeds. Allah's remembrance is the greatest (thing in life) and Allah knows what you do."
—Quran 29:45

muezzin: one who issues the call to prayer from the minaret of a mosque

salat: prayer performed five times each day

These Uzbek Muslims, like fellow believers across the world, perform their prayers five times each day.

mosque: a building used for public and community worship

khutba: sermon delivered in a mosque on Fridays

minbar: mosque pulpit from which khutba is preached

zakat: almsgiving

Ramadan: ninth month of Muslim calendar, during which Muslims fast

A muezzin calling the faithful to prayer in the city of Kashgar in western China.

On Friday, the noon prayer is a congregational prayer that usually takes place in a **mosque** (*masjid*, "place of prostration"). A special feature of the Friday prayer is a sermon (*khutba*), preached from a pulpit (*minbar*). Since there is no priesthood in Islam, any Muslim may lead the prayer. In many communities, larger mosques do have an imam who leads the prayer and is paid to look after the mosque.

3. *Almsgiving.* The third pillar of Islam is the *zakat*, almsgiving. As all Muslims share equally in their obligation to worship God, so too they all are duty bound to attend to the social welfare of their community by redressing economic inequalities. This is accomplished through an annual contribution of 2.5 percent of one's accumulated wealth and assets, not just on income. Strictly speaking, *zakat* is not charity, since almsgiving is seen not as voluntary but as a duty imposed by God, an act of spiritual purification and solidarity. Just as the Quran condemns economic exploitation, it warns against those who accumulate wealth and fail to assist others (Q. 3:180). Those who have benefited from God's bounty, who have received their wealth as a trust from God, are required to look after the needs of the less fortunate members of the Muslim community.

In most countries, Muslims determine to whom they will pay the *zakat*. However, in recent years, some governments, such as those of Pakistan, Sudan, and Iran, in the name of creating a more Islamic state, have collected and distributed the *zakat*. This has proved to be a point of contention, for some charge that the central government misappropriates funds, and others prefer to have the freedom to distribute it themselves to needy relatives, friends, or neighbors.

4. *The Fast of Ramadan.* Muslims are required to fast (*sawm*) during **Ramadan**, the ninth month of Islam's lunar calendar. From dawn to dusk, all healthy Muslims must abstain from food, drink, and sex. The primary emphasis is less on abstinence and self-mortification as such than on spiritual self-discipline, reflection, and the performance of good works.

The fast is broken at the end of the day by a light meal, called breakfast. In the evening, families exchange visits and share foods and sweets that are served only at this time of the year. The month of Ramadan comes to an end with a great celebration, the Feast of the Breaking of the Fast, Id al-Fitr, one of the great religious holy days and holidays of the Muslim calendar. Family members come from near and far to feast and exchange gifts in a celebration that lasts for three days.

5. *Pilgrimage to Mecca*. The pilgrimage season follows Ramadan. Every adult Muslim who is physically and financially able is expected to perform the pilgrimage (**hajj**) to Mecca in Saudi Arabia at least once in his or her lifetime. Those who are able may go more often. Just as Muslims are united five times each day as they face Mecca in worship, each year believers make the physical journey to this spiritual center of Islam, where they again experience the unity, breadth, and diversity of the Islamic community. In the twenty-first century almost 2 million Muslims gather annually from every part of the globe in Saudi Arabia for the *hajj*.

The focus of the pilgrimage is the Kaaba, the cube-shaped House of God that Muslim tradition teaches was originally built by the prophet Ibrahim (Abraham) and his son Ismail to honor God. The black stone is believed to have been given to Abraham by the angel Gabriel. Thus the stone is a symbol of God's covenant with Ismail and, by extension, with the Muslim community. Like *salat*, the pilgrimage requires ritual purification; no jewelry, perfume, or sexual activity is permitted. Pilgrims wear white garments, symbolizing for everyone, rich and poor alike, the unity and equality of all believers before God. Men and women worship together. There is no segregation of the sexes.

As the pilgrims near Mecca, they shout: "I am here, O Lord, I am here!" When they reach Mecca, they proceed to the Grand Mosque that houses the Kaaba. There they pray at the spot where Abraham, the patriarch and

hajj: annual pilgrimage to Mecca, in which all adult Muslims are expected to participate at least once if physically and financially able to do so

"Alms are for the poor, the needy, and those employed to administer the (funds); for those whose hearts are bound together; as well as for freeing slaves and [repaying] debts; spending in the cause of Allah and for the wayfarer: thus Allah commands, and Allah is All-Knowing and Wise."

—Quran 9:60

Muslims are required to abstain from food and drink from dawn to dusk during the month of Ramadan. At dusk each day during Ramadan, families gather to break the fast and share a meal. This practice is called "breakfast."

The pilgrimage to Mecca is one of the Five Pillars of Islam. All Muslims, health and wealth permitting, are expected to make the pilgrimage at least once in their lifetime.

The Kaaba. The pilgrimage (*hajj*) to Mecca, one of the Five Pillars of Islam, takes place during the first ten days of the twelfth month of the lunar calendar. The focus of the pilgrimage is the Kaaba, "the cube," also known as the House of God, which tradition says was built by Abraham and his son Ismail. Pilgrims circumambulate the Kaaba, located within the Great Mosque of Mecca. This is a ritual act that many believe symbolizes the angels' circling of God's throne in heaven.

father of monotheism, stood, and they circumambulate the Kaaba seven times. Another part of the *hajj* is a visit to the Plain of Arafat, the site of Muhammad's last sermon, where pilgrims seek God's forgiveness for their sins and for those of all Muslims throughout the world.

The pilgrimage ends with the celebration of the Feast of Sacrifice (Id al-Adha). The "great feast" commemorates God's testing of Abraham by commanding him to sacrifice his son Ismail (in the Jewish and Christian traditions it is Isaac who is put at risk). Commemorating God's final permission to Abraham to substitute a ram for his son, Muslims sacrifice animals (sheep,

Those who have made the *hajj* often use the honorific title *hajji*. Many, as demonstrated by this house in Jerusalem, decorate the facade with illustrations to show that the owner has been to Mecca.

goats, cattle) not only in Mecca but across the Muslim world. While some of the meat is consumed, most is distributed to the poor. The three-day Feast of Sacrifice is a time for rejoicing, prayer, and visiting with family and friends.

Women and Muslim Family Law

Few topics have received more popular attention than women and the family. If many Muslims speak of Islam as liberating women, others in the West as well as in Muslim countries decry the continuing oppression of women. The position of Muslim women must be viewed within the dual context of their status in Islamic law and the politics and culture of their societies. Islamic law itself reflects both the Quranic concern for the rights and protection of women and the family (the greater part of its legislation is devoted to these issues) and the traditions of the male-dominated society within which Islamic law was developed.

The Quran introduced reforms affecting the status of women both through new regulations and by teachings that led to the modification of prevailing customs. The Quran recognized a woman's rights to contract marriage, to receive and keep her

Jihad: The Struggle for God

Jihad, "to strive or struggle," is sometimes referred to as the sixth pillar of Islam, although it has no such official status. In its most general meaning, *jihad* refers to the obligation incumbent on all Muslims, as individuals and as a community, to exert (*jihad*) themselves to realize God's will, to lead a virtuous life, to fulfill the universal mission of Islam, and to spread the Islamic community through preaching Islam to convert others or writing religious tracts ("jihad of the tongue" and "jihad of the pen"). Thus, today it can be used to describe the personal struggle to keep the fast of Ramadan, to lead a good life, to fulfill family responsibilities. Popularly it is used to describe the struggle for educational or social reform—to establish good schools, to clean up a neighborhood, to fight drugs, or to work for social justice. However, it also includes the struggle for or defense of Islam, holy war. Although *jihad* is not supposed to include aggressive warfare, this tactic has been invoked by early extremists such as the Kharajites, by rulers to justify their wars of conquest and expansion, and by contemporary extremists such as Osama bin Laden and his *jihad* against America as well as *jihadi* organizations in Lebanon, the Persian Gulf, and Indonesia.

dowry, and to own and inherit property. No equivalent rights existed in Christianity or in Judaism during or long after the lifetime of the Prophet. In fact, women in the West did not gain inheritance rights until the nineteenth century. These Quranic reforms and others would become the basis for Muslim family law.

As the Five Pillars are the core of a Muslim's duty to worship God (*ibadat*), family law is central to Islam's social laws (*muamalat*). Indeed, Muslim family law has often been described as the heart of the *sharia*, reflecting the importance of the family in Islam. Because of the centrality of the community in Islam and the role of the family as the basic unit of society, family law has enjoyed pride of place in the development of Islamic law and in its implementation throughout history. Similarly, though the emergence of modern Muslim states has often seen the adoption of Western-oriented civil and commercial laws or legal systems, in most countries Muslim family law has remained in force. While in some countries family law has been reformed rather than replaced, often this reform has generated considerable conflict and debate. In the 1980s, the resurgence of Islam was often accompanied by attempts to return to the use of classical or medieval family law and to reverse modern reforms. Thus today, as in the past, the subject of women and the family remains an important and extremely sensitive subject in Muslim societies.

The status of women and the family in Muslim family law is the product of many factors: Arab culture, Quranic reforms, foreign ideas and values assimilated from conquered peoples, and the interpretation of male jurists in a patriarchal society. Regulations developed in the early centuries of Islamic history regarding marriage, divorce, inheritance, and bequests have guided Muslim societies, determining attitudes toward women and the family.

"For Muslim men and women—for believing men and women, for devout men and women, for true men and women, for men and women who are patient and constant, for men and women who humble themselves, for men and women who give in Charity, for men and women who fast (and deny themselves), for men and women who guard their chastity, and for men and women who engage much in Allah's praise—for them has Allah prepared forgiveness and great reward."

—Quran 33:35

The Quran teaches that men and women are equal before God in terms of their religious and moral obligations and rewards (Q. 33:35). However, husbands and wives are seen as fulfilling complementary roles, based on differing characteristics, capacities, and dispositions and their traditional roles in the patriarchal family. Men function in the public sphere, the "outside" world; they are responsible for the financial support and protection of the family.

A woman's primary role is that of wife and mother; she is responsible for the management of the household, raising her children and supervising their religious/moral training. In light of women's more sheltered and protected status and men's greater experience in public life and broader responsibilities, the Quran (and Islamic law) teaches that wives are subordinate to husbands (Q. 2:228), and in Islamic law the testimony of one man is worth that of two women. Similarly, because men in a patriarchal system were responsible for the economic well-being of all women and other dependents in the extended family, the male portion of inheritance was twice that of a female.

Marriage is a primary institution in Islam, regarded as incumbent upon all Muslims. It is a civil contract or covenant, not a sacrament. It safeguards chastity and the growth and stability of the family, legalizing intercourse and the procreation of children. Reflecting the centrality of the family and the identity and role of individual family members, marriage is not simply an agreement between two people but between two families. Thus, marriages arranged by the two families or by a guardian are traditional, although the majority of jurists agreed that a woman should not be forced to marry a man against her will.

Many non-Muslims are ignorant or unaware of Quranic reforms affecting women; indeed, most equate Islam with polygamy or, more accurately, polygyny. The Quran explicitly permits a man to marry four wives while in the same verse (Q. 43) noting that if all cannot be supported and treated equally, then only one is permitted. The purpose of this provision is not to discourage all men from practicing monogamy but to afford protection to unmarried women as well as to limit and regulate the unfettered rights of men. Islamic modernists in recent years have used this same spirit and another verse ("You are never able to be fair and just between women if that is your ardent desire," Q. 4:129) to argue that the Quranic ideal is monogamy and that plural marriages should be restricted or eliminated. In particular, they note that the original revelation was given to a premodern community in which losses in battle left many widows who needed protection. More important, many maintain that the demands of modern life make it extraordinarily difficult for any man to provide equally for more than one wife, especially in terms of time and affection.

Islamic law, reflecting the spirit of the Quran (Q. 4:35) and a saying of the Prophet ("of all the permitted things divorce is the most abominable"), regards divorce as permissible but reprehensible. One authoritative legal manual calls divorce "a dangerous and disapproved procedure . . . nor is its propriety at all admitted, but on the ground of urgency of relief from an unsuitable wife."[4] Islamic law itself, as if to underscore the seriousness of divorce, prescribes that a man must pronounce the words or formula of divorce three separate times to make it irrevocable.

The strong influence of custom can be seen in the more limited rights of divorce accorded women. The Quran had declared: "Women have rights similar to those (of men) over them; while men stand above them" (Q. 2:228). For example, while the *ulama* extended more limited divorce rights to women, in contrast to men, women had to go to court and present grounds for divorce far more specific than unsuitability; they were limited to charges like physical abuse, abandonment, and failure to provide adequate maintenance. Beginning in the 1920s, some Muslim governments relaxed these and other legal restrictions on women.

Historically, divorce rather than polygamy has proved to be the more serious social problem, especially since women have often been ignorant of their legal rights or unable to exercise them in male-dominated social environments. Historically, a woman's Quranic and legal rights to contract and dissolve her own marriage, to receive and control her dowry, or to inherit often disappeared under the pressures and mores of strong patriarchal societies. Thus custom tended to prevail over Islamic law as well as the letter and spirit of the Quran.

A major example of the interaction of custom and scripture is the veiling (or covering) and seclusion (***purdah***) of women. These customs, assimilated by Islamic practice from the conquered Persian and Byzantine empires, have been viewed by many, though certainly not all, as appropriate expressions of Quranic principles and values. The Quran does not stipulate the veiling and seclusion of women, although it does say that the wives of the Prophet should speak to men from behind a partition. It tells women to dress and behave modestly (Q. 24:30–31), but the admonition applies to men, as well.

purdah: seclusion of women from men who are not relatives

Veiling and seclusion have varied considerably across Muslim societies and in different historical periods. Originally veiling had been meant to protect women in upper-class urban surroundings, where they enjoyed mobility and opportunities to socialize. Village and rural women were slower to adopt the measure, which interfered with their ability to work in the fields.

Over the centuries, as the practices of veiling and seclusion spread, there were deleterious effects on the status of women religiously and socially. The institution of *purdah* served to cut off many women's access to the mosque, the social and educational center of the community, an isolation that further lowered their status. Poorer women were often restricted to small houses with limited social contacts. The serious negative impact of *purdah* in modern times was attested to in the 1940s by an Egyptian scholar and religious leader who bore the name of a distinguished predecessor. The twentieth-century Muhammad al-Ghazali (d. 1996) said: "Ninety percent of our women do not pray at all; nor do they know of the other duties of Islam other than their names."[5]

Although debate rages today in many Muslim societies about the status and character of "the Muslim woman," with greater opportunities for women's education and employment have come reforms to address the inequities of some Muslim laws that affect women only. Modernizing governments from the 1920s to the 1960s reformed Muslim family laws in marriage, divorce, and inheritance.

Reforms included measures that restricted a male's right unilaterally to divorce his wife as well as to practice polygyny. In fact, a wife was permitted to specify in her

The Sufi Path

At the heart of Sufism's worldview and spirituality is the belief that one must die to self to become aware of and live in the presence of God. For guidance in the way Sufis relied on a teacher or master (*shaykh* or *pir*), one whose authority was based on direct personal religious experience. The master leads his or her disciples through the successive stages of renunciation of the transient phenomenal world, purification, and insight. Along the way, God is believed to reward and encourage the disciple through special blessings and certain religious experiences or psychological states.

marriage contract that a husband must obtain her permission before taking another wife. A wife's grounds for divorce were increased, as well. These reforms were partial and were imposed from above through legislation. They were often resisted or reluctantly accepted by the *ulama*. Moreover, with the resurgence of Islam, more conservative religious forces and many Islamic activists have rejected family law reforms as Western inspired, calling instead for a return to classical Islamic laws and seeking again to limit and control women's role in society.

The Interior Path of Love: Islamic Mysticism

Alongside the path of law (*sharia*) is the interior path or way (*tariqa*) of Sufi mysticism, a major popular religious movement within Sunni and Shii Islam. Whereas the *sharia* provided the way of duties and rights to order the life of the individual and community, Sufism offered an esoteric path or spiritual discipline, a method by which the Sufi sought not only to follow God but also to know or to experience God's presence.

Islamic mysticism, like Islamic law, began as a reform movement. With the phenomenal success of Islam uniting the tribes of Arabia and conquering the Byzantine and Persian empires, the *ummah* entered another phase in its development. In a new capital, Damascus, the Umayyad caliphs set up a court characterized by an imperial lifestyle and material luxuries. Increasingly, pious Muslims in many locations saw these changes as evidence that God and submission to his will were being replaced in the royal courts of dynastic rulers by concerns for power and wealth. To counter this trend, the critics began to study the Quran, the traditions of the Prophet, and the performance of religious duties, with an emphasis on asceticism and love of God, reemphasizing the centrality of God over worship of the material world and its rewards.

Sufism: Islamic mysticism

The term **Sufism** comes from the coarse woolen garment (*suf*, "wool") worn by many of these early ascetics. The reformers did not reject the world so much as dependence on the things of this world; they did not wish to allow creation to obscure the Creator or to forget the Absolute Reality in the course of being swept along and away from God by material realities. Desiring a more faithful return to the purity and simplicity of the Prophet's time, men and women pursued a path of

Turkish Sufi order (Mawlawi *tariqah*), founded by Jalal al-Din Rumi (d. 1273), one of the most famous Sufi mystics. These men are popularly known as *whirling dervishes* because of one of their meditation rituals, a dance in which they revolve to the music of Sufi songs.

self-denial and good works. The **Sufis** were known for detachment from the material world, which they viewed as ephemeral, a transient distraction from the divine; repentance for sins; fear of God and the Last Judgment; and selfless devotion to the fulfillment of God's will.

● **Sufis:** Muslim mystics

Early emphasis on ascetic detachment (worldly renunciation) and meditation was complemented by the fusion of asceticism with an undying devotional love of God exemplified by Rabia al-Adawiyya (d. 801). The joining of the ascetic with the ecstatic permanently influenced the nature and future development of Sufism. An attractive and desirable woman, Rabia declined offers of marriage, not willing to permit anyone or anything to distract her from dedication and total commitment to God. Nothing captures better the selfless devotion she espoused than the following words attributed to her:

> O my Lord, if I worship Thee from fear of Hell, burn me in hell, and if I worship Thee in hope of Paradise, exclude me thence, but if I worship Thee for Thine own sake, then withhold not from me Thine Eternal Beauty.[6]

Over the years, a variety of ascetic and ritual practices were adopted as part of the mystic way, including fasting, poverty, silence, and celibacy. Among the Sufi techniques to "remember" God, who is always present in the world, are rhythmic repetition of God's name and breathing exercises that focus consciousness on God and place the devotee in the presence of God. Music and song as well as dance are also used to express deep feelings of love of God, to feel or experience his nearness, and to show devotion to God and Muhammad. The best-known use of dance is that of Turkey's whirling dervishes, who circle their master to imitate the divinely ordained motions of the universe.

One popular practice of Sufism is the veneration of Muhammad and Sufi saints as intermediaries between God and humanity. Despite the official Islamic belief that Muhammad was only a human being and not a miracle worker, his central role as the ideal model of Muslim life had generated stories of the Prophet's extraordinary powers. In Sufism these stories mushroomed and were extended to Sufi saints, the friends (**wali**) or protégés of God, who are said to have had the power to bilocate, cure the sick, multiply food, and read minds. The burial sites or mausoleums of Sufi masters became religious sanctuaries. Pilgrims visited them, offering petitions for success in this life and the next, and miracles were reported.

wali: Sufi term referring to a saint

The many faces of contemporary Islam include not only the more visible reassertion of Islam in Muslim politics but also the revitalization of Muslim piety and spirituality. These adherents of the Sufi Naqshbandi order at the Islamic Institute in Cairo represent one of the major mystical orders in Islam. Not only did they play an important role in reformist and anticolonialist movements throughout the Islamic world in the past, they also do so today.

Though Sufi spirituality complemented the more ritual and legalistic orientation of the *ulama* and the *sharia*, the relationship between the two was often tense. The *ulama* tended to regard Sufi masters and the mystic way as a challenge to their authority and their interpretation of Islam. Sufis tended to regard the *ulama's* legalistic approach to Islam as lesser, incomplete, and subordinate to the Sufi way.

The majority of the *ulama* reacted to these challenges to their authority and worldview by condemning Islamic mysticism in the name of Islamic orthodoxy. At this critical juncture a prominent Islamic scholar, Muhammad al-Ghazali (1058–1111), emerged to save the day.

Al-Ghazali spent many years traveling to major Sufi centers in Arabia and Palestine, practicing and studying Sufism. During this time, he wrote *The Revivification of the Religious Sciences*, in which he showed that law, theology, and mysticism were neither incompatible nor inconsistent with one another. This brilliant *tour de force* reassured the *ulama* about the orthodoxy of Sufism and countered the rationalism of the philosophers. In al-Ghazali's great synthesis, law and theology were presented in terms that the *ulama* could accept, but they were grounded in religious experience and interior devotion (Sufism). Rationalism was tempered by the Sufi emphasis on religious experience and love of God. Al-Ghazali reconciled the *ulama* and the Sufis, producing a religious synthesis that earned him the title "Renewer (**mujaddid**) of Islam." While the tension between many of the *ulama* and Sufism continued and, as we shall see, in later centuries led to attempts to reform or suppress Sufism, al-Ghazali had secured an important place for Sufism within Islam. Indeed, Sufism in the twelfth century and later swept across much of the Islamic world. Sufi orders became the great missionaries of Islam, and Sufism became integral to everyday popular religious practice and spirituality.

However, the strength of Sufism as a popular religious force also proved to be its weakness. Its flexibility, tolerance, and eclecticism, which enabled it to incorporate local religious practices and values as Islam spread to new regions, also led at times to the indiscriminate incorporation of superstitious and otherwise non-Islamic activities, ranging from magic and fetishism to drunkenness and sensuality. Sufism's concern about the dangers in the *ulama's* religious legalism and ritual formalism gave way to rejection, by some, of the official practices of Islam in favor of a highly individualistic and idiosyncratic brand of devotion. Emphasis on the limits of reason and the importance of religious practice and experience devolved into an anti-intellectualism that rejected all Islamic learning and authority and promoted superstition, passivism, and fatalism. Premodern reformers and modernists, both secular and Islamic, have blamed Sufism for the ills of the Muslim world, yet throughout much of the history of the *ummah*, Sufism has remained a vital spiritual presence and force.

> **mujaddid:** "renewer"; one who comes to restore and revitalize Islamic community and practice

Islam and the State

As we have seen, the early success and power of Islamic empires greatly influenced the development of Islamic law and mysticism. From Muhammad's establishment of the first Muslim community at Medina in 622 CE and down through the centuries, the faith of Islam became a central force in the development of state and society. The soldiers, traders, and Sufis of Islam spread God's word and rule, creating a vast land or region of

Sheikh Lotf Allah Mosque in Isfahan, Iran, completed in 1618, is one of the architectural masterpieces of Safavid Iranian architecture.

dar al-Islam: territory controlled and ruled by Muslims

Islam (***dar al-Islam***). The caliphate, with its centralized Islamic empires, the Umayyad (661–750) and Abbasid (750–1250) dynasties, was followed by an extensive series of Muslim sultanates extending from Timbuktu in Africa to Mindanao in Southeast Asia. During this period great medieval Muslim empires emerged: the Ottoman in the Middle East (1281–1924), the Safavid (1501–1722) in Iran, and the Mughal (1483–1857) in South Asia.

However different these empires and sultanate states, Islam constituted the basic framework for their political and social life. Islam provided legitimation, a religio-political ideology, and law, informing the state's political, legal, educational, and social institutions. The *caliph* or *sultan*, as head of state, was seen as the political successor of Muhammad. Though not a prophet, he was the protector of the faith who was to implement Islamic law and to spread Islamic rule. The *ulama* were the guardians of religion, its interpreters, and as such often served as advisers to *caliphs* and *sultans*. They were not an ordained clergy, nor were they associated with organized "congregations." Rather, they were a major intellectual and social force or class in society. They played a primary role in the state's religious, legal, educational, and social service institutions. The *ulama* were by this time theologians and legal experts, responsible for the application of the law and the administration of *sharia* courts. They ran the schools and universities that trained those who aspired to public as well as religious office. They administered funds that were applied to a broad range of services, from the

The Taj Mahal, the mausoleum built (1631–47) by the grief-stricken emperor Shah Jahan for his beloved wife Mumtaz Mahal, who died in childbirth. Situated in a forty-two-acre garden, it is flanked by two perfectly proportioned mosque complexes. This crowning achievement, a landmark of world architecture, symbolizes the wealth and splendor of the Mughal Empire. The project brought together craftsmen and calligraphers from the Islamic world who worked with Muslim and Hindu craftsmen from the empire.

construction and maintenance of mosques, schools, student hostels, and hospitals to roads and bridges. In time, they came to constitute a religious establishment alongside and often dependent on the political establishment. Indeed, in many empires the ruler appointed a senior religious leader, *Shaykh-al-Islam*, as head of religious affairs, a post that still exists in many Muslim countries today.

In an Islamic state, citizenship, or perhaps more accurately degree of citizenship, was also based on religious affiliation. Muslims were full citizens, enjoying all the rights and duties of this position. As discussed earlier, Jews and Christians as People of the Book, were also citizens, but they had the status of protected people (*dhimmi*). Islam also informed the international relations of the state. The spread of Islam as a faith and a religiopolitical system was legitimated by the Quran and by the teaching and example of Muhammad. Muslims sought to create a "Pax Islamica," much like the "Pax Romana" and what U.S. policy makers would later speak of as a "Pax Americana." Conquest and diplomacy, force, persuasion, preaching, and alliances were its means.

The obligation to strive (*jihad*) to follow and realize God's will entailed opposition to evil and injustice and included *jihad* as an armed struggle to defend Islam or the community and to spread Muslim rule and empire. As such, *jihad* became part and parcel of Islam's doctrine of war and peace. As Islamic empires spread, non-Muslims could pick one of three options: to convert to Islam, to become "protected people" and pay a poll tax, or to become enemies to be fought.

For the believer, the role of Islam in state and society was mirrored in the continuum of Muslim rule, power, and success from the time of the Prophet Muhammad to the dawn of European colonialism. Despite the contradictions of life, civil wars, impious rulers, and dynastic usurpers, the presence and continuity of an Islamic ideology and system, however different the reality might at times be from the ideal, validated and reinforced a sense of a divinely mandated and guided community with a purpose and mission. Thus for many Muslims the history of Islam is that of a vibrant, dynamic, and expansive faith. Islam and Muslim rule were extended over major areas of Africa; the Middle East; South, Southeast, and Central Asia; Spain; and southern Italy. As a result, Sunni Muslim history contains the belief that following the Islamic community's divine mandate to spread God's guidance and governance will lead to prosperity and power in this life as well as the promise of eternal life in heaven.

The rapid spread and expansion of Islam as a dynamic faith and imperial power challenged and was regarded as a theological and political threat to Christendom, epitomized by the launching of the Crusades.

Islam and the West (Christendom): The Crusades

Despite common religious roots and instances of cooperation, the history of Islam and Western Christendom has been marked more by confrontation than by peaceful coexistence and dialog. For the Christian West, Islam is seen as the religion of the sword; for many Muslims, the spirit of the Christian West was epitomized first by the Crusades and centuries later by a movement seen as largely equivalent, European colonialism.

Unlike Judaism or any other world religion, Islam constituted an effective theological and political challenge to Christendom and its hegemonic ambitions. Muslim armies overran the Byzantine Empire, Spain, and the Mediterranean, from Sicily to Anatolia. At the same time, Islam challenged Christian religious claims and authority. Appropriating Christianity's insistence that the New Testament describes a new covenant and revelation superseding that of the Jews, Muslims now claimed to represent a third major stage in God's revelation, a third covenant. Therefore, Christians and Jews should acknowledge that they had corrupted their original revelations from God and that the one, true God, in his mercy, had sent his revelation one final and complete time to Muhammad. Islam now claimed to have a divinely mandated universal mission to call all to worship God and to join the Islamic community and live under Islamic rule. From the seventh to the eleventh centuries, Islam spread rapidly, extending Muslim rule over Christian territories and winning Christian hearts, in time creating large numbers of converts. Christianity and Islam were on a collision course.

By the eleventh century, Christendom's response to Islam was twofold: the struggle to reconquer Andalusian Spain (1000–1492), where the coexistence of Muslims, Christians, and Jews had produced a cultural florescence, and the undertaking of the Crusades (1095–1453).

Jerusalem had been taken by Arab armies in 638. Thereafter, for five centuries, Muslims lived in peaceful coexistence with Christians and with Jews. Although banned by Christian rulers, Jews were permitted by Muslims to return to live and worship in

Courtyard of the Lions, Alhambra Palace, the fourteenth-century residence of the Nasrid dynasty in Granada, Spain, one of the remarkable monuments remaining from the several centuries of Muslim rule in Andalusia, when Muslims, Jews, and Christians coexisted and produced a high culture.

the city of Solomon and David. However, in the eleventh century political events and an imperial-papal power play that pitted Christendom against Islam began a period of misunderstanding and distrust that has spanned nearly a millennium.

In 1071, the Byzantine emperor Alexius I, whose army had been decisively defeated by a Seljuq (Abbasid) army, feared that all Asia Minor would be overrun. He called on other Christian rulers and the pope to come to the aid of his capital, Constantinople, by undertaking a "pilgrimage," or crusade, to free Jerusalem and its environs from Muslim rule. For the leader of the Western church, Pope Urban II, Jerusalem provided an opportunity to gain recognition of papal authority and the pontiff's role in legitimating the actions of temporal rulers. In addition, Christian rulers, knights, and merchants were driven by the promise of booty as well as trade and banking opportunities coming from the creation of a Latin kingdom in the Middle East. This enthusiastic response to the call for help by Alexius served to unite a divided Christendom in a holy war against the "infidel," ostensibly to liberate the holy city. The appeal to religion captured the popular mind and gained its support. This was ironic because, as one scholar has observed, "God may have indeed wished it, but there is certainly no evidence that the Christians of Jerusalem did, or that anything extraordinary was occurring to pilgrims there to prompt such a response at that time in history."[7]

Few events have had a more shattering and long-lasting effect on Muslim-Christian relations than the Crusades. Three myths pervade Western perceptions of the Crusades:

- that Muslims were the protagonists
- that Christendom triumphed
- the sole purpose of the Crusades was to liberate Jerusalem.

In fact, the Crusades were launched by Urban II and secular Christian rulers for causes as much political and economic as religious, and on balance Muslims prevailed.

For Muslims, the collective memory of the Crusades lives on as the clearest example of militant Christianity, an early harbinger of the aggression and imperialism of the Christian West, a vivid reminder of Christianity's early hostility toward Islam. If many regard Islam as a religion of the sword, Muslims down through the ages remember July 15, 1099, when the crusaders from Western Europe conquered Jerusalem, slaughtering all its Jewish and Muslim inhabitants in a massacre of unbridled violence. Western chroniclers spoke of Crusaders wading in blood up to their ankles. In Europe Christian monks hailed it as the greatest event in world history since the crucifixion of Christ. Muslims contrast this behavior with that of Salah al-Din (Saladin), the great Muslim general, who, in reconquering the holy city in 1187, spared noncombatants.

By the fifteenth century the Crusades had spent their force. Although ostensibly launched to unite Christendom and turn back Muslim armies, the opposite had occurred. One unintended result of the Crusades was the deterioration of the position of indigenous Arab Christian minorities in the Holy Land. These minorities had had rights and privileges under Muslim rule, but, after the establishment of the Latin Kingdom, they found themselves treated as "loathsome schismatics." In an effort to obtain relief from persecution by their fellow Christians, many Arabs abandoned their beliefs, and adopted either Roman Catholicism, or—the supreme irony—Islam.[8] Amid a bitterly divided Christendom, the Byzantine capital, Constantinople, fell in 1453 to Muslim armies, was renamed Istanbul, and became the seat of the Ottoman Empire. For Muslim-Christian relations, what actually happened in the Crusades is less important than how the period has been remembered. Each community (Islam and Christianity) sees the other as militant holy warriors, somewhat barbaric and fanatic in their religious zeal, determined to conquer, convert, or eradicate the other, and thus an enemy of God—an obstacle and threat to the realization of God's will. As we shall see, the history of their contention continued through the next wave of European colonialism and finally in the superpower rivalry that began in the twentieth century.

How do we get from a centuries-long history of Muslim vitality, creativity, power, and success vis-à-vis the West to a time in which much of the Muslim world is part of the developing rather than the developed world? How do we get from the confrontations of the past, on the one hand, and the coexistence and tolerance of Andalusia, on the other, to contemporary concerns about a clash of civilizations? Why is Islam equated by many with violence, religious extremism, and terrorism: from hostage taking and hijackings to holy wars, assassinations, and bombings?

Understanding Islam today requires an appreciation of key historical events from the eighteenth to the twentieth centuries as well as of the causes and nature of premodern and modern reform movements. Sacred texts and long-held religious beliefs, combined with the specific sociopolitical contexts of Muslim communities, have been critical factors in producing a diversity of Muslim experiences and interpretations of Islam.

Premodern Revivalist Movements

From the eighteenth to the twentieth centuries, the Islamic world witnessed a protracted period of upheaval and renewal. In many countries Muslim societies, already threatened by European colonialism, failed and declined for internal reasons, as well. Such crises sparked responses from religious social/political revivalist movements that quite literally spanned the breadth of the Islamic world: from the Mahdi in the Sudan, the Sanusi in Libya, the Fulani in Nigeria, the Wahhabi in Saudi Arabia, to the Padri in Indonesia. Though their political and socioeconomic conditions varied, all were concerned about religious, political, and social disintegration, and all were convinced that the cure for the societies was a renewal of the Islamic way of life.

Islamic revivalist movements draw on a long and rich history and tradition of revival (*tajdid*) and reform (*islah*). Throughout Islamic history, the failures of and threats to Muslim societies have given rise to individual reformers and to reformist movements led by scholars or mystics. Islamic revival and reform involve a call for a return to the fundamentals, the Quran and Sunnah, and the right to interpret (*ijtihad*, or use of independent judgment) these primary sources of Islam.

In the eighteenth and nineteenth centuries, this belief took on popular religious forms. While such Islamic renewers or revivalists claimed simply to return to the original teachings of the Quran and the Prophet Muhammad, in fact each one produced new religious interpretations and cultural syntheses needed to guide his age. We shall discuss the Wahhabi movement in Arabia and the Mahdiyya in Africa, perhaps the best known of the postmedieval revivalists. Each exerted a formative influence on modern Muslim states: the Wahhabi in what is now Saudi Arabia and Qatar and the Mahdist in Sudan.

A religious leader, Muhammad ibn Abd al-Wahhab (1703–92), and a local tribal chief, Muhammad ibn Saud (d. 1765), joined forces to produce a united, militant religiopolitical movement. Ibn Abd al-Wahhab was dismayed by the condition of his society, which he saw as having degenerated to that of pre-Islamic Arabia, the *jahiliyya*, or period of ignorance of Islam. He was appalled by such popular religious practices as the veneration of Sufi saints, which he believed compromised the unity or oneness of God, and he was very critical of the Islamic community in Arabia, which had fallen back into tribalism and tribal warfare. He condemned some devotional rituals as idolatry, the worst sin in Islam, and dismissed others as pagan superstitions. Abd al-Wahhab wished to purify Islam from all foreign un-Islamic practices.

The Wahhabi movement waged a rigorous holy war to subdue and unite once again the tribes of Arabia. Muslims who did not go along were declared enemies of God who must be fought. Unlike other revivalist movements, the Wahhabi chose to completely suppress rather than merely reform Sufism.

The Mahdi of the Sudan, on the other hand, was a charismatic Sufi leader who initiated a militant reformist religiopolitical movement. The founder of the Mahdiyya order, whose name was Muhammad Ahmad, proclaimed himself **Mahdi** ("divinely guided one") in 1881. Thus, he went beyond most other revivalist reformers who claimed the right to interpret Islam and instead said that he was a divinely appointed and inspired representative of God.

The *Mahdi* established an Islamic community, uniting his followers, who like the Prophet's Companions were called *Ansar* ("helpers"). He also justified waging holy war against other Muslims, declaring Sudan's Ottoman Muslim rulers infidels who "disobeyed the command of His messenger and His Prophet, . . . ruled in a manner not in accord with what God had sent, . . . altered the sharia of our master, Muhammad the messenger of God, and blasphemed against the faith of God."[9] During this period, Sufism was reformed, and alcohol, prostitution, gambling, and music were outlawed as foreign un-Islamic practices that had corrupted society. After a four-year struggle, Mahdist forces overcame Egyptian forces of the Ottoman Empire, and an Islamic state was established in Khartoum in 1885.

Geometric design plays a major role in Islamic art. Artists use circles, triangles, hexagons, and squares to create ornate patterns to express and reinforce the unity of the Islamic world vision. This striking illustration comes from a Moroccan Quran tablet.

Mahdi: "divinely guided one" who is expected to appear at the end of time to usher in a perfect Islamic society of peace and social justice

Islam and Modernity

By the nineteenth century, the decline of Muslim societies made them vulnerable to external powers. Sharing the fate of many, they fell victim to European imperialism, which ultimately did much to shape the modern Muslim world politically, economically, religiously, and culturally. When Europe overpowered North Africa, the Middle East, South Asia, and Southeast Asia in the nineteenth century, reducing most Muslim societies to colonies, many experienced these defeats as a religious crisis as well as political and cultural setbacks.

Colonialism brought European armies and Christian missionaries, who attributed their conquests not only to their military and economic power, but also to the superiority of Western civilization and the truth inherent in Christianity. The French spoke of a "mission to civilize" and the British of "the white man's burden." Thus the missionaries who accompanied the armies of bureaucrats, soldiers, traders, and teachers were quick to spread the message of the superiority of their religion and civilization.

Muslim responses to Europe's political/religious penetration and dominance varied significantly, ranging from resistance or warfare in "defense of Islam" to accommodation to Western values, if not outright assimilation. Some advocated following the example of the Prophet Muhammad, who in the face of rejection and persecution in Mecca chose initially to emigrate from Mecca to Medina and later to fight. However, the military defense of Islam and Muslim territory generally proved fruitless in the face of the large, modernized weapons of superior European forces; and emigration to a "safe, independent" Muslim territory was logistically and physically impossible for most.

The response of many Muslim rulers, from Egypt to Iran, was an attempt to emulate or adopt that which had made the West triumphant, its knowledge, science, and technology as well as its culture. From Muhammad Ali, an early nineteenth-century ruler of Egypt, to the shahs of Iran in the twentieth century, the goal was development of modernized societies with modern militaries. Even Muslim rulers who sought an end to Western hegemony seemed convinced of the superiority of the culture and were drawn by its accomplishments and power. Students were sent to the West to study, to learn the sources of its success. "Modern" schools and institutions, based on European models and curricula, were created in many parts of the Muslim world to provide a "modern" education for a new generation. As a result, a modern elite quickly emerged.

Modern Muslim elites, intellectually and culturally influenced by, if not dependent on, the West, regarded the traditional Muslim religious establishment, the *ulama* or scholars who interpreted Islam, as relics of the past, incapable of inspiring and responding to the demands of the day. Most advocated a Western, secular model of development, and to this end they favored appropriating Western political, economic, and social institutions. In addition, however, they wanted to introduce a process of secularization, entailing separation of church and state and the restriction of religion to private, rather than public, life.

Islamic Modernism

In the late nineteenth and early twentieth centuries, Islamic reformers sought to bridge the gap between conservative religious leaders and modernizing secular elites, to demonstrate that Islam was compatible with modernization. Islamic modernists advocated a bold reinterpretation (*ijtihad*) of religious doctrine and practice in light of the needs of modernizing societies through programs of religious, educational, and social reform. They rejected the tendency of many *ulama* to cling blindly to past traditions and religious interpretations no less than the indiscriminate Westernization promoted by many secular modernists.

Islamic modernism asserted the compatibility of faith and reason, of Islam and modernity. It provided an Islamic rationale for the reinterpretation of Islamic doctrine and law, for the adoption or adaptation of modern ideas, science, technology, and institutions. Declaring Islam to be a religion of reason, science, and progress, reformers called on Muslims to reclaim the beliefs, attitudes, and values that had made the Islamic community so successful in the past, contributing to the creation of Islamic empires and a world-class civilization.

Maintaining that the decline of the Muslim community was not due to Islam but to Muslims' departure from the dynamic faith of Muhammad, Islamic reformers advocated a process of purification and reconstruction, of renewal and reform, to overcome what they viewed as the prevailing static medieval religious worldview. Centers of Islamic modernist thought sprang up across the Muslim world from Cairo to Jakarta.

Islamic modernism challenged both the doctrines and the leadership of the conservative religious establishments, rejecting blind acceptance of the authority of the past. Many of these reformers were not traditionally trained religious scholars but modern educated "laymen" who claimed the right to interpret and reinterpret Islam. They repudiated the authority of the *ulama* as the sole "keepers of Islam" as well as the tradition that the *ulama's* legal doctrines/interpretations were binding.

The rationale of Islamic modernism was simple: The corpus of Islamic law consisted, on the one hand, of divinely revealed and thus immutable laws and, on the other, of laws that were human interpretations that met the needs of past historical and social contexts and were therefore subject to change to accommodate modern circumstances and conditions. Thus, they distinguished between the unchanging laws of God (observances governing prayer, fasting, pilgrimage) and social legislation or regulations that were capable of reformulation and change.

Islamic modernism inspired movements for religious reform and for national independence but remained primarily attractive to the intellectual elite. Its major contribution was to provide much of the vocabulary for Islamic reformism and to legitimate a modernist agenda. In particular, it stressed the compatibility of religion and reason, the need for reinterpretation of traditional sources, and thus the need for religious, political, and social reforms. Islamic modernism provided the precedent for accepting or Islamizing "modern" ideas and institutions (from the nation-state and parliamentary government to women's education) as well as the notion that those qualified to interpret Islam should be extended beyond the monopoly exercised historically by the *ulama*. However, it failed to produce a systematic reinterpretation of Islam or to develop effective organizations to preserve, propagate, and implement its message. These failures contributed to the emergence of revivalist activist organizations like the Muslim Brotherhood in Egypt and the Islamic Society in South Asia.

Modern Revivalist (Fundamentalist) Movements

The presence and power of Europe in the Muslim world and the seeming failure of reformers to block Western political and cultural penetration effectively spawned two major Islamic revivalist movements in the Middle East and South Asia in the 1930s, the Muslim Brotherhood (*Ikhwan al-Muslimin*) and the Islamic Society (*Jamaat-i-Islami*). Islamic activist organizations have been the driving force behind the dynamic spread of the contemporary Islamic resurgence. Their trailblazers, Hassan al-Banna (1906–49) and Sayyid Qutb (1906–66) of the Brotherhood and Mawlana Abul Ala Mawdudi (1903–79) of the *Jamaat*, have had an incalculable impact on the development of Islamic movements throughout the Muslim world. Both movements constructed an ideological worldview based on an interpretation of Islam that informed social and political activism. Their founders are the architects of contemporary Islamic revivalism, men whose ideas and methods have been studied and emulated by scholars and activists from the Sudan to Indonesia.

Hassan al-Banna, a schoolteacher, established the Muslim Brotherhood in Egypt in 1928, and Mawlana Abul Ala Mawdudi, a journalist, organized the *Jamaat-i-Islami* in India in 1941. Both leaders combined traditional Islamic educational backgrounds with knowledge of modern Western thought. Believing that their societies were dominated by and dependent on the West, politically and culturally, both al-Banna and Mawdudi posited an "Islamic alternative" to conservative religious leaders and modern elites, whose orientation was Western and secular. The *ulama* were generally regarded as passé, a religious class whose fossilized Islam and co-optation by governments was a major reason for the backwardness of the Islamic community. Modernists were seen as having traded away the very soul of Muslim society out of blind admiration for the West.

The Brotherhood and the *Jamaat* proclaimed Islam to be a self-sufficient, all-encompassing way of life, an ideological alternative to Western capitalism and Marxism. These movements did not simply retreat to the past. Joining thought to action, they provided Islamic responses, ideological and organizational, to their twentieth-century Muslim societies to address such issues as how best to respond to European colonialism and to revitalize the Muslim community. In contrast to Islamic modernists who justified adopting Western ideas and institutions because they were compatible with Islam, al-Banna and Mawdudi sought to produce new interpretations, using Islamic sources. For Hassan al-Banna and Mawlana Mawdudi, the cultural penetration of the West in education, law, customs, and values, which threatened the very identity and survival of the Muslim community, was far more dangerous in the long run than political intervention.

Though they opposed Westernization, the Brotherhood and the *Jamaat* were not against modernization per se. They engaged in modern organization and institution building, provided modern educational and social welfare services, and used modern technology and mass communications to spread their message and to mobilize popular support. Their message itself, though rooted in Islamic revelation and sources, was clearly written for a twentieth-century audience. It addressed the problems of modernity as seen through Muslim eyes: government accountability, the relationship of Islam to nationalism, democracy, capitalism, Marxism, modern banking, educational and legal reform, women and work, Zionism, and international relations.

Organizationally, the Brotherhood and the *Jamaat* believed that, like Muhammad and the early Muslim community in Mecca, they were a vanguard, righteous communities within the broader *ummah* of Islam. Both organizations recruited followers from mosques, schools, and universities: students, workers, merchants, and young professionals, primarily city dwellers from the lower middle and middle classes. The goal was to produce a new generation of modern, educated, but Islamically oriented leaders prepared to take their place in every sector of society.

RITUALS AND RITES: Ideological Origins of Contemporary Revivalism

Despite differences, Hassan al-Banna and Mawlana Mawdudi shared the following ideological worldview based on a historical tradition that has inspired and guided many contemporary reform movements.

1. Islam is a comprehensive way of life, a total, all-embracing ideology for personal and public life, for state and society.
2. The Quran, God's revelation, and the example (Sunnah) of the Prophet Muhammad are its foundations.
3. Islamic law (the sharia, the "path" of God), based on the Quran and Sunnah, is the sacred blueprint for Muslim life.
4. Faithfulness to the Muslim's vocation to reestablish God's sovereignty or rule through implementation of God's law results in success, power, and wealth of

the Islamic community (*ummah*) in this life as well as eternal reward in the next.

5. Muslim societies fail and become subservient to others because they have strayed from God's divinely revealed path, following the secular, materialistic ideologies and values of the West or of the East—capitalism or Marxism.
6. Restoration of Muslim pride, identity, power, and rule (the past glory of Islamic empires and civilization) requires a return to Islam, the reimplementation of God's law, and the acceptance of God's guidance for state and society.
7. Science and technology must be harnessed and used within an Islamically oriented and guided context to avoid the Westernization and secularization of Muslim society.

While al-Banna and Mawdudi viewed an Islamic revolution as necessary to introduce an Islamic state and society, they advocated a process of reform rather than violent political revolution. To establish an Islamic state required first the Islamization of society through a gradual process of social change. Both the Brotherhood and the *Jamaat* maintained that Muslims should not look to Western capitalism or communism and that faith in the West was misplaced. Western democracy had not only failed to check but also had contributed to authoritarianism, economic exploitation, corruption, and social injustice. These early Islamic activists believed that the inherent fallacy of Western secularism, separation of religion and the state, would be responsible for the moral decline and ultimate downfall of the West. Finally, the Brotherhood maintained that years of Arab subservience to the West had not prevented the West from betraying Arabs by supporting Israeli occupation of Palestine.

Radical Islam

The worldviews and interpretations of Hassan al-Banna and Mawlana Mawdudi were shaped by their historical and social contexts as much as by faith. The Muslim Brotherhood had a confrontation with the Egyptian state in the late 1950s and 1960s that caused a group within the movement to become more militant and radicalized. The chief architect of this transformation, Sayyid Qutb, recast the ideological beliefs of Hassan al-Banna and Mawlana Mawdudi into a rejectionist revolutionary call to arms.

Like Hassan al-Banna, Sayyid Qutb had studied at a modern college established to train teachers. A devout Muslim, he had memorized the Quran as a child. Like many young intellectuals of the time, he studied Western literature and grew up an admirer of the West. Qutb was a prolific writer and an active participant in contemporary literary and social debates.

In 1949, a turning point in his life, Qutb traveled to the United States to study educational organization. Although he had come to the United States out of admiration, Qutb's experiences convinced him that the sexual permissiveness, moral decadence, and anti-Arab bias, which he perceived in U.S. government and media support for Israel, had corrupted all of Western civilization. Shortly after his return to Egypt in 1951, Sayyid Qutb joined the Muslim Brotherhood.

During the 1950s, Qutb emerged as a major voice of the Muslim Brotherhood, especially influential among the younger, more militant members. Government harassment of the Brotherhood and Qutb's imprisonment and torture in 1954, for alleged involvement in an attempt to assassinate Egyptian strongman Gamal Abdel Nasser, increased his radicalization and made his worldview even more confrontational. During ten years of imprisonment, he wrote prolifically. In his most influential Islamic ideological tract, *Signposts*, or *Milestones*, he took the ideas of Hassan al-Banna and especially Mawlana Mawdudi to a militant radical revolutionary conclusion.

Qutb regarded Egypt and other Muslim governments as repressive and anti-Islamic. Society was divided into two camps, the party of God and the party of Satan, those committed to the rule of God and those opposed to it. There was no middle ground between the forces of good and of evil. Qutb advocated a vanguard, a group of true Muslims within the broader, corrupted society. The Islamic movement was a righteous minority adrift in a sea of ignorance and unbelief. Muslim governments and societies alike were seen as un-Islamic, atheist, or pagan entities.

Qutb maintained that the creation of an Islamic system of government was a divine commandment and therefore an imperative, not an alternative. Given the authoritarianism of many regimes, Qutb concluded that *jihad* as armed struggle was the only way to implement a new Islamic order. Islam, he declared, stood on the brink of disaster, threatened by repressive anti-Islamic governments and the neocolonialism of the West and the East. Qutb went beyond his predecessors when he declared Muslim elites and governments atheists as enemies of God, against whom all true believers should wage holy war. Many later radical groups have used Qutb's formulation of the two options to bring about change: evolution—a process that emphasizes change from below, or revolution—violent overthrow of established (un-Islamic) systems of government.

In 1966, Qutb and several other Muslim Brotherhood leaders were executed. Thousands of Brothers were arrested and tortured, while others went underground or fled the country. Many concluded that the Brotherhood had been crushed, a prediction that was to prove false a decade later.

It is difficult to overstate the impact of Hassan al-Banna, Mawlana Mawdudi, and Sayyid Qutb. Their worldviews and organizations became formative influences for contemporary Islamic movements. Combining religiopolitical activism with social protest or reform, contemporary Islamic movements represent a spectrum of positions from moderation and gradualism to radicalism and revolutionary violence, from selective criticism of the West to rejection and attacks on all that the West stands for. Indeed, these movements reflect the multiple issues facing Muslims in their struggle to determine the relationship of Islam to modern state and society:

- countering Western political and cultural hegemony
- dealing with the seeming challenge of modernity to Islamic belief
- redefining Islam and its relevance to modern life and society
- addressing the clash of cultures not only between the West and the Muslim world but within Muslim societies over religious and national identity and development

Islam and Postmodern Trends in a Postcolonial World

The Impact of the Islamic Resurgence

Since the last decades of the twentieth century, the Muslim world has experienced the impact of the contemporary resurgence of Islam. New Islamic governments or republics were established in Iran, Sudan, and Afghanistan. Rulers, political parties, and opposition movements used Islam in attempting to attract supporters. Islamic activists have led governments, served in cabinets and in the elected parliaments, and served as senior officials in professional associations. At the same time, a minority of radical Islamic organizations in Egypt, Algeria, Lebanon, the West Bank, and Gaza have engaged in violence and terrorism to topple governments or to achieve related goals. Extremists have left a legacy of kidnapping, hijacking, bombing, and murder from the Middle East to Southeast Asia, from Paris to New York and Washington. Understanding this complex and multifaceted phenomenon is often difficult and requires an awareness of its roots and sources. What were the causes and conditions that led to the contemporary resurgence of Islam?

Islam in Modern State and Society

A map of the modern Muslim world reveals both old and new realities and begins to explain visually the upheaval in Muslim societies. During the twentieth century, former Islamic empires and sultanates were replaced by modern nation-states, carved out by European colonial powers after World War I. By World War II, most of these newly designated states had won their independence, but it was an independence of artificial creations, and the new rulers, in Jordan, Syria, and Iraq had been placed on their thrones by Britain or France. Moreover, European education, culture, and values strongly influenced the elites in most states and societies. As a result, issues of government legitimacy as well as of national and cultural identity remained unresolved. After World War II, the stability of many rulers was due more to Western or Soviet support and strong military-security apparatus than to supportive indigenous culture or widespread political participation.

Once these modern nation-states had been created in the Muslim world, it was expected that they would generally follow a "modern," that is, Western, secular path of development. Outwardly, this seemed to be the general case. While Saudi Arabia proclaimed itself an Islamic state, based on the Quran and *sharia* law, most new nations adopted or adapted Western political, legal, social, economic, and educational institutions and values. In contrast to Saudi Arabia, Turkey positioned itself at the opposite end of the religion-versus-secularism spectrum. Under the leadership of Mustafa Kemal Ataturk, it suppressed Islamic institutions, banned Islamic dress and Islamic law, and transplanted Western secular laws and institutions to create its own version of a secular state.

However, Egypt, Syria, Iraq, Pakistan, Malaysia, and Indonesia created what may be called "Muslim states." In these and most other countries in the Islamic world, the majority populations are Muslim, but, despite some religious prescriptions, Western-inspired institutions have been adopted: parliaments, political party systems, legal codes, educational systems and curricula, banks, and insurance companies. Western dress, movies, and culture became prominent and pervasive among the wealthy and powerful in urban centers.

Throughout much of the twentieth century, progress and prosperity in Muslim societies were regarded by most governments and by those with key positions in government and society as dependent on the degree to which Muslims and their societies were "modern." The degree of progress and success for individuals, cities, and governments was measured in terms of conformity to Western standards and values. Based on these criteria, Turkey, Tunisia, Egypt, Lebanon, and Iran were often seen as among the more modern, advanced, and "enlightened," that is, Westernized and secular, countries. Saudi Arabia, the states of the Persian Gulf, Afghanistan, Bangladesh, and Pakistan were generally regarded as more traditional, religious, and thus "backward."

The Failure of Modernity and the Islamic Revival

The 1960s and 1970s shattered the hopes and dreams of many who believed that national independence and Western-oriented development would usher in strong states and prosperous societies. These were decades that proved a powerful catalyst for a religious resurgence and revival. The crises of many Muslim societies underscored the failure of many governments and societies to become strong and prosperous, even after national independence. The realities of many Muslim societies raised profound questions of national identity and the political legitimacy of rulers as well as of religious faith and meaning. Such pervasive conditions as poverty, illiteracy, failed economies, high unemployment, and unequal distribution of wealth could not be blamed entirely on Western influences.

The signs of these profound problems would not become fully appreciated in the West until the Iranian revolution of 1978–79. There were previews, however, during the preceding decade: the 1967 Arab-Israeli war, Malay-Chinese riots in Kuala Lumpur in 1969, the Pakistan-Bangladesh civil war of 1971, and Lebanon's civil war of the mid-1970s. Such catalytic events triggered a soul-searching reassessment among many Muslims. Their disillusionment and dissatisfaction were accompanied by an Islamic revival, a quest for self-identity and greater authenticity, as many reaffirmed the importance of Islam and Islamic values in their personal and social lives. Along with a reemphasis on religious identity and practice (prayer, fasting, dress, and values) came an equally visible appeal to Islam in politics and society made by governments as well as Islamic political and social movements. Islamic ideology, discourse, and politics reemerged as major forces in the development of the Muslim world, forces that both Muslim and Western governments have had to accommodate or contend with for several decades.

The return of Islam as an international political force was seen by many as signaling a return of God's guidance and favor. However, the fall of the shah and an *ulama*-led revolution were as threatening for many Sunni Muslim governments and elites, especially those in Gulf states like Iraq, Saudi Arabia, Bahrain, and Kuwait, which have significant Shia populations, as these events were to the West, America and Europe.

Perhaps the most significant symbolic event, which sparked Muslim disillusionment and dissatisfaction, was the 1967 Arab-Israeli war, now often called the Six-Day War. Israel defeated the combined forces of Egypt, Syria, Iraq, and Jordan in a "preemptive" strike, which the Israeli government justified as necessary to counter a planned Arab attack. The Arabs experienced a massive loss of territory: Sinai, Gaza, the West Bank, and in particular Jerusalem, the third-holiest city (after Mecca and Medina) of Islam.

Muslims, like Jews and Christians, for centuries have looked to Jerusalem, a city central to Muslim faith and identity, a place of religious shrines and pilgrimage. Muslims hold Jerusalem to be sacred because of its association with prophets (from David and Solomon to Jesus) and because of its central role in the Prophet Muhammad's Night Journey and ascension.

When Muslim armies took Jerusalem without resistance in 635, they built a large mosque (al-Aqsa) and then a magnificent shrine, the Dome of the Rock, on the site associated with the Night Journey and the biblical site of Abraham's sacrifice and Solomon's temple. Muslim loss of Jerusalem in the 1967 war was a traumatic experience, which made Palestine and the Arab-Israeli conflict not just an Arab Muslim and Arab Christian issue but a worldwide Islamic issue. Many who asked what had gone wrong also wanted to know why Israel had been able to defeat the combined Arab forces. Were the weakness and failure of Muslim societies due to their faith? Was Islam incompatible with modernity and thus the cause of Arab backwardness and impotence? Had God abandoned the Muslims? These were questions that had been raised before.

The Dome of the Rock in Jerusalem, a major holy site and place of pilgrimage erected by the Umayyad caliph Abd al-Malik, was completed in 692. The famous shrine is built on the spot from which Muslims believe Muhammad ascended to God and then returned to the world. In this story, one of the grand themes of Islamic scholarship and popular piety, the Prophet, in the company of the angel Gabriel, was transported at night from the Kaaba in Mecca to Jerusalem. From there, he ascended to the heavens and the presence of God.

As we have seen, from the seventeenth to the nineteenth centuries, internal threats to Muslim societies were followed by the external threat of European colonialism. The mid-twentieth century, however, was a period of independence and Muslim self-rule. The failures of the "modern experiment" led many to turn, or perhaps more accurately to return, to a more authentic, indigenous alternative to modern nationalism and socialism. Despite significant differences from one country to the next, many Muslims worldwide sought an Islamic alternative to Western capitalism and Soviet Marxism. In this context, Islam became a rallying cry and symbol for political organization and mass mobilization.

The Religious Worldview of Contemporary Islamic Activism

Islamic activists shared the following beliefs or points of ideology:

1. Islam, a comprehensive way of life, is and must be integral to politics and society.
2. The failures of Muslim societies were caused by departing from the path of Islam and depending on Western secularism, which separates religion and politics.
3. Muslims must return to the Quran and the example of the Prophet Muhammad and reintroduce Islamic laws.
4. Modern development must be guided by Islamic values rather than those that would lead to Westernization and secularization of society.

As Islamic symbols, slogans, ideology, leaders, and organizations became prominent fixtures in Muslim politics, religion was increasingly used both by governments and by reform and opposition movements to enhance their legitimacy and to mobilize popular support. Islamic movements and organizations sprang up across the Muslim world. A variety of opposition movements appealed to Islam: In Iran Ayatollah Khomeini led the "Islamic revolution" of 1979–80; militants seized the Grand Mosque in Mecca in 1979, calling for the overthrow of the government; religious extremists assassinated Egyptian President Anwar Sadat in 1981. At the same time, Afghan freedom fighters (*mujahideen*, "holy warriors") in the late 1970s and early 1980s led a resistance movement against the Soviet Union's invasion and occupation. Islamic movements and organizations throughout the 1980s created or extended their influence over religious, educational, social, cultural, and financial institutions as well as professional organizations of physicians, lawyers, and journalists.

The leadership of most Islamic organizations (particularly Sunni groups) was and remains outside the control of the *ulama*. Many have degrees in modern science, medicine, law, engineering, computer science, and education. Most Islamic organizations have attracted individuals from every stratum of society. While the majority of Islamic organizations work within the system, a minority of radical extremists insist that Muslim rulers are anti-Islamic and that violence and revolution are the only way to liberate society and impose an Islamic way of life.

From the Periphery to Mainstream Politics and Society

The 1980s were dominated by fear of "radical Islamic fundamentalism," embodied in Iran's announced desire to export its "Islamic fundamentalist revolution" and the activities of clandestine extremist groups. Feeding these fears were disturbances by Shiah in Saudi Arabia, Kuwait, and Bahrain; Iran's strong backing of a Lebanese Shiah group, Hezbollah, which emerged in response to the Israeli invasion and occupation of Lebanon; and a series of hijackings, kidnappings, and bombings of Western embassies. Although Muslim rulers and Western leaders alike were on edge, no other "Irans" occurred.

By the late 1980s and early 1990s, it was increasingly clear that a quiet, or nonviolent, revolution had taken place in many parts of the Muslim world. Islamic revivalism and activism had in many contexts become institutionalized in mainstream society. From Egypt to Malaysia, Islam played a more visible and important role in socioeconomic and political life. Islamically inspired social and political activism produced schools, clinics and hospitals, and social service agencies, such as day care, legal aid, and youth centers. Private mosques were established alongside those controlled by governments, and financial institutions such as Islamic banks and insurance companies appeared. In addition, an alternative elite emerged consisting of modern educated but Islamically (rather than secularly) oriented doctors, engineers, lawyers, businesspeople, university professors, military officers, and laborers. Perhaps nowhere was the impact of the Islamic revival experienced more visibly than in political elections.

The majority of Muslim countries are under authoritarian rule, a legacy of premodern Muslim history, European colonial rule, and post-independence. During the late 1980s, in response to "food riots," protests, and mass demonstrations over the economic failures of governments, elections were held in authoritarian countries like Jordan, Tunisia, Algeria, and Egypt. Participating Islamic organizations such as the Muslim Brotherhoods of Jordan and Egypt, Tunisia's Nahda (Renaissance) party, and Algeria's Islamic Salvation Front (FIS) emerged as the major political opposition.

In Algeria, the FIS swept municipal and, later, parliamentary elections and thus was poised to come to power peacefully, through the electoral process. The Algerian military intervened, however, installing a new government, canceling the election results, and imprisoning and outlawing the FIS. This set in motion a spiral of violence and counterviolence that polarized Algerian society and produced a civil war costing more than 100,000 lives.

By the mid-1990s, Islamic activists could be found in the cabinets and parliaments of many countries and in the leadership of professional organizations. In Turkey, the most secular of Muslim states, the Welfare (Refah) party swept mayoral elections, and in 1995 Turkey elected its first Islamist prime minister and also the leader of the

Welfare Party, Dr. Necmettin Erbakan. The Turkish military, claiming the need to save Turkish secularism, brought about the resignation of Erbakan and was influential in having the party outlawed and some of its leaders imprisoned.

The Road to 9/11

At the same time, radical extremist groups such as Egypt's *Gamaa Islamiyya* (Islamic Group) and Islamic Jihad attacked Christian churches, businesses, foreign tourists, and security forces. Extremists were convicted in the United States and Europe for terrorist acts, such as the 1993 bombing of the World Trade Center in New York. Terrorist attacks increased throughout the decade. Osama bin Laden was increasingly regarded as the "godfather" of global terrorism and a major funder of extremist groups. His involvement was suspected in the bombing of the World Trade Center in 1993, the killing of eighteen American soldiers in Somalia in 1993, and bombings in Riyadh in 1995 and in Dhahran in 1996. In February 1998, bin Laden and other militant leaders announced the creation of a transnational coalition of extremist groups, the World Islamic Front for Jihad Against Jews and Crusaders. His own organization, al-Qaeda, was linked to a series of acts of terrorism: the truck bombing of American embassies in Kenya and Tanzania in August 1998 that killed 263 people and injured more than 5,000, followed in October 2000 by a suicide bombing attack against the USS *Cole*, which killed seventeen American sailors.

September 11, 2001, would prove to be a watershed, signaling the extent to which Muslim extremists had become a global threat, in particular emphasizing the role of Osama bin Laden and al-Qaeda in global terrorism.[10]

Bin Laden's message appealed to the feelings of many in the Arab and Muslim world. A sharp critic of American foreign policy toward the Muslim world, he denounced U.S. support for Israel and sanctions against Iraq, which he said had resulted in the deaths of hundreds of thousands of civilians. He dismissed as the "new crusades" the substantial American military presence and economic involvement in his native Saudi Arabia. To these messages were added other populist reminders of Muslim suffering in Bosnia, Kosovo, Chechnya, and Kashmir.[11]

Al-Qaeda represented a new global terrorism, associated at first with the Muslims

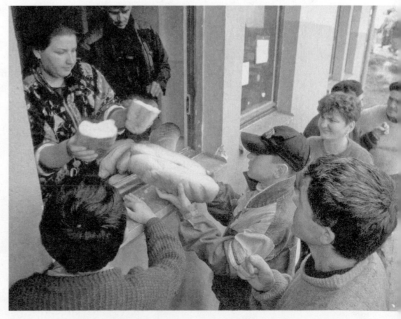

The ethnic warfare that accompanied the breakup of Yugoslavia had tragic effects in Bosnia, one of the oldest Muslim communities in Europe. Refugees of all ages, at Mihatovici, near Tuzla, line up to receive food.

CONTRASTING RELIGIOUS VISIONS

As the following contrasting visions indicate, every religious tradition is capable of generating both visions that encourage peace and understanding and visions that encourage conflict and violence.

Muhammad Iqbal (1876–1938)

Educated at Government College in Lahore, Pakistan, he studied in England and Germany, where he earned a law degree and a doctorate in philosophy. Iqbal's modern synthesis and reinterpretation of Islam combined the best of the East and the West, his Islamic heritage with Western philosophy. Both admirer and critic of the West, Iqbal acknowledged the West's dynamic spirit, intellectual tradition, and technology but was sharply critical of European colonialism as well as of the materialism and exploitation of capitalism, the atheism of Marxism, and the moral bankruptcy of secularism.

The Reconstruction of Religious Thought in Islam succinctly summarizes Iqbal's reformist vision, which can also be accessed in his extensive writings and poetry. Like other Islamic modernists, Iqbal rejected much of medieval Islam as static and stagnant. He saw Islam as emerging from 500 years of "dogmatic slumber" and compared the need for Islamic reform now to that confronting Christianity at the time of the Reformation. Iqbal emphasized the need to reclaim the vitality and dynamism of early Islamic thought and practice, calling for a bold reinterpretation (*ijtihad*) of Islam. He attempted to develop alternative Islamic models for modern Muslim societies. Thus, for example, drawing on Islamic traditions, he sought to "rediscover" Islamic principles and values that would provide the basis for Islamic versions of Western concepts and institutions such as democracy and parliamentary government.

Osama bin Laden (1957–2011)

Born in Riyadh, Saudi Arabia, bin Laden received a degree in public administration in 1981 from King Abdul-Aziz University. A major turning point in bin Laden's adult life occurred in 1979, when the Soviets occupied Afghanistan. From 1979 to 1982, he used his financial resources to support vigorously the *jihadi* resistance against the Soviets, providing construction materials, building roads and airfields, and then moving to Afghanistan to set up his own camps and command Arab *mujahideen* forces, who became known as "Arab Afghans." He later created al-Qaeda, "the base," to organize and track the fighters and funds being channeled into the Afghan resistance.

Bin Laden's opposition to the American-led coalition in the Gulf War of 1991 placed him on a collision course with the Saudi government and the West. In 1994 the kingdom revoked bin Laden's citizenship and moved to freeze his assets because of his support for militant fundamentalist movements. Bin Laden joined other dissident activists and religious scholars, moving to Sudan and then back to Afghanistan. Assuming a vocal leadership role in international terrorism, in 1996 he issued a Declaration of Jihad, created to drive the United States out of Arabia, overthrow the Saudi government, liberate Islam's holy sites of Mecca and Medina, and support revolutionary groups around the world. In 2000 he was among the founders of the World Islamic Front for the Jihad Against Jews and Crusaders, an umbrella group of radical movements across the Muslim world, and issued a *fatwa* emphasizing the duty of all Muslims to kill U.S. citizens and their allies.

who had gone to Afghanistan to fight the occupying Soviets in the 1980s, and re-flected in acts of terrorism in Central, South, and Southeast Asia, often attributed to the influence of Saudi Arabia and Wahhabi Islam. Bin Laden and other terrorists transformed Islam's norms about the defense of Islam and Muslims under siege to legitimate the use of violence, warfare, and terrorism. Their theology of hate espouses a bipolar view of a cosmic struggle between the armies of God and of Satan, the forces of good and evil, right and wrong, belief and unbelief: those who are not with them, Muslim or non-Muslim, are judged to be against them. These extremists "hijacked" the Islamic concept and institution of *jihad* in an attempt to lend legitimacy to their acts of violence and terror.

Globalization and Hijacking of *Jihad*

Since the late twentieth century the word *jihad* has gained remarkable currency. On the one hand, the term's primary Quranic religious and spiritual meanings became more widespread: *Jihad* was the "struggle" or effort to follow God's path, to lead a moral life, and to promote social justice. On the other hand, the idea of *jihad* as armed struggle has been widely used by resistance, liberation, and terrorist movements alike to legitimate their cause and recruit followers. Thus the Afghan *mujahideen* waged *jihad* in Afghanistan against the Soviet Union and subsequently among themselves; Muslims in Kashmir, Chechnya, the southern Philippines, Bosnia, and Kosovo have fashioned their struggles as *jihads*; Hezbollah, Hamas, and Islamic Jihad Palestine have characterized war with Israel as a *jihad*; and Osama bin Laden, speaking as head of al-Qaeda, declared global *jihad*, targeting Muslim governments as well as the West. Understanding the multiple meanings of *jihad* is critical to understanding Islam and Muslim politics today.

   Jihad is a term with multiple meanings and usages, both past and present. The central importance of *jihad* is rooted in the Quran's command to "struggle or exert" (the literal meaning of the word *jihad*) oneself in the path of God. *Jihad* has several major meanings. First and foremost it refers to the moral struggle to be virtuous, to do good works. Depending on circumstances, it also can mean fighting injustice and oppression, spreading and defending Islam, and creating a just society through preaching, teaching, and, if necessary, armed struggle. These two broad meanings of *jihad*, nonviolent and violent, are contrasted in a well-known tradition that reports that when Muhammad returned from battle, he told his followers, "We return from the lesser jihad to the greater jihad." The greater *jihad* is the more difficult and more important struggle against one's ego, selfishness, greed, and evil.

Jihad as Armed Struggle

The earliest Quranic verses dealing with the right to engage in a "defensive," armed *jihad* were revealed shortly after the *hijra* (emigration) of Muhammad and his followers to Medina. At a time when they were fleeing from persecution in Mecca and forced to fight for their lives, Muhammad is told in the Quran: "Leave is given to those who fight because they were wronged—surely God is able to help them—who were expelled from their homes wrongfully for saying, 'Our Lord is God'" (Q. 22:39–40). The defensive nature of *jihad* is emphasized in 2:190, "And fight in the way of God with those who fight you, but aggress not: God loves not the aggressors."

The Quran and Islamic law provide detailed guidelines and regulations regarding the conduct of war: who is to fight and who is exempted (48:17, 9:91); when hostilities must cease (2:192); and how prisoners should be treated (47:4). Verses such as 2:294 emphasize that warfare and the response to violence and aggression must be proportional: "Whoever transgresses against you, respond in kind." From the earliest times, it was forbidden in Islam to kill noncombatants as well as women and children and monks and rabbis, who were promised immunity unless they took part in the fighting.

But what of those Quranic verses, sometimes referred to as the *sword verses*, that call for killing unbelievers, such as "When the sacred months have passed, slay the idolaters wherever you find them, and take them, and confine them, and lie in wait for them at every place of ambush" (9:5)? This is one of a number of Quranic verses that are cited by critics to demonstrate the inherently violent nature of Islam and selectively used (or abused) by some Muslim religious extremists to develop a theology of hate and intolerance and to legitimate unconditional warfare against unbelievers. The privileging of the sword verses dates back to the early centuries of Islam.

During the period of expansion and conquest, many of the *ulama* (religious scholars) enjoyed royal patronage and provided a rationale for caliphs to pursue their imperial dreams and, in the name of spreading Islam, to extend the boundaries of their empires. Classical jurists argued that the sword verses (9:5 and 9:123) abrogated, or canceled, the earlier verses that limited *jihad* to defensive war, thus permitting unprovoked military action in the cause of God. However, the full intent of the sword verse "When the sacred months have passed, slay the idolaters wherever you find them" is missed or distorted. First, the verse refers to the specific context: The early Muslims were being persecuted and attacked by their Meccan enemy. The term *idolaters* here refers to the Meccan polytheists, not to "unbelievers" in general or, as extremists would hold, to Jews and Christians. Second, the tendency to quote the first part of the verse in isolation distorts the full intent of the passage, which is followed and qualified by: "But if they repent and fulfill their devotional obligations and pay the zakat [the charitable tax on Muslims], then let them go their way, for God is forgiving and kind" (9:5).

Bin Laden and other terrorists choose the selective militant interpretation of the so-called sword verses, ignore the criteria of Islamic law for a just *jihad*, and recognize no limits but their own. They reject the tenets of Islamic law regarding the goals and means of a valid *jihad*: that the use of violence must be proportional; that innocent civilians, noncombatants, should not be targeted; and that *jihad* can be declared only by a ruler or head of state. Today, extremists from Madrid to Mindanao legitimate unholy wars in the name of Islam itself, bypassing the Quranic requirement that authorization for *jihad* be given by a nation's ruler.

While bin Laden and al-Qaeda have enjoyed support from a significant minority of Muslims and religious leaders, the majority of Muslims and major Islamic scholars and religious leaders across the Muslim world condemned such attacks as unjustified. For example, the Gallup Organization in 2005–8 surveyed some thirty-five predominantly Muslim countries (from Morocco and Pakistan to Indonesia) as part of its World Poll. The vast majority (93 percent) of all those polled said the 9/11 attacks were unjustified; 7 percent said the attacks were completely justified. The Islamic Research Council at al-Azhar University, regarded by many as the highest moral authority in Islam, and other prominent religious leaders issued authoritative declarations (*fatwas*) against bin Laden's and other terrorists' initiatives:

> Islam provides clear rules and ethical norms that forbid the killing of non-combatants, as well as women, children, and the elderly, and also forbids the pursuit of the enemy in defeat, the execution of those who surrender, the infliction of harm on prisoners of war, and the destruction of property that is not being used in the hostilities.[12]

Timothy Winter (Abdul Hakim Murad), a British Muslim, Cambridge University professor, and prominent Muslim religious leader, represents many Muslims in his clear and straightforward rejection of Al-Qaeda as religiously illegitimate and inauthentic. Winter dismisses bin Laden and his right-hand man, Ayman al-Zawahiri, as unqualified, un-Islamic vigilantes who violate basic Islamic teachings:

> Their proclamations ignore fourteen centuries of Muslim scholarship, . . . [and they use] lists of anti-American grievances and of Koranic quotations referring to early Muslim wars against Arab idolators. . . . All this amounts to an odd and extreme violation of the normal methods of Islamic scholarship. . . . An insurrectionist who kills noncombatants is guilty of *baghy*, "armed transgression," a capital offence in Islamic law. A jihad can be proclaimed only by a properly constituted state; anything else is pure vigilantism.[13]

Suicide Bombing: War of the *Fatwas*

Few issues have been more contentious among religious authorities than suicide bombing, demonstrating the extent to which both sacred texts and human interpretation of sociopolitical contexts influence the formulation of *fatwas*. The issue of suicide bombing and the question of its legitimacy or illegitimacy crystallized in the Israeli-Palestinian conflict during the second intifada. Amid escalating Israeli and Palestinian violence, many Palestinians and other Arabs argued that suicide bombers were committing not an act of suicide but one of self-sacrifice, the only option for resistance and retaliation against an enemy with overwhelming military power and foreign support. As student posters at universities in the West Bank and Gaza declared: "Israel has nuclear bombs, we have human bombs."

Suicide attacks, especially those that target innocent civilians or noncombatants, have precipitated a sharp debate among prominent religious authorities in the Muslim world. Their advice and *fatwas* illustrate the debate today. Sheikh Ahmad Yasin, the late religious leader and founder of Hamas, as well as many other Arab and Palestinian religious leaders have argued that suicide bombing is necessary and justified when faced with Israel's illegal occupation and overwhelming military power.

Although Yusuf Qaradawi, a prominent religious scholar and public figure, condemns acts of terrorism and suicide bombings, he has made a clear exception when it comes to the Palestinian-Israeli conflict. His strong opposition to Israeli occupation and policies led to early support for suicide bombing in Israel. Qaradawi was one of the first religious scholars to issue a *fatwa* that justified suicide bombings in Israel, based on the premise that Israelis were not civilians but combatants in a war of occupation waged against the Palestinians.

In sharp contrast, Abdul-Aziz Al Al-Shaykh, the former Grand Mufti of Saudi Arabia, condemned all suicide bombing as un-Islamic and forbidden by Islam. Similarly, Timothy Winter rejects any use of suicide bombing and targeting of civilians as an aberration:

> This kind of targeting of civilians, for instance, the aberrant use of terrorist violence, is something that really is very new. . . . It hasn't gained much inroad into the leadership of the religion, but in the masses on the streets, as it were, particularly in very tense, unnatural places like Gaza, the slums of Baghdad, and other places, it does have a certain standing unfortunately. And this is the great challenge of the leadership of the religion—how to reassert orthodoxy in the face of a growing groundswell of fundamentalist revolt.[14]

Post 9/11: Impact and Response

The 9/11 bombings in the United States and subsequent acts of terrorism globally were accompanied in the United States and some European countries by an exponential growth of far right politicians, political commentators, media personalities, and some religious leaders who conflated mainstream Islam with terrorism. They fed an increase in discrimination against Islam and Muslims ("Islamophobia"), resulting in widespread suspicion of mainstream Muslims, hate crimes, and the belief that Islam, not just Muslim extremism, is a threat.

At a 2004 UN conference, "Confronting Islamophobia: Education for Tolerance and Understanding," Kofi Annan addressed the international scope of this problem, warning: "When the world is compelled to coin a new term to take account of increasingly widespread bigotry—that is a sad and troubling development. Such is the case with 'Islamophobia.'"

A *Washington Post*/ABC News poll in 2006 "found that nearly half of Americans—46%—have a negative view of Islam, seven percentage points higher than a few months after Sept. 11, 2001."

In Europe, Islam was overwhelmingly singled out as the religion most prone to violence, with percentages of those who agreed with this ranging from 63 percent in Britain to 87 percent in France and 88 percent in the Netherlands.

In the Gallup World Poll, when U.S. respondents were asked what they admire about the Muslim world, the most common response was "nothing" (33 percent); the second most common was "I don't know" (22 percent). Despite major polling by Gallup and PEW showing that American Muslims are well integrated economically and politically, a January 2010 Gallup Center for Muslim Studies report found that more than 4 in 10 Americans (43 percent) admit to feeling at least "a little" prejudice toward Muslims—more than twice the number who say the same about Christians (18 percent), Jews (15 percent), and Buddhists (14 percent). Nine percent of Americans admitted feeling "a great deal" of prejudice toward Muslims, while 20 percent admitted feeling "some" prejudice. Surprisingly, Gallup data revealed a link between anti-Semitism and Islamophobia, that contempt for Jews makes a person "about 32 times as likely to report the same level of prejudice toward Muslims."

Time Magazine and *The New York Times* in August 2010 reported that 33 percent of those interviewed believed that Muslim Americans were more sympathetic to terrorists and 60 percent had negative feelings about Muslims. Other studies from Gallup, the *Washington Post*, and the Pew Forum indicate similar findings.

Over the years, a common charge has been that Muslims do not condemn terrorism despite the fact that post 9/11 many statements have been issued by Muslim leaders and organizations from all over the world, including a major joint statement by global religious and intellectual leaders (the Amman Message). Unfortunately, major media outlets do not seem to find them "newsworthy," and thus they are relegated to the Internet. See, for example, http://www.ammanmessage.com/; http://www.cair-net.org/html/911statements.html; http://www.beliefnet.com/story/111/story_11121_1.html.

Over the past few decades, the vast majority of American Muslims have become economically and increasingly politically integrated into mainstream American society. Students account for 31 percent of the American Muslim population as compared to 10 percent in the general population; 40 percent have a college degree or more, compared to 29 percent of Americans overall. Muslim women are equal to men in holding college or postgraduate degrees and report incomes nearly equal to men.

Muslims span the socioeconomic spectrum: professionals (doctors, lawyers, engineers, and educators), corporate executives, and small business owners, as well as blue-collar workers. Only 2 percent of Muslims represent low-income families. Seventy percent have a job (paid or unpaid) compared to 64 percent of Americans overall.

Despite this integration, however, many American Muslims believe that they are singled out by the government for extra surveillance. This experience, however, has not soured the attitudes of the majority of Muslims, 71 percent of whom agree that most people who want to get ahead in America can succeed if they are willing to work hard. This is a higher proportion than the American public as a whole.

If some blamed the religion of Islam for the growth of radicalism and the appeal of bin Laden and other terrorist leaders, others identified U.S. and European policies in the Muslim world: uncritical support for authoritarian regimes, Palestinian-Israeli

In China, followers of traditional Islam (Gedimu, from the Arabic for "old," *qadim*) build communities around small central mosques. Muslim men meet here in Beijing for communal prayers in the central congregational mosque.

policies, and the West's double standard in promoting democratization as major catalysts.

That Osama bin Laden and many of the 9/11 hijackers were from Saudi Arabia and Saudi support for some Islamic groups and *madrasas* in countries like Afghanistan and Pakistan have raised questions about the role of Wahhabism in global terrorism. Wahhabi Islam, the official form of Islam in Saudi Arabia, is among the most ultraconservative interpretations of Islam.

As we have seen, the Wahhabi movement takes its name from Muhammad Ibn Abd al-Wahhab and the eighteenth-century revivalist movement. Over time, the ideas of many uncompromising interpreters of Wahhabi Islam have resulted in an ultraconservative or "fundamentalist" brand of Islam: literalist, rigid, puritanical, exclusivist, and intolerant. Wahhabis believe that they are right and all others (other Muslims as well as people of other faiths) are wrong. Presenting their version of Islam as the pristine, pure, unadulterated message of the Prophet, Wahhabis have sought to propagate and sometimes impose throughout the world their strict beliefs and interpretations, which are not shared by the majority of Muslims.

Since the last half of the twentieth century, domestic and foreign conditions have led to the emergence of militant, violent interpretations of Islam. In 1979, when militants seized the Grand Mosque in Mecca, they called for the overthrow of the Saudi monarchy. At the same time, Islamic activists from Egypt and other countries, often fleeing their home governments, had found refuge in Saudi Arabia, teaching in universities and religious schools or working in government ministries and organizations. As a result, alongside the puritanical Wahhabi Islam of the establishment, a radical brand of Wahhabi Islam, having both internal and external sources, infiltrated Saudi society. Its theology and worldview was one of militant *jihad*, domestic and global.

Both government-sponsored organizations and wealthy Saudi individuals have funded the export of Wahhabi Islam, in its mainstream and extremist forms, to other countries and communities in the Muslim world and in the West. Wahhabi theology, funding, and influence were exported to Afghanistan, Pakistan, the Central Asian Republics, China, Africa, Southeast Asia, the United States, and Europe. They offered financial aid for the building of mosques, libraries, and other institutions; funded and distributed religious tracts; and commissioned imams and religious scholars. At the same time, some wealthy businessmen and organizations in Saudi Arabia and the Gulf have provided financial support to extremist groups that actively promote a holy war ("jihadi") culture. The challenge is to distinguish between those who preach and propagate an ultraconservative Wahhabi theology and militant extremists and terrorist organizations. Similar divisions between mainstream Muslims and violent extremists exist in other religions, with Jewish, Christian, and Hindu fundamentalists sometimes acting in ways not condoned by the majority of their coreligionists.

In sharp contrast, in a world in which some in the Muslim world and in the West speak of or even promote a clash of civilizations between the Muslim world and the West, a historic event occurred on October 11, 2007. In a dramatic and groundbreaking display of interreligious solidarity, 138 of the world's most senior Muslim leaders wrote a letter, "A Common Word Between Us and You," to the heads of all Christian churches. The letter's authors—Muslims from around the world and from both the Sunni and Shiah, Salafi and Sufi traditions—declared their belief that with over half of the world's population consisting of Muslims and Christians, meaningful world peace can only come from peace and justice between the two largest global faiths despite their differences. The letter, based on a close study of both the Bible and the Holy Quran, was an open invitation to Christians to unite with Muslims to cooperate in creating peace and understanding and diffusing tensions, based on what is most essential to their respective faiths—the commandments of love: the shared belief of both Muslims and Christians in the principles of love of one God and love of neighbor.

Islam and the Arab Awakening: Between Authoritarianism and Pluralism

The "Arab Spring" or "Arab Awakening" marked a historic transition in the political makeup of countries like Tunisia, Egypt, Libya, and Syria. A broad sector of society, eager for change and democratic reforms, made their voices heard, reclaiming their dignity and national pride and insisting that they would decide the direction and the future of their countries. Though initially not among the leadership, in postuprising elections Islamist candidates and parties swept into power in Egypt (the Muslim Brotherhood's Freedom and Justice Party and Salafi, especially the Noor Party) and Tunisia (Ennahda, the Renaissance, Party), although not in Libya. If many voted for Islamists, many others were dismayed and feared Islamist rule would lead to increased religiosity in politics. Some asked: "Can the Islamists lead?"

Indeed, many in countries like Egypt and Tunisia agreed that election results, while polarizing, were the product of a free and fair process. Far from monolithic, Muslim Brotherhood and Ennahda and Salafis incorporate diverse currents, ideologically, politically, and socioeconomically. Many in leadership positions were challenged to move beyond the elder-dominated hierarchical structure and authority of the past and to engage in greater power sharing by bringing in support from younger representatives and opposition members. American and European policymakers were equally challenged to work with Islamically oriented government leaders. The question of "how" Islam and democracy will be compatible became even more real and relevant. New governments in both Egypt and Tunisia spoke of a civil state with an Islamic reference and equality of citizenship for all, and what that will mean regarding implementation of shariah and the rights and freedoms of religious minorities, secularists, and women. However, the ability of new governments to satisfy the expectations of diverse sectors of society, in particular to jump-start failed economies and address issues of high unemployment and now high expectations, was formidable. At the same time, the Egyptian and Tunisian governments were challenged by secular parties, including illiberal secularists, and especially the entrenched remnants of the Mubarak and Ben Ali regimes (military, police, judiciary, and a vast bureaucracy), often referred to as "the deep state," who remained in power.

By 2013, the Arab Spring began to look like an Arab winter. In Syria, the death toll in the struggle to oust the regime of Bashir Al-Assad and his opposition saw the death toll rise to 100,000, with vast destruction of the country. Both the governments of Egypt and Tunisia struggled to govern and to deal with opposition critics and movements. The hardest hit was Egypt, where a nationwide anti-Morsi and anti-Brotherhood protest movement galvanized on June 30, around the anniversary of Morsi's troubled first year in power.

The Morsi government made many mistakes and mishandled opportunities. The anti-Morsi opposition included many (liberals, marginalized revolutionary Arab youth, secularists and leftists, and Copts) with genuine concerns and grievances regarding the failure to reach out more effectively and build a more representative coalition government and to improve Egypt's failed economy, unemployment, poverty, and cost of living. However, the backbone of the movement consisted of individuals and institutions that represented the deep state legacy of the Mubarak regime (the military, the judges of the state constitutional court, the interior ministry, police, and state media as well as a strong contingent of illiberal secularists, including intellectuals, businessmen, and TV and media personalities). While some called for a second revolution, others warned of a civil war, and still others feared an end to the promises of Tahrir Square and democracy in Egypt. Politics became polarized into a growing "culture war" between the opposition and the Morsi government and its supporters. An opposition of millions in large-scale demonstrations across Egypt moved from demands for major reforms to violent clashes and a demand that Morsi resign or be driven from office, providing an excuse for a military-backed coup and a return to authoritarianism.

Three weeks after the military coup that removed President Mohamed Morsi and the Muslim Brotherhood from power, the interim government appointed nineteen generals as the governors of Egypt's provinces, and the military launched an operation against unarmed Muslim Brotherhood demonstrators, using lethal force that left more than 1,000 dead (other estimates ranged in the thousands), and thousands injured, the worst violence in Egyptian modern history.

On August 14, Egyptian security forces used lethal force against the Morsi supporter sit-in, killing more than 625 and injuring thousands. The interim government moved quickly to declare the Muslim Brotherhood a terrorist organization and attempted to totally suppress it, using mass arrests and military trials that drew sharp criticism from major international human rights organizations. The government cracked down and arrested foreign journalists and Egyptian critics and democracy activists. On March 24, 2014, an Egyptian court sentenced 529 members of the Muslim Brotherhood to death, the largest mass death sentence in modern Egyptian history.

Questions for Postmodern Times: Issues of Authority and Interpretation

The primary question for Muslims is not change, for most accept its necessity. Rather, it is how much change is possible or permissible in Islam and what kinds of change are necessary. This issue is central to virtually all the questions that Muslims face with respect to their faith in contemporary life: the relationship of Islam to the state, political participation or democratization, reform of Islamic law, promotion of religious and political pluralism, and the rights of women.

Although the sources and sacred texts of Islam, the Quran and the Sunnah of the Prophet, remain the same, the political, social, and economic contexts have changed. While all Muslims continue to affirm belief in God, Muhammad, and the Quran, Muslim interpretations of Islam today vary significantly. Some believe that Islam, like most faiths in the modern age, should be primarily a private matter; many others have struggled to implement Islam in public life as well. Although categories are not clear-cut and at times overlap, four general Muslim orientations or attitudes toward change may be identified: secularist, conservative traditionalists, Islamist or neofundamentalist, and Islamic reformist or neomodernist.

Like their counterparts in the West, secularists believe religion is a personal matter that should be excluded from politics and public life. Calling for the separation of religion and the state, they believe that Islam belongs in the mosque, not in politics, and that the mosque should solely be a place of prayer, not of political activism.

Conservatives emphasize following past tradition and are wary of any change or innovation that they regard as deviation, or *bida*, the equivalent of Christian heresy. Conservatives are represented by the majority (though certainly not all) of the *ulama* and their followers, who continue to assert the primacy and adequacy of centuries-old Islamic law. Advocating the reimplementation of Islamic law through the adoption of past legal doctrine, they resist substantive change.

Traditionalists or neotraditionalists, too, believe in the centrality of tradition and classical Islamic law, but they also believe that Islamic traditions based primarily on human interpretation rather than a sacred text can be reinterpreted, changed, or expanded in light of new social, economic, and political realities. Thus, for example, some prominent religious authorities, such as Sheikh Ali Gomaa, Grand Mufti of Egypt, have given *fatwas* that women may run for parliament or president and serve as judges.

Islamic activists or Islamists (often commonly referred to as fundamentalists) are in some respects similar to conservatives, though more flexible. They represent a broad spectrum, from ultra-orthodox, literalist, and puritanical movements to more flexible and reform-minded believers, from militant extremists to those who hold mainstream political and social positions. In contrast to conservatives, they are not wedded to the classical formulations of law. In the name of a return to the Quran and Sunnah, fundamentalists speak of purifying Muslim belief and practice by a rigorous and literalist embrace of the past, whereas more mainstream Islamists are prepared to interpret and reformulate Islamic belief and institutions.

Islamic activists emphasize the self-sufficiency of Islam over compatibility with the West. Few of their leaders are religious scholars or imams. Like the Muslim Brotherhood and other Islamic revivalist organizations from the twentieth century, their comprehensive understanding of Islam fosters social and political activism, often challenging the political and religious status quo.

In contrast to modernizers, neomodernists, despite some overlap with mainstream Islamists, are more open to substantive change and to borrowing from other cultures. Like Islamists, they root their reforms in the Quran and Sunnah and are not wedded to classical Islamic law. However, their approach to change is different. They distinguish more sharply between the principles and values of Islam's immutable revelation and certain historically and socially conditioned practices and institutions, which they believe can and should be subject to widespread change to meet contemporary circumstances.

fiqh: "understanding"; human interpretation of divine law (*sharia*)

At the heart of reformist approaches to Islam is the core issue, the relationship of the divine to the human in Islamic law. Thus reformers focus on the need to distinguish between the *sharia*, God's divinely revealed law, and *fiqh* ("understanding"), including the areas of human interpretation and application that are historically conditioned. Reformers go further than conservatives or traditionalists in their acceptance of the degree and extent to which classical Islamic law may be reinterpreted or changed. They place more emphasis on the finite nature of early doctrines. They argue that just as early Muslim jurists applied the principles and values of Islam to the societies of the past, again today a reinterpretation or reconstruction of Islam is needed. But who has the authority to do this work?

As in the past, both the *ulama*, the religious scholars of Islam, and Muslim rulers continue to assert their right to protect, defend, and interpret Islam. The *ulama* persist in regarding themselves as the guardians of Islam, the conscience of the community, its only qualified interpreters. Many rulers, through cooptation and coercion of religion, combine their obligation to protect and promote Islam with the state's power to influence, control, and impose a certain "brand" of Islam. Governments control and distribute funds used to build mosques and to pay the salaries of religious officials and functionaries. Even topics or outlines for Friday mosque sermons are subject to government approval.

Today, many argue that it is not rulers or the religious scholars but the laity and parliaments that should be major actors in the process of change. While the *ulama* base their authority on their training in traditional Islamic disciplines, lay Muslims

Islam and Democracy

A primary example of Islamic reformism and its method today is the debate over the relationship of Islam to democracy. Some Muslims reject any discussion of the question, maintaining that Islam has its own system of government. Others believe that Islam and democracy are incompatible, claiming that democracy is based on un-Islamic Western principles and values. Still others reinterpret traditional Islamic concepts like consultation (*shura*) and consensus (*ijma*) of the community to support the adoption of modern forms of political participation or democratization, such as parliamentary elections. Thus, just as it was appropriate in the past for Muhammad's senior Companions to constitute a consultative assembly (*majlis al-shura*) and to select or elect his successor through a process of consultation, Muslims now reinterpret and extend this notion to the creation of modern forms of political participation and government, parliamentary governments, and the direct or indirect election of heads of state. This process is sometimes called "Islamization." Similarly, in legal reform some Muslims believe that Islam is totally self-sufficient; they demand the imposition of Islamic law and reject any outside influences. Others argue that Islamic law can be reinterpreted today to incorporate new interpretations or formulations of law as well as laws from elsewhere that do not contradict the Quran and Sunnah.

counter that they possess the legal, economic, and medical qualifications necessary to address contemporary issues and should be counted among the "experts" along with the *ulama*.

Islam in the West[15]

As we discussed at the beginning of the chapter, Muslims have in modern times become part of the American and European landscapes.

Muslims were long an invisible presence in the West. Most came as immigrants. Many wanted to fit into their new societies, to be accepted, gain employment, raise families, and live quietly in their adopted countries. Others wished to live apart, to avoid any prospect of loss of identity or assimilation into a Western, non-Muslim society. Political events in the Muslim world reinforced a desire for a low profile in any country to which Muslims had relocated; in some cases Muslims found themselves on the defensive. Images and stereotypes from the past, of camels and harems, were replaced by modern impressions of violence and terrorism associated with the threat of militant "Islamic fundamentalism." The result has often been Muslim bashing and what some have called *Islamophobia*: harassment, discrimination, and violence toward Muslims on the basis of their faith or race.

Today, Muslims in Europe and America no longer live primarily in clusters of immigrants; rather they are members of second- and third-generation communities, participating in professional and civic life. Yet many continue to face issues of faith and identity as a religious minority.

For many years, Islam and other religions were suppressed and persecuted in Albania by a communist regime that declared the state officially atheist in 1967. Many mosques in this Muslim majority country were closed or destroyed, and religious symbols were banned. In 1990 the ban was lifted, and this and other mosques were rededicated and opened.

The Muslims of Western Europe

More than 44 million Muslims may be found in Europe. Because many, though certainly not all, wish to retain their religion, culture, and values, the presence and citizenship of Muslims in western Europe, as in America, have made assimilation, acculturation, integration, and multiculturalism major religious, social, and political issues.

In contrast to America, in Western Europe the Muslim presence is due in large part to immigration based on a vestigial colonial connection. After independence, many professionals and skilled laborers from former European colonies in Africa, South Asia, and the Arab world immigrated to Europe, seeking a better life. In the 1960s and 1970s, unskilled workers flooded into European countries whose growing economies welcomed cheap labor. In addition, from the 1970s onward, increasing numbers of Muslim students came to Europe, as they did to America, to study. While many returned home, others chose to stay for political or economic reasons.

The largest Muslim population in Western Europe is in France, with 4.7 million Muslims (70 percent of whom come from North Africa), followed by Germany (4.3 million) and the United Kingdom (2.9 million). The Muslims of France, comprising almost 7.5 percent of the population, now exceed Protestants and Jews in number and are second only to France's Catholic community. There are grand mosques in Paris and Lyon and more than a thousand mosques and prayer rooms throughout the country. The majority of Germany's 4.3 million Muslims are of Turkish origin (63 percent); Britain's 2.9 million Muslims come primarily from the Indian subcontinent.

The issue of Muslim identity has been particularly acute in France, where the government has taken a firm stand in favor of total assimilation or integration. The issue was symbolized in a celebrated case in which the wearing of a headscarf by Muslim female students was outlawed. In February 2004, France's National Assembly ignored protests and criticism from around the world and voted 494–36 to approve the controversial ban in public schools. Although the new law was aimed primarily at Muslims wearing the *hijab*, other religious apparel (large Christian crucifixes and Jewish skullcaps, or *yarmulkes*) was included; violators face suspension or expulsion. The government argued that this law is needed not only to protect France's secular traditions but also to ward off rising Islamic fundamentalism. Controversy over Islamic

In all Islamic communities, mosques are the social and community centers. Here, at the end of the Ramadan fast, women prepare to pray in the mosque in Regent's Park, London.

dress continued in 2010, when France, along with Belgium, moved to ban the *niqab*, wearing of a full face veil, in public places. The growth of far-right anti-immigrant political parties has created similar pressures in the Netherlands and elsewhere.

Islam in America

Islam is the fastest-growing religion in the United States. Many believe that in the first half of the twenty-first century, Islam will become the second-largest religion in America, after Christianity. The estimates of the number of American Muslims vary significantly, from 3 million to 7 million. Muslim Americans are racially diverse communities in the United States; two-thirds are foreign-born.[16] The majority of American Muslims, 60 percent, are South Asians (from the Indian subcontinent), and 35 percent are indigenous African Americans. The majority of American Muslims are Sunni, but there is a strong Shiah minority. Racial, ethnic, and sectarian differences are reflected in the demographic composition and politics of some mosques, as well: Many houses of worship incorporate the diversity of Muslims in America, but the membership of others is drawn along ethnic or racial lines.

Muslims were present in America prior to the nineteenth century. Perhaps 20 percent of the African slaves brought to America from the sixteenth to the nineteenth centuries were Muslim. However, most were forced to convert to Christianity. It was not until the late nineteenth century, with the arrival of waves of immigrant laborers from the Arab world, that significant numbers of Muslims became a visible presence in America. In recent decades many more have come from the Middle East and South

The Muslim community in America is a rich racial, ethnic, and cultural mosaic of indigenous believers, the majority of whom are African American, and immigrant Muslims. Thousands of Muslims from New York's varied ethnic communities pray next to Coney Island's landmark Parachute Jump to celebrate the Feast of Sacrifice (Id al-Adha). This major religious holiday commemorates God's command to Abraham to sacrifice his son Ismail.

Asia. In contrast to Europe, which attracted large numbers of Muslims as immigrant laborers in the 1960s and 1970s, many who have come to America in recent decades have been well-educated professionals, intellectuals, and students. Many have come for political and economic reasons, leaving behind the constraints of life under authoritarian regimes and failed economies.

The Transformation of "The Nation of Islam"

African American Islam emerged in the early twentieth century when a number of black Americans converted to Islam and established movements or communities. Islam's egalitarian ideal, in which all Muslims belong to a brotherhood of believers, transcending race and ethnic ties, proved attractive. Whereas Islam was seen as part of an original (African) identity, Christianity was associated with the legitimation of slavery and thus a legacy of white supremacy and oppression of black Americans that extended into the twentieth century. The early twentieth century saw the appearance of quasi-Islamic groups, combining a selective use of Islamic symbols with black nationalism. The most prominent and lasting movement, the Nation of Islam, was associated with Elijah Muhammad (formerly Elijah Poole, 1897–1975).

Elijah Muhammad had been a follower of Wallace D. Fard Muhammad, who preached a message of black liberation in the ghettos of Detroit in the early 1930s. After Fard mysteriously disappeared in 1934, Elijah Muhammad became the leader of the Nation of Islam. Adopting the title of the Honorable Elijah Muhammad, he claimed to be the messenger of God. Under his leadership, the Nation of Islam, popularly known as the Black Muslims, was redefined and transformed into an effective national movement. Elijah Muhammad preached black liberation and nationalism, black pride and identity, strength and self-sufficiency, black racial supremacy, and strong family values. The spirit and ethic of the Nation of Islam was embodied in the phrase "Do for self," a doctrine of economic independence that emphasized self-improvement and responsibility through hard work, discipline, thrift, and abstention from gambling, alcohol, drugs, and eating pork.

The Nation of Islam differed significantly from mainstream Islam in a number of basic beliefs. It claimed that Allah (God) was human—the black man named Wallace D. Fard—and that Elijah Muhammad (not the Prophet Muhammad) was the last messenger of God. The Nation taught black supremacy and black separatism, whereas Islam teaches the brotherhood of all believers in a community that transcends racial, tribal, and ethnic boundaries. The Nation did not subscribe to major tenets of the faith, such as the Five Pillars of Islam.

Three individuals epitomize the development and transformation of Elijah Muhammad's Black Muslim movement: Malcolm X, Wallace D. Muhammad (Warith Deen Muhammad), and Louis Farrakhan.

Malcolm X (1925–65), born Malcolm Little, exemplified the personal and religious transformation for which the Nation of Islam was noted. His experience of racism and prejudice led to his alienation from and rejection of American society. A prison sentence was the result of an early life of drugs and crime in the ghettos of Roxbury, Massachusetts, and later in New York's Harlem. It was during his incarceration (1946–52) that he became self-educated, reading widely in history, politics, and religion. Malcolm became convinced that Christianity was the "white man's religion" and that the Bible "[in the] white man's hands and his interpretation of it, have been the greatest single ideological weapon for enslaving millions of nonwhite human beings."[1] In 1948 he formally turned to Elijah Muhammad and accepted the teachings of the Nation of Islam. Malcolm Little became Malcolm X.

A gifted speaker, dynamic and articulate, and a charismatic personality, Malcolm X rose quickly through the ranks of the Nation of Islam to national prominence in the 1950s and early 1960s. He organized many of the Nation's temples; started its newspaper, *Muhammad Speaks*; and recruited new members, including the boxer Cassius Clay, renamed Muhammad Ali.

Malcolm X (d. 1965), also known as El-Hajj Malik El-Shabazz, African American Muslim leader, civil and human rights advocate. An early disciple of Elijah Muhammad, chief minister of the Nation of Islam, he became one of its most prominent leaders and spokespersons. He withdrew from the Nation in 1964, becoming a follower of Sunni Islam. He was assassinated in 1965 by members of the Nation of Islam.

However, Malcolm's increased involvement in domestic and international politics as well as his contacts with Sunni Muslims in America and in the Muslim world led to a gradual shift in his religious/ideological worldview. This development put him increasingly at odds with some of Elijah Muhammad's teachings. While Elijah Muhammad advocated separation and self-sufficiency that excluded involvement in "white man's politics," Malcolm came to believe that "the Nation of Islam could be even a greater force in the American Black man's overall struggle if we engaged in more action."[2] He spoke out forcefully on a variety of issues: the civil rights movement, the Vietnam War, solidarity with liberation struggles in colonial Africa. Such statements made him an easy target for those within the Nation who were jealous of his prominence, and as a result he found himself increasingly marginalized.

In March 1964 Malcolm X left the Nation of Islam to start his own organization and a month later went on pilgrimage to Mecca. Here Malcolm underwent a second conversion—to mainstream Sunni Islam. The pilgrimage brought Malcolm and the religious/separatist teachings of the Nation face to face with those of the global Islamic community, vividly exposing their conflicts and contradictions. Malcolm was profoundly affected by the Muslim emphasis, which he experienced firsthand during the hajj, on the equality of all believers.

The 1960s were a transitional period for the Nation of Islam. Not only Malcolm X but also Elijah Muhammad's son, Wallace D. Muhammad, each in his own way, questioned the teachings and strategy of the senior Muhammad. At one point, Wallace was excommunicated by his father. Despite their disagreements, however, Elijah Muhammad had designated his son as his successor, and in February 1975 Wallace D. Muhammad succeeded his recently deceased father as supreme minister. With the support of his family and the Nation's leadership, Wallace set about reforming the doctrines of the Nation and its organizational structure. He simultaneously integrated the Nation within the American Muslim community, the broader American society, and the global Islamic community.

Muhammad Ali, renowned heavyweight boxing champion of the world. Born Cassius Clay in 1942, he revealed in midcareer that he had become a member of the Nation of Islam and changed his name to Muhammad Ali. He became the most prominent and popular Muslim public figure in America and globally.

The Nation and its teachings were brought into conformity with orthodox Sunni Islam, and the organization was renamed the World Community of al-Islam in the West (WCIW). Wallace Muhammad made the pilgrimage to Mecca and encouraged his followers to study Arabic to better understand Islam. The community now observed Islam's Five Pillars. Black separatist doctrines were dropped as the community proceeded to participate in the American political process. The equality of men and women believers was reaffirmed; women were given more responsible positions in the ministry of the community. In 1980, as if to signal his and the community's new religious identity and mission, Wallace changed his name to Warith Deen Muhammad and renamed the WCIW the American Muslim Mission.

TALES OF SPIRITUAL TRANSFORMATION: Malcolm X

After leaving the Nation of Islam in March 1964, Malcolm X made the hajj, pilgrimage to Mecca. The experience transformed his life and changed his perspective on racism:

> There were tens of thousands of pilgrims, from all over the world. They were of all colors, from blue-eyed blondes to black-skinned Africans. But we were all participating in the same ritual, displaying a spirit of unity and brotherhood that my experiences in America had led me to believe never could exist between the white and the nonwhite.
>
> You may be shocked by these words coming from me. But on this pilgrimage, what I have seen, and experienced, has forced me to rearrange much of my thought patterns previously held, and to toss aside some of my previous conclusions. . . . During the past eleven days here in the Muslim world, I have eaten from the same plate, drunk from the same glass, and slept in the same bed (or on the same rug)—while praying to the same God with fellow Muslims, whose eyes were the bluest of the blue, whose hair was the blondest of blond, and whose skin was the whitest of white. And in the words and in the actions and in the deeds of the "white" Muslims, I felt the same sincerity that I felt among the black African Muslims of Nigeria, Sudan, and Ghana.
>
> We are truly all the same—brothers. All praise is due to Allah, the Lord of the worlds.

He returned a Muslim rather than a Black Muslim, changing his name to El Hajj Malik El-Shabazz. On February 21, 1965, Malcolm Shabazz was assassinated as he spoke to an audience in New York.

The transformation of the Nation of Islam under Warith Deen Muhammad did not occur without dissent. Louis Farrakhan (born Louis Eugene Walcott, in 1933), a bitter foe of both Malcolm and Wallace, broke with Wallace in March 1978. Farrakhan retained the name and organizational structure of the Nation of Islam as well as its black nationalist and separatist doctrines. However, from 1986 onward, while using many of the political and economic teachings and programs of Elijah Muhammad, he moved the Nation closer to more orthodox Islamic practices.

While Farrakhan's militancy and anti–Semitic statements brought condemnation and criticism, the effectiveness of the Nation in fighting crime and drugs in ghettos and in rehabilitating prisoners earned the Nation praise. Farrakhan's leadership of the Million Man March on Washington in 1995 received widespread media coverage and support among Christian as well as Muslim leaders and organizations. Though the Nation of Islam has far fewer members than Warith Deen Muhammad's American Muslim Mission, Farrakhan's persona and actions gave him a disproportionate amount of visibility and recognition as the twentieth century drew to a close.

Issues of Adaptation and Change

Islam and Muslim identity in North America reflect the diverse backgrounds of the community: from immigrants who came to America in pursuit of political, religious, or economic freedom to native-born African Americans seeking equality and justice. Muslims, like Hindus and Buddhists, have been challenged by an America that, despite separation of church and state, retains a Judeo-Christian ethos in which Judeo-Christian values are regarded as integral to American identity and Jewish and Christian holidays are officially recognized holidays. The tendency of some in America, as in Europe, to contrast American "national culture" with Islamic values further complicates the process of Muslim assimilation. Finally, the American media's disproportionate coverage of violence and terrorism (as reflected in the maxim "If it bleeds, it leads") has brushstroked mainstream Muslims and projected the image of Islam as a particularly militant religion, reinforcing those who talk of a clash of civilizations.

Islam in America provides many examples of significant change and reform. Both mosques and their leaders, or imams, have been transformed by the American experience. Because Friday is a workday and a school day in America, many Muslims are not able to attend the Friday congregational prayer. Therefore, for many, Sunday at mosques and Islamic centers is the day of congregational prayer, religious education ("Sunday school"), and socializing. Teaching materials and syllabi on Islam and Muslim life are available for the instruction of children and adults at mosques and in schools. Imams in America not only are responsible for the upkeep of mosques and leading of prayers, but often take on the duties of the clergy of other faiths, serving as counselors to military and as hospital and prison chaplains.

In the twenty-first century, Muslim-minority communities have become a global and permanent phenomenon. Today, American Muslims increasingly seek to empower themselves, participating in rather than simply reacting to life in America. Like American Jews and other minorities before them, Muslims are developing grassroots institutions that are responsive to their realities. The contemporary American Muslim community is increasingly more integrated both politically and economically. Muslim advocacy and public affairs organizations promote and lobby for Muslim rights and community interests.

Moreover, Muslim educational associations monitor textbooks and the teaching of Islam to ensure accuracy and objectivity. Public affairs organizations monitor publications and respond to misinformation in the media and to objectionable policies and actions by legislators and corporations. Islamic information services develop and distribute films, videos, and publications on Islam and Muslims in America to further better understanding. Some communities have primary and secondary Islamic schools.

Islam: Postmodern Challenges

Islam and Muslims today are again at an important crossroads. The struggle today, the world over, is one of faith, identity, and reform. What does it mean to be a Muslim in an increasingly globalized and pluralistic world and society? How should Islam's sacred sources and heritage be interpreted to respond to issues of religious authority, secularism, the role of *sharia*, the rights of women and minorities, religious extremism, and terrorism?

Like the other Children of Abraham, their Jewish and Christian cousins, Muslims face questions of faith and identity in a rapidly changing world. The process of reform bears witness to the fact that monotheistic does not mean monolithic. As in the past and as in all faiths, the unity of Islam embraces a diversity of interpretations and expressions, a source of dynamism and growth as well as contention and conflict among believers and, at times, with other faith communities. The challenge for all believers remains the rigorous pursuit in a world of diversity and difference of "the straight path, the way of God, to whom belongs all that is in the heavens and all that is on the earth" (Q. 42:52–53).

Like Catholic and Jewish communities before them, which created their own schools to safeguard and preserve the faith and identity of the younger generation, some Muslim communities have created Islamic schools that combine a standard academic curriculum with training in Arabic and Islamic studies.

While the Quran and Sunnah of the Prophet Muhammad remain normative for all Muslims, vigorously debated questions have been raised in the areas of interpretation, authenticity, and application. If some Muslims see little need to redefine past approaches and practices, others strike out into new territory. Some Muslim scholars distinguish between the Meccan and Medinan *surahs* (chapters). The former are regarded as the earlier and more religiously binding; the latter are seen as primarily political, concerned with Muhammad's creation of the Medinan state and therefore not universally binding. Still other Muslim scholars say that whereas the eternal principles and values of the Quran are to be applied and reapplied to changing sociopolitical contexts, many articles of past legislation addressed conditions in specific historical periods and are not necessarily binding today.

Although the example (Sunnah) of the Prophet Muhammad has always been normative in Islam, from earliest times Muslim scholars saw the need to examine critically and authenticate the enormous number of prophetic traditions (*hadith*). A sector of modern Western scholarship questioned the historicity and authenticity of the hadith, maintaining that the bulk of the Prophetic traditions are pious fabrications, written long after the death of the Prophet. Most Muslim scholars and some from outside the Islamic world have taken exception to this sweeping position. If many of the *ulama* continue to accept the authoritative collections of the past unquestioningly, other Muslim scholars have in fact become more critical in their approach and use of tradition (*hadith*) literature.

Contemporary Muslim discussion and debate over the role of Islam in state and society reflect a broad array of questions: Is there one classical model or many possible models for the relationship of religion to political, social, and economic development? If a new Islamic synthesis is to be achieved that provides continuity with past tradition, how will this be accomplished? Will it be imposed from above by rulers and/or

As in other world religions, in Islam marriage is solemnized in a religious ceremony. This Baghdad wedding is an occasion for great joy and celebration among the couple's family and friends.

the *ulama* or legislated in populist fashion through a representative electoral process? These questions are reflected in the debate over the nature and role of Islamic law in Muslim societies.

Islamization of the Law

What should the role of *sharia* be today? Does Islamization of law mean the wholesale reintroduction of classical law as formulated in the early Islamic centuries or the development of new laws derived from the Quran and Sunnah of the Prophet? Or can it include the acceptance of any laws, whatever their source (European, American, etc.), that are not contrary to Islam? Who is to define, determine, and oversee this process: rulers, the *ulama*, or parliaments?

The implementation of *sharia*, where it has occurred, has not followed a fixed pattern or set interpretation even among those countries dubbed conservative or fundamentalist, such as Iran, Sudan, Afghanistan under the Taliban, Pakistan, and Saudi Arabia. Women in Saudi Arabia cannot vote or hold public office. In Pakistan and Iran, despite other strictures and problems, women vote, hold political office in parliaments and cabinets, teach in universities, and hold responsible professional positions. However, Islamization of law has underscored several areas that have proved particularly problematic: the **hudud** (Quranically prescribed crimes and punishments for alcohol consumption, theft, fornication, adultery, and false witness), the status of non-Muslims and minorities, and the status of women. All potentially involve changes in Islamic law.

While some call for the reimplementation of the *hudud* punishments, other Muslims argue that harsh measures such as amputation for theft and stoning for adultery (not mentioned in the Quran) are, like stoning in the Old Testament or many

hudud: Quranically prescribed crimes and punishments adopted by some countries and advocated by some groups as evidence of the "Islamic" nature of their political rule and law

corporal punishments practiced by governments in centuries past, no longer suitable. Among those who advocate imposition of the *hudud*, some want it introduced immediately and others say that it should be contingent on the creation of a just society in which people will not be driven to steal to survive. Some critics charge that while appropriate relative to the time they were introduced, *hudud* punishments are unnecessary in a modern context.

Women and Minorities

As we have seen, one result of contemporary Islamic revivalism has been a reexamination of the role of women in Islam and, at times, a bitter debate over their function in society. More conservative religious voices among the *ulama* and many Islamists have advocated a return to veiling and sexual segregation as well as restrictions on women's education and employment. Muslim women are regarded as culture bearers, teachers of family faith and values, whose primary role as wives and mothers limits or prevents participation in public life. The imposition of reputed Islamic laws by some governments and the policies of some Islamist movements reinforced fears of a retreat to the past. Among the prime examples have been the enforcement of veiling, closure of women's schools, restriction of women in the workplace, and extremist attacks and killings. In fact, the picture is far more complex and diverse, revealing both old and new patterns.

Modern forms of Islamic dress have the practical advantage of enabling some women to assert their modesty and dignity while functioning in public life in societies where Western dress often symbolizes a more permissive lifestyle. It creates a protected, private space of respectability in crowded urban environments. For some

Queen Rania of Jordan (center) at prayer with other Muslim women.

GENDER FOCUS: Women and Empowerment

Muslim women in the twentieth century had two clear choices or models before them: the modern Westernized lifestyle common among an elite minority of women and the more restrictive traditional "Islamic" lifestyle of the majority of women, who lived much as their grandmothers and great-grandmothers had lived. The social impact of the Islamic revival produced a third alternative that is both modern and firmly rooted in Islamic faith, identity, and values. Muslim women, modernists, and Islamists have argued on Islamic grounds for an expanded role for women in Muslim societies. Rejecting the idea that Islam itself is patriarchal and distinguishing between revelation and its interpretation by all-male *ulama* in patriarchal

settings, Muslim women have reasserted the right to be primary participants in redefining their identity and role in society. In many instances, this change has been symbolized by a return to the wearing of Islamic dress or the donning of a headscarf, or *hijab*. Initially prominent primarily among urban middle-class women, this new mode of dress has become more common among a broader sector of society. For many it is an attempt to combine religious belief and Islamic values of modesty with contemporary freedoms in education and employment, to pair a much-desired process of social change with indigenous Islamic values and ideals. The goal is a more authentic rather than simply Westernized modernization.

Benazir Bhutto, former prime minister of Pakistan, was one of several Muslim women to have served as president or prime minister in an Islamic nation. She served two terms in the 1990s as prime minister (1988–October 1990), and again from 1993 until her final dismissal in November 1996. She was assassinated in 2007.

it is a sign of a real Islamic feminism that rejects what is regarded as the tendency of women in the West and elite Westernized Muslim women in many Muslim societies to go from being defined as restricted sexual objects in a male-dominated tradition to so-called free yet exploited sexual objects. Western feminism is often seen as pseudo-liberation, a new form of bondage to dress, youthfulness, and physical beauty, a false freedom in which women's bodies are used to sell everything from clothing to automobiles to cell phones. Covering the body, it is argued, defines a woman and gender relations in society in terms of personality and talents rather than physical appearance.

New experiments by educated Muslim women to orient their lives more Islamically have also resulted in more women "returning to the mosque." In the past, when women were restricted to the home and allowed only limited education, they did not participate in public prayer in mosques. While some attended the Friday congregational prayer, sitting separately from the men, it was more common for women to pray at home and to leave religious learning to men. Today in many Muslim countries and communities, particularly those that have been regarded as among the more modernized, such as Egypt, Jordan, Malaysia, and the United States, women are forming prayer and Quran study groups, which are led by women. To justify these public activities, women cite the examples of Muslim women in early Islam who fought and prayed alongside their men and of women who were held in high repute for their knowledge and sanctity. Women from the United States to Malaysia, as individuals and in organizations, are writing and speaking out for themselves on women's issues. They draw on the writings and thought not only of male scholars but also, and

The Quran and Islamic tradition enjoin modesty, and thus everyone is required to wear modest dress. The diversity of attire found across the Muslim world is reflected in this group of young Muslim women in the United States. Though all are dressed modestly, some wear a headscarf (*hijab*) while others do not.

most importantly, on a growing number of women scholars who utilize an Islamic discourse to address issues ranging from dress to education, employment, and political participation.

Contemporary Muslim societies reflect both the old and the new realities. Old patterns remain strong and are indeed reasserted and defended by those who call for a more widespread return to traditional forms of Islamic dress and segregation or seclusion of women (*purdah*). However, at the same time, Muslim women have become catalysts for change. While the women's literacy rate in Pakistan is anywhere from 12 percent to 40 percent (vs. 69 percent for men), women's literacy rates are much higher in Egypt (63.5 percent), Iran (70 percent), Saudi Arabia (81 percent), and as high as 89 percent in Jordan and 85 percent in Malaysia. In the United Arab Emirates, as in Iran, the majority of university students are women. Women have increasingly empowered themselves by entering the professions, running for elective office, and serving in parliament, becoming students and scholars of Islam, and establishing women's professional organizations, journals, and magazines. Women's organizations such as Women Living Under Muslim Laws, based in Pakistan but international in membership; Musawah: Global Movement for Equality and Justice in the Muslim Family; and Malaysia's Sisters in Islam are active internationally in protecting and promoting the rights of Muslim women.

Islamic Reform

Islamic reformers face formidable challenges and obstacles, including the discrediting of militant ideas and ideologies and the reform of *madrasas* and universities that perpetuate

Indonesia has the largest Muslim population in the world. These women from the province of Aceh, contestants seeking to become Miss Indonesia, learn how to perfect the application of makeup.

a "theology of hate" and train so-called jihadists. Another obstacle to reform, however, is the ultraconservatism of many (though not all) *ulama*, which hinders reform in the curriculum and training of religious scholars, leaders, and students.

The struggle of Islam is between the competing voices and visions of over a billion mainstream Muslims and a dangerous and deadly minority of terrorists. While the extremists dominate the headlines and threaten Muslim and Western societies, the vast majority of Muslims, like other religious believers, wish to pursue normal, everyday activities. For decades, quietly, persistently, and effectively, a group of reform-minded Muslims have articulated a variety of progressive, constructive Islamic frameworks for reform. These intellectual activists represent voices of reform from North Africa to Southeast Asia and from Europe to North America. They respond to the realities of many Muslim societies, the challenges of authoritarian regimes and secular elites, the dangers of religious extremism, and the dead weight of well-meaning but often-intransigent conservative religious scholars and leaders.

Islamic reform is a process not only of intellectual ferment and religious debate but also of religious and political unrest and violence. The lessons of the Protestant Reformation, the Catholic Counter-Reformation, and more recently Vatican II demonstrate that religious reformations take time and are often fraught with conflict

TEACHINGS OF RELIGIOUS WISDOM: A Bosnian Prayer

Our Lord
Do not let success deceive us
Nor failure take us to despair!
Always remind us that failure is a temptation
That precedes success!
Our Lord
Teach us that tolerance is the highest degree of
   power
And the desire for revenge
The first sign of weakness! . . .
Our Lord

If we sin against people,
Give us the strength of apology
And if people sin against us,
Give us the strength of forgiveness!
Our Lord
If we forget Thee,
Do not forget us!

Source: A Bosnian Prayer cited by Mustafa Ceric, Grand Mufti of Bosnia-Herzegovina, in his "Judaism, Christianity, Islam: Hope or Fear of Our Times," in James L. Heft, ed., *Beyond Violence* (New York: Fordham University Press, 2004), pp. 54–55.

and even danger. Generations of reformers, often a minority within their communities, struggle today against many powerful forces, including conservative religious establishments, with their medieval paradigms; authoritarian regimes able to control or manipulate religion, education, and the media; and political and religious establishments that often see reformers as a threat to their power and privilege.

Conclusion

With 1.8 billion members, one-fourth of the world's population, the global Muslim community is second only to Christianity's 2.3 billion. Despite setbacks, for fifteen centuries Islam has proven vibrant and dynamic, growing spectacularly as a faith and empire, from the time of the Prophet Muhammad. Islam's message and way of life has attracted followers of every race and culture, adapting to diverse cultures from Africa to Asia and Europe to America. Unity of faith has been accompanied by a diversity of expressions. In the twenty-first century, Islam is at a crossroads. Muslims face yet another watershed as they struggle to implement their faith and practice within the realities and challenges of contemporary life.

The struggle for reform is religious, intellectual, spiritual, and moral. But it must be a more rapid and widespread program of Islamic renewal that not only builds on past reformers but also more forcefully follows the lead of today's enlightened religious leaders and intellectuals and more effectively engages in a wide-ranging process of reinterpretation (*ijtihad*) and reform.

The pace of reform has been slow in many countries and societies that are dominated by authoritarian regimes, entrenched elites, and a global politics in which Western governments, despite their democratic principles and values, are often willing to support autocrats to protect their own national interests. The process has been compounded by the threat and attacks of Muslim extremists within Muslim countries and in the West.

In contrast to Christianity's centuries-long Protestant Reformation and Vatican II in Roman Catholicism, the forces of globalization and development today necessitate a more rapid process of change. At the same time, religious, like political, reform often brings heat as well as light. Religious reformations often include not only bitter and divisive theological debates, but also, as in Christianity, the religious wars (1516–1750) between Protestants and Catholics. The result of theological and legal differences can be seen in the results—the many Christian denominations and the various branches of Judaism: ultra-orthodox, orthodox, conservative, reform, reconstructionist, and humanistic.

While the trajectory of Islamic reform and its outcome remain uncertain, Muslims are challenged to exemplify the Quranic prescription that the Islamic community (*ummah*) pursue a just and middle (*wasat*) path: "Thus We have made you a just community, that you may witness to humanity" (2:143) as, like those before them, it seeks to follow "the straight path, the way of God, to whom belongs all that is in the heavens and all that is in the earth" (42:52–53).

Discussion Questions

1. Identify and describe the Five Pillars of Islam.

2. What are the differences between Sunnis, Shiah, and Sufis?

3. What is the difference between the *sharia* and *fiqh*? What impact have these aspects of Islam had on modern revivalism and reformism?

4. What are the origins of the Crusades? Explain their long-term effects on Muslim-Christian/Western relations.

5. Discuss the impact of European colonialism on the Muslim world. What are some of the ways in which Muslims responded to it?

6. What is *ijtihad*? Why is this concept at the heart of the question of the relationship between Islam and modernity?

7. Describe the different themes and techniques used for the revival and reform of Islam in the eighteenth century.

8. Discuss the basic tenets and significance of the Muslim Brotherhood and the *Jamaat-i-Islami*.

9. What are the causes and conditions that led to the contemporary resurgence of Islam?

10. How is Islam used both to support and to oppose the state? Give examples.

11. Describe the diverse meanings of *jihad*. How has the concept been used by different Islamic movements to justify their activities?

12. Discuss the origin and development of the Nation of Islam. Do African American Muslims differ from mainstream Muslims?

13. How has Islam affected or changed the status of women? How are women influenced by Islamic movements today? How are they influencing these movements?

14. What are some of the major issues facing Muslims living in non-Muslim-majority countries today, particularly in Europe and America?

15. Identify and discuss several key areas of Islamic reform.

Key Terms

Allah	*dhimmi*	*hadith*
caliph	*fatwa*	*hajj*
dar al-Islam	*fiqh*	*hijra*

hudud	*muamalat*	*sharia*
ibadat	*muezzin*	Shiah
ijma	*mufti*	Sufi
ijtihad	*mujaddid*	Sufism
imam	Muslim	Sunnah
Islam	People of the Book	Sunni
jahiliyya	*purdah*	*surah*
jihad	*qiyas*	*tawhid*
khutba	Quran	*ulama*
Mahdi	Ramadan	*ummah*
minbar	*salat*	*wali*
mosque	*shahadah*	*zakat*

Suggested Readings

Armstrong, Karen. *Islam: A Short History* (New York: Modern Library, 2002).

Brown, Jonathan. *Hadith: Muhammad's Legacy in the Medieval and Modern World* (Oxford: Oneworld Publications, 2009).

———. *Very Short Introduction: Muhammad* (Oxford: Oxford University Press, 2010).

Donohue, John, and John L. Esposito, eds. *Islam in Transition: Muslim Perspectives*, 2nd ed. (New York: Oxford University Press, 2006).

Esposito, John L. *The Future of Islam* (New York: Oxford University Press, 2010).

———, ed. *Islam: The Straight Path*, 4th rev. ed. (New York: Oxford University Press, 2010).

———. *The Islamic World: Past and Present*. 3 vols. (New York: Oxford University Press, 2004).

———, ed. *The Oxford History of Islam* (New York: Oxford University Press, 2000).

———. *Unholy War: Terror in the Name of Islam* (New York: Oxford University Press, 2000).

———. *What Everyone Needs to Know About Islam*, 2nd ed (New York: Oxford University Press, 2011).

——— with Dalia Mogahed. *Who Speaks for Islam? What a Billion Muslims Really Think* (New York: Gallup Press, 2008).

Lings, Martin. *What Is Sufism?* (London: I. B. Tauris, 1999).

Nasr, Seyyed Hossein. *The Heart of Islam: Enduring Values for Humanity* (San Francisco: Harper, 2002).

The Quran: A Modern English Version, trans. Majid Fakhry (Berkshire, UK: Garnet, 1996).

The Qur'an, trans. Haleem, M. A. S. Abdul (Oxford: Oxford University Press, 2008).

Ramadan, Tariq. *Western Muslims and the Future of Islam* (New York: Oxford University Press, 2005).

Sonn, Tamara. *A Brief History of Islam* (Malden, MA: Wiley–Blackwell, 2010).

Notes

1. Ibn Hisham, quoted in Philip K. Hitti, *History of the Arabs*, 9th ed. (New York: St. Martin's Press, 1966), p. 120. For the text within the context of a major biography of the Prophet

Muhammad, see Ibn Ishaq, *The Life of Muhammad*, trans. A. Guillaume (London: Oxford University Press, 1955), p. 651.

2. Bernard Lewis, ed. and trans., *Islam: From the Prophet Muhammad to the Capture of Constantinople* (New York: Harper & Row, 1974), pp. 179–81.

3. Seyyed Hossein Nasr, *Muhammad: Man of God* (Chicago: Kazi Publications, 1995), p. 90.

4. *The Hedaya*, trans. Charles Hamilton, 2nd ed. (Lahore, Pakistan: Premier Books, 1957), p. 73.

5. As quoted in Reuben Levy, *The Social Structure of Islam* (Cambridge: Cambridge University Press, 1955), p. 126.

6. Margaret Smith, *Rabia the Mystic and Her Fellow-Saints in Islam* (Cambridge: Cambridge University Press, 1928), p. 30.

7. Francis E. Peters, "Early Muslim Empires: Umayyads, Abbasids, Fatimids," in Marjorie Kelly, ed., *Islam: The Religious and Political Life of a World Community* (New York: Praeger, 1984), p. 85.

8. Roger Savory. "Christendom vs. Islam: Interaction and Coexistence," in Roger Savory, ed., *Introduction to Islamic Civilization* (Cambridge: Cambridge University Press, 1976), p. 133.

9. John O. Voll. "The Sudanese Mahdi: Frontier Fundamentalist," *International Journal of Middle East Studies* 10 (1979), p. 159.

10. For perceptive discussions of Osama bin Laden, see A. Rashid, *Taliban: Militant Islam, Oil, and Fundamentalism in Central Asia* (New Haven, CT: Yale University Press, 2000), and J. K. Cooley, *Unholy Wars: Afghanistan, America and International Terrorism* (London: Pluto Press, 2000).

11. Osama bin Laden, "From Somalia to Afghanistan, March 1997," in *Messages to the World: The Statements of Osama Bin Laden*, ed. Bruce Lawrence (New York: Verso, 2005), 44–57.

12. *Al-Hayat*, November 5, 2001.

13. http://groups.colgate.edu/aarislam/abdulhak.htm.

14. Timothy Winter, "The Poverty of Fanaticism," available at http://www.islamfortoday.com/murad02.htm (accessed 19 May 2011).

15. This section is adapted from John L. Esposito, *Islam: The Straight Path*, 3rd ed. (New York: Oxford University Press, 1998), and *Muslims on the Americanization Path* (New York: Oxford University Press, 1999).

16. http://en.wikipedia.org/wiki/Islam_in_the_United_States#cite_note-PewForum -60#cite_note-PewForum-60 (accessed May 14, 2011).

Additional Resources

Oxford Islamic Studies Online (http://www.oxfordislamicstudies.com). A comprehensive scholarly resource for the study of Islam.

Oxford Bibliographies Online (http://oxfordbibliographies.com). Developed cooperatively with scholars and librarians worldwide, the "Islamic Studies" portal at this site is an excellent starting point for research and further understanding.

Islamicity (http://www.islamicity.com). This extensive site provides a nonsectarian, comprehensive, and holistic view of Islam and Muslims to a global audience.

CDs

Michael Sells, *Approaching the Qur'an* (contains CD of Qur'an recitation)
Sami Yusuf, *Without You* (http://www.youtube.com/watch?v=7-ROGqpdRf8)
Zain Bhika, *Allah Knows* (http://www.youtube.com/watch?v=RpjIsSdsT6A)

Films/DVDs

Cities of Light: The Rise and Fall of Islamic Spain (http://www.pbs.org/programs/citiesoflight/)
Great World Religions: Islam
    (http://www.thegreatcourses.com/tgc/courses/course_detail.aspx?cid=6102)
Inside Islam: What a Billion Muslims Really Think
    (http://www.youtube.com/watch?v=FFDyDHSlTfc)
Islam: Empire of Faith (www.pbs.org/empires/islam)
Muhammad: Legacy of a Prophet
    (http://upf.tv/about-upf/our-work/shop/shop-muhammad-dvd.html)
National Geographic, *Inside Mecca*,
    (http://video.google.com/videoplay?docid=-6916375781663065887)

GLOBALIZATION

From New to New Age Religions

6

Overview

Debbie belongs to a Baptist church in Atlanta and regularly attends services on Sunday mornings and Wednesday evenings. However, she has other religious interests as well. Indeed, she regularly checks her astrological chart in the newspaper to see what kind of day she can expect to have. And on Tuesday nights she practices Zen Buddhist meditation with a small Zen group that meets at the house of her friend Sherry. Indeed, Sherry, who happens to be Jewish, is in fact the organizer and leader of the group, or "sangha," as Buddhists call it. Moreover, next week, she and her friend are going for a three-day Zen meditation retreat that she hopes will help deepen her spirituality both as a Christian and as a practitioner of Zen. Last week, Debbie's friend Michael talked her into going to a program led by a psychic medium who offers to put people in touch with their dead relatives. She is not sure what she thinks about this but is open to giving it a try. Likewise, Debbie has been reading *Dianetics*, by Scientology founder L. Ron Hubbard, just to see what it is all about.

All these activities mark Debbie as one of countless individuals who are on a personal quest that is typical of new age religion: They are eager to explore the mystery of the "self" and its perfection. Debbie has another friend, Marcus, who thinks she is too self-absorbed and needs to pay more attention to issues of social justice in a global culture dominated by mass media and multinational corporations, and marred by racial and economic exploitation. Marcus is trying to get her involved in a small interracial activist group inspired by the life and teachings of Martin Luther King Jr.

The group meets at Ebenezer Baptist Church in Atlanta, where Martin Luther King Jr.'s father was once the pastor and Martin the co-pastor. These activities of Debbie and her friends, as we shall see, could all be grouped together under the heading of *new age religion.*

In this chapter we will first explore what we mean by "new" religions and then focus primarily on "new age religions"—the distinctive forms that new religions and new ways of being religious have taken in response to globalization. New religions represent the integration of influences from multiple religions and cultures, resulting in the creation of new variations and expressions of known religious practices. In one familiar pattern, a new prophet or sage reveals new understandings of an existing tradition, given to him or her in religious experiences or revelations.

In the past the messages of prophets and sages reflected primarily local situations—typically the incursion of elements imported from nearby religions and cultures. Today, however, many new religious movements reflect not just a response to local diversity—to this or that movement that has entered the environment of a relatively stable culture. Rather, they are indicative of an awareness of global religious diversity as a whole, past and present. This awareness is fostered by mass communications, especially the Internet and cable television, and widespread access to international transportation, made possible by modern science and technology.

It is in this new environment of the awareness of the diversity of human religious experience that the "new age" religions are emerging, both accommodating and integrating diverse elements of varying, often quite dissimilar, existing traditions. Some movements, however, represent the attempt to reassert particular forms of past

A Pagan outdoor ceremony with a flaming pentagram at a stone circle in England. The ceremony is held on the full moon closest to the summer solstice.

religious expression that adherents believe have been neglected but should be operative in the new age of global interdependence. Contemporary interest in shamanism
and goddess worship would be examples of this. What these movements typically have
in common is the belief that humanity is indeed entering a "new age" in which global
harmony must be achieved, not only with other religions and cultures but also with
the natural environment.

Encounter with Modernity: The Challenge of Global Diversity to the "Purity" of Tradition

In the twenty-first century, Christianity, like all other religious traditions, seeks to
communicate its understanding of truth on a variety of websites. Many of these websites address the concerns of those who hold fundamentalist beliefs and seek to educate
their believers against the dangers of "new age religion." Such websites often contain
warnings such as "'New Age' Religions and Why Christians Can't Participate." Such
websites warn a Christian like "Debbie" (described above) that she is in danger of
worshipping false gods. She is warned that she is failing to be faithful to the Gospel of
Jesus Christ, who offers the one and only path to God and salvation. In postmodern
societies, Christianity is not alone in facing the problem of keeping its followers "true
to the tradition." Other traditions, especially the monotheistic traditions of Judaism
and Islam, also warn their "faithful" to "be faithful" and keep to the way of Torah or
the way of the Quran, as the case may be.

Globalization presents challenges to believers of all traditions. These challenges
come from intimate exposure to the beliefs of other cultures and traditions, which are
now commonly found in everyone's hometown. The challenge of new age religions
is a challenge to the purity of tradition. Persons involved in postmodern spirituality do
not see themselves in an "either/or" situation. They do not see themselves as having
to choose one spiritual practice or path to the exclusion of others. In fact, they see
themselves in a "both/and" situation. For the new age believer, one can be a Jew and
still engage in Buddhist rituals and meditation; one can be a Catholic and still practice
Hindu meditation and ritual; and so on.

The problem of keeping the tradition "pure" may be more challenging for monotheistic religions than it is for the religious traditions of India and China, where different religious paths have often interpenetrated. Nevertheless, people of all religions
and cultures often have reservations when they see their children departing from
strict adherence to the "sacred traditions" as they have known and practiced them. In
every tradition this can seem quite threatening. The issue presented by globalization
is whether it shall lead to greater understanding and cooperation among religions and
cultures or greater defensiveness, prejudice, and even violence. The answer, as we
shall see, is that globalization can lead to both.

New Religions

Old Religions and New Religions in the History of Religions

From a historical perspective, as this book has amply indicated, no religion has ever managed to remain unchanged. Indeed, while every chapter in this book began with an "overview" description of the religious beliefs and practices of the tradition, in every case we went on to say that such a snapshot was no more than a broad generalization that did not accurately reflect the tremendous diversity found among practitioners, yesterday or today. There is not one Judaism but many, not one Buddhism but many—likewise there are many Christianities, many Islams and Hinduisms, many Daoisms and Confucianisms.

New religions test and transform boundaries. Every tradition tolerates a tremendous amount of diversity. An emerging movement that at first is treated as a form of error may finally be accepted into the fold or at least tolerated as a distant cousin. It may, for example, be seen as a reform within the tradition to bring it back to its original purity. But then there are other movements, perhaps brought about by new religious experiences and extraordinary revelations, whose "errors" seem too great. Changes that had started out as reforms may present such a dramatic break with past beliefs and practices that they come to be perceived not as a continuation of the old tradition but as a fatal error—a deviation from the true path. The new tradition, of course, sees the error lying not in itself but in the old tradition, which had somehow lost its way.

Although before the common era there was more than one form of Judaism, Christianity, which began as a Jewish sect called the *Nazarenes*, came to be seen, and to see itself, as crossing a boundary that made it no longer a Jewish alternative but a "new religion." And while Christianity also encompasses tremendous diversity, when Islam emerged in Arabia in the seventh century it was seen by Christians as a new and heretical religion, even though Muslims recounted many of the same biblical stories and saw their faith as the continuation and culmination of God's revelations handed down through Moses and Jesus. Moreover, Islam developed two major branches, Sunni and Shiah, as well as many schools of theology and law. However, in nineteenth-century Persia, when the Baha'i movement claimed to bring a final revelation that included all the religions, East and West, it came to be viewed as "not true Islam," but a new belief system.

When we look at Asian religions we find the same pattern. Hinduism encompasses great diversity, yet as Buddhism grew and developed it was seen, and came to see itself, as a "new religion." Buddhism, too, splintered into many Buddhisms, some claiming to be more advanced than others.

In every tradition, some movements emerged and then disappeared. Even so, in century after century, many of "today's" new religions become tomorrow's old and established religions. We can illustrate the character of new religions with a few examples before turning to our primary concern, examples of "new age" religions that have appeared in our emerging global civilization. The relatively recent history of Christianity in North American culture presents an interesting illustration of how a new religion comes to be.

In the 1800s, Christian denominationalism began to emerge as a way of moving beyond the hostile sectarianism that had divided Christians, and by the late twentieth century there was a broad spectrum of "acceptable" religious diversity in America. Nevertheless, a number of very distinctive religious movements that originated in the nineteenth century tested the limits of denominationalism. As a rule, contemporary mainline Christian denominations (i.e., those representing widely established, long-accepted church traditions in America, such as the Methodists, Presbyterians, and Episcopalians) tend to regard these unique movements as having strayed beyond the boundaries of Christianity. Mormonism provides us with a good example; Jehovah's Witnesses provides another.

The Church of Jesus Christ of Latter-day Saints: A New American Christianity

The Church of Jesus Christ of Latter-day Saints, or Mormonism, was established on April 6, 1830, by Joseph Smith Jr. It appears to have arisen in response to the confusion and conflict created by the incredible sectarian diversity of nineteenth-century Christianity. Joseph Smith believed he had been led by angels to discover a revelation that would overcome this confusion. The new revelation, contained in the Book of Mormon, was understood by Smith and his followers as a continuation of the revelation given in the Bible. It was a revelation that had been given first to Native Americans, as descendants of the lost tribes of ancient Israel. Mormons believe that these tribes had migrated to the North American continent, where the risen Christ visited them and gave them new revelations. Eventually the book containing these pronouncements was buried by a Native American named Mormon, who was killed by tribesmen who rejected the new message and wanted to suppress it. It was these "pagan" natives who met Columbus in 1492. But the revelation could not be suppressed forever, and so Joseph Smith was guided by angels to find the Book of Mormon so that it could flourish once more.

Earlier, in Chapter 4, we noted the incorporation into Christianity of traditions specific to Africa and Asia. Similarly, Mormonism links biblical religion to the history of an indigenous population—in this case producing a distinctively

Joseph Smith Jr. receiving the sacred plates of the Book of Mormon from the Angel Moroni.

American Christianity, one that includes visits of the risen Christ and several of the risen apostles to a new land, to guarantee the purity of Mormon revelation and so set it apart from existing "human interpretations" of Christianity. The capstone of the message was the promise that at the end of time, in the "latter days," Christ would return to establish a "New Jerusalem" in America. The growing stature of Mormonism in America is illustrated by Mitt Romney as the first Mormon candidate for President of the United States in 2012. Mormonism, with its emphasis on family, community, and healthy, wholesome living, flourishes today, with well over 10 million members worldwide.

Jehovah's Witnesses—Another American Vision of the End Time

The nineteenth century saw the emergence of other apocalyptic movements looking for the coming of a New Jerusalem in America. William Miller (1782–1849), a farmer in upstate New York, considered the founder of the Seventh Day Adventists, predicted the second coming of Christ would occur on March 21, 1843. When that did not happen, he recalculated and predicted March 21 a year later. Another, Charles Taze Russell (1852–1916) was swept up in the apocalyptic fervor of movements similar to the Millerites. Charles Taze Russell may have learned from the failure of those predictions, for he embraced an interesting twist on the apocalyptic belief that Christ was coming soon, suggesting that Christ had already spiritually returned as an invisible presence in 1874, initiating a 40-year period for the ingathering of true believers, culminating in 1914, the beginning of World War I as the beginning of the time of apocalyptic sufferings that would announce the second coming.

Charles Taze Russell, founder of the original Watchtower Bible and Tract Society.

Russell began publishing his beliefs in a journal called *Zion's Watch Tower and Herald of Christ's Presence* in 1879. Small congregations following his teachings began holding annual conventions in 1891. Beginning in Allegheny, Pennsylvania, the movement established headquarters in Brooklyn, New York, by 1909. After Russell's death the movement was led by Joseph Franklin Rutherford (1869–1942). In the twentieth century Jehovah's Witnesses grew into a significant international movement with a presence in Europe, Asia, Latin America, and the Middle East. In the year 2000, the Watch Tower Society separated out from the Watch Tower Bible and Tract Society and the new Watch Tower Society's governing board assumed leadership authority in the global movement.

The Jehovah's Witnesses take their name from the Hebrew name for God, the four letters of the tetragrammerton—YHWH. There are no vowels in biblical Hebrew, so they adopted the practice of pronouncing this as "Yehovah." They refer to themselves as Yehovah's Witnesses, those who are called to champion the oneness of God. Although they consider themselves Christians, they do not adhere to the teachings of the ancient church councils that affirmed the trinitarian theology accepted by both the Catholic and mainline Protestant Reformation traditions, which consider God to be one, yet three—Father, Son, and Holy Spirit, all equal in status. For Jehovah's Witnesses, "trinity" is not found in the Bible. In the New Testament, they argue, Jesus is not equal to God but is "first born of all creation" (St Paul's Letter to the Colossians, 1:15) and the "Holy Spirit" simply refers to the active power of God at work in the world. For similar reasons they do not celebrate traditional Christian holidays like Christmas and Easter, which they see as later pagan nonbiblical additions to Christianity.

Like the Millerites or Seventh Day Adventists, Jehovah's Witnesses are distant inheritors of the traditions of the Anabaptist wing of the sixteenth-century Protestant Reformation, who were known for their distrust of government as the work of the devil. Indeed, the Jehovah's Witnesses have a reputation as "conscientious objectors" who refuse to cooperate with any government's conscription into military service. They have also been responsible for several U.S. Supreme Court decisions protecting the separation of church and state. Perhaps most well known among these was securing the right to refuse blood transfusions, which they believe are forbidden by the Bible.

Also, like the Adventists, Jehovah's Witnesses strongly identify with the Jewishness of early Christianity, before its explicit doctrinal move into Trinitarianism. Russell saw 1914, the beginning of World War I, as a spiritually pivotal time which marked the end of the gentile domination over Israel and the beginning of the difficult end times predicted in the Bible. Indeed, Adventists present in Nazi Germany during World War II were courageous in their resistance to the Nazis and Nazi anti-Semitism. Like Jews, they became targets for imprisonment in the death camps.

Civil Religion in China—A Blend of Confucianism and Marx's Secular Apocalyptic Vision

Civil religions represent yet another form in which new religious traditions can play very traditional roles in a society. In most times and most places throughout the history of civilization, religion and politics permeated all of culture and were like two sides of the same coin. It was, as we have seen, modernity that introduced secular nation-states and the idea that government should not impose on citizens the obligation to join or practice any particular religion. But having removed religion as a legitimizer of their own authority, these modern states faced a new problem—winning loyalty from their citizens without the traditional appeal to religion. The result has been the creation of a distinct entity we shall call *civil religion*. Civil religion reintroduces religion under the disguise of "indigenous cultural history and tradition" to reinforce the authority of new and more secular political social orders.

Thus a civil religion is based on a sacred narrative of the state's founding, in which the development of the state is portrayed as a just, moral enterprise, in harmony with

Mao Zedong, founder of the People's Republic of China.

ideals of the religious traditions shared by most citizens. Typically, the state's leaders developed a set of national rituals and yearly holidays (holy days) that celebrate and allow the regular, solemn reliving of key events in the nation's history. Such civil religions come to expression in national anthems and patriotic songs, school textbooks that emphasize the righteousness of the country's founders, and war memorials honoring those who sacrificed their lives for the nation.

In many cases, the cultural pattern from one tradition (Christianity, Islam, Confucianism, etc.) clearly comes to underlie the nation's civil religion, though seldom to the extent of specific endorsement. What is striking is how nearly all the great ideas in the history of religions (e.g., sacrifice, sage, prophet, martyrdom, sacred center, "chosen people," rebirth, *millennialism*—the belief in an age of peace and perfection at the end of time) have been adopted across the world in the service of creating and sustaining the civil religions that support modern nations. Chinese communist civil religion provides a helpful example of this.

When the Red Army gained control of the mainland of China in 1949, Communist Party leader Mao Zedong ascended the southern gateway to the emperor's old palace (the Forbidden City) to proclaim the creation of the People's Republic of China. This moment was later pictured on currency and in popular prints, and soon thereafter an immense portrait of Chairman Mao was mounted over the ancient gateway. Over the next twenty-five years, the Communist Party drew on a variety of religious conceptions to legitimate its position in China and to wield power. Essential to this was the communist millennial doctrine imported from Russian revolutionaries. They in turn drew upon Karl Marx's modernist grand narrative derived from Joachim of Fiore's apocalyptic-biblical vision of the three ages of the human race as a story of progress ending in a final new age. Paradise on earth was inevitable if the people changed their ways and lived in thoroughgoing cooperation. Citizens who sacrificed themselves for the common good were immortalized as "heroes of the people," and their dying was said to hasten the arrival of the new age.

Early on, the government integrated this with ancient Confucian imperial doctrine to promote the cult of Mao himself as the sage-philosopher leader of the nation. His words and teachings were pivotal for national salvation, and his character radiated the morality of communist truth. Statues of Mao were put up in public spaces around the nation, his portrait replaced images of family ancestors in home shrines, and during the Cultural Revolution (1966–76) his "Little Red Book" became a sacred text to be memorized, followed, and always possessed. Officially, the Communist Party disavowed religion as superstition and railed at long-dead Chinese emperors as feudal exploiters of the masses. Nevertheless, it is not hard to see how party strategists adapted powerful religious ideas from both European and Chinese traditions to create a civil religion to confirm the legitimacy of its dictatorship.

The New Age and New Age Religions

Postmodernism and the New Age

The collapse of colonialism, especially after World War II, was followed by the emergence of globalization. This globalization was fostered by the development of international corporations, global mass transportation, and global mass media, carrying modern science and technology around the world. Logically enough, then, since the 1960s and 1970s new patterns of religion have appeared that reflect a global consciousness. These religions shaped by science and technology as well as by the traditional considerations, although incredibly diverse, are often grouped together under the title *new age religions*. Not all new age religions are postmodern as we have defined that term. Indeed, many are content to continue the modernist pattern of privatization rather than seek a new public role for religion. But global consciousness has been a significant factor in the emergence of all new age religions. In this section and the next, we will look at examples of modernist and postmodernist new age religions.

In the first chapter we cited Jean-François Lyotard's definition of *postmodernism* as the collapse of metanarratives, the grand stories or myths that gave each civilization a sense of meaning, purpose, and identity. The great metanarratives created a relationship of identity between religion and culture, giving us Hindu civilization, Christian civilization, Islamic civilization, and so on. Each civilization was centered in its own grand stories and the social practices that came from the vision of life the stories promoted. Modernism, with its myth of scientific progress, was a relatively recent addition.

The resurgence of religions around the globe since the 1970s may well represent the need to fill the vacuum created by the tendency of secularization to purge events of meaning. The problem with a secular understanding of time, history, and society is that the significance and drama provided by the grand narratives of religions are missing. Pluralism may have collapsed the grand metanarratives into smaller stories, but there is still a great hunger for such stories, and new age religions help people discover the meaning and significance of time and their place in it. New age religions provide a rich feast for the religious imagination as seekers attempt to penetrate the mysteries of their time and to explore the wonders they offer.

Postmodern culture represents the loss of a normative center in every culture that has been touched by global mass media, international corporations, and global mass transportation. Postmodern culture is pluralistic, relativistic, and eclectic—seemingly without any public norms or standards. The choice between "truths" is said to be intellectually "undecidable" and so is decided pragmatically, in terms of "what works for me." Truth, goodness, and beauty are in the eye of the beholder. People mix and match beliefs, practices, and aesthetic choices to their own taste in all areas of life—whether music, clothing, architecture, intellectual beliefs, or religion.

Globalization provides the social context of postmodernism. Globalization "marbleizes" all cultures so that the world's religions are accessible in everyone's hometown.

A young Buddhist monk at a school in Burma looks at his photo on a laptop.

Today, much more than in the past, in the same community you will find Jews, Christians, Muslims, Hindus, Buddhists, and many others. Such pluralism is a powerful social force inducing the collapse of metanarrative, whereby a story that was once embraced by almost all people in a given culture is now simply one of many stories. In this situation religions are challenged first to relinquish their position of being identical with the culture and then to accommodate an existing cultural pluralism. In this context, almost all religious communities have had to embrace denominational type identities, accepting the existence of other beliefs and practices, although fundamentalist communities strive mightily to resist such an accommodation. This denominational accommodation, we said, was what sociologist Peter Berger meant by saying that all religions have become "Protestant." But for most new age groups their religious practices have gone a step further, moving from organizational pluralism (denominationalism) to eclecticism.

Many of the "new age" religions, like older "new religions," represent the integration of the diverse influences from different traditions. The new age religions are not based solely on the great world religions; often they incorporate elements of primal religions, exhibiting a special interest in shamanism. Moreover, today these eclectic belief systems typically reflect not only global religious diversity but the global influence of science and technology as well.

A group in the Netherlands performs a ritual based on the Thirteen Moon calendar of the Maya.

The New Age—Modern and Postmodern?

New age religious movements can be divided into modernist forms, which continue to privatize religion, and postmodernist public forms of religious practice, which seek an active role, socially and politically, in transforming society. Most modernist new age religions are highly diverse in their practices and beliefs, with minimal organizational structure. Nevertheless, there are some very important instances of highly structured new age movements; as we shall see, Scientology is one and Baha'i is another. What unites new age seekers, despite their diversity, however, is the quest for the perfection of the self. Their goal is to realize a "higher self" through intense personal experiences of transformation.

Many new age seekers are not interested in joining religious organizations. They typically integrate a variety of interests into their personal style of spiritual practice. Many read "spiritual" books and go to workshops and seminars intended to guide them to self-realization. Modernist "new agers" are interested in such shamanistic practices as channeling information from other-worldly spiritual beings, contacting the dead through mediums, spiritual healing, and the cultivation of ecstatic out-of-body experiences (sometimes referred to as *astral projection*). They are also interested in the mystical traditions and meditation practices of all religions as well as the ancient divination practice of astrology. Some combine these interests with the teachings and practices of transpersonal psychologists such as Abraham Maslow (1908–70) and Fritz Perls (1894–1970); others embrace speculative visions that combine the "new physics" with religion, believing that science itself is finally coming to discover and affirm ancient religious and metaphysical insights. The final test of each seeker's synthesis is personal experience and pragmatically evaluated usefulness.

Modernity, we learned in Chapter 4, on Christianity, emerged out of the splitting of the medieval unity of faith and reason into the *via moderna* of empirical rationality and the *devotio moderna* of personal emotional experiences of transformation (mysticism, pietism, and the experience of being "born again"). The first path became dominant in the Enlightenment and the second in the Romantic movement, as a reaction to the Enlightenment. The growth of new age religiousness is deeply rooted in this Romantic reaction to the rationalism of the Enlightenment.

The Enlightenment emphasized universal rationality (i.e., the sameness of human nature everywhere), science, and progress. Its philosophers rejected the ancient, the archaic, the traditional, the idiosyncratic, and the nonrational. The Romantic reaction, a stage we are still in, did just the opposite, embracing in all their diversity the emotional, the experientially transformational, the historically unique and particular, as well as the "primitive" and traditional aspects of human history.

Like fundamentalist forms of evangelical Christianity, modernist forms of new age religions are expressions of the human need for transformative experience, a need as old as shamanism and as recent as the Romantic reaction to Enlightenment rationalism and its expression in evangelical pietism. Both deemphasize rationality and focus on the experiential transformation and perfection of the self through deeply emotional experiences of the kind we have called religious. And both share the conviction that all social change begins by changing the self (i.e., by being born again).

The Age of Apocalypse or the Age of Aquarius?

Two new age models of religious meaning are playing a role in our emerging global civilization—the apocalyptic and the astrological. These models share a vision of the conflict and discord of the past and present giving way to a future era of global peace and harmony. Among Christian evangelicals the popularity of the belief that the end of time is near is evidenced by sales of tens of millions of books such as Hal Lindsey's *The Late Great Planet Earth* and the *Left Behind* series of novels. As indicated by the popularity of biblical prophecies of the end times among evangelical Christians, there are still many heirs to the apocalyptic religious vision of the medieval monk Joachim of Fiore, who anticipated a "third age" (the age of the Spirit) as a time of global peace and harmony. However, the third age will be preceded by the biblical apocalypse, which in turn will bring the cataclysmic end of time. The belief that there will be a cataclysmic end to time followed by a new age of peace and harmony is also illustrated in such late-twentieth-century movements such as Aum Shinrikyo (to be reviewed shortly). But first we will turn to the alternative vision—the astrological vision of the age of Aquarius.

A gentler vision of the new age, the age of Aquarius, has been offered by some astrologers in recent decades:

> We are passing out of 2,000 years of Piscean astrological influence into the influence of Aquarius, which will affect all aspects of our culture as we move from Piscean structures of hierarchical devotion to more fluid and spontaneous relationships that dance to an Aquarian rhythm.[1]

Predictions of the coming of a new age by others not of the apocalyptic tradition include the writings of José Argüelles. In his book *The Mayan Factor*, this new age author used ancient Mayan and Aztec astrology to calculate that the age of Aquarius would begin in 1987, on August 16 or 17.[2] When that did not happen, new interpretations or perhaps misinterpretations of Mayan texts emerged predicting a more traditional apocalyptic view of the end of the world which would occur when the Mayan calendar ends (according to some) on December 21, 2012. As of 2013, that has not happened either. In these Aquarian times, many forms of new age religion tap into a very ancient type of religious experience found in primal animistic and early urban polytheistic religious practices—that of the shaman. As we saw in Chapter 2, in his or her ecstatic or out-of-body experiences, the shaman explores the spirit world, the realm of contact with spiritual beings and dead ancestors.

Everywhere in the world, shamanism appears to be the earliest form of religious experience. And everywhere, the great world religions emerge with the discovery that the realm that a shaman visits when he or she leaves her physical body to travel to the domains of the spirits and of dead ancestors is really an intermediate spiritual realm between the earthly physical world and a higher unitary reality. For example, in the Vedas of Hinduism the highest realities are the many gods and goddesses of nature, but in the Upanishads the discovery is made that the gods are part of the order of this world of samsara and that there is a higher power beyond their realm, the reality of Brahman.

The emergence of monotheism out of polytheism in the Mediterranean world (in Judaism, Christianity, and Islam) provides another example. The polytheistic realm of the gods was not denied. It could not be denied because many people continued to have shamanistic-type experiences of another realm inhabited by spiritual beings. So this realm of the deities was reassigned to a different kind of spiritual being and renamed the realm of angels and demons. Like the devas or gods of Hinduism, angels were recognized as spiritual beings, yet they were part of the cosmic order created by a higher reality, God. In China this concept of a higher unitary reality was given the impersonal name of Dao.

For all the differences between ancient urban religious cultures and religions in postmodern society, there is at least one profound similarity between them: Both pre-modern urban society, as typified, for instance, by the polytheistic culture of ancient Rome, and postmodern society, with its myriad eclectic religious practices, lack an integrating center. In both, being religious is not so much about belonging to "a religion" as it is about selecting from the chaotic variety of available beliefs and practices, a mix that will serve the pragmatic purposes of finding health, happiness, and meaning, that is, of having the unseen powers that govern your destiny on your side.

Wicca and the Resurgence of Goddess Worship

Determining how many people "practice new age religion" is next to impossible. This is because it is quite common for nominal adherents to one of these belief systems to practice several different forms in their private life while perhaps also belonging to a traditional church or synagogue. One form this eclectic spirituality can take is sometimes called *neopaganism*, which is vividly exemplified in a return to the practice of witchcraft, or attunement to the sacred powers of nature, a pattern found in all premodern societies. The most prominent such practice today is Wicca, which appears to be a self-conscious reconstruction of ancient pagan religious practices. The Wiccan movement can be traced back to England in the 1940s and the writings of Gerald Gardener, who claimed to be an initiate of a Wiccan coven, authorized to reveal its teachings and practices to the public. Two students of Gardener's brought the practice to America in the 1960s. By 1965 a church of Wicca was established in Mississippi, and by 1978 the handbook for U.S. military chaplains included Wicca in its list of religions.

Wiccans see the world ordered by sacred forces that can be accessed through ritual magic. These powers are personified as gods and goddesses. Wiccan rituals involve the

High priestess and priest Gypsy and Richard Ravish sit at a Wiccan altar dedicated to magick in Salem, Massachusetts.

elaborate use of chant, dance, drumming, and meditation. By following the ancient Celtic agricultural cycle of festivals for the seasons of the year, these rituals enable Wiccans to reconnect with the rhythms of nature and to experience its hidden unity. Many tend to see their ritual practice as an outward expression of the fundamental truth of the interconnectivity of all things, a view that they believe modern science also affirms. One particular strand of Wicca, Dianic Wicca, presents itself as a feminist religion that rejects references to gods in favor of goddess worship and has radicalized its practice by banning male membership.

J. Z. Knight and the Ramtha School of Enlightenment

The Ramtha movement begun by J. Z. Knight provides another example of new age religion that appeals to pre-Christian shamanistic practices. It is a very good example of what is called "channeling," in which a spiritual being takes over and speaks through the body of a person. Knight is considered by her followers to be the psychic medium who channels Ramtha, a 35,000-year-old warrior, who speaks through her, revealing an ancient wisdom. It is said that when Ramtha possesses her, Knight's entire personality, her voice quality, and all her mannerisms change, as if she is another person altogether. Like the shamans of tribal cultures, she is revered by her followers as one who communicates between two worlds, the physical and the spiritual. Ramtha is an ancient warrior who supposedly lived in the city of Lemuria and defeated the armies of the ancient city of Atlantis. Ramtha was wounded in battle, and during the seven years of his recovery he had profound out-of-body spiritual and enlightenment experiences and finally transcended human form to become a being of light. The teachings of Ramtha are embodied in a text known as *The White Book*.

The vision of Ramtha appears to have much in common with the teachings of Gnosticism from ancient Greece and Rome. The highest spiritual reality, for instance, is said to be both male and female; the spiritual realm is said to be made up of seven levels; and Ramtha is said to be a being of light. All of these are characteristic teachings of ancient Gnosticism. Ramtha's revelation to Knight is intended to help people realize their true divine nature. Once upon a time people had divine powers to create objects in the world simply by thinking them. However, humans lost their awareness of the divine core of their being and became imprisoned in the material world. Ramtha has come to help them rediscover their true spiritual nature and their true powers and so overcome "the ditch of limitation."

J. Z. Knight was born in Roswell, New Mexico, a city famed for the belief among flying saucer enthusiasts that in 1947 an alien spaceship crashed and was examined by the military, which has kept the findings secret. Knight's mother is said to have had the power to foretell the future through dreams. Furthermore, the stories of Knight's childhood include one that says an elderly Yaqui Indian woman predicted that the infant Knight would grow up to be one who sees "what no one else sees." In addition, a psychic predicted that Knight would move to a mountainous area covered in pine trees, which Knight saw fulfilled when she was offered a job in the Tacoma, Washington, area. It was there that Knight experienced the manifestation of Ramtha for the first time in 1973. Five years later she made her first public appearance as the medium or channeler of Ramtha. Knight has become famous, publishing books, making TV appearances, and so on. Eventually, she established a kind of Ramtha retreat or teaching center on her ranch in Yelm, Washington. There she teaches Ramtha's followers that they can perfect themselves. There is no need to be trapped in their limitations. Everyone should realize their true divine powers.

Madame Helena Petrovna Blavatsky, founder of the theosophy movement.

Theosophy, Christian Science, and the Unity School of Christianity

The precedents for the Ramtha school and many other forms of new age religion go back to the interest in esoteric religious beliefs and practices that flourished in the nineteenth century, when historical and ethnographic researchers were just beginning to catalog the diverse practices of primal (tribal) and archaic (early urban) religions. From Europe, the teachings of Emanuel Swedenborg (1688–1772) and Franz Anton Mesmer (1734–1815) spread belief in the validity of the shamanistic experience of other worlds and in the animistic unity of all things, which made spiritual healing possible. In America, Ralph Waldo Emerson (1803–82) and others popularized a school of thought called *transcendentalism*, which integrated certain Asian religious beliefs (especially Hinduism) with American philosophy, affirming the existence of a "world soul" that all beings shared. In this context the practice of spiritualism also flourished, with psychic mediums performing in private séances the ancient shamanistic rituals for contacting spirit beings and dead relatives.

One of the most important movements to emerge at this time was theosophy, founded in New York by Helena Petrovna Blavatsky (1831–91) in 1875. Like the transcendentalists, theosophists found great spiritual wisdom in esoteric teachings, especially in the ancient teachings of Hinduism, with their focus on the interconnectedness of all beings through the universal Brahman. In the theosophical view, all world religions have a hidden unity of message and metaphysical reality, which could be sought through the truths of esoteric texts as well as through the help of leaders who claimed to receive guidance from "living masters," residing in the Himalayas. The theosophists had considerable influence among Asian reformers who were trying to modernize Buddhism. This growing interest in global religious wisdom is illustrated by the first Parliament of World Religions in Chicago in 1893, at which representatives of all the world's religions convened to share their views.

This historical milieu gave birth to two important nineteenth-century precursors of new age religion, both with roots in the New Thought movement: the Church of Christ, Scientist (Christian Science) and the Unity School of Christianity. Women were leaders in both movements. Mary Baker Eddy was the founder of the Christian Science movement, and Emma Curtis Hopkins, a former disciple, broke with Eddy to form the Unity School. The two movements drew on popular forms of philosophical idealism, and the Unity School emphasized Hindu teachings, as well. These influences were integrated with an aura of "science" to affirm the higher reality of mind over matter and therefore the possibility of spiritual healing and spiritual control over the events of one's life.

Emma Curtis Hopkins, founder of the Unity School of Christianity.

Scientology

As the new age religions began to appear in the twentieth century, the religious fascination with the authority of "science" broke free of its earlier linkage to Christianity in movements of the "Christian Science" type. One result was the emergence of *Scientology*, founded by L. Ron Hubbard (1911–86). In 1950 Hubbard published *Dianetics: The Modern Science of Mental Healing*, in which he claimed to have discovered a cure for all human psychological and psychosomatic ills through the realization of a state of mind he called "Clear." Hubbard went on to establish the Hubbard Dianetic Research Foundation in Elizabeth, New Jersey. Later he moved the organization to

"The lofty reasonings of Science are the sunshine of the Spirit. They are the works of Truth. Truth is in us. Let it shine. Truth performs great tasks. Let it shine on miracles of health, cheering, enlightening the nations."

—Emma Curtis Hopkins

Phoenix, Arizona, where the Hubbard Association of Scientologists was founded in 1952.

Although born in Tilden, Nebraska, Hubbard was exposed to Asian religion and culture as a child because he traveled with his father, who was in the navy. As a young man with an adventurous spirit, Hubbard was involved in three Central American ethnological expeditions. He received a commission in the navy during World War II, during which service he was pronounced dead twice. In one instance he apparently had something like a shamanistic out-of-body experience in which he acquired spiritual knowledge that gave him his life's mission.

In *Dianetics: The Modern Science of Mental Healing*, which became the foundation for Scientology, we learn that the mind is made up of two parts, the analytic and the reactive. Traumatic experiences in early life or even in the womb are said to imprint themselves on the reactive mind as *engrams*, which cause psychological and psychosomatic problems if they are not dissolved. The way to dissolve these traumatic impressions is to work with a counselor called an *auditor*, who leads the individual into reenacting the events that caused the trauma, thus releasing or liberating the individual from the engrams' negative effects. Hubbard called this state of release "Clear," and devotees of Scientology work hard to attain it.

Mary Baker Eddy, founder of the Church of Christ, Scientist (Christian Science).

Scientology, however, went beyond the psychological orientation of Dianetics to develop an elaborate mythology according to which all humans were once advanced beings Hubbard called *Thetans*. These are all-powerful, eternal, and omniscient beings. The first Thetans relieved their boredom by playing mind games in which they used imagination to create different physical worlds. However, they soon forgot their true identity as creators and found themselves trapped in these worlds, living as mortals who died, only to be reincarnated again and again. At each reincarnation, people accumulated more psychological baggage, or engrams. To be liberated from this pattern and realize one's true identity, it is necessary to gain insight into one's engrams. Upon finally achieving the "Clear" state of mind, a person gains control over both mind and life. The auditing process that leads to this liberation came to involve the use of a machine that works somewhat like a lie detector. This device, the E-meter, it is believed, measures reactions of resistance to words and other symbols that reveal undissolved engrams. After achieving "Clear," one can go on to higher states that involve out-of-body experiences.

In 1954 Hubbard established the first Church of Scientology in Washington, DC, and in 1959 he started the Hubbard College of Scientology in England. Whereas many new age religious movements stress individualism and are quite loosely organized, Scientology has an elaborate bureaucratic global organization, similar to that of Roman

TALES OF SPIRITUAL TRANSFORMATION: A Scientologist's Account of Achieving "Clear"

As with other religious movements throughout history, Scientologists seek to undergo spiritual death and rebirth, or being "born again." In such rebirth experiences the old way of experiencing the world is replaced by a dramatically new one. The following example is taken from a publication of the Church of Scientology of California dated 1970.

There is no name to describe the way I feel. At last I am at cause. I am Clear—I can do anything I want to do. I feel like a child with a new life—everything

is so wonderful and beautiful. Clear is Clear! It's unlike anything I could have imagined. The colors, the clarity, the brightness of everything is beyond belief. Everything is so new, I feel newborn. I am filled with the wonder of everything.

Source: Quoted in Robert S. Ellwood and Harry Partin, eds., *Religious and Spiritual Groups in America*, 2nd ed. (Upper Saddle River, NJ: Prentice Hall, 1988), p. 140.

Catholicism or Mormonism. Perhaps an even better analogy is to the modern international business corporation, with its penchant for technical language, efficient organization, and the dissemination of polished communications to interface with the world. And yet all this organization and efficiency is focused on bringing about a powerful experience of enlightenment or rebirth that perfects the self and opens it to the spiritual world that shamans have traversed throughout the ages. Scientologists have also shown a keen interest in Buddhist teachings, there may be Taoist influences as well, and of course the parallels of the auditing practices to depth psychology are obvious. The achievement of "Clear" shows the movement's affinity with both Western experiences of being "born again" and Eastern experiences of enlightenment.

Scientology is, in many ways, the perfect illustration of the global eclectic integration of the elements that make up new age religions: science (especially psychology), technology (corporate and technical structure), Asian religions (reincarnation and the quest for liberation), and shamanism (out-of-body spiritual explorations). A Thetan, according to Hubbard, goes "through walls, barriers, vanishes space, appears anywhere at will and does other remarkable things."[3]

L. Ron Hubbard, founder of Scientology

"Philosophic knowledge is only valuable if it is true or if it works. . . . A philosophy can only be a *route* to knowledge. It cannot be crammed down one's throat. If one has a route, he can then find what is true for him. And that is Scientology."

—L. Ron Hubbard

The Baha'i Global Religious Vision

As we transition from the nineteenth through the twentieth and into the twenty-first century, the Baha'i tradition presents us with a powerful example of the embrace of globalization in a new religious movement that links the biblical religions of Judaism, Christianity, and Islam in a sweeping vision that comes to embrace the religions of Asia as well.

The Baha'i tradition emerged in nineteenth-century Persia (Iran today) in a world dominated by Islam. There is a kind of logical development that goes on among the biblical religions. Arising out of the religious traditions of an ancient Israel, Judaism began to emerge after the Babylonian Exile as the first biblical witness to the oneness of God through its Torah and eventually Talmud. In the first century, Christianity, starting as a Jewish sect, broke off from Judaism to become a new religion. Christians claimed that Jews had failed to recognize Jesus as Messiah and Son of God, who fulfills the ancient Jewish prophecies which Christians believe are contained in the Torah. For Christians, Jesus is the final fulfillment of the Bible; nothing and no one else is needed after him. So Christians added the New Testament to the Torah to make a new Bible in two parts: Old Testament (an adaptation of the Torah) and New Testament.

Then in the seventh century, in Arabia, Muhammad emerged as a new prophet, who teaches that both Jews and Christians have strayed from the straight path God had laid out in his revelations in history. Muslims believe God sent the "seal of the prophets," Muhammad, as the last and final prophet to reveal the truth of God's will. Just as Christianity did not deny that God revealed himself to Jews first, but asserted Jesus completed God's revelation in Christianity, so Muslims argue that revelation is only completed by God's revelation through the "seal of the prophets," Muhammad. The Quran, like the New Testament, embraced the great figures of biblical revelation, such as Adam, Abraham, Isaac, Jacob, Moses, David, and Jesus and even recognizes Jesus as the Messiah who will return at the end of time, but it does not call him, as Christians do, Son of God.

In the nineteenth century in Persia, a new religious movement, Baha'i, emerged and claimed to be founded on a new revelation to the Bab in 1844. The Baha'i emerge out of Shiite Islam, which emphasizes the primacy of political leadership by divinely inspired Imams rather than the Sunni Ulama or scholars sharing authority with political leaders or Caliphs. One Shiite branch, The Twelvers, held that there would be twelve such Immams. The twelfth disappeared and is said to have gone into occulatation, a state of being not unlike Jesus' ascension into heaven, to come again at the end of time. In fact, some teach that Jesus and the twelfth Imam—the Madhi—will appear together at the end of time. Around this time this messianic expectation for the reappearance of the twelfth Imam—Mohammad al Madhi—was heating up, leading to the expectation that since it was one thousand years since the disappearance of the "hidden Imam" his promised return was eminent.

Shirazi Sayid Ali Muhammad, who came to be known as the Bab, was the first Shiite Muslim messianic leader to break away from Islam to forge a new religious movement and was seen by some as the hoped-for revelation of the hidden Imam. He was executed for his attempt in 1850. The followers of the Bab (a word meaning "gate") were initially known as the Babis. The Bab, who came to play a role similar to John the Baptist in the Christian story of Jesus, is said to have prophesied that his disciple, Mirza Husayn ali Nuri (1817–1892), was to be the promised one—*He Who God Will Manifest*—a new messenger of God. Mirza Husayn ali Nuri was imprisoned in Tehran during a persecution of the Babis in 1852. While in prison he came to believe he was indeed called to be a divine messenger. He became known as

Bahaaullah—"the splendor or glory of God." He authored the *Kitab al-aqdas* or the "Most Holy Book" of the Baha'i faith. In 1863, while in exile in Baghdad, he publicly embraced his role as God's promised messenger. He was imprisoned in Acre for nine years and later settled in Haifa in what is now Israel. He died in 1892. Haifa is now the site of the Baha'i World Center.

Baha'i teaching claims that God's revelation did not end with Jesus, nor with Muhammad, nor even with Bahaaullah, but God provides a new messenger or "Manifestation" for each new age of humanity. Naturally, Muslims take exceptions to the idea that Muhammad is not the seal of the prophets, just as Christians reject the Muslim view that Islam corrects and supersedes Christian teachings, and just as Jews take exception to Christian and Muslim claims to have superseded Judaism. The teachings of the Baha'i complicate this picture further by arguing that God has provided other revelations in Asian religions, like Hinduism and Buddhism through

The Baha'i Gardens and the Shrine of the Bab in Haifa, Israel.

Krishna and Buddha, that are a part of God's "Great Covenant" of continuing revelations to all humanity. Baha'i is just the most recent example. According to Baha'i teaching, all these prophets or "mirrors" of God are part of God's continuing manifestations leading the whole human race into a new global unity. The global vision of the Baha'i teaches the oneness of God, the oneness of all God's prophets around the world, and the oneness of humanity. Baha'i calls on all to establish this oneness as a fact in a global harmony beyond all divisions of nationality, religion, race, or gender.

Baha'i teaching offers a parallel to the vision of history of progress through the three ages of the human race. This view, rooted in Joachim of Fiore's account of the Book of Revelation in Christianity, was adopted in Western Enlightenment philosophical thought by figures like Immanuel Kant, G. W. F. Hegel, and Karl Marx. The great Enlightenment philosopher Immanuel Kant was perhaps the first philosopher to see the ethical significance of an emerging global consciousness. At the end of the eighteenth century, in his "Idea for a Universal History from a Cosmopolitan Point of View" (1784) and in his essay on "Perpetual Peace" (1795), Kant argued that living on a round earth we cannot escape from each other. Rather, we are forced to recognize our equality and interdependence with each other as human beings. Kant was a severe critic of Western colonialism and called for the creation of a "league of nations" to promote our common human rights and bring an end to all war. He brought together the Stoic dream of cosmopolitan citizenship with the Christian millennial hope that at the end of time all the tribes of the earth would live together in perpetual peace. Kant's ideals came to be embodied in the experiment with the League of Nations from 1920 to 1946 and the birth of the United Nations in 1945.

Parallel commitments are expressed in Baha'i teachings that have established a global "House of Justice" and Spiritual Assemblies to provide a model for—and encouragement of—the global unification of the human race in peace and universal harmony. Baha'i teachings do not see the teachings of Bahaaullah as competing with these other trends toward globalization but rather see in them the multiple instances in which God is working to unify the human race in confirmation of the Baha'i vision. It was, Abdul-Baha, Bahaaullah's son and successor in spiritual teaching, who appointed his grandson, Shoghi Effendi, as the Guardian of the Baha'i Community and it was Effendi who established the Universal House of Justice. Under his guidance the laws and institutions needed to promote the unity of the human race became organized into "the Administrative Order" of the Baha'i community. This institution exists at the local, national, and finally the international level through which Baha'i's work promotes the establishment of world harmony and God's kingdom on earth. This emerging kingdom, they believe, will pass from a stage of crisis through a lesser peace gradually established by agreements among the nations, to the "Most Great Peace," which results from finally realizing the truth of Bahaaullah's teaching by the masses as a "coming of age" of the whole human race. Baha'i teaching and practice provides global leadership through The World Centre of Baha'i Faith and its "International Teaching Center" in Haifa in Israel. The estimated population of Baha'i's in the world today is over 5 million.

East Goes West: Zen in America

Yogic meditation, whether in its Hindu or Buddhist forms, has made surprising inroads into American religious life in the "new age." Transcendental Meditation is an example of the first, while Zen Buddhism is an example of the second. Both are examples of a new "methodism" in American culture. As we learned in Chapter 4, Methodism was one of the most successful evangelical forms of Christianity transplanted from England to America. Evangelical Christianity originated as a rebellion against religious dogmatism and the religious wars that dogmatism had caused in Europe. It emphasized the spiritual practices of piety and prayer (praying regularly or "methodically") and the religious experience of being "born again" as more important than religious dogma. And evangelicals saw the test of true faith as demonstrating the fruit of that experience by exercising ethical compassion toward all others. In this way Methodism prepared the way for new forms of methodism in an age of globalization in America. Zen is one way in which the "methodist impulse" of pragmatic Americans looking for experiential religion finds expression in the new age. Like Methodism, it minimizes belief and maximizes spiritual practice leading to transformative experience and ethical compassion.

"Zen" is a Japanese translation of the word *Ch'an*, which is the Chinese translation of the Sanskrit *dhyana*, meaning "meditation." Zen is rooted in the practice of yogic meditation that has its origins in India. The core of this spiritual practice is emptying the mind of all thoughts, which begins by simply focusing one's mind on following one's breathing. Unlike the Hindu tradition, however, Zen Buddhist practice requires meditating with your eyes open, emphasizing that Zen is about transforming how you see and experience the world around you. Zen emphasizes the spiritual practice of sitting cross-legged (in the "lotus position") with an empty mind free of all emotional attachments so as to remain "mindful" or open to every new experience as you engage in your everyday activities.

Bodhidharma is said to have brought Buddhism from India to China in the fifth century CE as the first patriarch of the Chinese tradition of Ch'an. He defined Zen as a transformative experience rather than a religion of doctrines to be believed. The goal of meditation was to lead one to experience "no self," or "emptiness of all self." He emphasized that the self could not be defined, only experienced in its emptiness and immediacy or "suchness." So he said that Zen was

A special tradition outside the scriptures;
No dependence upon words or letters;
Direct pointing at the soul of man;
Seeing into one's own nature, and the attainment of Buddhahood.

The "enlightened" person is one who is "born again" (to use an evangelical phrase)—one who experiences his or her interdependence with all beings. Such a person sees everything with astonishment and wonder, as if for the first time, and knows that no one has an independent self. This experience is said to lead one to embrace all beings with compassion.

A famous Zen *koan* is "What is the sound of one hand clapping?" A Zen master gives this koan or spiritual puzzle to Zen disciples and asks them to meditate on it until they have an answer. Then the disciples are to come back to have their answers tested. The problem is that there is no "rational" answer. This spiritual puzzle is meant to defeat the rational mind and its abstract conventional beliefs in order to startle each disciple into a direct experience of reality. According to Zen teaching, you cannot know who you are and what reality is by "believing" some doctrines or truths. You can only know your true nature and the true nature of all reality by experiencing a breakthrough (called *kensho* or "enlightenment") that forces you to abandon all conventional beliefs and experiences for a direct experience of reality that cannot be put into words.

Zen Buddhism began to establish itself in America in the 1930s, at first to serve immigrant Japanese communities in California. But Buddhism did not become an American phenomenon until the 1950s and 1960s. The stories of Zen as a spiritual practice that challenges conventional religion and conventional forms of experience

Buddhist scholar and writer D. T. Suzuki at work.

and authority appealed to the "Beat generation" or "beatniks" of the 1950s (novelists and poets such as Jack Kerouac and Gary Snyder) and the "counterculture" of the "hippies," who carried their irreverent attitude toward "conventional" middle-class life in America into the 1960s and beyond. Authors such as Alan Watts and D. T. Suzuki played a major role in bringing Zen to popular attention in the 1960s and 1970s. Almost a half century later Zen communities can be found in most large cities around the world. Zen in America tends to be less monastic and far more open to the leadership of women than would be the case in Japan. It is not unusual, in the spirit of the "new age," for American Zen communities or sanghas to have many members who continue to practice their Judaism or Christianity as well. Also, many atheists and agnostics are attracted to it as a way to be religious without having to be theistic. These communities seem to have integrated Zen into the middle-class lifestyle of a now-postmodern culture that encourages diversity and experimentation in a way that the conformist America of the 1950s, protested by "beatniks," did not.

West Goes East: The Aum Shinrikyo Movement

The new age religions we have looked at so far have been more Aquarian than apocalyptic. They have been rooted in the nature-oriented religions deeply attuned to the cycles of nature, like the astrological tradition that posits the Aquarian age. But other new age religions reflect the pattern of the eastward migration of biblical apocalyptic traditions, leading to some interesting integrations of West and East. The Japanese religion Aum Shinrikyo is a good example. An apocalyptic new age vision has taken root in this new religion, which achieved global notoriety and terrorist status when some members released deadly sarin gas into the Tokyo subway system in 1995. As a child in a school for the blind, Aum Shinrikyo founder Chizuo Matsumoto boasted that he would one day be prime minister of Japan. Yet the early years of the severely sight-impaired youth were not promising. After two failures to enter the Japanese university system, he joined a new religious movement called *Agonshu*, which mixed Buddhist, Daoist, and Hindu teachings. In 1984 he broke with Agonshu and developed a personal religious vision, integrating elements of Hindu yoga, Buddhist meditation, and Christian apocalyptic beliefs. He visited India in 1986 and had what he believed to be a powerful enlightenment experience. Convinced that he was destined to be a great spiritual master, Chizuo Matsumoto, then the leader of his own small movement, took on the name Shoko Asahara and named his group Aum Shinrikyo.

In 1986 Shoko Asahara registered the Aum Shinrikyo ("Supreme Truth") movement as a religion with the Japanese government. Having done this, he attracted additional followers by writing extensively in his country's new age religious publications, promising to teach seekers out-of-body shamanistic skills such as clairvoyance and teleportation. He had a charismatic personality, and his movement, which has had an extraordinary appeal among the university-educated professional class, quickly became one of the fastest-growing new religions in Japan.

Shoko Asahara, founder
of Aum Shinrikyo

Through a well-developed bureaucracy, with Asahara at the top, Aum Shinrikyo established monastic-like separatist communities throughout Japan, where the most devoted followers congregated, having left their families and given all their earthly belongings to the movement. Descriptions of the initiation rituals have mentioned the heavy use of hallucinogens, the drinking of vials of Asahara's blood, and a total surrender to Asahara as the spiritual master.

In the beginning Asahara taught that the world would end soon and that it was the task of his followers to save humanity through their hard work in Aum business ventures and through purification by personal spiritual practices. After Asahara and some of his handpicked leaders were decisively defeated in an attempt to win seats in Japan's parliament in 1990, Asahara's teachings took a darker turn, seeking to destroy what he believed were the demonic forces that opposed his movement.

By 1993 Aum Shinrikyo had plants producing automatic weapons as well as chemical and biological weapons, ostensibly to protect Japan against its enemies. Believing that the United States was about to trigger an apocalyptic nuclear war, Aum scientists traveled to Russia and Africa in search of biological and nuclear weapons. Aum Shinrikyo's following in Russia by 1995 was estimated at 30,000, roughly three times its membership in Japan. The group's terrorist plans, however, were known only to a small, mostly Japanese, elite.

Asahara came under legal scrutiny for his varied activities, especially after authorities learned that the worth of Aum's assets exceeded $1 billion. In 1994, convinced that the Japanese government's special police force had set out to destroy him, Asahara ordered the assassination of three judges by releasing poison gas in their neighborhoods. The judges survived, but some innocent bystanders were killed. The next year, after the Tokyo subway gassing, he was arrested.

Asahara integrated Japanese Shinto beliefs with Hinduism and Tibetan Buddhism in a way that appealed to many young Japanese professionals (including scientists) by calling into question modern materialism as well as the stress and decadence of modern life. Indeed, influenced by the science fiction of Isaac Asimov, Asahara developed a vision of the role of scientists in building an elite secret society that would save civilization from cataclysmic wars. To this he added a strong dose of Christian apocalyptic expectations (mixed with the predictions of Nostradamus) about the imminent end of the world in a battle between good and evil. He justified his murderous assaults on his fellow citizens by pronouncing that killing those who are creating bad karma was actually doing them a spiritual favor, since it stopped them before they produced even more negative karma.

To his followers, Asahara declared himself to be Jesus Christ, come to bring judgment on the world. In preparation for the global nuclear war he believed the United States was plotting, he bought land in Australia. There his followers could start to build a new civilization as they waited out the years of lethal radiation in a devastated Northern Hemisphere. Ultimately, Asahara was convicted for having masterminded the Tokyo sarin gas attack. He was sentenced to death in 2004, and the movement, which regrouped under the name *Aleph* ("the beginning"), still reveres him as its spiritual leader.

Like Scientology, Aum Shinrikyo illustrates the integration of shamanism and Eastern mysticism with scientific research and technological applications organized by a highly efficient globally oriented bureaucratic organization. The difference between them is equally important, for Asahara's eclectic religious vision adds elements of Western apocalyptic thought colored by his own paranoid vision of himself as the rejected prophet and spiritual master. The result was dangerously violent.

Conclusion: The Postmodern Challenge— Can There Be a Global Ethic in a World of Religious Diversity?

In 2010 various atheist groups in the United States and Britain began an advertising campaign, affirming on billboards and other media that you can be "Good Without God." This, of course, was shocking to many pious people in both countries. However, from the perspective of the comparative study of religions, atheism appears to be a culturally relative phenomenon. It seems to depend on the versions of monotheistic belief generated by the biblical religions of Judaism, Christianity, and Islam. Many Buddhists, it is often noted, have no belief in God yet are deeply religious and morally courageous. One of the attractions of Buddhism in a world shaped by modern science is to offer educated persons a way to be religious without believing in God. The real question for the global future of religions is this: Can there be a shared global ethic in a world of diverse worldviews, whether theistic or nontheistic?

Beyond Atheism: The Challenge of Postmodern Secular Relativism

As we noted in the first chapter, religion is about what people hold sacred, and what they hold sacred is their way of life. God, gods, or spirits are often introduced in sacred stories to explain why a group's way of life is sacred, but that way of life may be considered sacred even if such beings are not appealed to. A good example of this, noted in Chapter 4, is the Russian revolution under Stalin, which declared itself an atheist state whose idea of good was the mass extermination of its own citizens that rivaled the devastation of the Holocaust. The Soviet Union was an atheist state that considered its way of life sacred and so executed countless numbers who threatened the new communist way of life.

The interesting question is not whether one can be good without God but whether one can be good without being religious—and here the answer seems to be no. For even those who champion a secular humanist morality hold some things sacred, especially human dignity and human rights. In the United States, atheists have sometimes embraced a kind of fundamentalism. Some have challenged whether a city council, a state government, or even the U.S. Senate violates the First Amendment to the U.S. Constitution by beginning proceedings with a prayer. Many championing atheism have argued that no prayer should ever be said as part of a government proceeding. The First Amendment, however, forbids two opposing things in one sentence—(1) "the establishment of religion" (where the government gives official preference to one religion over all others) and (2) any attempt to restrict the "free exercise of religion" by the government. According to the Constitution, the state should show no preference but should support religious diversity. If we understand that even atheists hold their values and way of life sacred, then they are religious and should be neither forbidden nor favored by government. Globalization relativizes all worldviews, including atheistic ones. The true challenge to religion in a global civilization is not atheism but relativism. If all views, whether theistic or atheistic, are relative, then who can say how human beings ought to live? If good is in the eye of the beholder, then even Hitler and Stalin can be made to seem good. To affirm human dignity against the brutality of such figures is to reject relativism and affirm the sacredness of human dignity.

Among religious modernists a different solution was sought to the challenge of scientific rationality and theistic belief. As explained in Chapter 4, on Christianity, the difference between fundamentalists and modernists stems from an argument about the impact of science on traditional religious beliefs. Theistic fundamentalists often seem to believe they must oppose science to reaffirm traditional religious beliefs, while atheistic fundamentalists seem to believe that they must oppose religion in order to affirm scientific beliefs. Modernists attempt to embrace science, preferring to find a rational balance between science and religious beliefs.

Traditional theistic fundamentalists generally had no objection to the use of science to invent things like the automobile or for the creation of better medications. When science impinged on religious beliefs concerning the origins of humanity and the right way to order society, however, many drew a line. If the human self and society do not have sacred origins but are the result of biological evolution and human decisions, then the human self and society seem to be set adrift in a relativistic world without meaning, purpose, or ethical norms.

As modern science and technology—and the worldview they foster—were carried around the world by colonialism, the impact of modernity was felt in different ways in different societies and cultures. Not every religious tradition emphasizes orthodoxy ("right beliefs") the way Christianity does. For example, Hinduism, Judaism, and

Islam place far more emphasis on orthopraxy ("right actions"), the maintenance of a sacred way of life. Thus the most common feature of the fundamentalist reaction to modernity across religions and cultures is the desire to preserve the premodern sacred "way of life" against the threat of secularization and the normless relativism it seems to engender.

The social sciences of the nineteenth century promoted a technological understanding of society. According to this understanding, society itself can be redesigned through public policy decisions, just as engineers periodically redesign cars. While the use of scientific and technological inventions per se was relatively uncontroversial, many rejected the way social science treated the social order in a secular and technological fashion, as if society could or should be shaped and reshaped by human choices, without regard to the sacred ways of one's ancestors. In our chapter on Christianity (Chapter 4), we pointed to the emergence of existentialism as a watershed moment in the history of modernization, opening the door to postmodern relativism by calling into question the idea of *human nature*. For many, this seeming disappearance of human nature is terrifying, suggesting that we as human beings know neither who we are nor what we ought to do. This is the mindset Nietzsche was addressing when he said that "modern man" had murdered God and so now wandered the universe without a sense of direction. In fact, as we noted in the chapter on Christianity, the one thing Christian fundamentalists and Nietzschean atheists have in common (unlike Christian modernists) is that both see science and the Bible as incompatible. Depending on which camp you are in, either God or science has to be rejected. For many theistic fundamentalists today, it seems that the secular "technologized" understandings of self and society can only lead to moral decadence—a decadence in which the family and the fabric of society will be destroyed. Those who believe that secularization is robbing humanity of an understanding of its sacred origins and destiny reject scientific-technologized understandings of self and society. As an antidote, they favor a return to the sacred fundamental truths about human nature that governed life in premodern times.

Modernization is often presented in terms of a story about the secularization of society, that is, the liberation of the various dimensions of cultural life from the authority of religion. Since religion in premodern societies preserves the sacred by governing every aspect of life, modernization and secularization are threats to traditional societies everywhere. Nevertheless, sacralizing society to protect a divinely ordered way of life is not the only role religion has played in history. Moreover, as we have noted, secular ways of life that appeal to the rationality of science have also become sacred. Paradoxically, the most successful critiques of the sacralization of society have come from religions. The great sociologist Max Weber pointed out that religion not only sacralizes and reinforces the unchanging "routine" order of society (as the French sociologist Émile Durkheim held); sometimes it also "charismatically" desacralizes and transforms society. Religion, like reason, sometimes criticizes and transforms sacred order rather than functioning as its defender. Brahmanic Hinduism sacralized caste society in ancient India, but Buddhism began as a movement to desacralize the priestly elite and see all persons in the caste system as equal and capable of achieving spiritual deliverance. Sacralization readily accommodates hierarchies (e.g., a caste system, or hierarchical social order), whereas desacralizing breaks with caste, inviting pluralism and equality.

Because religions (even in the same traditions) often manifest dramatically opposing values and orientations, the sociologist Jacques Ellul has argued that it is helpful in understanding the role of religion in society to distinguish between two terms that are typically used interchangeably: sacred and holy. In his view, the experience of the sacred leads to a view of society as an order that is itself sacred and must be protected from all profane attempts to change it. The experience of the holy, on the other hand, calls into question the very idea of a sacred order. It desacralizes (or secularizes) society and seeks to introduce change in the name of a higher truth and/or justice. According to this view, the same religious tradition can express itself in opposite ways in different times and places. In India, early Buddhism called into question the sacred order of Hindu caste society, but later Buddhist societies developed their own sacred orders. Early Daoists in China called into question the sacred hierarchical order of Confucianism but later also integrated themselves into the sacred order of Confucian society by means of a neo-Confucian synthesis.

In the West, early Christianity, sharing a common ethos with Judaism, called the sacred order of Roman civilization into question, but medieval Christianity resacralized Europe. Then later, Protestantism desacralized the medieval European social order and unleashed the dynamics of modernism, which is also in danger of sacralization. From this perspective, the struggle between fundamentalism and modernism in the modern world that we have surveyed in this textbook is an example of the conflict between the sacralizing and desacralizing (secularizing) roles of religion.

Traditional religious fundamentalists express the desire to preserve the sacredness of human identity in a rightly ordered society against what they perceive as the chaos of today's decadent, normless secular relativism. Secular fundamentalists express a desire to preserve the sacredness of the scientific and rational way of life against the chaos introduced into society by diverse forms of religious absolutism. To restore the sacred normative order, religious fundamentalists tend to affirm the desirability of achieving the premodern ideal of one society, one religion. In the case of secular fundamentalism, what is to be preserved is the sacredness of the way of life made possible by scientific rationality in an age of progress. Both religious and secular or atheistic fundamentalists remain uncomfortable with the religious diversity that thrives in a secular society.

Religious modernism as it emerged in the West rejected the fundamentalist ideal, adopted from premodern societies, of identity between religion and society. Instead of dangerous absolutism, modernists looked for an accommodation between religion and modern secular society. They argued that it is possible to desacralize one's way of life and identity in a way that creates a new identity that preserves the essential values or norms of the past tradition, but in harmony with a new modern way of life. Modernists secularize society and privatize their religious practices, hoping by their encouragement of denominational forms of religion to ensure an environment that supports religious diversity.

What we are calling religious postmodernism, like religious modernism, accepts secularization and religious pluralism. But religious postmodernism, like fundamentalism, rejects the modernist solution of privatizing religious belief and practice and seeks a public role for religion. It differs from fundamentalism, however, in that it rejects the domination of society by a single religion. Religious postmodernists insist that there is a way for religious communities in all their diversity to shape the public order and so rescue society from secular relativism. The chief example of this option is the model established by Mohandas K. Gandhi. Because his disciples rejected the privatization of religion while affirming religious diversity, Gandhi's movement must be defined as a postmodern new age religious movement rather than a modernist one.

"Passing Over": A Postmodern Spiritual Adventure That Responds to the Challenge of Globalization

All the great world religions date back a millennium or more, and each provided a grand metanarrative for the premodern civilization in which it emerged—in the Middle East, in India, and in China. In the past these world religions were relatively isolated from one another. There were many histories in the world, each shaped by a great metanarrative, but no global history.

The perspective of religious postmodernism arises from a dramatically different situation. We are at the beginning of a new millennium, which is marked by the development of a global civilization. The diverse spiritual heritages of the human race have become the common inheritance of all. Modern changes have ended the isolation of the past, and people following one great tradition are now very likely to live in proximity to adherents of other faiths. New age religion has tapped this condition of globalization but in two different ways. In its modernist forms it has privatized the religious quest as a quest for the perfection of the self. In its postmodern forms, without rejecting self-transformation, it has turned that goal outward in forms of social organization committed to bettering society, bringing personal and social transformation into balance.

The time when a new world religion could be founded has passed, argues John Dunne in his book *The Way of All the Earth*. What is required today is not the conquest of the world by any one religion or culture but a meeting and sharing of religious and cultural insight. "The holy man of our time, it seems, is not a figure like Gautama [Buddha] or Jesus or Mohammed, a man who could found a world religion, but a figure like Gandhi, a man who passes over by sympathetic understanding from his own religion to other religions and comes back again with new insight to his own. Passing over and coming back, it seems, is the spiritual adventure of our time."[4]

This postmodern spiritual adventure occurs when we pass over into another's religion and culture and come to see the world through another's eyes. When we do this, we "come back" to our own religion and culture enriched with new insight not only into the other's religion and culture but also into our own—insight that builds bridges of understanding, a unity in diversity between people of diverse religions and cultures. The model for this spiritual adventure is found in the lives of Leo Tolstoy (1828–1910), Mohandas K. Gandhi (1869–1948), and Martin Luther King Jr. (1929–68).

Two of the most inspiring religious figures of the twentieth century were Mahatma Gandhi and Dr. King. They are the great champions of the fight for the dignity and rights of all human beings, from all religions and cultures. Moreover, they are models for a different kind of new age religious practice, one that absorbs the global wisdom of diverse religions, but does so without indiscriminately mixing elements to create a new religion, as is typical of the eclectic syncretism of most new age religions. Yet clearly these religious leaders initiated a new way of being religious that could occur only in an age of globalization.

Martin Luther King Jr. often noted that his commitment to nonviolent resistance, or civil disobedience, as a strategy for protecting human dignity had its roots in two sources: Jesus' Sermon on the Mount and Gandhi's teachings of nonviolence derived from his interpretation of the Hindu sacred story called the *Bhagavad Gita*. Gandhi died when King was a teenager, but Dr. King did travel to India to study the effects of Gandhi's teachings of nonviolence on Indian society. In this he showed a remarkable openness to the insights of another religion and culture. In Gandhi and his spiritual heirs, King found kindred spirits, and he came back to his own religion and culture enriched by the new insights that came to him in the process of passing over and coming back. Martin Luther King Jr. never became a Hindu, but his Christianity was profoundly transformed by his encounter with Gandhi's Hinduism.

Just as important, however, is the spiritual passing over of Gandhi himself. As a young man, Gandhi went to England to study law. His journey led him not away from Hinduism but more deeply into it, for it was in England that Gandhi discovered the *Bhagavad Gita* and began to fully appreciate the spiritual and ethical power of Hinduism.

Having promised his mother that he would remain a vegetarian, Gandhi took to eating his meals with British citizens who had developed similar commitments to vegetarianism through their fascination with India and its religions. It is in this context that Gandhi was brought into direct contact with the nineteenth-century theosophical roots of new age globalization. In these circles he met Madame Blavatsky and her disciple Annie Besant, both of whom had a profound influence on him. His associates also included Christian followers of the Russian novelist Leo Tolstoy, who, after his midlife conversion, had embraced an ethic of nonviolence based on Jesus' Sermon on the Mount (Matthew 5–7).

At the invitation of his theosophist friends, Gandhi read the *Bhagavad Gita* for the first time, in an English translation by Sir Edwin Arnold, entitled *The Song Celestial*. It was only much later that he took to a serious study of the Hindu text in Sanskrit. He was also deeply impressed by Arnold's *The Light of Asia*, recounting the life of the

> "I simply want to tell the story of my numerous experiments with truth, and my life consists of nothing but these experiments. . . . They are spiritual, or rather moral; for the essence of religion is morality."
>
> —M. K. Gandhi

Buddha. Thus, through the eyes of Western friends, he was first moved to discover the spiritual riches of his own Hindu heritage. The seeds were planted in England, nourished by more serious study during his years in South Africa, and brought to fruition on his return to India in 1915.

From his theosophist friends, Gandhi not only learned to appreciate his own religious tradition but came to see Christianity in a new way. For unlike the evangelical missionaries he had met in his childhood, the theosophists had a deeply allegorical way of reading the Christian scriptures. This approach to Bible study allowed people to find in the teachings of Jesus a universal path toward spiritual truth that was in harmony with the wisdom of Asia. The power of allegory lay in opening the literal stories of the scripture to reveal a deeper symbolic meaning based on what the theosophists believed was profound universal religious experience and wisdom. From the theosophists, Gandhi took an interpretive principle that has its roots in the New Testament writings of St. Paul: "The letter killeth, but the spirit giveth life" (2 Corinthians 3:6). This insight would enable him to read the *Bhagavad Gita* in the light of his own deep religious experience and find in it the justification for nonviolent civil disobedience.

Gandhi was likewise profoundly influenced by Tolstoy's understanding of the Sermon on the Mount. The message of nonviolence—love your enemy, turn the other cheek—took hold of Gandhi. And yet Gandhi did not become a Christian. Rather, he returned to his parents' religion and culture, finding parallels to Jesus' teachings in the Hindu tradition. And so he read Hindu scriptures with new insight, interpreting the *Bhagavad Gita* allegorically, as a call to resist evil by nonviolent means. And just as King would later use the ideas of Gandhi in the nonviolent struggle for the dignity of black citizens in North America, so Gandhi was inspired by Tolstoy as he led the fight for the dignity of the lower castes and outcasts within Hindu society and for the liberation of India from British colonial rule.

Gandhi never became a Christian and King never became a Hindu. Nevertheless, Gandhi's Hindu faith was profoundly transformed by his encounter with the Christianity of Tolstoy, just as King's Christian faith was profoundly transformed by his encounter with Gandhi's Hinduism. In the lives of these twentieth-century religious activists we have examples of "passing over" as a transformative postmodern spiritual adventure. Whereas in the secular forms of postmodernism all knowledge is relative, and therefore the choice between interpretations of any claim to truth is "undecidable," Gandhi and King opened up an alternate path. While agreeing that in matters of religion, truth is undecidable, they showed that acceptance of diversity does not have to lead to the kind of ethical relativism that so deeply troubles fundamentalists. For in the cases of Gandhi and King, passing over led to a sharing of wisdom among traditions that gave birth to an ethical coalition in defense of human dignity across religions and cultures—a global ethic for a new age.

Mohandas K. Gandhi, whose techniques of nonviolent civil disobedience led to the liberation of India from British colonial rule in 1947.

By their lives, Gandhi and King demonstrated that, contrary to the fears raised by fundamentalism, the sharing of a common ethic and of spiritual wisdom across traditions does not require any practitioners to abandon their religious identity. Instead, Gandhi and King offered a model of unity in diversity. Finally, both Gandhi and King rejected the privatization of religion, insisting that religion in all its diversity plays a decisive role in shaping the public order of society. And both were convinced that only a firm commitment to nonviolence on the part of religious communities would allow society to avoid a return to the kind of religious wars that accompanied the Protestant Reformation and the emergence of modernity.

The spiritual adventure initiated by Gandhi and King involves passing over (through imagination, through travel and cultural exchange, through a common commitment to social action to promote social justice, etc.) into the life and stories and traditions of others, sharing in them and, in the process, coming to see one's own tradition through them. Such encounters enlarge our sense of human identity to include the other. The religious metanarratives of the world's civilizations may have become "smaller narratives" in an age of global diversity, but they have not lost their power. Indeed, in this Gandhian model, it is the sharing of the wisdom from another tradition's metanarratives that gives the stories of a person's own tradition their power. Each person remains on familiar religious and cultural ground, yet each is profoundly influenced by the other.

Tolstoy, Jesus, and "Saint Buddha": An Ancient Tale with a Thousand Faces

Although at first glance the religious worlds of humankind seem to have grown up largely independent of one another, a closer look will reveal that hidden threads from different religions and cultures have for centuries been woven together to form a new tapestry, one that contributes to the sharing of religious insight in an age of globalization. In *Toward a World Theology*, Wilfred Cantwell Smith traces the threads of this new tapestry, and the story he tells is quite surprising.[5] Smith notes, for example, that to fully appreciate the influence on Gandhi of Tolstoy's understanding of the Sermon on the Mount, it is important to know that Tolstoy's own conversion to Christianity, which occurred in a period of midlife crisis, was deeply influenced not only by the Sermon on the Mount but also by the life of the Buddha.

Tolstoy was a member of the Russian nobility, rich and famous because of his novels, which included *War and Peace* and *Anna Karenina*. Yet in his fifties, Tolstoy went through a period of great despair that resolved itself in a powerful religious conversion experience. Although nominally a member of the (Russian) Orthodox Church, Tolstoy had not taken his faith seriously until he came to the point of making the Sermon on the Mount a blueprint for his life. After his conversion, Tolstoy freed his serfs, gave away all his wealth, and spent the rest of his life serving the poor.

As Wilfred Cantwell Smith tells it, a key factor in Tolstoy's conversion was his reading of a story from the lives of the saints. The story was that of Barlaam and

Josaphat. It is the story of a wealthy young Indian prince by the name of Josaphat who gave up all his wealth and power and abandoned his family to embark on an urgent quest for an answer to the problems of old age, sickness, and death. During his search, the prince comes across a Christian monk by the name of Barlaam, who tells him a story. It seems that once there was a man who fell into a very deep well and was hanging onto two vines for dear life. As he was trapped in this precarious situation, two mice, one white and one black, came along and began to chew on the vines. The man knew that in short order the vines would be severed and he would plunge to his death.

Leo Tolstoy, the famous Russian novelist, whose writings on Jesus' Sermon on the Mount inspired Gandhi.

The story was an allegorical parable of the prince's spiritual situation. Barlaam points out that the two mice represent the cycle of day and night, the passing of time that brings us ever closer to death. The paradox is that like the man in the well, Josaphat cannot save his life by clinging to it. He must let go of the vines, so to speak. He can save his life only by losing it. That is, if he lets go of his life now, no longer clinging to it but surrendering himself completely to the divine will, his spiritual death will lead to a new life that transcends death. This story and its parable touched the deeply depressed writer and led him to a spiritual surrender that brought about his rebirth. Out of this rebirth then came a new Tolstoy, the author of *The Kingdom of God Is Within You*, which advocates a life of nonviolent resistance to evil based on the Sermon on the Mount.

The story of the Indian prince who abandons a life of wealth and power and responds to a parable of a man about to fall into an abyss is of course a thinly disguised version of the life story of the Buddha. Versions of the story and the parable can be found in almost all the world's great religions, recorded in a variety of languages (Greek, Latin, Czech, Polish, Italian, Spanish, French, German, Swedish, Norwegian, Arabic, Hebrew, Yiddish, Persian, Sanskrit, Chinese, Japanese, etc.). The Greek version came into Christianity from an Islamic Arabic version, which was passed on to Judaism as well. The Muslims apparently got it from members of a Gnostic cult in Persia, who got it from Buddhists in India. The Latinate name *Josaphat* is a translation of the Greek *Loasaf*, which is translated from the Arabic *Yudasaf*, which comes from the Persian *Bodisaf*, which is a translation of *Bodhisattva*, a Sanskrit title for the Buddha.

The parable of the man clinging to the vine may be even older than the story of the prince (Buddha) who renounces his wealth. It may well go back to early Indic sources at the beginnings of civilization. It is one of the oldest and most universal stories in the history of religions and civilizations. Tolstoy's conversion was brought about in large part by the story of a Christian saint, Josaphat, who was, so to speak, really the Buddha in disguise.

The history of the story of a great sage's first steps toward enlightenment suggests that the process leading to globalization goes back to the very beginnings of civilization.

Therefore the line between new religions and new age (globalized) religions may not be as sharp as previously assumed. We can see that the practice of passing over and coming back, of being open to the stories of others, and of coming to understand one's own tradition through these stories is in fact very ancient. Therefore, when Martin Luther King Jr. embraced the teachings of Gandhi, he embraced not only Gandhi but also Tolstoy and, through Tolstoy, two of the greatest religious teachers of nonviolence: Jesus of Nazareth, whose committed follower King already was, and Siddhartha the Buddha. Thus from the teachings of Gandhi, King actually assimilated important teachings from at least four religious traditions—Hinduism, Buddhism, Judaism, and Christianity. This rich spiritual debt to other religions and cultures never in any way diminished King's faith. On the contrary, the Baptist pastor's Christian beliefs were deeply enriched, in turn enriching the world in which we live. The same could be said about Gandhi and Hinduism.

Gandhi's transformation of the *Bhagavad Gita*—a Hindu story that literally advocates the duty of going to war and killing one's enemies—into a story of nonviolence is instructive of the transforming power of the allegorical method that he learned from his theosophist friends. The *Bhagavad Gita* is a story about a warrior named Arjuna, who argues with his chariot driver, Krishna, over whether it is right to go to war if it means having to kill one's own relatives. Krishna's answer is yes—Arjuna must do his duty as a warrior in the cause of justice, but he is morally obliged to do it selflessly, with no thought of personal loss or gain. Gandhi, however, transformed the story of Arjuna and Krishna from a story of war as physical violence into a story of war as active but nonviolent resistance to injustice through civil disobedience.

If the message of spiritual realization in the *Gita* is that all beings share the same self (as Brahman or Purusha), how could the *Gita* be literally advocating violence, for to do violence against another would be to do violence against oneself? The self-contradiction of a literal interpretation, in Gandhi's way of thinking, forces the mind into an allegorical mode, where it can grasp the *Gita*'s true spiritual meaning. Reading the *Gita* allegorically, Gandhi insisted that the impending battle described in the Hindu classic is really about the battle between good and evil going on within every self.

Krishna's command to Arjuna to stand up and fight is thus a "spiritual" command. But for Gandhi this does not mean, as it usually does in "modern" terms, that the struggle is purely inner (private) and personal. On the contrary, the spiritual person will see the need to practice nonviolent civil disobedience: that is, to replace "body force" (i.e., violence) with "soul force." As the *Gita* suggests, there really is injustice in the world, and therefore there really is an obligation to fight, even to go to war, to reestablish justice. One must be prepared to exert Gandhian soul force by putting one's body on the line, but in a nonviolent way, through civil disobedience. In so doing, one leaves open the opportunity to gain the respect, understanding, and perhaps transformation of one's enemy.

The lesson Gandhi derived from the *Gita* is that the encounter with the other need not lead to conquest. It can lead, instead, to mutual understanding and mutual respect. King's relationship to Gandhi and Gandhi's relationship to Tolstoy are models of a postmodern spirituality and ethics that transform postmodern relativism and eclecticism into the opportunity to follow a new spiritual and ethical path—"the way of all the earth"—the sharing of spiritual insight and ethical wisdom across religions and cultures in an age of globalization.

On this path, people of diverse religions and cultures find themselves sharing an ethical commitment to protect human dignity beyond the postmodern interest in personal transformation fostered by the modernist ideal of privatization. Gandhi and King were not engaged in a private quest to perfect the self (although neither neglected the need for personal transformation). Rather, each man embarked on a public quest to transform human communities, socially and politically, by invoking a global ethical commitment to protect the dignity of all persons. The religious movements associated with both men fit the pattern of the holy that affirms the secularization of society in order to embrace religious pluralism. Gandhi and King recovered the premodern ideal of religion shaping the public order but now in a postmodern mode, committed to religious pluralism.

The Children of Gandhi: An Experiment in Postmodern Global Ethics

In April 1968, Martin Luther King Jr., sometimes referred to as "the American Gandhi," went to Memphis to support black municipal workers in the midst of a strike. The Baptist minister was looking forward to spending the approaching Passover with Rabbi Abraham Joshua Heschel. Heschel, who had marched with King during the voter registration drive in Selma, Alabama, three years earlier, had become a close friend and supporter. Unfortunately, King was not able to keep that engagement. On April 4, 1968, like Gandhi before him, Martin Luther King Jr., a man of nonviolence, was shot to death by an assassin.

The Buddhist monk and anti–Vietnam War activist Thich Nhat Hanh, whom King had nominated for a Nobel Peace Prize, received the news of his friend's death while at an interreligious conference in New York City. Only the previous spring, King had expressed his opposition to the Vietnam War, largely at the urging of Thich Nhat Hanh and Rabbi Heschel. King spoke out at an event sponsored by Clergy and Laymen Concerned about Vietnam, a group founded by Heschel, Protestant cleric John Bennett, and Richard Neuhaus, then a Lutheran minister. Now another champion in the

Martin Luther King Jr., who led the civil rights movement for racial equality in the United States, using the techniques of nonviolent civil disobedience inspired by Gandhi.

struggle against hatred, violence, and war was dead. But the spiritual and ethical vision he shared with his friends, across religions and cultures, has continued to inspire followers throughout the world.

These religious activists—a Baptist minister who won the Noble Peace Prize for his leadership in the American civil rights movement, a Hasidic rabbi and scholar who narrowly escaped the death camps of the Holocaust, and a Buddhist monk who had been targeted for assassination in Vietnam but survived to lead the Buddhist peace delegation to the Paris peace negotiations in 1973—are the spiritual children of Gandhi. By working together to protest racial injustice and the violence of war, they demonstrated that religious and cultural pluralism do not have to end in ethical relativism and, given a commitment to nonviolence, can play a role in shaping public life in an age of globalization. The goal, Martin Luther King Jr. insisted, is not to humiliate and defeat your enemy but to win him or her over, bringing about not only justice but also reconciliation. The goal, he said, was to attack the evil in systems, not to attack persons. The goal was to love one's enemy, not in the sense of sentimental affection or in the reciprocal sense of friendship, but in the constructive sense of seeking the opponent's well-being.

Nonviolence, King argued, is more than just a remedy for this or that social injustice. It is, he was convinced, essential to the survival of humanity in an age of nuclear weapons. The choice, he said, was "no longer between violence and nonviolence. It is either nonviolence or nonexistence."

Truth is to be found in all religions, King said many times, and "injustice anywhere is a threat to justice everywhere. We are caught in an inescapable network of mutuality, tied in a single garment of destiny. Whatever affects one directly affects all

A Buddhist monk meditates during a moment of silence near the finish line of the Boston Marathon bombings on the one-week anniversary of the April 22, 2013 attack.

TEACHINGS OF RELIGIOUS WISDOM: Thich Nhat Hanh on the Shared Wisdom of Buddhism and Christianity

Thich Nhat Hanh was nominated by Martin Luther King Jr. for the Nobel Peace Prize for his nonviolent struggle to establish peace between North Vietnam and South Vietnam during the Vietnam War in the 1960s. During this time Thich Nhat Hanh also engaged in dialogue with the famous Catholic Christian monk Thomas Merton about the similarities and differences between Buddhist and Christian monastic spirituality. Since then Hanh's influence has become global. In his writings, especially *Living Buddha, Living Christ*, he insists that religious language is about direct religious experience, not about abstract metaphysical beliefs. On this, he says, both Buddhist and Christian contemplative monks agree.

Once the ultimate is touched, all notions are transcended: birth, death, being, non-being, before, after, one, many and so forth. Questions like "Does God exist?" or "Does nirvana exist" are no longer valid. God and nirvana as concepts have been transcended. . . . For the one who has had an experience of God or nirvana, the question "does God exist?" is an indication of the lack of insight. (p. 189)

Buddhists and Christians know that nirvana or the Kingdom of God is within their hearts. Buddhist sutras speak of Buddha nature as the seed of enlightenment that is already in everyone's consciousness. The Gospels speak of the Kingdom of God as a mustard seed planted in the soil of consciousness. The practices of prayer and meditation help us touch the most valuable seeds that are within us and they put us in contact with the ground of our being. . . . When the energy of mindfulness is present, transformation takes place. When the energy of the Holy Spirit is within you, understanding, love, peace, and stability are possible. God is within. You are, yet you are not, but God is in you. This is interbeing. This is non-self. (p. 167–68)

Source: Thich Nhat Hanh, *Living Buddha, Living Christ* (New York: G. P. Putnam and Sons, Riverhead Books), 1995.

indirectly."[6] The scandal of our age, said Abraham Joshua Heschel, is that in a world of diplomacy "only religions are not on speaking terms." But, he also said, no religion is an island, and all must realize that "holiness is not the monopoly of any particular religion or tradition."[7]

"Buddhism today," writes Thich Nhat Hanh, "is made up of non-Buddhist elements, including Jewish and Christian ones." And likewise with every tradition. "We have to allow what is good, beautiful, and meaningful in the other's tradition to transform us," the Vietnamese monk continues. The purpose of such passing over into the other's tradition is to allow each to return to his or her own tradition transformed. What is astonishing, says Thich Nhat Hanh, is that we will find kindred spirits in other traditions with whom we share more than we do with many in our own tradition.[8]

The Future of Religion in an Age of Globalization

Will the global future of religion and civilization be shaped by this Gandhian model of new age spiritual practice? It clearly offers an alternative to both traditional denominational modernist religions and the more privatistic modernist forms of new age religion. The Gandhian model also offers an alternative to the fundamentalist rejection of modernization and secularization by showing that religious pluralism does not have to lead to relativism. On the contrary, it can lead to the sanctification of life and the promotion of an ethic of human dignity across religions and cultures. The challenge is that the sharing of spiritual wisdom does require seeing the religions and cultures of others as having wisdom to share, and not all will accept this presupposition. Nevertheless, the emergence of religious postmodernism means that in the future, the struggle among religions will most likely be not so much between fundamentalism and modernism, nor between theists and atheists, but between religious fundamentalist exclusivism and postmodern religious pluralism—both as forms of religion that shape not only private but also public life.

Discussion Questions

1. What is the difference between a "new religion" and a "new age religion"?

2. How do modernist new age religious belief and practice differ from postmodernist new age religious belief and practice? Give an example of each.

3. How does new age religion relate to the split between faith and reason (the *via moderna* and the *devotio moderna*) that shaped the emergence of the modern world through the Enlightenment and the Romantic reaction it provoked?

4. In what sense is "civil religion" a new way of being religious, and in what sense is it a very old way of being religious?

5. What do the authors mean by suggesting that in a postmodern society, atheism can itself become a form of fundamentalism?

6. In what way is the postmodern path of religious ethics opened up by M. K. Gandhi and Martin Luther King Jr. similar to fundamentalist ideals for society, and in what way is it different?

Suggested Readings

Bruce, Steve. *Religion in the Modern World* (New York: Oxford University Press, 1996).

Dunne, John S. *The Way of All the Earth* (1972; rpt., Notre Dame, IN: University of Notre Dame Press, 1978).

Ellwood, Robert S., and Harry B. Partin, eds. *Religious and Spiritual Groups in Modern America*, 2nd ed. (Upper Saddle River, NJ: Prentice Hall, 1973, 1988).

Fasching, Darrell J. *The Coming of the Millennium* (San Jose, CA: Authors Choice Press, 1996, 2000).

————. "Stories of War and Peace: Sacred, Secular and Holy," in Sarah Deets and Merry Kerry, eds., *War and Words* (Lanham, MD: Rowman and Littlefield, 2004).

Fasching, Darrell J., Dell deChant, and David Lantigua. *Comparative Religious Ethics: A Narrative Approach to Global Ethics*, 2nd ed. (Oxford: Blackwell, 2011).

Jones, Lindsay, ed. *Encyclopedia of Religion*, 2nd ed., 15 vols. (Detroit: Macmillan Reference USA, 2005).

Juergensmeyer, Mark. *Terror in the Mind of God* (Berkeley: University of California Press, 2000).

Laderman, Gary, and Luis Leon, eds. *Religion and American Cultures*, vol. 1 (Santa Barbara, CA: ABC Clio, 2003).

Lewis, James R., ed. *The Oxford Handbook of New Religious Movements* (New York: Oxford University Press, 2004).

Melton, J. Gordon. *Finding Enlightenment* (Hillsboro, OR: Beyond Words Publishing, 1998).

Rothstein, Mikael, ed. *New Age Religion and Globalization* (Aarhus, Denmark: Aarhus University Press, 2001).

Notes

1. William Bloom, *The New Age: An Anthology of Essential Writings* (London: Rider/Channel 4, 1991), p. xviii. Quoted in Steve Bruce, *Religion in the Modern World* (Oxford: Oxford University Press, 1996).

2. Sarah Pike, "New Age," quoted in Robert S. Ellwood and Harry B. Partin, eds., *Religious and Spiritual Groups in Modern America*, 2nd ed. (Upper Saddle River, NJ: Prentice Hall, 1988), p. 140.

3. L. Ron Hubbard, *Scientology: The Fundamentals of Thought* (Edinburgh: Publications Organization Worldwide, 1968); originally published 1950. Quoted in Ellwood and Partin, *Religions and Spiritual Groups in Modern America*, p. 147.

4. John Dunne, *The Way of All the Earth* (Notre Dame, IN: University of Notre Dame Press, 1978), p. ix.

5. Wilfred Cantwell Smith, *Toward a World Theology* (Philadelphia: Westminster Press, 1981), chap. 1.

6. Martin Luther King Jr., "Letter from Birmingham Jail," in King, *I Have a Dream: Writings and Speeches That Changed the World*, ed. James M. Washington (San Francisco: HarperSanFrancisco, 1992), p. 85.

7. Abraham Joshua Heschel, *Moral Grandeur and Spiritual Audacity: Essays [of] Abraham Joshua Heschel*, ed. Susannah Heschel (New York: Farrar, Straus & Giroux, 1996), pp. 241, 247.

8. Thich Nhat Hanh, *Living Buddha, Living Christ* (New York: G. P. Putnam and Sons, Riverhead Books, 1995), pp. 9, 11.

Additional Resources

Cults a.k.a. New Religious Movements, Ontario Consultants on Religious Tolerance (http://www.religioustolerance.org/cultmenu.htm)

This site devoted to religious tolerance offers comprehensive, balanced information on new religions, "cults," and the anti-cult and counter-cult movements. Principal new religions are profiled, including their history, beliefs, practices, publications, and conflicts with government or other groups. Offers an overview of the conflicts, including references supporting the various sides of the conflicts.

Religious Movements, University of Virginia (http://cti.itc.virginia.edu/~jkh8x/soc257/)

This archive provides detailed profiles of more than 200 different religious groups and movements. The founding editor of the Religious Movements Homepage Project, Jeff Hadden, passed away in 2003. The new editor-in-chief is Douglas E. Cowan, who is at the University of Waterloo in Ontario Canada (http://artsweb.uwaterloo.ca/~decowan/). Through the work of an advisory board of internationally recognized scholars of new religious movements, the data are being expanded and updated.

GLOSSARY

al-haram al-sharif: the noble sanctuary

Allah: God

al-Quds: the holy city (i.e., Jerusalem)

animism: religious tradition whose basic perception entails belief in an inner soul that gives life and ultimate identity to humans, animals, and plants and that places primary emphasis on experiential rituals in which humans interact with other souls

Ashkenazi: Jews whose traditions originated in central and eastern Europe

Augustinian: refers to views of St. Augustine, for example, his view of the separation of church and state, in which the state is answerable to the church in religious matters while the church is answerable to the state in secular matters, yet both exist to promote the spread of the Gospel

bar/bat mitzvah: the rite of passage for boys (bar mitzvah) whereby they become full members of the religion of Judaism who are able to read and interpret Torah; in modern times a parallel rite for girls (bat mitzvah) has been established in some forms of Judaism

Bwiti: a West Central African religion that incorporates animism, ancestor worship, and Christianity into its belief system, along with a specially cultivated hallucinogen

caliph (khalifah): successor of Muhammad as the political and military head of the Muslim community

Catholic: those churches that define their Christian authenticity through apostolic succession

Christ: from Greek translation of the Hebrew word meaning "messiah" or "anointed one," the title Christians apply to Jesus of Nazareth

circular time: the awareness, more prevalent in hunter-gather than in industrial societies, that life is governed by the rising and the setting of the sun, the phases of the moon, and the seasons of the year

circumcision: the cutting of the foreskin of the penis as a sign of the covenant of Abraham

Constantinian/Constantinianism: view of the unity of church and state attributed to the first Christian Roman Emperor, Constantine, in which the state exists to rule over and protect the church as the official religion of the empire

cosmogony: mythological account of the creation

covenant: the agreement between God and the people of Israel whereby they are chosen to be God's people; God agrees to guide and protect them; the people agree to follow God's commandments (*halakhah*)

***dar al-Islam*:** the house or abode of Islam, as opposed to the house of war; territory controlled and ruled by Muslims

deism: Enlightenment view that God created the world the way a watchmaker creates a clock and leaves it to run on its own without interference

***dhimmi*:** literally, protected non-Muslim peoples; refers to Jews and Christians (later extended to others) who were granted "protected" status and religious freedom under Muslim rule in exchange for payment of a special tax

Diaspora: the dispersion of a religious people outside their geographic homeland, where they must live as a minority among others

divine: representative of the gods

Dreamtime: in Aboriginal legend, the time when the world was being created

dual Torah: the scriptures of Rabbinic Judaism, composed of the written Torah (Tanak) and the oral Torah (Talmud)

evangelical: refers to pietistic Christian movements that arose in response to the Enlightenment and also dogmatic divisions within Protestantism; emphasizes the unifying power of conversion as an emotional transformation rather than a rational/dogmatic one

***fatwa*:** legal opinion or interpretation issued on request by legal expert (*mufti*) to either judges or private individuals

***fiqh*:** understanding; science of Islamic law; jurisprudence; human interpretation and application of divine law

fundamentalist: term first emerged to refer to evangelical Protestants who believed that certain fundamental truths of the Gospel were threatened by modern interpreters; in general, fundamentalist movements in all religions see modernity as corrupting the fundamental truths and practices of a society as they were expressed in the premodern stage of their respective traditions

Gemara: *see* Talmud

gentile: anyone not Jewish

Ghost Dance: a shaman-led nationwide movement aimed at reviving the indigenous nations of North America; ended in 1890 when the U.S. Cavalry massacred up to 300 of the men, women, and children gathered for the Ghost Dance at Wounded Knee, South Dakota

globalization: for the purposes of world religions, the idea that all the world's religions have members in every country or society; anyone using the Internet can view the major temples, shrines, churches, mosques, or monasteries from around the world and offer ritual prayers or make monetary offerings to them

Gospel: literally, "good news"; usually refers to the four Gospels of the New Testament, which retell the words and deeds of Jesus of Nazareth; can also refer to other, similar ancient writings not included in the Christian scriptures

grace: expresses the idea of unmerited divine love and assistance given to humans

hadith: narrative report of Muhammad's sayings and actions

hajj: annual pilgrimage to Mecca; all Muslims should make the *hajj* at least once in their lifetime, but it is recognized that individual circumstances may make compliance impossible

halakhah: the commandments of God revealed in the Tanak and commented on in the Talmud; the word means "to walk in the way of God" by obeying his commands or laws

haredim: Jewish ultra-Orthodox movements that reject all modernist forms of Judaism

Hasidism: a form of Judaism emerging in the eighteenth century, focused on piety and joy, with strong roots in Jewish mysticism

heresy: comes from the Greek term that means "choice"; came to be used as a negative term for choosing to believe doctrines viewed as erroneous by those who considered themselves to be "more orthodox"

heretic: from the ancient Greek, meaning "to choose"; in our postmodern world every religious person becomes a heretic, that is, one who is not simply born into a given religion or identity but must choose it, even if it is only to choose to retain the identity offered by the circumstances of his or her birth

hijab: Arabic word for veil or external covering; can consist of headscarf alone or full body covering; also known as *chador* (in Iran) or *burqa* (in Afghanistan)

hijra: migration; Muhammad's *hijra* from Mecca to Medina in 622 marks the first year of the Muslim lunar calendar

Holocaust: meaning "burnt sacrifice," one name given to the attempt by Nazi Germany to eliminate the Jewish people

Homo religiosus: religious humanity; a term coined by comparative religions scholar Mircea Eliade to indicate that religious practice was universal to all humans

homoousios/homoiousios: first term was used to assert that the Word of God through which all things were created is "the same as" God; second term was used to assert that this Word was "like God"; Council of Nicaea (325 CE) affirmed the first and rejected the second

hudud: Quranically prescribed crimes and punishments for consumption of alcohol, theft, fornication, adultery, and false witnessing; some countries have adopted these punishments as evidence of the "Islamic" nature of their political rule and law

ibadat: worship, ritual obligations

ijma: consensus; in Islamic law, refers to agreement of scholars on interpretation of legal questions; some have reinterpreted this principle to justify the right of a parliament to enact legislation

ijtihad: human interpretation or independent reasoning in Islamic law

imam: in Sunni Islam, the prayer leader and the one who delivers the Friday sermon; in Shiah Islam, refers to Muhammad's descendants as legitimate successors, not prophets, but divinely inspired, sinless, infallible, and the final authoritative interpreter of God's will as formulated in Islamic law

incarnation: the eternal Word of God is embodied in the flesh of Jesus during his earthly life; there were two basic formulations of this: "the Word became flesh" and "the Word bodily dwells in the flesh" of Jesus

Islam: submission or surrender to God

Israel: either Jews as a religious people or the land and state of Israel, depending on the context

jahiliyya: the period of ignorance in which justice is guaranteed and administered not by God but by threat of retaliation by family or tribe

jihad: to strive or struggle; exerting oneself to realize God's will, lead a virtuous life, fulfill the universal mission of Islam, and spread Islam through preaching and/or writing; defense of Islam and Muslim community; currently often used to refer to the struggle for educational and social reform and social justice as well as armed struggle, holy war

justification by faith: Protestant Reformation doctrine formulated by Martin Luther, asserting that humans are saved by faith as a gift rather than through works of obedience to the law

Kabbalah: Jewish mysticism; the most important Kabbalistic work is the *Zohar*; for Kabbalists, God is the *En Sof*, the limitless or infinite, who manifests himself in the world through his *Shekinah*, or "divine presence" in all things; the reunion of all with the infinite through mystical contemplation will bring about nothing less than the messianic kingdom

khatam: seal or last of the prophets; Muhammad

khutba: sermon delivered at Friday prayer session in the mosque

Kingdom of God: the kingdom occurs whenever humans live in accord with the will of God and especially at the end of time, when God will be all in all

kosher: what is *halal*, suitable or fit, used especially in reference to foods permitted by Jewish dietary laws

liberation theology: liberation theology emerged in Latin America in the twentieth century; the goal was to show that the Gospel was more radical than Marxism in its promotion of justice for the poor

Mahdi: expected or awaited one; divinely guided one who is expected to appear at the end of time to vindicate and restore the faithful Muslim community and usher in the perfect Islamic society of truth and justice

Marranos: the Jews of Spain who were forced to convert to Christianity during the Inquisition but secretly continued to practice their Jewish faith

metanarrative: a grand cosmic and/or historical story accepted by the majority of a society as expressing its beliefs about origin, destiny, and identity

millennialism: beliefs about an age of peace (1,000 years) at the end of time that have their origin in the New Testament Book of Revelation

minbar: pulpit in the mosque from which the Friday sermon (*khutba*) is preached

Mishnah: *see* Talmud

mitzvot: the commandments of God requiring deeds of loving kindness

modern: a civilization that separates its citizens' lives into public and private spheres, assigning politics to public life while restricting religion to personal and family life; a dominant scientific metanarrative provides the most certain public truths people believe they know; society and politics are governed by secular, rational, and scientific norms rather than religion

morality: the rightness of any human action

mosque (*masjid*): Islamic temple, from *masjid*, "place of prostration"

muamalat: social interactions

muezzin: one who issues the call to prayer from the top of the *minaret*

mufti: legal expert, adviser, or consultant; one who issues *fatwas* to judges and litigants

mujaddid: renewer; one who comes to restore and revitalize the Islamic community; one who purifies and restores true Islamic practice; one *mujaddid* is to be sent at the beginning of each century

mujtahid: expert in Islamic law; one who exercises *ijtihad*, or independent reasoning, in legal matters; one capable of interpreting Islamic law

Muslim: one who submits or surrenders himself or herself to God and his will; one who follows Islam

myth: from the Greek *mythos*, meaning "story"; a symbolic story about the origins and destiny of human beings and their world; myth relates human beings to whatever powers they believe ultimately govern their destiny and explains to them what the powers expect of them

n/um kausi: shamans of the Kung people

Native American Church: a "Pan-American" movement among American Native peoples that has factions related in varying ways to Christianity but that are united in their ceremonial use of the cactus peyote as the group's own communal sacrament

neopaganism: modern adaptations of ancient pagan (polytheistic and animistic) beliefs

new age religions: religions that emerge by breaking with traditional beliefs and practices, typically through the influence of other religious practices around the globe due to the influence of modern science, global media, and global travel

new religions: religions that arise as new revelations within a tradition that change it in ways that traditional adherents do not accept, often through the influence of new religious prophets and the influence of other religions in their local environment

nonviolence: a strategy for dealing with the violence of others through nonviolent acts of civil disobedience

numinous: the human perception of the sacred

original sin: the sin of Adam and Eve, who disobeyed the command of God not to eat the fruit of the tree of knowledge of good and evil; said to have affected all human beings by corrupting their will so that they are often unable to do the good they intend

orthodoxy: acceptance of "right beliefs" or "doctrines" based on sacred texts as formulated by religious authorities

orthopraxy: the practice of "right actions" or rituals as prescribed by sacred traditions

passing over: the act of imagination whereby one sees the world through the eyes of another's religion and thereby gains new insight into one's own religion

Pentecostal: refers to churches that emphasize possession by the Holy Spirit and speaking in tongues

People of the Book (*ahl al-kitab*): those possessing a revelation or scripture from God; typically refers to Jews and Christians, Muslims, and sometimes includes Zoroastrians

postmodern: a society typified by diversity in both beliefs and social practices that has no single dominant metanarrative (other than the narrative of diversity) and is skeptical of finding either certain knowledge or norms in any public form of truth, whether religious, ethical, or scientific

premodern: a civilization in which there is no separation between religion and society; a dominant religious metanarrative provides the most certain truths people believe they know; by being a member of that culture, one automatically participates in its religious vision and lives by its religious norms

Protestant: the churches, beginning at the time of Martin Luther, that teach salvation by faith rather than works and also reject the mediation of the church through apostolic succession as necessary for salvation in favor of a direct personal relationship with God in Christ

Protestant ethic: term coined by sociologist Max Weber, who noted that the Calvinist branch of the Reformation fostered a belief in working hard and living simply for the glory of God and as proof that one was among those destined to be saved; such an attitude, Weber said, contributed to the accumulation of wealth needed for investment and fueled the Industrial Revolution and the flourishing of capitalist societies

purdah: seclusion of women from men who are not relatives; segregation of the sexes

qiyas: legal term for analogical reasoning

Quran: revelation, recitation, message; Muslim scripture

Rabbinic: a rabbi is a teacher; the name came to designate the Judaism of the *dual Torah* introduced by the Pharisees, which came to be normative in the premodern period

Ramadan: month of fasting; ninth month of the Muslim calendar

redemption: root meaning is "to be rescued or freed," especially from slavery; used in both a literal and a metaphorical sense: God redeemed Israel from slavery in Egypt and exile in Babylonia; God redeems sinners from punishment and death due to sin

religion: from the Latin *religare*, meaning "to tie or bind," and the root *religere*, which has the connotation of "acting with care"; expresses a sense of being "tied and bound" by obligations to whatever powers are believed to govern one's destiny— whether those powers be natural or supernatural, personal or impersonal, one or many; ancient peoples everywhere believed that the powers governing their destiny were the forces of nature

ritual: actions that connect the individual and the community to each other, through the sacred

sacraments: ritual actions, such as baptism and holy communion, said to impart the grace of God to Christians, usually through the mediation of ordained clergy

salat: official prayer or worship performed five times each day

Second Coming: belief that Jesus, who died on the cross, arose from the dead, and ascended into heaven, will return at the end of time to raise the dead and establish a new heaven and a new earth

secular: sociologically used to mean "nonreligious"

Sephardic: Jews whose traditions originated in Spain and Portugal

shahadah: declaration of faith, witness, testimony; refers to the declaration of Muslim faith: "There is no god but God and Muhammad is His Messenger"

shaman: *see* spirit medium

shamanism: the traditions focused on individuals who can leave their bodies to enter the realm of the afterlife and spirits where they can learn higher spiritual truths and the arts of healing to bring back to one's people; has its roots in ancient animistic and polytheistic cultures

sharia: Islamic law; straight path

Shema: the essential declaration of monotheistic faith as found in Judaism: "Hear O Israel, the Lord our God, the Lord is One"

Shiah or Shii: follower(s), partisan(s); refers to those who followed the leadership of Ali, the nephew and son-in-law of Muhammad, as Muhammad's successor;

those who believe that leadership of the Muslim community should belong to Muhammad's descendants

Son of God: title applied to Jesus of Nazareth

sorcerers: mediums who manipulate the spirit world and coerce the supernaturals without their consent, often for their own benefit and against community values

spirit flight: "soul journey"; a shaman's attempt to locate another person's soul, perhaps because it has wandered off in this world or needs assistance to reach the afterlife of the clan's ancestors

spirit medium: person who communicates with deities and spirits through ritually induced trance

Sufi: literally "one who wears wool"; Muslim mystic or ascetic

Sufism: Islamic mysticism or asceticism

Sunnah: example; typically refers to Muhammad's example, which is believed by Muslims to be the living out of the principles of the Quran; *Sunni* is derived from this word

Sunni: those who accept the *sunna* and the historic succession of the Caliphs; the majority of the Muslim community

surah: chapter, particularly of the Quran

sympathetic imagination: empathy; necessary to understand the religious languages and messages of different times and places

synagogue: a community centered on the study of Torah and prayer to God; the buildings used to house these activities also came to be known as synagogues

syncretism: the weaving together of alien and indigenous religious beliefs and practices; or the combining of elements from different practices to create a new religion

syncretistic: the identification of the gods of one religion with the gods of another so that one's own gods are seen as the same as those of the other's religion but under different names

taboo: forbidden

Talmud: the oral Torah, recorded in the *Mishnah*, and the commentary on the *Mishnah* called the *Gemara*; there are two Talmuds: the Bavli (Talmud of Babylonia) and the Yerushalmi (the Jerusalem Talmud); the former is considered the more comprehensive and authoritative

Tanak: the written Torah, or Hebrew Bible, made up of Torah (the first five books, from Genesis to Deuteronomy), Neviim (the prophets and historical writings such as Jeremiah and 1 and 2 Kings), and Ketuvim (the wisdom writings, such as Proverbs, Job, etc.)

Tannaim: the generation of sages, beginning with Hillel and Shammai, that created the *Mishnah*

tawhid: oneness, unity, and uniqueness of God; absolute monotheism

temple: a place to worship God or the gods in diverse religions; in Judaism only one temple was allowed for the worship of God in Jerusalem, whereas each Jewish community would have a synagogue for study and prayers

Tisha B'Av: a day of mourning to commemorate tragedies affecting the Jewish people, particularly the fall of the First and Second Temples in Jerusalem

totem: symbol taken from the natural world that stands for a social group possessing a common origin and essence

transcendent: beyond all finite things

Trinity: God as Father, Son, and Holy Spirit; meant to suggest that the transcendent God can be immanent in the world without losing his transcendence—when God acts in the world (as Son or Spirit), God does not cease to be father and Creator of the universe; therefore, God is not many gods but one God in three persons

tutelary spirit: a supernatural agent, often an ancestral spirit, whose help is required by a shaman to perform the difficult soul journeys, negotiate with evil spirits, compel a soul to return, or increase the shaman's healing powers

two natures, one person: doctrine affirmed by Council of Chalcedon (451 CE); in the one person of Jesus are two natures (divine and human) said to coexist in unity but without confusion or mixture, so Jesus is fully human in everything except sin, and yet the fullness of God is also present in him and united to him

Tzaddik: in the Hasidic tradition, a "righteous man," as powerful as the rabbi in a traditional Talmudic community but revered for mystical piety and devotion, not Talmudic scholarship; for the Hasidim, the Tzaddik was especially chosen by God as a direct link between heaven and earth, whose holiness was so powerful that, like Moses (Exodus 32:11–14), he could intervene on behalf of the faithful and change the mind of God

ulama **(sing.** *alim***):** religious scholars

ultimate reality: that which is the highest in value and meaning for the group

ummah: Muslim community of believers

"Venus" figurines: prehistoric Eurasian small stone sculptures of females with large breasts and hips, often with their genitalia emphasized, thought to indicate a worship of fertility in small communities

via analogia: a way of knowing spiritual reality through the use of analogy, for example, "God is my shepherd"

via negativa: the mystical way of knowing the highest spiritual reality (God, Brahman, etc.) by negating all finite qualities and characteristics; Hindus, for instance, say Brahman is "neti . . . neti"—not this and not that (i.e., Brahman is not a thing, Brahman is no-thing and therefore is pure nothingness, Brahman is beyond imagination and cannot be imaged, Brahman can only be known by a mystical experience of unknowing)

wali: friend or protégé of God; Sufi term referring to saint; one reputed to have the power to bilocate, cure the sick, multiply food, and read minds

white shamans: Westerners who create global organizations propagating a purported "universal" shamanic tradition, charging high fees for tours, courses, initiations, and healing services, some pledging to use some of the proceeds to assist indigenous shamans

zakat: almsgiving, one of the Five Pillars of Islam: 2.5 percent tithe of one's net worth to help the poor is required of all Muslims

Zionism: the desire to return to the land of Israel as a homeland; in modern times, the secular movement started by Theodor Herzl that led to the formation of the state of Israel

Zohar: major book of Jewish Kabbalism: *The Book of Splendor*

ART CREDITS

INDEX